W9-CKT-451

Parnassus

Parnassus:
Twenty Years of
Poetry in Review

Herbert Leibowitz, Editor

Columbia College Library
600 South Michigan Avenue
Chicago, IL 60605

Ann Arbor

THE UNIVERSITY OF MICHIGAN PRESS

Grateful acknowledgment is made to the following authors and publishers for permission to reprint materials published elsewhere.

"Walt Whitman an American," from *Geography of the Imagination* by Guy Davenport. Copyright © 1981 by Guy Davenport. Reprinted by permission of Pantheon Books, a division of Random House, Inc.

"Vesuvius at Home: The Power of Emily Dickinson," reprinted from *On Lies, Secrets, and Silence, Selected Prose 1966–1978* by Adrienne Rich, by permission of the author and W. W. Norton & Company, Inc. Copyright © 1979 by W. W. Norton & Company, Inc.

Copyright © 1994 by the University of Michigan
All rights reserved
Published in the United States of America by
The University of Michigan Press
Manufactured in the United States of America
♾ Printed on acid-free paper

1997   1996   1995   1994   4   3   2   1

A CIP catalogue record for this book is available from the British Library.

Library of Congress Cataloging-in-Publication Data

Parnassus : twenty years of poetry in review / Herbert Leibowitz, editor.
      p.   cm.
   Includes bibliographical references and index.
   ISBN 0-472-09577-3 (alk. paper). — ISBN 0-472-06577-7 (pbk. : alk. paper)
      1. American poetry—20th century—History and criticism.
   2. Poetry, Modern—History and criticism. I. Leibowitz, Herbert A.
PS325.P34   1994
811'.5409—dc20   94-30760
                                                                 CIP

811.5409 P256L

Parnassus

For Nick Lyons, wise friend, lover of poetry and fine prose, who inspired me to take the long, exhilarating climb up Parnassus, with gratitude and love

Contents

Introduction

Poetry magazines often announce their arrival on the scene with a manifesto promising, like the Dadaists, to sweep away antiquated styles and conventional rules or to defend, like the New Formalists, traditional practices seen as under siege by misguided zealots. Whether glossy, mimeographed, or electronic, these magazines serve as a portable stage for the display of new work and the recruitment of readers. In this heady, often fractious atmosphere, poets can take their first fumbling—or bold—steps to push their verse into unmapped terrain, exchange ideas, form alliances. William Carlos Williams, for example, credited poetry magazines with saving his career from disappearing into a black hole of neglect and willful misunderstanding.

When *Parnassus* was started in 1973, new books of poetry were greeted grudgingly, like distant cousins, and assigned cramped space or ejected into the cold. Relegated to the back of book supplements in Sunday newspapers, poetry reviews often seemed perfunctory, three unrelated volumes arbitrarily herded into a rickety omnibus. What could a serious reviewer do with such a claustrophobic form but settle for a simplistic formula: a few tentative generalities about theme and language, a little quotation as ocular proof, and finally a smattering of judgments, all in a lackluster prose that the reader forgot instantly. (With a few noble exceptions the situation has worsened over the last fifteen years.) The responsible literary magazines published poetry chronicles each quarter, but books under review seemed chosen by a kind of triage.

Parnassus' editorial mission from its first issue sprang from a number of quixotic premises: that American poetry should not be treated with contempt or indifference; that each issue of the magazine should be a Hyde Park Corner where contrary ideas and diverse voices—the political and the aesthetic, the operatic and the intimate, the philosophical and the colloquial—might blend into a harmonious ensemble; that although language is rooted in local soil and translation is a diabolical art, poetry is increasingly an interdependent universe, its poets and literate readers crossing national borders to study and be influenced by Tsvetayeva, Celan, Vallejo, Zagajewski, Paz—*Parnassus* has stationed itself at the frontier of this international exchange: and that all reviews should possess the density, clarity, and incandescence of works of art. I have preached with scriptural fervor the ideal that reviewers should be guides—quirky, witty, informed, spellbinding—who persuade not by labored exegesis or chatty journalism but by a spirited cantabile that does not sacrifice an ounce of intellectual weight or acumen. Learning should perch lightly but firmly like a falcon on a writer's wrist.

My models for such an enterprise were Marianne Moore, Ezra Pound, and Randall Jarrell, in whose hands the review became a distinctive art form. With surgical precision and subtle argument Moore could masterfully dissect the poems of Williams, Stevens, Hart Crane, laying bare the basic principles—and the damaging flaws—of their poetics. She invited imagination to the critic's table. Veering in one paragraph from the playfully didactic to the peevishly opinionated, Pound could deride slipshod writing or launch a young poet before the public; offer a brilliantly concise lecture on metrics or excavate an exquisite ancient Chinese poem from some musty scholarly tome. In his most dazzling digressions, he never lost the Ariadne's Web of logic. Jarrell's stern judgments—he did not spare his friends Robert Lowell and John Berryman when he reviewed their books; they hung on his words as if they were messages (and rebukes) from Yahweh—would have been a cruel flaying were it not for the exhilarating ride of discovery we share as he cracks open secrets encoded in syllables, patterns of syntax, repetition and accident, and rhythms inert or sturdy as a heartbeat.

After twenty years editing *Parnassus,* I am still combating the commonly held view that poetry reviewing does not require the care and invention of poetry. To my consternation, this attitude corrupts even poets' critical prose. The signs are easy to spot: stodgy rhythm, anemic vocabulary, uniform syntax, humorless piety, clotted jargon, puffery, long-winded explication. Dullness presides over the interminable proceedings like a bureaucrat. All the acoustical and metaphoric resources, the rich sensibility, that poets should normally command mysteriously desert them as if they were seized by a sudden amnesia or agreed with the academic theorists who claimed that the authorial voice was a fraud, a construct, that subjectivity itself was criminally suspect. But when after much encouragement poets strike off these self-imposed shackles, their prose grows engaging: it has presence, charm, suppleness, edge.

I am often asked what accounts for *Parnassus'* survival when the life expectancy for literary magazines is so grim. There are, I believe, several reasons. Parnassus has avoided the taints of sectarianism, logrolling, cant, and fashion. It is hospitable to the adversary mind that does not shrink from controversy or caustic truth-telling yet knows how to praise a poet's work with analytic grace. Uncowed by reputation, given generous space to hone their arguments or advocacy, *Parnassus'* reviewers are usually discerning skeptics. (The rotating of assignments among men and women of different tastes ensures that no party line will be parroted.) Whether brandishing a poison-tipped polemical scimitar or judiciously assessing a young poet's first flight, *Parnassus'* reviews and essays prove that passion, part of the circuitry of style, is compatible with intellectual rigor. Our reviewers have roamed the back roads of poetry as well as its urban centers, trusting in the genial power of lilting prose and the nimble mind that keeps us unsure where it will next leap.

In selecting the essays and reviews for this collection, I have drawn heavily on poets and novelists whose scintillating prose illustrates the satisfying partnership between knowledge and style that makes *Parnassus* unique. (I wish I had room to include some of the superb essays from our Words and Music issue.) There are retrospectives, perhaps the magazine's specialty, that scrape away the encrustations from a poet's verse and allow us to see it from an entirely new angle; short reviews and landmark discussions of Whitman and Dickinson; an imaginative and imaginary interview with a dead poet; extended meditations on "Metaphysical" poetry, the element of chance, and the contemporary lyric; poetic prose; an argument against translation facing off with interpretations of French, Italian, Russian, and Polish poets. Theodore Roethke complained of the burdens of "lugging pork up Parnassus." Readers of this book will spend their time more pleasurably in the company of writers blessed with the gift of tongues.

Part I

Walt Whitman an American

GUY DAVENPORT

His rooms in Camden were shin-deep in wadded paper; nonchalance was one of the household gods. Visitors, wading in, knew the others so numinously there around the old man with so much white hair and beard, so freckled and so barbaricly slouched on a buffalo robe: the ghosts of Rossini and Scott, of Lincoln and Columbus, of Anacharsis Cloots and Elias Hicks, and two supreme goddesses, Artemis Philomeirix and Eleutheria whose *eidolon* was erected in his sixty-third year on Bedloe's Island, a gift from the French, three hundred and two feet tall, statue and pediment together, the work of Frédéric-Auguste Bartholdi, at the sight of which millions of eyes would water in gray dawns with an anguish of hope which only Whitman's poetry can duplicate ("Not a grave of the murdered for freedom but grows seed for freedom . . . in its turn to bear seed, Which the winds carry far and re-sow, and the rains and the snows nourish"), Liberty.

Lincoln on horseback tipped his hat to him in Washington one day, a gazing stranger whom Lincoln must have supposed was some office seeker. or underling in one of the departments, perhaps a geologist with that grizzled a beard. It was the republican equivalent of Napoleon looking in on Goethe to talk history and poetry.

He attended Poe's funeral, standing toward the back of the mourners. He comforted the dying in the War (like Henry James) and wrote letters home for them (like Ezra Pound at Pisa). Not until he was an old man did anyone care or know who he was. George Collins Cox came and photographed him hugging children (and copyrighted the photograph, as if Walt were Niagara Falls or Grand Canyon); Thomas Eakins came and did a masterpiece of a portrait. Young men came and learned what they might do with their lives, John Burroughs being the star pupil.

Like Poe, he has always been suspect in his own country. To name the Walt Whitman Bridge the authorities had to sidestep the objections of Christians and Patriots that his morals were un-Ameri-

From *Parnassus* (vol. 5, no. 1, 1976).

can. Emerson, who once strolled through the Louvre without stopping in front of a single picture, was at pains to have it known that he was not a close friend of Whitman's. Thoreau wrote in his journal, December 1, 1856: "As for the sensuality in Whitman's 'Leaves of Grass,' I do not so much wish that it was not written, as that men and women were so pure that they could read it without harm."

"Whitman," Kafka told his friend Gustav Janouch, "belongs among the greatest formal innovators in the modern lyric. One can regard his unrhymed verse as the progenitor of the free rhythms of Arno Holz, Émile Verhaeren, and Paul Claudel . . . the formal element in Walt Whitman's poetry found an enormous echo throughout the world. Yet Walt Whitman's significance lies elsewhere. He combined the contemplation of nature and of civilization, which are apparently entirely contradictory, into a single intoxicating vision of life, because he always had sight of the transitoriness of all phenomena. He said: 'Life is the little that is left over from dying.' So he gave his whole heart to every leaf of grass. I admire in him the reconciliation of art and nature. . . . He was really a Christian and—with a close affinity especially to us Jews—he was therefore an important measure of the status and worth of humanity."*

"Have you read the American poems by Whitman?" Van Gogh wrote to his sister-in-law in September 1888. "I am sure Theo has them, and I strongly advise you to read them, because to begin with they are very fine, and the English speak about them a good deal. He sees in the future, and even in the present, a world of healthy, carnal love, strong and frank—of friendship—of work— under the great starlit vault of heaven a something which after all one can only call God—and eternity in its place above this world. At first it makes you smile, it is all so candid and pure; but it sets you thinking for the same reason.

"The 'Prayer of Columbus' is very beautiful."**

The range of sensibilities that responded to his is impressive and a bit puzzling: Henry James, Melville, Swinburne, Tennyson, Victor

*Gustav Janouch, *Conversations with Kafka*, translated by Goronwy Rees, New Directions, 1971, p. 167.

**Complete Letters of Vincent Van Gogh*, Vol. III, New York Graphic Society, 1958, p. 445.

Hugo, John Hay, Yeats, the Rossettis. He was a force useful to talents as diverse as those of William Carlos Williams and Dino Campana, Guillaume Apollinaire and Hart Crane. He had freed poetry from exclusive commitments to narrative and the ode. He closed the widening distance between poet and audience. He talks to us face to face, so that our choice is between listening and turning away. And in turning away there is the uneasy feeling that we are turning our backs on the very stars and on ourselves.

He succeeded in making himself a symbol of American idealism as bright as and in many ways far more articulate than Jefferson or Jackson. But as an ideal figure he turned out to be risky currency. Thoreau and Emerson were safer, more respectable, and more apt to remain in the realm of ideas.

Whitman, Jack Yeats complained, was bad for the American spirit because it seemed to him that we indulged all too naturally in what Whitman urged us to wallow. Beerbohm caricatured this view of Whitman (". . . inciting the American eagle to soar"), and the young Ezra Pound in his pre-Raphaelite suit thought Whitman much too much, while intelligently suspecting that there was something there that the critics weren't seeing.

There are lots of things the critics haven't seen. It is for instance worthwhile reading Whitman against the intellectual background he assumed his readers knew and which is no longer remembered except sporadically: the world of Alexander von Humboldt from which Whitman takes the word *cosmos;* Louis Agassiz, for whom Thoreau collected turtles; Volney's *Ruins,* the historical perspective of which is as informative in Whitman as in Shelley; Fourier; Scott. A great deal that seems naive and spontaneous in Whitman has roots and branches.

His age still read Plutarch as part of its education, and Whitman's understanding of erotic camaraderie looks different (less personal and eccentric) beside a knowledge of the Theban Sacred Band under Pelopidas and Epameinondas, whose conversations in Elysium with Freud one would like to hear, those heroes whose names were terror to the Spartan infantry, who were Pythagoreans who believed, in the Master's dictum, that a friend is another self, who were sworn to chastity, and who passed daily the palace of an old king named Oedipus.

And they were, as they said in their language, democrats.

Whitman's fond gaze was for grace that is unaware of itself; his constant pointing to beauty in common robust people was a discovery. Custom said that beauty was elsewhere. Women in his time were pathologically interested in their own looks, especially in well-to-do families, because that would be their sole achievement, aside from motherhood, on this earth. They were laced breathlessly into corsets, caged in hoopskirts, harnessed into bustles. Their bodies were girt about with bodices, drawers, bloomers, stockings, gloves, petticoats. Their shoes were always too small. They took no more exercise than aged invalids. Their hair was curled with irons heated in an open fire, then oiled, then shoved into a bonnet it would tire a horse to wear. Their flesh never met the light of the sun. They fainted frequently and understandably. How in the world did they pee?

In Plutarch you could read about Spartan girls who wrestled with boys, both naked. It was the opinion of the Spartans that clothing on such an occasion would be indecent. (We know of a Philadelphia woman in the time of Dr. Benjamin Rush who chose to die in modesty rather than let a doctor see her breasts.)

One suspects that Thoreau would have married a woodchuck or a raccoon, if the biology of the union could have been arranged; Whitman might, given the opportunity, like Clarence King or Lafcadio Hearn, have married a black woman. It was one of his fantasies that he had had one for a mistress.

Freud's replacing one Calvinism with another pretty much the same should not fool us into thinking we can say that Whitman's love for handsome boys was a psychosis which we can then subtract from his book, like Victoria looking at da Vinci's notebooks with the anatomical drawings decorously covered by brown paper. That love is the very heart of his vision. He was re-inventing a social bond that had been in civilization from the beginning, that had, in Christian Europe, learned various dodges, and met its doom in Puritanism and was thus not in the cultural package unloaded on Plymouth Rock.

As in the ancient world Whitman had no patience with the pathic (as his word was), the effeminate. He wanted in men and women a love that was unaware of itself, as heroism is unaware of itself, as children are unaware of their own beauty. What Whitman was observing as the mating habits of the species was a debased form of Courtly Love that the industrial revolution had entwined with commerce (a pretty wife was an asset to a rich man, indeed, she was part of his wealth). Women were caught in a strange new myth, as if Pluto were the most eligible husband for Persephone.

There was accuracy in Whitman's turning to those spirits that were free to be lively, lusty, inventive. He loved, as Nietzsche said of the Greeks, the health of the race. His race was like none before. It stood at a unique place in history. It joined the two halves of the world. Whitman's great vision culminated in his celebration of the spanning of our continent with rails, the closing of the gap between Europe and America with the transatlantic cable, and the opening of the Suez Canal. These completed the circle Columbus had drawn the first brave arc of. More than commerce would flow along that new route that at last belted the whole earth. Why should not ideas as archaic as man himself immigrate along that line?

One reason Whitman is so interesting right now is that we do not yet know if that band around the earth is an umbilicus or a strangling cord. Albert Speer explained at Nuremberg that radio and telephone had amplified Hitler's scope and accelerated the implementation of his orders so far beyond any such power available to previous tyrants that we need a new kind of imagination to grasp how so much evil could have been done in those twelve infernal years. The first hell allowed by the world belt was Whitman's own Civil War, an old feud of the English that infected the new world and broke out with renewed vigor, Round Head and Cavalier, North and South, industrialist and planter.

Whitman's fellow nurse in the Union hospitals, Henry James, would live until 1916, another hell caused by easy scope of movement. Modernity seems to sink Whitman's vision of a cohesive society further and further back into the past while isolating its essential purity and brilliance. The final sterilizer of his vision would seem to be the internal combustion engine, which has made all movement restless and capricious.

And at the center of all Whitman's poetry there is movement. His age walked with a sprier step than ours; it bounced in buckboard and carriage; a man on a horse has his blood shaken and his muscles pulled. A man in an automobile is as active as a sloth; an airplane ride offers no activity more strenuous than turning the pages of a magazine. Dullness, constant numbing dullness, was the last thing Whitman would have thought of America, but that is what has happened.

In his second letter to Emerson Whitman objected at length to "writers fraudulently assuming as always dead what everyone knows to be always alive." He meant sex; I wonder if the assumption might not now be valid of the mind. From Whitman onward there is a distrust of the poet in the United States. The art of genteel America was to be fiction, the movies, and *Schlagsahne*. There is a bewildering irony in New England Transcendentalism's fathering both Whitman and the current notion that poetry is cultural icing, spiritual uplift, wholly unrelated to anything at all. What was useful to middle-class frumpery was trivialized for anthologies, and the rest dismissed to the attention of professors and idealists.

Within a few miles of each other in the 1880s Whitman was putting last touches to his great book, Eadweard Muybridge was photographing movements milliseconds apart of thousands of animals, naked athletes, and women, and Thomas Eakins was painting surgeons, boxers, musicians, wrestlers, and Philadelphians. Mary Cassatt, who might have been among them, had moved to France, permanently. In a sense Muybridge and Eakins were catching up with Whitman's pioneering. Their common subject, motion, the robust real, skilled and purposeful action, was distinctly American, an invention. Eakins and Muybridge worked together; Eakins came over to Camden and photographed and painted Whitman. Their arts ran parallel, shared a spirit and a theme. Muybridge's photographs, the monumental *Zoopraxia*, kept Degas and Messonier up all night looking at it. There has been no finer movement in American art, nor a more fertile one (from Muybridge, through Edison, the whole art of the film), and yet their impact was generally felt to be offensive. Eakins and Muybridge were forgotten for years; Whitman persisted.*

*Muybridge inscribed the double-folio *Zoopraxia: Men and Animals in Motion* as a gift to Haverford College, eccentric soul that he was. The good Quakers wrapped it in brown paper and hid it on the shelves of the library among outsized books, omitting to list it in the card catalogue. I found the bulky parcels there in an idle moment in 1964. Once I saw what I'd found, I commanded three hale students

Grass: "a uniform hieroglyphic." Meaning in *Leaves of Grass* is an interpretation of symbols. The poet's work encompasses the undertaking of the most primitive transcriptions of nature into signs as well as contemporary decipherings of science, which had "great saurians" to explain, electricity, new planets. The double continuum of time and space became in Whitman's imagination a coherent symbol with perspectives to range.

Emerson's "He seems a Minotaur of a man" and Thoreau's "He occasionally suggests something a little more than human" (both remarks were in letters to friends, not public print) catch Whitman in what would become traditional opinions: that his idealism was inappropriate to his rough matter, and that the roughness of his matter offended the idealism of his cultivated readers. No woman, it was assumed, could ever read him; Lowell insisted that the book, if placed in libraries, be kept from seminarians.

Is he so big that no one has yet taken his size? The cooperative struggle to measure Melville revealed greatness upon greatness. Where Whitman's tone is rich we can see his mastery: there is nothing anywhere like "Out of the Cradle Endlessly Rocking" (Hugo at his most resonant and symbolic sounds thin beside it; Leopardi, a plausible rival, could not have achieved the wildness, the lonely openness of the poem). Nor does "When Lilacs Last in the Dooryard Bloom'd," for all its Tennysonian color and voice, have an equal.

There are 390 poems in *Leaves of Grass* as Whitman left it. Modern editions add 42 others that he had rejected or not yet included; the Blodgett and Bradley Comprehensive Reader's Edition (Norton, 1965) adds 123 more pages of fragments, deletions, and notebook drafts.

He threw away:

> I am that halfgrown angry boy, fallen asleep,

---

to help me carry it to my apartment. I then called the great kinesiologist Ray L. Birdwhistell, Jr., who dropped everything and came out. We spread the sheets all over the floor and in hours of looking I listened to Birdwhistell's analysis of how nineteenth-century people moved, what they did with shoulders, elbows, hips, eyebrows, toes, knees. Sherlock Holmes would have fallen down and worshipped. Any reading of Whitman is vastly enriched by a knowledge of Eakins and Muybridge; their arts can now be seen as complementary. Whether the Quakers have catalogued their Muybridge, sold it for the thousands of dollars it is worth, or put it back in its plain brown paper on the back shelves of the library I have never asked.

The tears of foolish passion yet undried upon my cheeks

and

Him of The Lands, identical, I sing, along the single thread . . .

in which the full timbre of his voice is undiminished. Had Whitman written entirely in his strong, aria-like, lyric mode, he would have fared far better with the critics (who speak of his formlessness) and fellow poets (who complain of the catalogues, the dross, the talk), but he would have been little more than an American Victorian, Tennyson with a twang.

We have paid too little attention to Whitman's subjects, especially when they smack of the prosaic. Consider "Outlines for a Tomb (G. P., Buried 1870)," which imagines various tableaux for a million-aire philanthropist's tomb, a poem thoroughly traditional, a classical eulogy to which Chaucerian pictured rooms have been added. The poem comes into stereoptic focus when we go to the trouble to discover that G. P. is George Peabody (1795–1869). The curious "buried 1870" becomes clear when we know that Peabody died in London and was brought home in a British war ship, with full honors. An apprentice to a dry-goods firm at eleven, he worked his way up in the world until, as head of a banking firm with offices in Baltimore, Philadelphia, New York, and London, he was able to become one of the first great merchant philanthropists. He gave two million to the English for housing for the poor, a museum to Harvard, and a museum to Yale. Yale got her museum to house the paleontological collection of Othniel Marsh, who was Peabody's nephew; Harvard got hers to house Agassiz's biological specimens. Harvard was not originally a beneficiary; it was only after the pious Peabody discovered that Marsh was a Darwinian that he tried to counteract this heresy by bestowing equal funds on Harvard, where Agassiz, Darwin's superior as a zoologist, declined to accept the great theory without further proof. Yet you will not find George Peabody in the *Britannica*.*

---

*You will in *The Columbia Encyclopedia*. For an account of Peabody in his scientific context, as well as for a splendid history of paleontology in the age of Whitman, see Robert West Howard's *The Dawnseekers*, Harcourt Brace Jovanovich, 1975. You can also see in this book a photograph of Edgar Allan Poe inspecting the fossil skeleton of a prehistoric horse: a discovery still unknown to the Poe scholars.

As Whitman's world faded into a dimness, a great deal of his poetry was rendered meaningless except as general or abstract statement. Things vivid to him and his readers, such as Transcendentalism, the philosophy of Fourier and Owen, the discovery of dinosaurs in the west by Cope and Marsh, phrenology, photography, telegraphy, railroads, have fused into a blur. A technological era was beginning to articulate itself and Whitman was its poet. It was not a time to which one inside it could easily give a name, or a direction. Whitman's only certainty was that he was living in a new kind of society, that tore itself asunder in the tragedy of the Civil War, but did not thereby abandon its original intention to be a democratic republic.

> Quicksand years that whirl me I know not whither,
> Your schemes, politics, fail, lines give way, substances
>   mock and elude me,
> Only the theme I sing . . .

The theme. A music of sensations, songs containing catalogues of things, as if creation could be summoned and praised by chanting the name of everything there is, the constructing of a context, like Noah's ark, where there is a place for everything, a compulsion to confront every experience with innocent eyes—no one phrase is ever going to label Whitman's theme. The base on which it stands is Christian: a sympathy whose scope is rigorously universal, a predisposition to love and understand. Young admirers fancied him an American Socrates, but of course he is the very opposite. He was like those Greeks in love with the immediate, the caressable (always with the eye), the delicious, who, to St. Paul's distress, worshipped each other when free from placating and begging from a confusion of gods.

And he was decidedly pagan, always ready with a good word for "the rhythmic myths of Greece and the strong legends of Rome." A pagan is not a godless man; he is a man with many gods. Whitman could easily (as he liked to imagine) kneel with the Muslim, hear the Law with the Jew, sit in silence with the Quaker, dance with the Pawnee.

This splendid sympathy with forms knits his book together. Grass is the one universal plant, absent only in the deserts of the poles. Classifying and naming the grasses of the world has kept botanists overworked since Linnaeus, and the end is nowhere in sight. Leaves: we use the word for the pages of books, and the first paper was leaves of grass, papyrus. Grass is a symbol for life throughout the Bible, integral with the metaphor of shepherd and sheep.

There were "nations ten thousand years before these States"; we are carrying something on. And of this past "not a mark, not a record remains—and yet all remains." From the people in the deep forgotten past,

> Some with oval countenances learn'd and calm,
> Some naked and savage, some like huge collections of insects,

our heritage is unknown but there is no doubt of there being a heritage.

Charles Fourier, who thought civilization a mistake, said that man's first duty is to keep the Sacred Flame, which he understood to be both our kinship to God and those livelinesses of spirit man himself had invented—the dance, poetry, music, mathematics, communal genius like French cuisine, Cretan stubbornness, Scotch scepticism, Dutch housekeeping. Whitman knew Fourier only in the washed and bowdlerized versions of his thought discussed at Brook Farm, and in the writings of Blaine, Greeley, and Margaret Fuller. Perhaps he believed Emerson's warning that Fourier was basically unsound. Yet Whitman and Fourier were of the same historical moment, and much of their thought rhymes, though with many a dissonance. Fourier died (in Montmarte, while saying his prayers, kneeling against his bed, surrounded by his cats) when Whitman was 18. In those eighteen years Fourier was writing texts that would have interested Whitman immensely—they were not published until 1957, and some are still unpublished. They describe a world, the New Harmony as Fourier called it, that has kept the flame. It is a world divided up into beehives of communities, each of which is a family of human beings and animals. All work is done by everybody, an hour at a time. The days are rhythmic and contain a little of everything good. All sexual predilections are arranged for and honored for their diversity. Ceremonial honors are given to those whose passionate nation encompasses the widest range. All are friend and servant to all. Children learn every skill by age 10, yet the dominant note of the community is play.

Fourier's vision was an opposite to the commercial world in which he lived and suffered. In utopian design his is the most extreme yet achieved. It can be explained by noting that Fourier's every detail intends to save the individual from that dullness and quiet despair which was the immediate and alarming result of the Industrial Revolution.

If the world was to belong to the rapacious, civilization was then little more than the jungle. Rapacity, in any case, as Fourier thought, was alternative action symbolizing and disguising warmer passions unacceptable to civilization. Marriage, for instance, is a reproductive not a social unit. A true family is an enormous gathering of people, like a primitive tribe, where congeniality can have a large scope, and where everybody knows he belongs. The city was to disappear, and we may already have cause, watching the cities rot and revert to the jungle, to wonder whether Fourier's small communities could possibly by this time have rotted with such Spenglerian gangrene as Detroit and St. Louis.

To keep the sacred flame. The image is taken from antiquity, when the household fire was a god, part of which was given to each member of the family as they went away to new homes. Symbolically this fire was the family spirit, guardian of its integrity and survival. Fourier talks about it as if it were spirit itself, and he designed his Harmony to preserve the liveliness of the child into old age; he saw no reason why it should drain away. He is the only philosopher interested in happiness as the supreme human achievement. A good nature should be the whole concern of government.

It was compliant, insouciant, easy good nature that Whitman admired most in a society. And nineteenth-century industrial culture had begun to erase the possibilities of Whitmanian good nature. Ruskin noted the characteristic sulk on American girls' faces, the pout, the petulance. Look at the Steichen photograph of J. P. Morgan, 1903, the one with the dagger. Slow-burning rage, not charming insouciance, was to be the standard American state of mind.

An American publisher remembered in old age "a large-boned old man in a sombrero" shuffling into the Hotel Albert (the anecdote is Ford Madox Ford's, and is therefore suspect). "I am Walt Whitman," said the old man, "if you'll lend me a dollar you'll be helping immortality to stumble on." (The dollar would have been equally useful upstairs in the hotel, where Ryder hovered over his visions: American culture has the eerie habit of passing itself, in narrow corridors, ghostlike.) Whitman's personal loneliness and destitution became part of the legend quite early. "a fine old fellow in an iron land" begins Rubén Darío's sonnet to Whitman. Garcia Lorca:

> Not for a single moment, handsome old Walt Whitman,
> have I lost the vision of your beard full of butterflies,
> your corduroy shoulders wasted by the moon
> your thighs of virginal Apollo,
> your voice like a column of coarse ashes;
> old man beautiful as mist*

Crane in *The Bridge* lets his evocation of Whitman walking on the beach "Near Paumanok—your lone patrol . . . " blend with another beach, Kitty Hawk. Even if the Gasoline Age had not changed the world into the Slope of Sisyphus, it would still be arguable if any society could have lived up to Whitman's idealism. Like Thoreau's, it is an idealism for individuals rather than conglomerates. For all its acceptance of the city crowds and the bustle of commerce, it is in essence pastoral, following natural rhythms, with sympathies that depend on the broad and easy freedom of country people. Never again could a major American poet comprehend, much less repeat, Whitman's vision. Yet many began there and were nourished on its honey before they ate of the tree of the knowledge of good and evil. Charles Ives did, set some of the poems as songs, but abandoned his *Walt Whitman Overture,* if he ever indeed began it. Pound's *Cantos* are a version of "A Passage to India" written in finer historical detail and transposed into a tragic mode. *Paterson* is Whitman's vision after a devastating rain of acid vulgarity. Olson's *Maximus* records the awful fact that Whitman's prophecy for a coherent democratic society remains unfulfilled in any sense, as we now live in an incoherent industrial society that has discovered that death is much better for business than life. The largest American

*Geoffrey Dutton's translation, in his *Whitman,* Grove Press, 1961, p. 111.

business is the automobile, the mechanical cockroach that has eaten our cities; that and armaments.

Of the delights celebrated in "A Song of Joys," most are accessible now only to the very rich, some are obsolete, some are so exploited by commerce as to be no longer joys for anybody except the stockbroker, two are against the law (swimming naked, sleeping with "grown and part-grown boys"), and one is lethal ("the solitary walk").

Whitman is a kind of litmus paper, perhaps a seismograph. Reading him, we become aware of an awful, lost innocence, and are not certain whether the innocence was real or in Whitman's imagination. He gave his whole life to a book, he freed literature to go courses that were until Whitman unsuspected. He had the power to move even unwilling hearts (witness Gerard Manley Hopkins reading him because he couldn't not read him, knowing the author to be "a scoundrel" and the poetry to be wicked). Pound in the cage at Pisa remembered a University of Pennsylvania philologist who was surprised at attitudes toward Whitman, as "even the peasants in Denmark know him." The Japanese publish a journal devoted to him. The Russian Futurists and Mayakovsky considered Whitman to be the founder of their school.

Many excellent books have been written about him, his place in world literature is assured. He is still, however, a renegade, disreputable still. That he was a master of words and rhythms is affirmed and denied with equal passion. His cults come and go. He is, like Goethe in Germany and Victor Hugo in France, inextricably part of our history. Like Jefferson and Franklin he has been woven into our myth. He is our archetypal poet, our great invention in literature, our lyric voice. I like to think that eventually he will shame us into becoming Americans again.

Vesuvius at Home: The Power of Emily Dickinson

ADRIENNE RICH

I am travelling at the speed of time, along the Massachusetts Turnpike. For months, for years, for most of my life, I have been hovering like an insect against the screens of an existence which inhabited Amherst, Massachusetts, between 1831 and 1884. The methods, the exclusions, of Emily Dickinson's existence could not have been my own; yet more and more, as a woman poet finding my own methods, I have come to understand her necessities, could have been witness in her defense.

"Home is not where the heart is," she wrote in a letter, "but the house and the adjacent buildings." A statement of New England realism, a directive to be followed. Probably no poet ever lived so much and so purposefully in one house; even, in one room. Her niece Martha told of visiting her in her corner bedroom on the second floor at 280 Main Street, Amherst, and of how Emily Dickinson made as if to lock the door with an imaginary key, turned and said: "Matty: here's freedom."

I am travelling at the speed of time, in the direction of the house and buildings.

Western Massachusetts: the Connecticut Valley: a countryside still full of reverberations: scene of Indian uprisings, religious revivals, spiritual confrontations, the blazing-up of the lunatic fringe of the Puritan coal. How peaceful and how threatened it looks from Route 91, hills gently curled above the plain, the tobacco-barns standing in fields sheltered with white gauze from the sun, and the sudden urban sprawl: ARCO, MacDonald's, shopping plazas. The country that broke the heart of Jonathan Edwards, that enclosed the genius of Emily Dickinson. It lies calmly in the light of May, cloudy skies breaking into warm sunshine, light-green spring softening the hills, dogwood and wild fruit-trees blossoming in the hollows.

From *Parnassus* (vol. 5, no. 1, 1976).

From Northampton bypass there's a 4-mile stretch of road to Amherst—Route 9—between fruit farms, steakhouses, supermarkets. The new University of Massachusetts rears its skyscrapers up from the plain against the Pelham Hills. There is new money here, real estate, motels. Amherst succeeds on Hadley almost without notice. Amherst is green, rich-looking, secure; we're suddenly in the center of town, the crossroads of the campus, old New England college buildings spread around two village greens, a scene I remember as almost exactly the same in the dim past of my undergraduate years when I used to come there for college weekends.

Left on Seelye Street, right on Main; driveway at the end of a yellow picket fence. I recognize the high hedge of cedars screening the house, because twenty-five years ago I walked there, even then drawn toward the spot, trying to peer over. I pull into the driveway behind a generous 19th-century brick mansion with wings and porches, old trees and green lawns. I ring at the back door—the door through which Dickinson's coffin was carried to the cemetery a block away.

For years I have been not so much envisioning Emily Dickinson as trying to visit, to enter her mind, through her poems and letters, and through my own intimations of what it could have meant to be one of the two mid-19th-century American geniuses, and a woman, living in Amherst, Massachusetts. Of the other genius, Walt Whitman, Dickinson wrote that she had heard his poems were "disgraceful." She knew her own were unacceptable by her world's standards of poetic convention, and of what was appropriate, in particular, for a woman poet. Seven were published in her lifetime, all edited by other hands; more than a thousand were laid away in her bedroom chest, to be discovered after her death. When her sister discovered them, there were decades of struggle over the manuscripts, the manner of their presentation to the world, their suitability for publication, the poet's own final intentions. Narrowed-down by her early editors and anthologists, reduced to quaintness or spinsterish oddity by many of her commentators, sentimentalized, fallen-in-love with like some gnomic Garbo, still unread in the breadth and depth of her full range of work, she was, and is, a wonder to me when I try to imagine myself into that mind.

I have a notion that genius knows itself; that Dickinson chose her seclusion, knowing she was exceptional and knowing what she needed. It was, moreover, no hermetic retreat, but a seclusion which included a wide range of people, of reading and correspondence. Her sister Vinnie said, "Emily is always looking for the rewarding person." And she found, at various periods, both women and men: her sister-in-law Susan Gilbert, Amherst visitors and family friends such as Benjamin Newton, Charles Wadsworth, Samuel Bowles, editor of the Springfield *Republican,* and his wife; her friends Kate Anthon and Helen Hunt Jackson, the distant but significant figures of Elizabeth Barrett, the Brontës, George Eliot. But she carefully selected her society and controlled the disposal of her time. Not only the "gentlewomen in plush" of Amherst were excluded; Emerson visited next door but she did not go to meet him; she did not travel or receive routine visits; she avoided strangers. Given her vocation, she was neither eccentric nor quaint; she was determined to survive, to use her powers, to practice necessary economies.

Suppose Jonathan Edwards had been born a woman; suppose William James, for that matter, had been born a woman? (The invalid seclusion of his sister Alice is suggestive.) Even from men, New England took its psychic toll; many of its geniuses seemed peculiar in one way or another, particularly along the lines of social intercourse. Hawthorne, until he married, took his meals in his bedroom, apart from the family. Thoreau insisted on the values both of solitude and of geographical restriction, boasting that "I have travelled much in Concord." Emily Dickinson—viewed by her bemused contemporary Thomas Higginson as "partially cracked," by the 20th century as fey or pathological—has increasingly struck me as a practical woman, exercising her gift as she had to, making choices. I have come to imagine her as somehow too strong for her environment, a figure of powerful will, not at all frail or breathless, someone whose personal dimensions would be felt in a household. She was her father's favorite daughter though she professed being afraid of him. Her sister dedicated herself to the everyday domestic labors which would free Dickinson to write. (Dickinson herself baked the bread, made jellies and gingerbread, nursed her mother through a long illness, was a skilled horticulturalist who grew pomegranates, calla-lillies, and other exotica in her New England greenhouse.)

Upstairs at last: I stand in the room which for Emily Dickinson was "freedom." The best bedroom in the house, a corner room, sunny, overlooking the main street of Amherst in front, the way to her brother Austin's house on the side. Here, at a small table with one drawer, she wrote most of her poems. Here she read Elizabeth Barrett's "Aurora Leigh," a woman poet's narrative poem of a woman poet's life; also George Eliot; Emerson; Carlyle; Shakespeare; Charlotte and Emily Brontë. Here I become, again, an insect, vibrating at the frames of windows, clinging to panes of glass, trying to connect. The scent here is very powerful. Here in this white-curtained, high-ceilinged room, a redhaired woman with hazel eyes and a contralto voice wrote poems about volcanoes, deserts, eternity, suicide, physical passion, wild beasts, rape, power, madness, separation, the daemon, the grave. Here, with a darning-needle, she bound these poems—heavily emended and often in variant versions—into booklets, secured with darning-thread, to be found and read after her death. Here she knew "freedom," listening from above-stairs to a visitor's piano-playing, escaping from the pantry where she was mistress of the household bread and puddings, watching, you feel, watching ceaselessly, the life of sober Main Street below. From this room she glided downstairs, her hand on the polished bannister, to meet the complacent magazine editor, Thomas Higginson, unnerve him while claiming she herself was unnerved. "Your scholar," she signed herself in letters to him. But she was an independent scholar, used his criticism selectively, saw him rarely and always on *her* premises. It was a life deliberately organized on her terms. The terms she had been handed by society—Calvinist Protestantism, Romanticism, the 19th-century corseting of women's bodies, choices, and sexuality—could spell insanity to a woman genius. What this one had to do was retranslate her own unorthodox, subversive, sometimes volcanic propensities into a dialect called metaphor: her native language. "Tell all the Truth—but tell it Slant—." It is always what is under pressure in us, especially under pressure of concealment— that explodes in poetry.

The women and men in her life she equally converted into metaphor. The masculine pronoun in her poems can refer simultaneously to many aspects of the "masculine" in the patriarchal world— the god she engages in dialogue, again on *her* terms; her own creative powers, unsexing for a woman, the male power-figures in her

immediate environment—the lawyer Edward Dickinson, her brother
Austin, the preacher Wadsworth, the editor Bowles—it is far too
limiting to trace that "He" to some specific lover, although that was
the chief obsession of the legend-mongers for more than half a
century. Obviously, Dickinson was attracted by and interested in
men whose minds had something to offer her; she was, it is by
now clear, equally attracted by and interested in women whose minds
had something to offer her. There are many poems to and about
women, and some which exist in two versions with alternate sets
of pronouns. Her latest biographer, Richard Sewall, while rejecting
an earlier Freudian biographer's theory that Dickinson was essentially
a psycho-pathological case, the by-product of which happened to
be poetry, does create a context in which the importance, and validity,
of Dickinson's attachments to women may now, at last, be seen in
full. She was always stirred by the existences of women like George
Eliot or Elizabeth Barrett, who possessed strength of mind, articu-
lateness, and energy. (She once characterized Elizabeth Fry and
Florence Nightingale as "holy"—one suspects she merely meant,
"great.")

   But of course Dickinson's relationships with women were more
than intellectual. They were deeply charged, and the sources both
of passionate joy and pain. We are only beginning to be able to
consider them in a social and historical context. The historian
Carroll Smith-Rosenberg has shown that there was far less taboo
on intense, even passionate and sensual, relationships between women
in the American 19th-century "female world of love and ritual,"
as she terms it, than there was later in the 20th century. Women
expressed their attachments to other women both physically and
verbally; a marriage did not dilute the strength of a female friendship,
in which two women often shared the same bed during long visits,
and wrote letters articulate with both physical and emotional longing.
The 19th-century close woman friend, according to the many diaries
and letters Smith-Rosenberg has studied, might be a far more
important figure in a woman's life than the 19th-century husband.
None of this was condemned as "lesbianism." We will understand
Emily Dickinson better, read her poetry more perceptively, when
the Freudian imputation of scandal and aberrance in women's love
for women has been supplanted by a more informed, less misogynistic

attitude toward women's experiences with each other.

But who, if you read through the seventeen hundred and seventy-five poems—who—woman or man—could have passed through that imagination and not come out transmuted? Given the space created by her in that corner room, with its window-light, its potted plants and work-table, given that personality, capable of imposing its terms on a household, on a whole community, what single theory could hope to contain her, when she'd put it all together in that space?

"Matty: here's freedom," I hear her saying as I speed back to Boston along Route 91, as I slip the turnpike ticket into the toll-collector's hand. I am thinking of a confined space in which the genius of the 19th-century female mind in America moved, inventing a language more varied, more compressed, more dense with implications, more complex of syntax, than any American poetic language to date; in the trail of that genius my mind has been moving, and with its language and images my mind still has to reckon, as the mind of a woman poet in America today.

In 1971, a postage stamp was issued in honor of Dickinson; the portrait derives from the one existing daguerrotype of her, with straight, center-parted hair, eyes staring somewhere beyond the camera, hands poised around a nosegay of flowers, in correct 19th-century style. On the first-day-of-issue envelope sent me by a friend there is, besides the postage stamp, an engraving of the poet as popular fancy has preferred her, in a white lace ruff and with hair as bouffant as if she had just stepped from a Boston beauty-parlor. The poem chosen to represent her work to the American public is engraved, alongside a dew-gemmed rose, below the portrait:

> If I can stop one heart from breaking
> I shall not live in vain
> If I can ease one life the aching
> Or cool one pain
> Or help one fainting robin
> Unto his nest again
> I shall not live in vain.

Now, this is extremely strange. It is a fact, that in 1864, Emily Dickinson wrote this verse; and it is a verse which a hundred or more

19th-century versifiers could have written. In its undistinguished language, as in its conventional sentiment, it is remarkably untypical of the poet. Had she chosen to write many poems like this one we would have no "problem" of non-publication, of editing, of estimating the poet at her true worth. Certainly the sentiment—a contented and unambiguous altruism—is one which even today might in some quarters be accepted as fitting from a female versifier—a kind of Girl Scout prayer. But we are talking about the woman who wrote:

> He fumbles at your Soul
> As Players at the Keys
> Before they drop full Music on—
> He stuns you by degrees—
> Prepares your brittle Nature
> For the Ethereal Blow
> By fainter Hammers—further heard—
> Then nearer—Then so slow
> Your breath has time to straighten—
> Your brain—to bubble Cool—
> Deals—One—Imperial—Thunderbolt—
> Then scalps your naked Soul—
>
> When winds take Forests in their Paws—
> The Universe—is still—

(#315)

Much energy has been invested in trying to identify a concrete, flesh-and-blood male lover whom Dickinson is supposed to have renounced, and to the loss of whom can be traced the secret of her seclusion and the vein of much of her poetry. But the real question, given that the art of poetry is an art of transformation, is how this woman's mind and imagination may have used the masculine element in the world at large, or those elements personified as masculine—including the men she knew; how her relationship to this reveals itself in her images and language. In a patriarchal culture, specifically the Judeo-Christian, quasi-Puritan culture of 19th-century New England in which Dickinson grew up, still inflamed with religious revivals, and where the sermon was still an active, if perishing, literary form, the equation of divinity with maleness was so fundamental that it is hardly surprising to find Dickinson, like many an early mystic, blurring erotic with religious experience and imagery. The poem I just read has intimations both of seduction and rape merged with the intense force of a religious experience. But are these metaphors for each other, or for something more intrinsic to Dickinson? Here is another:

> He put the Belt around my life—
> I heard the buckle snap—
> And turned away, imperial,
> My Lifetime folding up—
> Deliberate, as a Duke would do
> A Kingdom's Title Deed
> Henceforth, a Dedicated sort—
> Member of the Cloud.
>
> Yet not too far to come at call—
> And do the little Toils
> That make the Circuit of the Rest—
> And deal occasional smiles
> To lives that stoop to notice mine—
> And kindly ask it in—
> Whose invitation, know you not
> For Whom I must decline?

(#273)

These two poems are about possession, and they seem to me a poet's poems—that is, they are about the poet's relationship to her own power, which is exteriorized in masculine form, much as masculine poets have invoked the female Muse. In writing at all—particularly an unorthodox and original poetry like Dickinson's—women have often felt in danger of losing their status as women. And this status has always been defined in terms of relationship to men—as daughter, sister, bride, wife, mother, mistress, Muse. Since the most powerful figures in patriarchal culture have been men, it seems natural that Dickinson would assign a masculine gender to that in herself which did not fit in with the conventional ideology of womanliness. To recognize and acknowledge our own interior power has always been a path mined with risks for women; to acknowledge that power and commit oneself to it as Emily Dickinson did was an immense decision.

Most of us, unfortunately, have been exposed in the schoolroom to Dickinson's "little-girl" poems, her kittenish tones, as in "I'm Nobody! Who Are You?" (a poem whose underlying anger translates itself into archness) or

> I hope the Father in the skies
> Will lift his little girl—
> Old fashioned—naughty—everything—
> Over the stile of "Pearl."
>
> (#70)

or the poems about bees and robins. One critic—Richard Chase—has noted that in the 19th century "one of the careers open to women was perpetual childhood." A strain in Dickinson's letters and some— though by far a minority—of her poems was a self-diminutization, almost as if to offset and deny—or even disguise—her actual dimensions as she must have experienced them. And this emphasis on her own "littleness," along with the deliberate strangeness of her tactics of seclusion, have been, until recently, accepted as the prevailing character of the poet: the fragile poetess in white, sending flowers and poems by messenger to unseen friends, letting down baskets of gingerbread to the neighborhood children from her bedroom window; writing, but somehow naively. John Crowe Ransom, arguing for the editing and standardization of Dickinson's punctuation and typography, calls her "a little home-keeping person" who, "while she had a proper notion of the final destiny of her poems . . . was not one of those poets who had advanced to that later stage of operations where manuscripts are prepared for the printer, and the poet's diction has to make concessions to the publisher's style-book." (In short, Emily Dickinson did not wholly know her trade, and Ransom believes a "publisher's style-book" to have the last word on poetic diction.) He goes on to print several of her poems, altered by him "with all possible forbearance." What might, in a male writer—a Thoreau, let us say, or a Christopher Smart or William Blake—seem a legitimate strangeness, a unique intention, has been in one of our two major poets devalued into a kind of naïveté, girlish ignorance, feminine lack of professionalism, just as the poet herself has been made into a sentimental object. ("Most of us are half in love with this dead girl," confesses Archibald MacLeish. Dickinson was fifty-five when she died.)

It is true that more recent critics, including her most recent biographer, have gradually begun to approach the poet in terms of her greatness rather than her littleness, the decisiveness of her choices instead of the surface oddities of her life or the romantic crises of her legend. But unfortunately anthologists continue to plagiarize other anthologies, to reprint her in edited, even bowdlerized versions; the popular image of her and of her work lags behind the changing consciousness of scholars and specialists. There still does not exist a selection from her poems which depicts her in her fullest range. Dickinson's greatness cannot be measured in terms of twenty-five or fifty or even 500 "perfect" lyrics, it has to be seen as the accumulation it is. Poets, even, are not always acquainted with the full dimensions of her work, or the sense one gets, reading in the one-volume complete edition (let alone the three-volume variorum edition) of a mind engaged in a lifetime's musing on essential problems of language, identity, separation, relationship, the integrity of the self; a mind capable of describing psychological states more accurately than any poet except Shakespeare. I have been surprised at how narrowly her work, still, is known by women who are writing poetry, how much her legend has gotten in the way of her being re-possessed, as a source and a foremother.

I know that for me, reading her poems as a child and then as a young girl already seriously writing poetry, she was a problematic figure. I first read her in the selection heavily edited by her niece which appeared in 1937; a later and fuller edition appeared in 1945 when I was sixteen, and the complete, unbowdlerized edition by Johnson did not appear until fifteen years later. The publication of each of these editions was crucial to me in successive decades of my life. More than any other poet, Emily Dickinson seemed to tell me that the intense inner event, the personal and psychological, was inseparable from the universal; that there was a range for psychological poetry beyond mere self-expression. Yet the legend of the life was troubling, because it seemed to whisper that a woman who undertook such explorations must pay with renunciation, isolation, and incorporeality. With the publication of the *Complete Poems*, the legend seemed to recede into unimportance beside the unquestionable power and importance of the mind revealed there. But taking possession of Emily Dickinson is still no simple matter.

The 1945 edition, entitled *Bolts of Melody*, took its title from a poem which struck me at the age of sixteen and which still, thirty years later, arrests my imagination:

> I would not paint—a picture—
> I'd rather be the One
> Its bright impossibility
> To dwell—delicious—on—
> And wonder how the fingers feel
> Whose rare—celestial—stir
> Evokes so sweet a Torment—
> Such sumptuous—Despair—
>
> I would not talk, like Cornets—
> I'd rather be the One
> Raised softly to the Ceilings—
> And out, and easy on—
> Through Villages of Ether
> Myself endured Balloon
> By but a lip of Metal
> The pier to my Pontoon—
>
> Nor would I be a Poet—
> It's finer—own the Ear—
> Enamored—impotent—content—
> The License to revere,
> A privilege so awful
> What would the Dower be,
> Had I the Art to stun myself
> With Bolts of Melody!

(#505)

This poem is about choosing an orthodox "feminine" role: the receptive rather than the creative; viewer rather than painter, listener rather than musician; acted-upon rather than active. Yet even while ostensibly choosing this role she wonders "how the fingers feel/ whose rare-celestial—stir—/ Evokes so sweet a Torment—" and the "feminine" role is praised in a curious sequence of adjectives: "Enamored—*impotent*—content—." The strange paradox of this poem—its exquisite irony—is that it is about choosing not to be a poet, a poem which is gainsaid by no fewer than one thousand seven hundred and seventy-five poems made during the writer's life, including itself. Moreover, the images of the poem rise to a climax (like the Balloon she evokes) but the climax happens as she describes, not what it is to be the receiver, but the maker and receiver at once: "A Privilege so awful/ What would the Dower be/ Had I the Art to stun myself/ With Bolts of Melody!" —a climax which recalls the poem: "He fumbles at your soul/ As Players at the Keys/ Before they drop full Music on—" And of course, in writing those lines she possesses herself of that privilege and that "dower." I have said that this is a poem of exquisite ironies. It is, indeed, though in a very different mode, related to Dickinson's "little-girl" strategy. The woman who feels herself to be Vesuvius at home has need of a mask, at least, of innocuousness and of containment.

> On my volcano grows the Grass
> A meditative spot—
> An acre for a Bird to choose
> Would be the General thought—
>
> How red the Fire rocks below—
> How insecure the sod
> Did I disclose
> Would populate with awe my solitude.

(#1677)

Power, even masked, can still be perceived as destructive.

> A still—Volcano—Life—
> That flickered in the night—
> When it was dark enough to do
> Without erasing sight—
>
> A quiet—Earthquake style—
> Too subtle to suspect
> By natures this side Naples—
> The North cannot detect
>
> The Solemn—Torrid—Symbol—
> The lips that never lie—
> Whose hissing Corals part—and shut—
> And Cities—ooze away—

(#601)

Dickinson's biographer and editor Thomas Johnson has said that she often felt herself possessed by a demonic force, particularly in the years 1861 and 1862 when she was writing at the height of her drive. There are many poems besides "He put the Belt around my Life" which could be read as poems of possession by the daemon—poems which can also be, and have been, read, as poems of possession by the deity, or by a human lover. I suggest that a woman's poetry about her relationship to her daemon—her own active, creative power—has in patriarchal culture used the language of heterosexual love or patriarchal theology. Ted Hughes tells us that

> the eruption of (Dickinson's) imagination and poetry followed when she shifted her passion, with the energy of desperation, from (the) lost man onto his only possible substitute, —the Universe in its Divine aspect . . . Thereafter, the marriage that had been denied in the real world, went forward in the spiritual . . . just as the Universe in its Divine aspect became the mirror-image of her "husband," so the whole religious dilemma of New England, at that most critical moment in its history, became the mirror-image of her relationship to him, of her "marriage" in fact.*

This seems to me to miss the point on a grand scale. There are facts we need to look at. First, Emily Dickinson did not marry. And her non-marrying was neither a pathological retreat as John Cody sees it, nor probably even a conscious decision; it was a fact in her life as in her contemporary Christina Rossetti's; both women had more primary needs. Second: unlike Rossetti, Dickinson did not become a religiously dedicated woman; she was heretical, heterodox, in her religious opinions, and stayed away from church and dogma. What, in fact, *did* she allow to "put the Belt around her Life"—what *did* wholly occupy her mature years and possess her? For "Whom" did she decline the invitations of other lives? The writing of poetry. Nearly two thousand poems. Three hundred and sixty-six poems in the year of her fullest power. What was it like to be writing poetry you knew (and I am sure she did know) was of a class by itself—to be fuelled by the energy it took first to confront, then

*A Choice of Emily Dickinson's Verse, p. 11.

to condense that range of psychic experienc
then to copy out the poems and lay them
few here and there to friends or relatives
as gestures of confidence? I am sure she
she indicates in this poem:

> Myself was formed—a carpenter—
> An unpretending time
> My Plane—and I, together wrought
> Before a Builder came—
>
> To measure our attainments
> Had we the Art of Boards
> Sufficiently developed—He'd hire us
> At Halves—
>
> My Tools took Human—Faces—
> The Bench, where we had toiled—
> Against the Man—persuaded—
> We—Temples Build—I said—

> (#488)

This is a poem of the great year 1862, the year in which she first
sent a few poems to Thomas Higginson for criticism. Whether it
antedates or postdates that occasion is unimportant; it is a poem
of knowing one's measure, regardless of the judgments of others.

There are many poems which carry the weight of this knowledge.
Here is another one:

> I'm ceded—I've stopped being Theirs—
> The name They dropped upon my face
> With water, in the country church
> Is finished using, now,
> And They can put it with my dolls,
> My childhood, and the string of spools,
> I've finished threading—too—
>
> Baptized before, without the choice,
> But this time, consciously, of Grace—
> Unto supremest name—
> Called to my Fill—the Crescent dropped—
> Existence's whole Arc, filled up
> With one small Diadem.

> My second Rank—too small the first—
> Crowned—Crowing—on my Father's breast—
> A half unconscious Queen—
> But this time—Adequate—Erect—
> With Will to choose—or to reject—
> And I choose—just a Crown—

(#508)

Now, this poem partakes of the imagery of being "twice-born" or, in Christian liturgy, "confirmed"—and if this poem had been written by Christina Rossetti I would be inclined to give more weight to a theological reading. But it was written by Emily Dickinson, who used the Christian metaphor far more than she let it use her. This is a poem of great pride—not pridefulness, but *self*-confirmation—and it is curious how little Dickinson's critics, perhaps misled by her diminutives, have recognized the will and pride in her poetry. It is a poem of movement from childhood to womanhood, of transcending the patriarchal condition of bearing her father's name and "crowing—on my Father's breast—." She is now a conscious Queen, "Adequate—Erect/ With Will to choose, or to reject—."

There is one poem which is the real "onlie begetter" of my thoughts here about Dickinson; a poem I have mused over, repeated to myself, taken into myself over many years. I think it is a poem about possession by the daemon, about the dangers and risks of such possession if you are a woman, about the knowledge that power in a woman can seem destructive, and that you cannot live without the daemon once it has possessed you. The archetype of the daemon as masculine is beginning to change, but it has been real for women up until now. But this woman poet also perceives herself as a lethal weapon:

> My life had stood—a Loaded Gun—
> In Corners—till a Day
> The Owner passed—identified—
> And carried me away—
>
> And now We roam in Sovereign Woods—
> And now We hunt the Doe—
> And every time I speak for Him—
> The Mountains straight reply—
>
> And do I smile, such cordial light
> Upon the Valley glow—

It is as a Vesuvian face
Had let its pleasure through—

And when at Night—our good Day done—
I guard My Master's Head—
'Tis better than the Eider-Duck's
Deep Pillow—to have shared—

To foe of His—I'm deadly foe—
None stir the second time—
On whom I lay a Yellow Eye—
Or an emphatic Thumb—

Though I than he—may longer live
He longer must—than I—
For I have but the power to kill,
Without—the power to die—

(#754)

Here the poet sees herself as split, not between anything so simple as "masculine" and "feminine" identity but between the hunter, admittedly masculine, but also a human person, an active, willing being, and the gun—an object, condemned to remain inactive until the hunter—the *owner*—takes possession of it. The gun contains an energy capable of rousing echoes in the mountains and lighting up the valleys; it is also deadly, "Vesuvian;" it is also its owner's defender against the "foe." It is the gun, furthermore, who *speaks for him.* If there is a female consciousness in this poem it is buried deeper than the images: it exists in the ambivalence toward power, which is extreme. Active willing and creation in women are forms of aggression, and aggression is both "the power to kill" and punishable by death. The union of gun with hunter embodies the danger of identifying and taking hold of her forces, not least that in so doing she risks defining herself—and being defined—as aggressive, as unwomanly, ("and now we hunt the Doe") and as potentially lethal. That which she experiences in herself as energy and potency can also be experienced as pure destruction. The final stanza, with its precarious balance of phrasing, seems a desperate attempt to resolve the ambivalence; but, I think, it is no resolution, only a further extension of ambivalence.

Though I than he—may longer live
He longer must—than I—

> For I have but the power to kill,
> Without—the power to die—

The poet experiences herself as loaded gun, imperious energy; yet without the Owner, the possessor, she is merely lethal. Should that possession abandon her—but the thought is unthinkable: "He longer *must* than I." The pronoun is masculine; the antecedent is what Keats called "The Genius of Poetry."

I do not pretend to have—I don't even wish to have—explained this poem, accounted for its every image; it will reverberate with new tones long after my words about it have ceased to matter. But I think that for us, at this time, it is a central poem in understanding Emily Dickinson, and ourselves, and the condition of the woman artist, particularly in the 19th century. It seems likely that the 19th-century woman poet, especially, felt the medium of poetry as dangerous, in ways that the woman novelist did not feel the medium of fiction to be. In writing even such a novel of elemental sexuality and anger as *Wuthering Heights*, Emily Bronte could at least theoretically separate herself from her characters; they were, after all, fictitious beings. Moreover, the novel is or can be a construct, planned and organized to deal with human experiences on one level at a time. Poetry is too much rooted in the unconscious; it presses too close against the barriers of repression; and the 19th-century woman had much to repress. It is interesting that Elizabeth Barrett tried to fuse poetry and fiction in writing "Aurora Leigh"—perhaps apprehending the need for fictional characters to carry the charge of her experience as a woman artist. But with the exception of "Aurora Leigh" and Christina Rossetti's "Goblin Market"—that extraordinary and little-known poem drenched in oral eroticism—Emily Dickinson's is the only poetry in English by a woman of that century which pierces so far beyond the ideology of the "feminine" and the conventions of womanly feeling. To write it at all, she had to be willing to enter chambers of the self in which

> Ourself behind ourself, concealed—
> Should startle most—

and to relinquish control there, to take those risks, she had to create a relationship to the outer world where she could feel in control.

It is an extremely painful and dangerous way to live—split between a publicly acceptable persona, and a part of yourself that you perceive as the essential, the creative and powerful self, yet also as possibly unacceptable, perhaps even monstrous.

> Much Madness is divinest sense—
> To a discerning Eye—
> Much sense—the starkest Madness.
> 'Tis the Majority
> In this, as All, prevail—
> Assent—and you are sane—
> Demur—you're straightway dangerous—
> And handled with a chain—

(#435)

For many women the stresses of this splitting have led, in a world so ready to assert our innate passivity and to deny our independence and creativity, to extreme consequences: the mental asylum, self-imposed silence, recurrent depression, suicide, and often severe loneliness.

Dickinson is *the* American poet whose work consisted in exploring states of psychic extremity. For a long time, as we have seen, this fact was obscured by the kinds of selections made from her work by timid if well-meaning editors. In fact, Dickinson was a great psychologist; and like every great psychologist, she began with the material she had at hand: herself. She had to possess the courage to enter, through language, states which most people deny or veil with silence.

> The first Day's Night had come—
> And grateful that a thing
> So terrible—had been endured—
> I told my soul to sing—
>
> She said her Strings were snapt—
> Her Bow—to Atoms blown—
> And so to mend her—gave me work
> Until another Morn—
>
> And then—a Day as huge
> As Yesterdays in pairs,
> Unrolled its horror in my face—

Until it blocked my eyes—

My Brain—begun to laugh—
I mumbled—like a fool—
And tho' 'tis years ago—that Day—
My brain keeps giggling—still.

And Something's odd—within—
That person that I was—
And this One—do not feel the same—
Could it be Madness—this?

(#410)

Dickinson's letters acknowledge a period of peculiarly intense personal crisis; her biographers have variously ascribed it to the pangs of renunciation of an impossible love, or to psychic damage deriving from her mother's presumed depression and withdrawal after her birth. What concerns us here is the fact that she chose to probe the nature of this experience in language:

The Soul has Bandaged moments—
When too appalled to stir—
She feels some ghastly Fright come up
And stop to look at her—

Salute her—with long fingers—
Caress her freezing hair—
Sip, Goblin, from the very lips
The Lover—hovered—o'er—
Unworthy, that a thought so mean
Accost a Theme—so—fair—

The soul has moments of Escape—
When bursting all the doors—
She dances like a Bomb, abroad,
And swings upon the hours . . .

The Soul's retaken moments—
When, Felon led along,
With shackles on the plumed feet,
And staples, in the Song,

The Horror welcomes her, again,
These, are not brayed of Tongue—

(#512)

In this poem, the word "Bomb" is dropped, almost carelessly, as a correlative for the soul's active, liberated states—it occurs in a context of apparent euphoria, but its implications are more than euphoric—they are explosive, destructive. The Horror from which in such moments the soul escapes has a masculine, "goblin" form, and suggests the perverse and terrifying rape of a "bandaged" and powerless self. In at least one poem, Dickinson depicts the actual process of suicide:

> He scanned it—staggered—
> Dropped the Loop
> To Past or Period—
> Caught helpless at a sense as if
> His mind were going blind—
> Groped up—to see if God was there—
> Groped backward at Himself—
> Caressed a Trigger absently
> And wandered out of Life.
>
> (#1062)

The precision of knowledge in this brief poem is such that we must assume that Dickinson had, at least in fantasy, drifted close to that state in which the "Loop" that binds us to "Past or Period" is "dropped" and we grope randomly at what remains of abstract notions of sense, God, or self, before—almost absent-mindedly—reaching for a solution. But it's worth noting that this is a poem in which the suicidal experience has been distanced, refined, transformed through a devastating accuracy of language. It is not suicide that is studied here, but the dissociation of self and mind and world which precedes.

Dickinson was convinced that a life worth living could be found within the mind and against the grain of external circumstance: "Reverse cannot befall/ That fine prosperity/ Whose Sources are interior—." (#395) The horror, for her, was that which set "Staples in the Song"—the numbing and freezing of the interior, a state she describes over and over:

> There is a Languor of the Life
> More imminent than Pain—
> 'Tis Pain's Successor—When the Soul
> Has suffered all it can—

A Drowsiness—diffuses—
A Dimness like a Fog
Envelopes Consciousness—
As Mists—obliterate a Crag.

The Surgeon—does not blanch—at pain
His Habit—is severe—
But tell him that it ceased to feel—
That creature lying there—

And he will tell you—skill is late—
A Mightier than He—
Has ministered before Him—
There's no Vitality.

                                    (#396)

I think the equation surgeon-artist is a fair one here; the artist can work with the materials of pain; she cuts to probe and heal; but she is powerless at the point where

After great pain, a formal feeling comes—
The nerves sit ceremonious, like Tombs—
The stiff Heart questions was it He, that bore,
And Yesterday, or Centuries before?

The Feet, mechanical, go round—
Of Ground, or Air, or Ought—
A Wooden way
Regardless grown,
A Quartz contentment, like a stone—

This is the Hour of Lead
Remembered, if outlived
As Freezing persons, recollect the Snow—
First—Chill—then Stupor—then the letting go—

                                    (#341)

For the poet, the terror is precisely in those periods of psychic death, when even the possibility of work is negated; her "occupation's gone." Yet she also describes the unavailing effort to numb emotion:

Me from Myself—to banish—
Had I Art—
Impregnable my Fortress
Unto All Heart—

But since Myself—assault Me—
How have I peace
Except by subjugating
Consciousness?

And since We're mutual Monarch
How this be
Except by Abdication—
Me—of Me?

(#642)

The possibility of abdicating oneself—of ceasing to be—remains.

Severe Service of myself
I—hastened to demand
To fill the awful longitude
Your life had left behind—

I worried Nature with my Wheels
When Hers had ceased to run—
When she had put away her Work
My own had just begun.

I strove to weary Brain and Bone—
To harass to fatigue
The glittering Retinue of nerves—
Vitality to clog

To some dull comfort Those obtain
Who put a Head away
They knew the Hair to—
And forget the color of the Day—

Affliction would not be appeased—
The Darkness braced as firm
As all my strategem had been
The Midnight to confirm—

No drug for Consciousness—can be—
Alternative to die
Is Nature's only Pharmacy
For Being's Malady—

(#786)

Yet consciousness—not simply the capacity to suffer, but the capacity to experience intensely at every instant—creates of death not a blotting-out but a final illumination:

This Consciousness that is aware
Of Neighbors and the Sun
Will be the one aware of Death
And that itself alone

Is traversing the interval
Experience between
And most profound experiment
Appointed unto Men—

How adequate unto itself
Its properties shall be
Itself unto itself and none
Shall make discovery.

Adventure most unto itself
The Soul condemned to be—
Attended by a single Hound
Its own identity.

(#822)

The poet's relationship to her poetry has, it seems to me—and I am not speaking only of Emily Dickinson—a twofold nature. Poetic language—the poem on paper—is a concretization of the poetry of the world at large, the self, and the forces within the self; and those forces are rescued from formlessness, lucidified, and integrated in the act of writing poems. But there is a more ancient concept of the poet, which is that she is endowed to speak for those who do not have the gift of language, or to see for those who—for whatever reasons—are less conscious of what they are living through. It is as though the risks of the poet's existence can be put to some use beyond her own survival.

The Province of the Saved
Should be the Art—To save—
Through Skill obtained in themselves—
The Science of the Grave

No Man can understand
But He that hath endured
The Dissolution—in Himself—
That man—be qualified

To qualify Despair
To Those who failing new—

Mistake Defeat for Death—Each time—
Till acclimated—to—

(#539)

The poetry of extreme states, the poetry of danger, can allow its
readers to go further in our own awareness, take risks we might
not have dared; it says, at least: "Someone has been here before."

The Soul's distinct Connection
With immortality
Is best disclosed by Danger
Or quick Calamity—

As Lightning on a Landscape
Exhibits Sheets of Place—
Not yet suspected—but for Flash—
And Click—and Suddenness.

(#974)

Crumbling is not an instant's Act
A fundamental pause
Dilapidation's processes
Are organized Decays.

'Tis first a cobweb on the Soul
A Cuticle of Dust
A Borer in the Axis
An Elemental Rust—

Ruin is formal—Devil's work
Consecutive and slow—
Fail in an instant—no man did
Slipping—is Crash's law.

(#997)

I felt a Cleaving in my Mind
As if my Brain had split—
I tried to match it—Seam by Seam—
But could not make them fit.

The thought behind, I strove to join
Unto the thought before—

But Sequence ravelled out of Sound
Like Balls—upon a Floor

(#937)

There are many more Emily Dickinsons than I have tried to call
up here. Wherever you take hold of her, she proliferates. I wish
I had time here to explore her complex sense of Truth; to follow
the thread we unravel when we look at the numerous and passionate
poems she wrote to or about women; to probe her ambivalent feelings
about fame, a subject pursued by many male poets before her; simply
to examine the poems in which she is directly apprehending the
natural world. No one since the 17th century had reflected more
variously or more probingly upon death and dying. What I have
tried to do here is follow through some of the origins and consequences
of her choice to be, not only a poet but a woman who explored
her own mind, without any of the guidelines of orthodoxy. To say
"yes" to her powers was not simply a major act of nonconformity
in the 19th century; even in our own time it has been assumed
that Emily Dickinson, not patriarchal society, was "the problem."
The more we come to recognize the unwritten and written laws
and taboos underpinning patriarchy, the less problematical, surely,
will seem the methods she chose.

Eiron *Eyes*

WILLIAM HARMON

If the Hindus are right and the destiny of every creature in the universe is governed by an inescapably just Karma that dictates the types and durations of an indefinite succession of reincarnations inflexibly delivering rewards and punishments that match what one has done in previous existences, then Harriet Monroe (1860–1936), founder of *Poetry* magazine, will by now have undergone any number of rebirths, via the wombs of a crawling insect (for her pedestrian imagination), flying insect (capriciousness and inability to sit still), jellyfish (occasional spinelessness and tendency to sting the innocent), tortoise (taking too much time with some important chores), jay (hysteria plus silly litigiousness), third-world churchmouse (to compensate for excessive wealth), and chairpersoness of the Greater Teaneck Arts Council and Begonia Guild (on general principles plus two counts of suffering Morton Dauwen Zabel gladly).

Any schoolchild today can look back at Ms. Monroe's errors in just the single year of 1915 and think, "Jesus! How could she have been such a ninny? She sat on 'Prufrock' for eight months before burying it in the back pages, all the while showcasing Arthur Davison Ficke and similar jiveturkeys. Deaf to the essential integrity of the original eight-stanza 'Sunday Morning,' she made Stevens omit three stanzas, so that he felt constrained to rearrange the remaining five. She was a poet of zero talent herself, and she so overrated Masters, Sandburg, and Robinson that she had insufficient I.Q. left when the time came to give Hart Crane the appreciation and sympathy that he frantically needed."

We—you and I—can be sure, can't we, that *we* would never be guilty of such mistakes; we'd have "Prufrock" right up there in the front of the magazine with no eight-month delay (if, that is, we had ever mustered the courage and resources to get a magazine going); we'd keep "Sunday Morning" intact all along without putting Stevens and his obviously brilliant poem through what must have been a humiliating and emasculating experience; if we had been calling the shots, Hart Crane would probably still be alive, surrounded by sycophants gaily helping to celebrate his

Review of Louis Zukofsky's "*A*" from *Parnassus* (vol. 7, no. 2, 1979).

45

eightieth birthday with a cake in the shape of a big Life Saver; and . . . and, well, and *everything.*

You bet.

My point is that, if the Hindus are right, Ms. Monroe ought to be about due for some release from her punishing passage through all those mortifying wombs, some recognition for the things she managed to do at least half-right. Death's first minister and chief of data processing, old Citragupta, will be on hand to recite evidence from his scrupulous printout that Ms. Monroe *did,* after all, found the magazine and run it vigorously for many years; she paid her contributors; she *did,* after all, print Eliot and Stevens and dozens of other first-rate poets; she *did* have the perspicacity to accept the advice of Ezra Pound when he was twenty-six (exactly half her age), even before he got so buddy-buddy with Yeats. And she *did,* early in 1924, publish a sonnet that had been written by a teenage prodigy in New York City:

> "Spare us of dying beauty," cries out Youth,
> "Of marble gods that moulder into dust—
> Wide-eyed and pensive with an ancient truth
> That even gods will go as old things must."
> Where fading splendor grays to powdered earth,
> And time's slow movement darkens quiet skies,
> Youth weeps the old, yet gives her beauty birth
> And molds again, though the old beauty dies.
> Time plays an ancient dirge amid old places
> Where ruins are a sign of passing strength,
> As in the weariness of aged faces
> A token of a beauty gone at length.
> Yet youth will always come self-willed and gay—
> A sun-god in a temple of decay.
>
> ("Of Dying Beauty")

You guessed it: Louis Zukofsky (1904–1978). And your verdict is correct: not bad—for a kid (he turned twenty in January 1924 but the poem was written earlier) not bad at all. He may have absorbed too much Santayana, he may have affected the dark-fantastic too much, but he was no damned ego-freak (no "I" mars the poem) and he knew how to write a good dignified sonnet.

Scarcely seven years later, Ms. Monroe turned her magazine over to the same prodigy for a special number (February 1931) devoted to "Objectivist" poetry along with some modest polemics that provoked from her in the next issue a few condescending but indulgent remarks about the arrogance of youth (she was seventy, her guest-editor twenty-seven). But she *did* let Zukofsky edit a whole issue, even though nobody had any very prismatic idea of what an "Objectivist" poem may be (years later Kenneth Rexroth summarized the contributors as "anybody who would say yes and didn't write sonnets," but some of Zukofsky's own offerings were sonnets; and the point was in no way cleared up by the publication of Zukofsky's *An "Objectivists" Anthology* in 1932). Here is a poem from the special issue of *Poetry*:

> The moving masses of clouds, and the standing
> Freights on the siding in the sun, alike induce in us
> That despair which we, brother, know there is no withstanding. . . .

The note on the contributor of those lines says, by the way: "Whittaker Chambers, of Lynbrook, N.Y., was born in 1901. He has appeared in *The Nation, The New Masses,* and is a translator of note." Small world.

Zukofsky's own contribution to these "Objectivist" enterprises was a part of a long poem called *"A"* of which seven movements were finished by 1930. To approach a discussion of the whole poem, I want to start by looking at the original opening of the second movement:

> The clear music—
> Zoo-zoo-kaw-kaw-of-the-sky,
> Not mentioning names, says Kay,
> Poetry is not made of such things,
> Old music, itch according to its wonts,
> Snapped old cat-guts from Johann Sebastian,
> Society, traduction twice over.

The version, called *"A"*-2 in the eventual book form, shows some interesting adjustments:

> —Clear music—

> Not calling you names, says Kay,
> Poetry is not made of such things,
> Music, itch according to its wonts,
> Snapped old catguts of Johann Sebastian,
> Society, traduction twice over.

I want first to note that the poet had put his own name into the poem but in a mangled form, like the cries of beasts and birds: "Zoo-zoo-kaw-kaw-of-the-sky"; later he eliminated the name entirely, here and in other passages. Such a distortion of one's name followed by effacement of it impresses me as the gesture of a particular sort of personage, the *eiron* of antiquity who was both an ethical and a theatrical type.

Aristotle (*Nicomachean Ethics* 4) described the *eiron* and other such types so as to outfit a kind of Central Casting for life and literature. Zukofsky's generation, *Epigonoi* coming after a generation of giants like Stevens, Williams, Pound, and Eliot, may seem particularly rich in pure types: Charles Olson a *philosophus gloriosus et maximus,* Beckett a tragic clown, Rexroth a lordly pedant of incredible erudition in sixty-seven languages, and Zukofsky himself, in person and in print, the classic *eiron* described in Northrop Frye's *Anatomy of Criticism*: self-deprecating, seldom vulnerable, artful, given to understatement, modest or mock-modest, indirect, objective, dispassionate, unassertive, sophisticated, and maybe foreign (all of these terms apply to the *eiron* both as author and as character). The derivation of *eiron* from a Greek word meaning "to say" (and kin to "word," "verb," "verve," "rhematic," and "rhetor") suggests that irony is chiefly a kind of speech and that the *eiron* is recognized chiefly by a manner or habit of speaking. He—whether Socrates, Swift, or Art Carney in the role of Ed Norton—says less than he means; now and then he says the reverse. He may be Prufrock, crying, "It is impossible to say just what I mean!" or Polonius, knowing how we "With windlasses and with assays of bias,/ By indirections find directions out."

Now, from an objective or Objectivist point of view, epic contains history along with one or another measure of myth. The greater the measure of myth, the higher the status of the epic poet himself, so that Moses, Homer, and Vyāsa (who was said to have compiled the *Mahā-bhārata*) are themselves legendary, as, in modern times, such poets as Milton, Whitman, and Pound have become. So grand is the epic enterprise, indeed, that the author thereof threatens to turn into a boastful *alazon,* ordering the Muses around and organizing gods and devils in overweening patterns. Besides, these poets make up among themselves a kind of hermetic society of trade secrets and inside dope, a tradition of precursors, guides, and counsellors, each one becoming *"mio Virgilio"* for the next one, who becomes *"il miglior fabbro"* for his associate, and so on. Since 1700, we have seen a succession of secularized or individualized epics or mock-epics, all of them more or less inconsistent and turbulent (if they are not outright flops), and they test the possibility of a sustained poem without a sustaining body of supernatural lore. The question seems to have been: What, other than a system of myth-dignified ideological conflicts and resolutions, can keep a long poem going?

The obvious answer from the *eiron*'s viewpoint: *Nothing.* A somewhat less obvious addendum from the viewpoint of the modern *eiron* would be: *But it doesn't make any difference.* There persists an article of faith that supposes that we have somehow lost a paradise, that Homer or Dante or Milton could write tremendous poems because the poet and his audience *in illo tempore,* in that spell of magic and an organic oral tradition, shared a whole complex of beliefs capable of organizing and running an epic poem. That's a crock. If Homer, Dante, and Milton have anything in common, it is that they seem, fitfully, to have entertained beliefs that nobody could share. A cursory look at the debates among their audiences and successors will show very quickly that their appeal was not based on any shared system of beliefs, opinions, or even historical data. Their appeal was and still is based on their extremely powerful presentation of artworks so compelling that they overwhelm our disbelief with enchantment, and we—if we believe anything short of suicidal nihilism—assent.

Nothing is lost, but things can change and centers can shift around among comedy, tragedy, romance, and irony. It looks as though the general drift since 1700 has been toward irony, maybe because of the rise of science and the spread of middle-class commerce. In any event, we have been privileged witnesses to a prolonged flowering of ironies, some very amusing and some very touching. The general environment is a diachronic matrix, so to speak, in which mythic meanings have fled from literature to music, and a modernist-ironist like Zukofsky can best orient his own most ambitious literary work by going back two centuries—from 1928 to 1729—pick up a moment of metamorphosis ("traduction twice over," which means the two ironically contrasted meanings of "traduction"—

from Old and New Testament to German to English—along with the
transferral of energy from score to performance to repeated performance)
and to chase that moment or movement as a fugue:

> A
> Round of fiddles playing Bach.
> *Come, ye daughters, share my anguish—*
> Bare arms, black dresses,
> *See Him! Whom?*
> Bediamond the passion of our Lord,
> *See Him! How?*
>
> . . . .
>
> The Passion According to Matthew,
> Composed seventeen twenty-nine,
> Rendered at Carnegie Hall,
> Nineteen twenty-eight,
> Thursday evening, the fifth of April.
> The autos parked, honking.

These lines of condensed polyphonic counterpoint enact the marriage
of music and irony. For whatever reason (and reasons are legion), the *eiron*'s
art—irony—amounts to saying two or more things at one time, so that an
auditor with 20/20 ears ought to hear an ironic utterance as a chord of
sorts, one that displays its own meaning in its own sound as harmonies
among *cord* and *chord, accord* and *a chord,* even *choral* and *coral.* (In the case
of Zukofsky's introductory "Round," we are dealing with a fact. In 1928,
Seder was Wednesday, 4 April, and Passover began the next day, which
was also Maundy Thursday for Christians, and on that evening in Carnegie
Hall there was a performance of Bach's St. Matthew Passion by the Detroit Symphony Orchestra and Choir, conducted by Ossip Gabrilowitsch.
Olin Downes's enthusiastic review the next day noted that the conductor
"had requested plain dark dress and a silent reception of the masterpiece.")

At times, the drawing together of many meanings in one word amounts
to an ecstatic joining of ostensible opposites, as when Hopkins, in "The
Windhover," uses "buckle" to mean, simultaneously, both "fall apart"
and "come together." Freud, in a note based on some pretty unruly
speculations of the linguist Karl Abel, explored the possible psychic mean-

ing of the "antithetical sense of primal words," such as the English "let,"
"fast," and "still" (or those contrasting twin daughters of a single mother,
"queen" and "quean"). The presence of such Siamese chords permits the
approach of monophonic language to polyphonic music. Oddly, "fugue"
itself is fugal, because it means both "a polyphonic musical style or form"
and "a pathological amnesiac condition" (both meanings derive from the
concept of "chase" or "flight"). Whether perfidious or merely economical, the capacity in language for such halvings and doublings will give a
high rhetorical valence to such figures as zeugma and syllepsis (which
don't mean *quite* the same thing) and such devices as parallel plots and
contrast-rhymes ("hire"-"fire," "town"-"gown," "womb"-"tomb," and
so forth).

What the solo modern prose voice at the beginning of *"A"* accom-
plishes is, then, to suggest both irony and fugue complexly: by talking
about a piece of vocal-instrumental polyphony and by doing so in ways
that are themselves fugal or quasi-fugal:

A
Round of fiddles playing Bach.

"A" equals air *(aria)* with different values in ancient and modern English,
or in English and other European languages, or in English itself variable
according to stress. Prefixed in this way or that, it means "with" and it
means "without." It means "one" and "he" and "they" and "of." Here,
right off the baton, it plays "around" against "a round," which is iridescent with musical, poetic, geometric, and mundane meanings. The part-
for-whole figure of "fiddles" (for "fiddlers") plays against the whole-for-
part figure of "Bach" (for "a work by Bach"), and "playing," as I have
been leaking none too subtly, means everything that both "work" and
"play" can mean, including the ideas of performance and impersonation
and contest. (At about the same time, Yeats was scrutinizing near-by
ranges of meaning in "play" and "labor" in another poem that has to do
with time, memory, age, youth, and music: "Among School Children,"
which moves from an ironic "I walk" to an ecstatic "dance?").

Then, hundreds of pages later, in an interpolation in *"A"*-21 (p. 474),
Zukofsky resumes the theme of roundness by means of a related word,
"rote":

> there cannot be too much
> music R—O—T—E
> rote, fiddle
>
> like noise of surf . . .

Let me confess that I went for most of my life with only one meaning for "rote," one phrase ("learn by rote"), and one circumscribed connotation (bad). I took that verbal poverty with me to a study of Eliot's "The Dry Salvages" and appraised the line "The distant rote in the granite teeth" as a very effective figure of speech that rendered the sound of water against a rock as a lesson mechanically repeated (*rota:* circle). In fact, English "rote" has three meanings, of which Eliot, writing in 1942, used two and Zukofsky, in 1967, used all three. It also means "a medieval stringed instrument" and "the sound of surf breaking on the shore" *(American Heritage Dictionary).* (It could appear in the name of an enterprise called POTH, if that name be Greek.) The verbal chord may be tabulated:

rote 1	routine	ME from Lat. *rota,* wheel	IE *ret*—to run, roll
rote — rote 2	surf	ON *rauta,* to roar	IE *reu*—to bellow
rote 3	instrument	OF from Gmc.	IE *krut*—
			instrument

Such an etymological history of three words converging in a single sound—*rote*—may be seen as a model of Zukofsky's main themes and techniques in *"A."* No modern ironic poem of any length could possibly be self-standing, and Zukofsky's resembles those by Williams, Pound, and Eliot in including precursors and companions. A shrewd programmer should design a map that would show Pound appearing in Eliot's and Williams' poems (and, later, in Lowell's and Berryman's), Eliot and Williams in Pound's (and Lowell's and Berryman's), and so on, in a serial *agon* that is at the same time an old-boy network. As is noted in *"A"*-1, Zukofsky's poem gets going not long after the death of Thomas Hardy in January 1928. Some unconscious ironist says of the most conscious ironist of modern letters, "Poor Thomas Hardy he had to go so soon" (which is ironic because he had been born in 1840). But that note is enough to suggest that the long poem at hand will carry on the work of *The Dynasts,* Hardy's immense epic drama that could be called "The

Convergence of the Twain," because it traces, in a somewhat fugal staggered form, the fate of two men born in 1769, Napoleon and Wellington, whose paths finally cross, or collide, at Waterloo. As Hardy is dying, the successors maintain the ironic dynasty, and Zukofsky launches his long poem by assimilating the techniques of Pound, Eliot, Williams, and Hardy. With Zukofsky, the focus is on technique and the fabric of the language itself, but the notion of tellingly ironic convergence remains as it had been in Hardy's poems.

Zukofsky begins his poem on a particular April evening in 1928, and for him—as for Whitman, Yeats, and Eliot before him—this paschal time of Passover and Passion, converging in the syncretism of Eos-East-Easter with its terrible beauty, furnishes an ideal prism for seeing the world clearly and for intelligently hearing its ironies and harmonies. (Of "When Lilacs Last in the Dooryard Bloom'd," "Easter 1916," *The Waste Land, Ulysses,* and *The Sound and the Fury* alike, one could say that the typical modern literary work begins and centers on a particular day in spring. Oddly, for both Faulkner and Zukofsky, the focus happens to be the same few days in April 1928.) Given this matrix of ideal convergences, the *eiron*'s eyes and ears can subject language to a detailed inquisition, though it hardly takes the full third degree to remove hide and hair from verbal surfaces. In a sixty-year career, Zukofsky experimented with every species of rhematic and thematic irony as ways of saying more than one thing at a time, and he devoted an inordinate amount of his genius to the transfiguration into English of various foreign texts. Since Zukofsky tried to preserve sound and sense alike—which is impossible—"translation" is not quite the correct word for this process. Pound's "creative translations" showed the path here, especially in versions of Old English and Latin (to which I shall come back in a few moments), but Pound is only one member of a large modern club that has trafficked in the Englishing and modernizing of many sorts of foreign and ancient texts. Some years ago, for instance, there was a black film version of "Carmen" called "Carmen Jones," in which Escamillo became "Husky Miller." Any number of modern characters, in their names if not otherwise, show this sort of metempsychosis: Shaw's John Tanner out of Don Juan Tenorio, O'Neill's Ezra Mannon out of Agamemnon, Eliot's Harcourt-Reilly out of Heracles, Faulkner's Joe Christmas out of Jesus Christ, Updike's Caldwell out of Chiron. Zukofsky's refinement, which may echo certain Talmudic or Cabalistic techniques of interpretation, has been to apply this principle of

nomenclature to whole texts, typically ironic or comic-lyric, and to produce a complete *Catullus* by this method, as well as a version (appearing
as "A" -21) of Plautus' *Rudens,* which is evidently a reworking of a lost
Greek play by Diphilus.

One of those shipwreck-and-lost-daughter comedies, *Rudens* (i.e., *The
Rope*) resembles Shakespeare's *Pericles* (although it is not, strictly speaking,
the source of *Pericles,* as one critic has stated). At any rate, we may note
here that Volume II of Zukofsky's *Bottom: On Shakespeare* is a musical
setting for *Pericles* by Zukofsky's wife, Celia. One may regard all of *Bottom*
as a long poem that works as an appendix to *"A."* It is typically ironic of
Zukofsky to see all of Shakespeare through the eyes of Nick Bottom,
big-mouthed weaver and man of the theatre (not to mention part-time ass
and boyfriend of the fairy queen).

Zukofsky's novel handling of Latin and other foreign languages has
been duly admired by some, but I have to say that I think his Catullus and
Plautus are dull distortions. Their purpose may be to breathe (literally)
new breath through their consonants and vowels, but the result is a high-
handed botch.

I am not qualified to discuss the fine points of this complicated problem
of translation. It's just that sound and sense cannot be transferred from one
language to another, and it may also be true that not even sense by itself
can be moved. Now and then, as in the acoustic and semantic nearness of
Hebrew *pāsaḥ,* Latin *passiō,* and English *pass,* there seems to be a linguistic
kinship that resembles the connection among *Pesach, Passion,* and *Passover;* but such harmonies are rare. More commonly, even "cognates" from
closely related languages may not be good translations for one another,
especially in the realm of abstractions. *Stupor Mundi* just isn't "stupor of
the world."

Consider these two lines from *Rudens,* in which Charmides (a *senex*) is
needling his friend, the pimp Labrax, about a shipwreck:

> *Pol minime miror, navis si fractast tibi,*
> *scelus te et sceleste parta quae vexit bona.*

"Pol" is a faint oath that abridges something like "by Pollux." "Minime"
is an adverb meaning "least" (or "not at all"). "Miror" (as some may
recall from their high-school Latin version of "Twinkle, Twinkle, Little
Star") is the present first-person singular declarative of a deponent verb

(hence the passive form) meaning "I wonder." "Well, by God, I'm not a bit surprised," as you might say. The Loeb translation by Paul Nixon captures all of these meanings: "Gad! I don't wonder at all that your ship was wrecked, with a rascal like you and your rascally gains aboard." Zukofsky:

> Pole! minimal mirror! the ship
> fractured from your ill-begot goods.

Well: "Pole! minimal mirror!" does preserve the general sound pattern of "Pol minime miror," and it may preserve some of the sense (if calling one "Pole" and "minimal mirror" suggests that he doesn't do much reflecting). But at what price? This: the subordination of sense to sound, which is exactly what Imagists and Objectivists complain about in the verse of sonneteers and what Olson complained about in Pound's later Chinese translations. And this: the sacrifice of the character's personal style. Kept up doggedly for seventy pages, Zukofsky's Plautus' Diphilus' *Rudens* is the most tiresome part of *"A."*

The next most tiresome part is *"A"*-24, which is another fugal experiment. *"A"*-21 amounts to a superposed transmogrification of the folk theme of the recovered daughter with Greco-Roman voices joined by synthetic English (a tricky sort of technique that Pound was intelligent enough, in Canto I, to limit to seventy-six lines and to carbonate, ad lib, with matter, rhythms, and "cross-lights" from sources other than his Greek-Latin-English triad). *"A"*-24, which was composed by Celia Zukofsky (with help from the Zukofsky's brilliant son, Paul) before Louis Zukofsky wrote *"A"*-22 and *"A"*-23, is not so much the real conclusion of *"A"* as a kind of addendum called *L. Z. Masque*, "a five-part score—music, thought, drama, story, poem." The score is presented contrapuntally with music in two staves (treble and bass) above four verbal lines in type of varying sizes. The music is Handel's, the words from Zukofsky's *Prepositions* (thought), *Arise, Arise* (drama), *It was* (story), and *"A"* itself (poem). The two acts are divided into nine scenes named for characters and musical forms (Cousin: Lesson, Nurse: Prelude & Allegro, Father: Suite, Girl: Fantasia, Attendants: Chaconne, Mother: Sonata, Doctor: Capriccio, Aunt: Passacaille, and Son: Fugues). The text is about 240 pages, with an indicated duration of about 70 minutes. Presumably, a harpsichord plays while four voices speak the words ("The words are NEVER

SUNG to the music. . . . Each voice should come through clearly"). I have taken some pains to describe *"A"*-24, because I don't want to be judged indifferent or careless when I say that the thing is unreadable. I have done my best, line-by-line and also measure-by-measure, and in my cranial studio I get only the effect of five non-profit educational stations going at one time. I'll keep at it, but for the present I can't find anything to admire. In both *"A"*-21 and *"A"*-24 the fugue fails.

That failure is more than disappointing. It is heartbreaking. As the ironic poem progresses through its early and middle phases, its moments of greatest tenderness and beauty coincide with the moments of most concentrated attention on Zukofsky's marriage to Celia Thaew in 1939 and the birth, on 22 October 1943, of their son, the *Wunderkind* violinist Paul Zukofsky, whose childhood experiences contributed to Louis Zukofsky's novel called *Little*. *Baker's Biographical Dictionary of Musicians,* edited by Nicolas Slonimsky, praises Paul Zukofsky's sympathy for contemporary music and the "maximal celerity, dexterity, and alacrity" of his playing. Even so, the Plautus translation, which was probably done as the Catullus was—by Louis and Celia Zukofsky together—and the five-part happening of *"A"*-24, in which all three Zukofskys had a part, subtract from the overall integrity and intensity of *"A."*

The remaining twenty-two sections add up to about five hundred pages of poetry that takes the initial fugal subjects and styles through a forty-five-year development, conditioned by external historical and personal events but never, I think, completely irrelevant to the promises potently implicit in

A
Round of fiddles playing Bach.

Earlier I suggested a number of the possible meanings, but I did not mention the chance that the fiddles are playing B A C H, which, in a peculiar German style of notation used at one time before the seven-note nomenclature was adopted, would sound as B-flat, A, C, B-natural. J. S. and C. P. E. Bach used this sequence as a musical subject, as did Schumann, Liszt, Rimsky-Korsakov, and a score (ha) of other composers. Zukofsky's use of this musical acrostic to organize the very long (135 pages) *"A"*-12—

Blest
Ardent
Celia
       unhurt and
Happy—

brings us back to the alphabet and its gifts and challenges to the ironic
poet.

Bach's adding his "signature" to a piece of music is an uncommon but
not a unique phenomenon. It is recorded that Bach, who may have written
a four-note "cruciform" motif for the Crucifixion in the *St. Matthew
Passion,* once sketched out a canon formula for a friend named Schmidt.
Translating *Schmidt* into the Latin *faber,* Bach then canonized his friend in
the form of F A B E Repetatur, then signed the formula with the tribute,
Bonae Artis Cultorem Habeas. It is said that the *paytanim,* composers of
Hebrew liturgical poetry, "signed" their works by placing their names or
anagrams thereof as an acrostic at the beginning of each line. It is also said
that certain Jewish names may have been formed as acronyms drawn from
devotional formulae, as "Atlas" from *akh tov leyisrael selah* ("Truly God
is good to Israel") and not from the Greek name of the world-bearing
Titan or the German word for "satin." That may belong in the same
uncertain category as the oddity of the King James version of Psalm 46,
written when Shakespeare was 46 years old: the forty-sixth word from the
beginning is "shake," the forty-sixth from the end "spear." It is certain,
however, that writers now and then have used their own names or initials
to "sign" their works internally, as it were, as well as on the title page.
Shakespeare and Donne used "will" and "done" in poems as puns on their
own first or last names. Robert Browning used his initials for *The Ring and
the Book,* and T.S. Eliot may have had a variation of the same policy in
mind when he titled a play *The Elder Statesman.* J. D. Salinger once named
a character Jean de Daumier-Smith, and Martin Gardner's fascinating
column in *Scientific American* is called "Mathematical Games."* In modern
prose's grandest ironic epic, Mann's *Doktor Faustus,* the composer Lever-
kühn repeatedly uses certain notes, Bach-fashion, to trace non-musical

---

*Two further examples: The Boy Scouts chose a motto with initials to match those of their
founder, Lord Baden-Powell; and in the graphic arts, Al Hirschfeld always weaves the name
of his daughter Nina into his caricatures, hidden there among wrinkles or ruffles or extrava-
gant coiffures.

meanings over musical themes; and at the end of the book, in the *Nach-schrift*, the author's own names rises touchingly through the prose of his rather foolish narrator, "Dr. phil. Serenus Zeitblom": *"Es ist getan,"* he says. He now writes as *"ein alter Mann, gebeugt. . . ."* Pound reversed the process once, in Canto IV, when he alluded to Whitman's "Beat! beat! . . . whirr and pound" but changed the wording to "Beat, beat, whirr, thud." Later, though, he made up for this avoidance of his own name by putting three archaic Chinese characters on the title page of *Thrones: pao en tê*, pronounced, more or less, "Pound."

So what? So the work of art inherently resists being used for autobiography or any other kind of direct representation. Only by certain tricks can an artist register his own presence in a self-willed medium, especially if he is an *eiron* approaching that medium and its social environment from below or outside. The *eiron*'s infra-structural position resembles the alien's extra-structural condition, so that if one has to be both—a talented son, say, of Yiddish-speaking immigrants—then one's ears will, with luck, be attuned to speech as a foreign entity and, particularly, to American English as the native property of others. "Abcedminded," then, as it says in *Finnegans Wake*, verbal comedy leads ironic outsiders of various sorts to write *The Comedian as the Letter C* and an uproarious novel called *V.* and a long poem called *"A"* (just as Stephen Dedalus contemplated calling his novels by letters of the alphabet). This is elevated comedy, a plane of discourse where linguistic perspicuity and literally broken English are joined in rapturous wedlock. Here Gandhi, mindful of the gentry's "plus fours," will describe his loincloth as "minus fours," and Vladimir Nabokov will notice how, on more than one level, "therapist" may equal "the rapist." The fine ear of Zukofsky's Wisconsin friend Lorine Niedecker will pick up and decoct the miraculous fission of language when it is forced through the double warp of music and translation:

> O Tannenbaum
> the children sing
> round and round
> one child sings out:
> atomic bomb

(This is, incidentally, part of a garland, *For Paul*, written for Zukofsky's son.) Poetry tests the language as language tests the world.

An ironic epic, accordingly, is going to be partly an ordeal for words themselves, starting, conventionally enough, with the virtually pure air of the first letter and first vowel, *a*. The purpose of the ordeal, from the viewpoint of ironic skepticism, will be to follow the contours of language without undue distortion, so that most of Zukofsky's prosody is a natural-seeming measure of syllables-per-line or words-per-line with no twisting, chipping, or padding to fit an imposed meter that may depend on an arbitrary Morse of qualitative or quantitative dots and dashes given further shape by a rhyme scheme. Once the measure by syllable-unit or word-unit is established along with a modest devotion to short lines, however, the purest music of consonant and vowel, stress and pitch, fancy and plain can come through with an effect, usually, of delicacy, eloquence, accuracy, and fidelity.

Such an idiom works best with its inherent data of ambiguity, inquisition, and multiple irony. These data are most lucidly presented in fairly short poems (like Zukofsky's, and like those of Cid Corman and Robert Creeley, both of whom owe much to Zukofsky's example) in which the courtesy and modesty can balance the potentially injurious clarity of perception and memory. The idiom does not work so well in longer flights, in which it tends to become otiose or academic. (*"A"* comes equipped with an index, but it quirkily omits some important items. Lorine Niedecker seems to be in the poem—pp. 165 and 214–15, for example—but is not in the index; neither is "A friend, a Z the 3rd letter of his (the first of my) last name"—p. 193—who I think must be Charles Reznikoff.) Yet another difficulty with this idiom is the way it refreshingly insists on seeing everything anew, with unprejudiced eyes; but that means the propagandist for the idiom, whether in lyric or in critical writing, had better be sure he is original. Often, however, Zukofsky seems merely derivative. His *A Test of Poetry,* for instance, promises to chuck out academic biases but winds up as little more than a replay of Pound's "How to Read" and *A B C of Reading,* even to the extent of repeating Pound's dogmatic concentration on Book XI of the *Odyssey.* A teacher can get a funny feeling when a bold student merely repeats the once-original gestures of Creeley, say, and justifies them on principles that really are "academic" in the worst sense: "I do this because Creeley does, because Olson and Zukofsky told him, because they got it from Pound, because Pound thought Fenollosa was right," etc. I am not sure that originality is very important. I am not even sure it is quite possible. But if you make a fuss about it, then you ought to be able to do some other thing than imitate, echo, and repeat.

At his best, Zukofsky dissolves illusion and punches sham to pieces. He breaks things up into particles and articles: under his testing, for example, the ambiguity-loaded *anathema* is analyzed into *"an, a, the—"* (p. 397). Once the alphabet has been taken apart, though, the problem is how to put it back together with honest energies and designs. Zukofsky's life must have confirmed some of his early ironic suspicions; after twenty years at a technical school, he retired as an associate professor, and for a long time he "was not well." The one time I met him, in June 1975, he was frowning through the sickliest-looking yellow-green complexion I think I have ever seen; but his voice was very youthful, his wit intact. On the whole, though, I think he found himself on the receiving end of an enjoyable destiny. He was brilliant, he loved his noble father, he found the perfect wife, his son appeared with the New Haven Symphony at the age of eight, and his work tended after all in the direction suggested by the title of a late poem: "Finally a valentine."

As *"A"*-24 is arranged, the whole book ends on a nicely cadenced C-minor chord in the harpsichord, the drama voice saying, "New gloves, mother?" and the poem voice repeating the end of *"A"*-20, "What is it, I wonder, that makes thee so loved." Finally, with "love" sounding simultaneously in "gloves" and "loved," a valentine, indeed.

Well, I must be churlish. I prefer consigning *"A"*-24 to the status of appendix or addendum, because I think the poem itself (if not the life of the poet) finds a more authentic and convincing conclusion in the end of *"A"*-23, which was the last part written by Zukofsky. It does not end, *Heldenleben*-style, with a survey and synthesis of the artist's life-in-work, but with a return to the alphabetical keynote that started *"A"*-1. What we have is a scrupulously measured twenty-six-line alphabet-stretto:

> A living calendar, names inwreath'd
> Bach's innocence longing Handel's untouched.
> Cue in new-old quantities—'Don't
> bother me'—Bach quieted bothered;
> since Eden gardens labor, For
> series distributes harmonies, attraction Governs
> destinies. Histories dye the streets:
> intimate whispers magnanimity flourishes: doubts'
> passionate Judgment, passion the task.

Kalenderes enlumined 21-2-3, *nigher . . fire*—
Land or—sea, air—gathered.
Most art, object-the-mentor, donn'd one—
smiles ray *immaterial Nimbus . . Oes*
sun-pinned to red threads—thrice-urged
posato (poised) 'support from the
source'—horn-note out of a
string (Quest returns answer—'to
rethink the Caprices') *sawhorses silver*
all these fruit-tree tops: consonances
and dissonances only of degree, never-
Unfinished hairlike water of notes
vital free as Itself—impossible's
sort-of think-cramp work x: moonwort:
music, thought, drama, story, poem
parks' sunburst—animals, grace notes—
z-sited path are but us.

This garland names names (Bach, Handel) and suggests others without quite pronouncing them outright (Landor, Mozart, maybe Anaximander, John Donne inwreathed, as is fitting, with Don Juan). It covers instruments, voices, plants, animals (including a goat inside "Caprices" and an A-shaped sawhorse that is a Wooden Horse too: a running theme through the poem, so to speak). I don't know what all is included in "z-sited," aside from the author's and alphabet's final monogram, but I suspect it may include a reminder that the early Semitic and Greek character for *zayin-zeta* looked like this: I, which may be pronounced "eye" or "I," which is roughly what the Hebrew *zayin* still looks like—hence "eyesight." "Are but us" looks and sounds like a re-vision of "arbutus" with an adumbration of widespread (if not universal) identity, community, and harmony.

That hermetic hint is, I think, a more satisfying conclusion than an adventitious pun on "love." We have come too far through too many agonies and mazes at too much intellectual and emotional expense to accept at the end the weakly established assertion that love matters or some similar Hallmark sentiment. It's like the Calvin Coolidge whom one can imagine in Purgatory taking a look at Pound's sweet little Canto CXX. "What's it about, Cal?" "Forgiveness." "What's he say?" "He's for it."

One of these days a scholarly critic with time on his hands is going to discover or invent a tabular schema. In *"A"*-12 there is evidence that

Zukofsky had the twenty-four-book 'plan in mind by 1950 and possibly somewhat earlier. There too (p. 258) there is a recognition that both of Homer's epics have been divided into twenty-four books by scholars, and it would not surprise me to learn that Zukofsky knew that Bach's *St. Matthew Passion* can be divided into twenty-four scenes: Schweitzer calculated it as "twelve smaller ones, indicated by chorales, and twelve larger ones, marked by arias." But Zukofsky's general design does not gracefully fall into twenty-four shapely parts. With or without the marginal *"A"*-21 *(Rudens)* and *"A"*-24 *(L. Z. Masque),* the shape of the whole is asymmetrical. The contour may match that of a diary or revery, but there is no essential literary progression. Such development as may emerge is more along the lines of an experimental fugue and variations, with room along the way for one poem 135 pages long (*"A"*-12) and another four words long (*"A"*-16). *"A"*-6 asks:

> *Can*
> The design
> Of the fugue
> Be transferred
> To poetry?

When the "plot" has to include a piece of history—such as the death of Williams or the assassination of President Kennedy—then the writing slackens, and the grief seems perfunctory. In other stretches, the author's vigor and sincerity seem to thin out and his wordplay ("Pith or gore has" for "Pythagoras") nosedives towards the asymptote of crossword puzzles and tricks like Henny Youngman's superseding "diamond pin" with "dime and pin."

The scholiasts have their work cut out for them. For all I know, the audience for poems like Zukofsky's may be nothing but scholiasts. I hate to think that world poetry today amounts to nothing more than a hundred people writing something for an audience of a hundred (probably the same hundred). The dismal situation would be no less dismal if that figure were a thousand or even a million, because the proportion is so small up against the whole human race. Maybe the University of California Press ought to keep a few copies of the full *"A"* available for specialists, and they may be wise to market it in an ugly Clearasil-pink dust jacket, to keep amateurs at arm's length. But maybe the publisher should also issue a

250-page volume of selections. I would suggest that 1–7, 9–11, 15–18, and 20 could be kept as wholes, 21 and 24 done without, and the rest given in generous selections. That sort of book would reach more people with a more concentrated representation of a fine poet's best work. Whatever is planned in the way of new editions, the Index should be re-done to provide a better key to main themes, motifs, and characters (including those in any number of alphabets).

Djuna Barnes at the Stake:
An Imaginary Retort

Paul West

Is there any sense in which, not writing for its own sake, you have actually written about something, not to evince your presence at the table, in front of the paper, but to make a specific point, or even a precise epitome of life?

If *inter*viewed, I would insist on being *viewed* beforehand, in a warm room full of purple sponges. I would be naked, supine, and the sponges would be squeezing or draining purple ink all over me. Only then would I consent, when the interviewer had bowed to the crumpled smile I sit upon, the smile that sits atop the closed parenthesis of my bowed-out legs. See how the little puckered mouth sits inside the wide one of my legs, both of which I have dried and daubed with red lipstick. A human might move through that *bouche de jambes,* on the way to my other mouth or off home, right beneath my hams. I am not the lady I was.

Now I am kvetchy, touchy, curt. No this is not the interview, this is the complaint about interviewers. I no longer wish to be bothered, diddled, licked, loved. Not even to be flattered. It all comes back, like oysters repeating, but I do not feel like its proprietor. What was it that Joyce told me about Wilde? In the morning he studied the Restoration through a microscope and then repeated it through a telescope in the evening. By evening, the Restoration shows up better, like a cut-rate Pleiades on the dried-out chest of a dead and nutbrown nun. Well, I have seen Restorations aplenty, and there is nothing restorative about them. Had it been I, I would have used the telescope in the daytime, to distance things, and the microscope at night, to make them bigger when everything had been humbled and shrunken by the *congé* of one not wholly charismatic star. How could *I* be Oscar anyway? He could always, as men can, volunteer to be made a eunuch, whose voice without overtones is so important to the church. But clitoridectomy, dear, is quite different, doing absolutely nothing for the voice. Twig it? There is nothing left to play with, whereas—dreams, dreams. I am a woman whose tragedy, like *Hamlet,* has been told from the viewpoint of the ghost.

Is *this* the interview, then? Has it begun? Why are we rehearsing the rehearsal? You have such faith in my longevity, in my very Evity. It was

From *Parnassus* (vol. 15, no. 1, 1989).

Joyce again, naked on his back with a full saucer of warm tea on his naked and very flat belly. "By the toime it's cool," he told me, "Oi'll have the notion I want." I thought a better trick than getting the notion was to lift the saucer off one's belly without spilling a drop. Should it not have been perched, instead, on what was lower down: the impartial addenda of foliage? A saucer not to be upset in any way, of good sweet thick Indian called Morning Thunder, dark as nun's chest.

Joyce was a friend, Nora too. We talked of death, rats, horses, languages, climates, the sea. To me he looked like a half-blind pilot in goggles, both eyes in glass cockpits, the blind eye wide open, the good eye shut, but on his face a look of preposterously benighted accuracy. A compass steered his face, making him give that little jeer now and then, lifting and rounding his upper lip. His children were large, always growing taller so as to reach up and touch with their head-tops the red magic carpet of hair that Nora cruised beneath, *spushally* (as she said) *whun* there was wind. They could all have flown to China on it. He drank his cool thin wine through cool thin lips that seemed to narrow into a pencil line and then retract altogether into his head. Heavily thin, he: how the portly might look if regularly squassated by the silly Inquisition.

Mister Joyce was not my only friend.

There was Guido Bruno, who published my *Book of Repulsive Women* and interviewed me about my play *Three from the Earth*. "Why so morbid, Djuna," he said. "You, of all the people I have known, have had your fill of joy in this world." "I have had no joy in my twenty-six years," I told him. He praised my "slovenly doggedness." To the stake with him.

And there was Jack Dempsey, plucking his eyebrows for his next fight, with pretty-boy Georges Carpentier. Women, he instructed me, like to see a head punched in, but they want it to have a smattering of seven languages in it, and a taste for poetry. "A woman howls twice as convincingly as a man," he said. "It's longer and higher. You can get it above the pounding of blood in your ears. And then I like to hear a feminine sigh when it's all over; a man just grunts."

"It?" I said.

"Yeah," he answered. "Ladies are great on the cold steel look, in the eye. Do you speak French?" That day, when I took tea, I took it in an inverted cup, in that little narrow-gauge hollow in the base, taking it up with my tongue's tip: a little algebraic refinement in honor of all feminine sighs. With his hair, *en brosse,* one could have cleaned out the Augean stables and left not a cowpat intact.

I was interviewing, for money, see, like you. Diamond Jim Brady, Lillian Russell, D. W. Griffith, Mother Jones, Lunt and Fontanne, Flo Ziegfeld, Yvette Guilbert, Alfred Stieglitz, Frank Harris. I never tried to do a good one. I never placed them in their period. "Back behind the scenes," I wrote, "where the blue of Herod's court lay chilly upon wilted palms that clung to dingy netting—" and then added "the tropics just out of mothballs." I knew it by heart the instant I thought of it. The play was *Salome,* after all. I tried to think of what these stiffs would *never* say, and then I wrote it in their mouths. I made Flo Ziegfeld define a vampire as "a woman who eats lightly of uncooked things; who walks out between tall avenues of spears to die, and doesn't"—hold the noise down, you guys—"and finally spends the evening in an orgy of virtuous dreams." Oh yes. All kinds of tricks like that. Why, I even said to Donald Ogden Stewart in 1930 that I wouldn't really mind dying.

"You would take it in good part," he said.

"I would achieve metallurgical composure," I said. "I wouldn't mind. I would receive it in any part it knocked at."

"Well, *I* would," he said, stepping back into the limelight as we felt the shades of oblivion lapping at our chins, "I am famous just now, and I like it." He dabbed a pinch of talcum powder on the back of his neck. He was one of those actors made relentless with time's ponderous approval. I saw the taupe, happy eyes, slightly bulbous with success, and just then he added "Isn't it simply perfection it happens to be me who is with you, and there's going to be more of me tomorrow?" We continued with our royal plural and crushed out our cigarette with a weary heel. I was not so much an interviewer as a vampire lady; I did not suck them, however, I blew blood *into* their veins, just to keep them going during the interview. Only Joyce was good, and Frank Harris. I outlived them all because I was able to chew the dry grass of envy. I brought myself forward while obfuscating them. I invented their minds.

It was different with Harris, though; he seemed to have lived. He had a mustache like a mural. He was a corridor of a man. Thousands had strolled through him, even in time of war, which it was: 1917. We talked politics for a while, like people eating smoked salmon. Then he raved about the beauty of the diamond mines in South Africa.

"I'll see you swinging yet," I told him, "in Kimberley. See you swinging by the neck in Kimberley." It had a Kipling rhythm to it. Joyce could have sung it.

"That's the way to die," he said. "Go out like a fine, brave fruit, not like a worm." I wished Donald Ogden Stewart had been there then.

When you asked Frank questions, he became a quivering anatomical district, like Père Lachaise transplanted to Bombay. Other questions and their answers. Forgotten, all. Then to Shaw and Shakespeare, whose worst play, he said, was done hundreds of times *in his life* for every *Hamlet*. "And *Lear* only once or twice," he said. "*Titus Andronicus,* I mean."

At the mantlepiece he sighed and said "Ah," the ejaculation of a man who did not weep when his heart was full. I had just said "You believe that the endowment of art produces artists, and the endowment of literature writers of genius?" He and I both had a little reverence for the beautiful and a little *love* for the things that are *terrible.*

I had drawn myself: not quartered, just drawn. High cheekbones forcing the *retroussé* nose a little too far forward, as if an elephant were trying to void an afterbirth. I made the philtrum too deep, too much a runnel, see. Lips not bad, although with too much truculent steadiness. The whole aspect came out rather too oriental, not English enough. Or did I mean squawlike? Eskimo even. It was not what I had intended myself to be. I thought of myself as bladelike, with faint lines of suet trapped in the engravings on the blade. In fact I looked Irish, earnest, and pudgy-mouthed: a face born to scold, even when at its happiest above a polkadotted frock of enormous busyness. I always looked so clean, so laundered. My clothes looked full of starch. It was the English blood in me. I never worked in colors, so you can see, I could not draw the red cheeks, I said, or the grey eyes, or the ginger hair. I had good legs—I should have drawn them draped around my face, bringing the neat little holster from below up to the small pucker of the upstairs mouth. I was a bonfire waiting to crown. My self-portrait is inaccurate in that it made my lower face recede too much, as if drawn back by some diffidence in the jaws. It was a disabused face that was going to be used, and then thrown away, and then found again, and used, and so on, until the last collection of refuse.

How did my life go? (Where did it go?) No, I mean its gait? What sort
of walk did it have? I always expected it to get better, so I always hastened
away to the next rendezvous, and there was never anyone there. Only
people to interview or to love. I always hoped for ideas to come pouring
out of the firmament right into my lap, but the people I ran into (who ran
into me) never had ideas; they had hands, lips, tongues, organs of insertion
and other organs merely fricative that you could not insert into anything.
No ideas, I moaned. Nobody thinks, everybody talks. Would you remember who Vernon and Irene Castle were? They danced a lot, and all
America copied everything they did. When Irene went into hospital, she
bobbed her hair, and women followed suit. When she kept her hair in
place with a ribbonlike band of pearls, everybody copied. Here is the most
important conversation they ever had.

> VERNON: "Are you content?"
> IRENE: "Yes."
> "Are we—*living?*" He fed her yet another egg sandwich.
> "I think so."
> "And what shall we do—in the end?"
> "Keep more dogs."
> "And after that?"
> IRENE, WHOSE NAME MEANT PEACE: "Keep—still."

What I wanted to know about them was when did they ride, drive, walk,
talk, think, dream, hope, relax, pace, rest, rise, run, brood, row, kiss, fight,
hug, hate, pun? When did they cooperate over the aluminum? I always
wanted to know what went on behind what people did, what they said.
That was what fiction was for, I said: speculative mindreading. How did
the Castles' mind work when the Castles weren't using it for some *purpose?*
How did anyone's mind work then? I thought of them and all I could think
of was their prowling puppies. Being English-born drove Vernon crazy.
It was the war. He simply had to volunteer for the R.F.C. and was killed
in 1918 training flyers in Houston.

Another Anglo, born in Derby, was the actor and playwright Charles
Rann Kennedy, the elastic cherub with his feet up on the fender of fame;
he laid bare a white, quivering ultrapersonality. He occasionally said
things: "Our mouths take on the shape of a rubber ring over the iniquity
of our neighbors." Imagine. He rewrote one act seventy-three times,

which I would call elephantiasis of the timid side. Who counted the revisions? If I were that timid, I would be scared of getting the addition wrong.

Lillian Russell was a perfume daubed all over with woman. She swayed like a big, languorous harebell, musing on her porcelain Buddha, saying "I could never be lonely without a husband, but without my trinkets, my golden gods, I could find abysmal gloom." Compared with the Castles, she was a thinker. She told me how to cook mushrooms with onion and lemon and cream, and I half-expected a small version of herself to come bubbling up from the mass, such was the expression of her face while talking about it: a thick-whipped, fungus-crushing *volupté*. In the back somewhere I heard the spit-spit of a chafing dish; I felt I had interrupted a kitchen ritual, but she made no move for the dish, and no servant appeared in order to turn it down or to serve. Her clocks ran on cream, her mind ran on purple gloom. When she began to get fat, I knew on what. When I drew her (as I drew practically everybody I settled mothlike on), I stranded her thick-lipped rotund beauty between two enormous padded arms of a chair, like the adenoids of an ogre inflated to flank her, behind her two buxom caryatids with snake faces. Miss Russell's lower trunk dissolved into legs that liquefied on to the rug, as if she were dwindling into hemorrhage, and I drew my name, a mélange of flowers and stemmed petals, to the right of the puddle. "When a woman is busy," she told me, "she hasn't time to fasten the straps about the wrists of the infamous." Was this an image from electrocution or the straitjacket? I never knew, but that lumpish incense of her presence stayed with me for days; she was like musky cottage cheese, and she often hated mirrors. I made a note to include at least the aroma of her in an otherwise visual paragiraffe.

Diamond Jim Brady, now *he* was visual, with ten hankies in each hip pocket to protect him from people who tried to bump into him when he was dancing, which he loved to do, having been taught it by the Castles. They tried to bump the diamonds off him. These hankie-mounds he called bunkers. A similar principle dictated his overall shape, at which he worked, smothering his oysters with clams, and his steaks with veal cutlets. Round as he was, I drew him as a pudgy diamond, a man of many facets whose only regret was the disappearance (he said) of Bohemia. I made prisms of him, as if sucking up to the light. When Johns Hopkins cut the kidney stone out of him, he did not have it mounted, or even add it to the avoirdupois of his plump, turquoise-plagued hand, and I could not fathom why, considering how much room there remained upon him, and how fast he kept on swelling. He could have worn it as a warning. You can always identify a cream-lover: they smell like babies, fresh from the nipple, and that faintly sour bouquet comes off them all the time, as if white essence of pure Mamma had been leaking through the aureole for years. Brady had no ideas at all. He knew you could live and die without ever having a single one, and you could do this because no one else noticed their absence. That is called fellow-feeling. In the end I put all the world's talkers into one talker, the doctor in *Nightwood,* and he got all their ideas as well. Stieglitz, it was, I think, who said he believed in woman, not in women, whereas Swift said the opposite. There are your lumpers-together and there are your sifters-out. Stieglitz always bundled us all together. "You women," he would say, "play with the mouse, but you never eat it." Just as he seceded from the standard notion of a photograph, I seceded from his standard notion of woman. Talking categories, though, was like wiping an empty glass over and over again, whereas what I liked to do was study mouths, and I said to myself, Stieglitz has that fine and sudden stoppage of the lip seen mostly in southern Germany. I like to see a mouth that is a personality upon a person, rather like the quotation mark of a vagina against the big hoop of one's legs when one squats in that particular way. Microcosm and macrocosm. Microlap and macrolap. Stieglitz was an idiosyncratic breather too, which was hard to notice because he said so many unusual things with that quick hesitancy of his, from having "to bleed one's own blood" (he *would* tell *that* to a woman) to having a gallery with horrors along one wall and idylls along the other. That was how he got to know what his friends were really like: The psychopaths hovered before the idylls, the sane before the horrors. One by one he lost all his friends to make new ones, he said. A lake was the most human thing he knew—since it had neither brains nor heart. And it was while talking to him, listening to him, and thinking to myself this is yet another experience of listening to someone else assuming I am heedful of their ideas, that I realized that I like to listen to my own only. Cold, lonesome, and full of sorrow (caught from men like a disease, older men mainly), I felt I could keep it in no longer, that I was sealed up, would never hear or see again, even if flattered by an older man whom my hat never frightened. The only "wisdom" I ever knew was simply the over-charge, the superplus, not of bright and exonerating ideas, oh no, but only of what the system can no longer abide, accommodate. Out it comes, and people say: Oh, is *that* what you think? And I would always say: No, that is what I *exude,* what I am obliged to spill. It is what is unbearable to me now, and it stays outside me like something given birth, going naturally into prose to become the redeeming munition of some future social order in which there will be no more great droning bores of men, no more murky women hissing over editions of Emerson and Longfellow.

You see what ideas can bring me to, how they bring me down; but my prose was never a little squabbling, wet dog. It was the fog of all my sad precisions.

I loved silence, not that I was ever part of the cult. I would sit there in that ridiculous apartment of mine and try to isolate a pure moment of it, in which to write, without some hammer, some voice, some truck, some bird, some neutral angel shot down in flames. I used to think we should do our writing, if we could, in the few seconds after birth, although we would have to cut out the post-partum screaming for that, and in the few seconds at the end of dying. I mean the kind of silence you want to hug, make your very own, and write like a demon in it, as if you were stuck in the dead center of an iceberg out in the Atlantic. And your ears almost but not quite pinged with all the whiteness. I never had such peace, which was why my prose style always seemed to want to assert itself against other things, shove them aside, preempt them. It was like having an Elizabethan link-boy going ahead of you, telling them to clear the street. Or La Grande Horizontale in Paris, whose bosom arrived fifteen minutes before she did, it was so huge. "Get out of the way," my prose said. "Watch me in the act of going by, like a procession of gorgeous animals whose flanks catch the insensate sun." When you feel like that, you can't afford to write too many sentences such as "Polly, put the kettle on," though one every hundred is a relief, like a crashed monoplane riding to the tip of Niagara.

So many called me morbid, but it only means soft rottenness. *Morbidezza,* one pound sliced, I say; it sounds like a cheese. The Lunts got upset when I said to her, the Lady Lynn, "Would you go on playing were Lord Alfred called away to a better land? Would Lord Alfred continue his career were you but dust?" First, she marked out her mouth, plating it thick: such an excellent foundation for scarlet. "What a head you have for horror. My Lord and I are alive and together, and we seek the perfect play." I wanted to explain to her that, far from trying to shock anyone, I was merely curious as to how people would behave if someone revealed to them the plot of the farce in which they were starring. Life has no plot, which is why we go grovelling to the feet of fiction. We like things to have shape, design. We want to die into a planned universe, not one that kills at random like M. Breton shooting his revolver into a crowd. Lady Lynn told me that she had rehearsed so often that she talked to herself even when crossing the street, and I thought, yes, Lady Lynn, all your rehearsals are bows to a play you won't be able to rehearse. You won't have a chance. Is that why we like the theater too? We always know what's coming, if we've been there before, at the same play. We like theater because, mostly, the actors go home to supper alive, themselves. Acting, they are briefly beyond their own possession. The opera star Mary Garden told me that some women, masters of their art (art of love), "have been loved to the coffin's edge," but Yvette Guilbert, the singer, more than *soi-disant diseuse,* taught me that Pierrot's roots go deep and wind around "the eternal corpse of the world, as a ribbon is wound around a lovely gift." This was better than the usual actress fluff Miss Barnes had to write down, and then up.

It was fall in Manhattan, but it was spring for all the hothouse flowers; having been reticent all year, they obeyed the sun and, tropismically, went for broke. "Europe," she told me, "is an immense field of fragments, and these fragments are moving." A simple enough statement, it told of shredded metal, dismembered men, plundered countries, broken voices, and broken minds. She was thinking of the corpses of all nations, lying there "in the four corners of the Earth," like dust. She spoke of what she called "the face hospital," where she had seen red slanting planes that used to be faces, out of which (her words) "in the place where the mouth should be, oozes a little saliva and blood—a cross section of flesh." She chided us, "You Americans," for not being patient in the presence of life, for always rushing on to the next sensation because, as she said, "Everything real shocks you." She seemed to think that Americans, having created their new country, thought they had created a land exempt from the rumbling huffs of the destroyer, as if the American dream had abolished death. So, if anything went wrong with our brawling little paradise, it was a social matter and could be fixed, whereas in Europe they knew that mayhem wasn't sociological at all. It came from the lust to kill, just like a dirt complex. Being an old lady, a kind of veteran even, with a crotchety temper, I had seen some wars, but had waited almost ninety years before I heard the true words of abomination, spoken in Vienna: Second-hand, a merely reported obscenity, this, but fresh from sauntering, blood-and-wine Vienna, where some neologist-psychopath had referred to the few surviving Viennese Jews—still living there—as "gaschamber-shirkers." It must have been meant as a joke, but it was the most lethal of jokes, telling *me* that nobody learned anything ever, and that it was probably no use writing any more books to tell them so. When I was told that, I was gassed a little too, and I could ill-afford to die even a little. It was gol-darned unthinkable, I told myself, using an old euphemism of ours. What would they have done with the likes of me? A girl who looked like a mutinous chambermaid, so Irish and common? They would have gassed me too, as a decadent, a *maudite,* of course, and all my morbidity would have been for nothing.

It took me most of a long life to realize that I liked to see fictional characters as emblems of some metaphysical relationship between them and the chemical matrix. This sounds pompous, and perhaps it is. They are not so much people as imagistic devices installed, for me, between the angels and the mud: the angels up yonder, the mud under our shoes. I stole this notion from the Renaissance thinker Pico della Mirandola, whose life others stole from him at an early age. This is not a theory but a persuasion. Many characters do not touch bottom or top, but hover in between, like most people, neither profane nor exalted. Some touch the bottom only, like Céline. Some touch only the top, like Simone Weil. Some, like Cartesian divers, are in constant motion, touching bottom or top, yet never elongated enough to touch both at the same time. I think I am one of the Cartesian divers in this, no sooner an earthy metaphysician than a highbrow earthworm. It would be almost fashionable to say that the most appealing characters are those who maintain contact with both on a sustained basis, but I suspect the really dramatic characters are the extremists: the angels or the devils, the highbrows or the worms. I cannot prove any of this, but I have a keen sense of how heraldic people, or their imitations, can be—there to fill the void with pageantry, not answers.

If you are interested in the energy of the universe, you will look to the extremists, but if you care most about the ferocious agonies and blissful antinomies of the human fix, then you will settle for those who are wired in above and have feet of clay holding them down. How be both? Milton's Satan fell, but his agony consisted in his knowing what he had fallen from. To put it another way: Voluptuous aversion is the most frequent state of mind I have felt. Can one be wise without being paradoxical? I mean the sun can't keep on making itself up from helium all the time; it has to start its process of self-perpetuation with a couple of hydrogen atoms, which pair up, then link to another, making a trio, after which the first trio looks for another trio, and of the resulting sextet four members go on as helium while the two ejected ones start off again looking for a third. Now, wouldn't you think that the sun, needing helium, would have evolved some less tricky way of making it—anyway, some way of not having to deal with hydrogen at all? Not that I am knocking hydrogen. But no: Proton-proton reaction is the sun's way of doing things, and evermore shall be so. What I like most about the sun is that helium was named for it (*helios* is Greek for *sun,* and we may well wonder why): The sun is mostly hydrogen (seventy or eighty percent). They should have called the sun *hydrogios.* Helium is not unique to the sun, either. We have it here on earth, but no one knew that until the very late Nineteenth Century. Aren't we like the sun, then? Mostly water, but helplessly, narcotically in need of ideas? I wouldn't pursue too far my analogy of ideas as helium, but you get my drift. The sun is no more homogeneous than we are, and we are not microcosms of it, but we make our energy by devouring something, and so in that sense are loose replicas. It is time to prepare for the next question, which I am sure is going to be less hospitable than the first, although I think that first one would have upset others a great deal more than it upsets me. It was maliciously maieutic, my dears. Like a green mamba, it threw itself at me, and I became coiled up with it. This voluntary, like a scar, marks the place where the green mamba bit me and learned nothing from the encounter.

At the very end, or toward it, a determined woman from Harper and Row, the publishers, came and took me out of the nursing home my relatives had thrust me into, and surrounded me with round-the-clock West Indians, all uninsultable and impervious to screaming, so I was able to go on making helium to the end. What did you wish to ask now? Why don't you ask me about the unwritten novel with the helium nucleus and the two missing protons? Why don't you ask me something else?

High Adventures of Indeterminacy

JOAN RETALLACK

We've been looking for ways to get out of ruts for as long as we've been in them. About the third century B.C., when Epicurus had his prescient vision of a rush-hour stupor of atoms commuting through the void, bumper to bumper at uniform speed in parallel lanes spanning the cosmos, he surely cried out "there must be more to life than this!" We do know that he came up with the "swerve." For no reason at all, but often enough to account for variety and change in the universe, atoms just ran amok, swerving into adjoining traffic, creating in the mess of collision, new structures. Enter onto the scene of Western thought (albeit for a cameo appearance), indeterminacy and its refreshing artifacts, alleviating briefly the claustrophobia we've always been prone to in the confines of our small worlds. Is there nothing new under the sun?, we groan. Yes, more things than are dreamt of by Reason alone, says Epicurus, foreshadowing Shakespeare's reply to Ecclesiastes.

Despite Renaissance zest for play, the fragile spirit of indeterminacy seemed destined to be squeezed out between the Judeo-Christian God (who for some reason needed to know it all in advance) and the great weight of evidence brought to bear on everything during the Enlightenment and its aftermath. We've had problems ever since dealing with things like spontaneity, intuition, and, most of all, change. Does change really occur? How can it be possible? Is it really advisable? Determinism, Rationalism, Logical Positivism are such reassuringly traditional bedtime stories. All the well-wrought prose of history seems to be on their side.

Review of Marjorie Perloff's *The Poetics of Indeterminacy*, Gertrude Stein's *The Yale Gertrude Stein*, and John Cage's *For the Birds* and *Themes and Variations* from *Parnassus* (vol. 11, no. 1, 1983).

We are obsessed with law—since Moses came down from the mountain with our first lawbooks; since Plato in his senescence wrote *The Laws,* his sequel to the *Republic,* to ensure that nothing would be left to the imagination. Somewhere along the way we invented laws of chance, confident there was nothing we couldn't tame. Einstein alarmed us with relativity but then reassured us: God doesn't play dice. Heisenberg's "uncertainty" principle, we are relieved to know, describes an uncertain observer, not uncertain events. Even sub-atomic behavior must be law-abiding and, hopefully, any day will enter the fold of the respectably predictable.

Predictable. But isn't that a synonym for dull? All this docility, this good citizenship, all this predictability should begin to make us a bit uneasy. Must we really resign ourselves to the same old patterns—birth, struggle, a few laughs, and old devil death, generation after generation, *ad nauseam?* Well, yes: but perhaps there could be a few more laughs, we say in all modesty. Or perhaps the struggle can take a new form, says the revolutionary. Suddenly there is hope—declarations of independence, manifestoes, constitutions, utopias filled with good will and free-play, not all practical, but envisioning something other than the structures we inhabit, the habits of our structures.

Buckminster Fuller has said that a structure is simply a division of an outside from an inside. If nothing else, we are curious about what lies outside. The more so since Whorf and others showed us the extent to which structures of language and culture engender and delimit our understanding of reality. Along with our tendencies toward biological conservatism, we harbor a genuine wish to enlarge the range of the possible. There will always be revolutionaries, anarchists, deconstructionists, experimentalists of one sort or another. In short, an avant garde, defying the gravity of established order or just ignoring it, reinventing invention. There they are, folks, swerving into view, climbing up to the high wire—philosophical daredevils, *bêtes blanches, artistes noires*—a death defying act.

Meanwhile, down on the ground floor ("low culture" some call it) indeterminacy never did go out of style. Lots and dice and other forms of courting chance have been a firmly entrenched institution since ancient times. Never mind the rantings of preachers and teachers and police. We're no fools. We know you can't leave everything to logic. The willful indeterminist act in literature, however, of the sort we find in the work of Gertrude Stein or John Cage, appears to be a relatively recent development. Marjorie Perloff dates it from Rimbaud, though Hugh Kenner makes an intriguing case for an accidental indeterminacy that we've been negotiating as readers for as long as our pile of books has included works written in other cultures or other times.

First let me explain that much of what Perloff discusses under the rubric "indeterminacy" has to do with the effect of a text on the reader. This effect, which she sometimes calls "undecidability," is (in contrast to Heisenberg's particles) lodged in the nature of the event, the text, which because of random references or syntactical dislocations or illogical juxtapositions, resists the reader's attempts to pin down a coherent exegesis. (Text as irreducible enigma.) The reader may not even be able to perceive a correspondence of references to referents, signifiers to signifieds. All of this implies a theory of meaning in literature entirely different from the one we are accustomed to. Or does it?

In *The Pound Era,* Kenner claims there is a high degree of "undecidability" in any text removed from our experience, either through historical accident (the not so accidental passage of time transporting it beyond certainty) or cultural remove. It seems that we are in fact accustomed to reading with a surprisingly high tolerance for non-comprehension of one sort or another. We "intuitively grasp" while letting slip and slide the great deal that we don't understand; or radically misunderstand what we think is perfectly clear. But this doesn't inhibit our enjoyment in the least. It may even enhance it.

Take Shakespeare for instance. Kenner gives an example from *Cymbeline,* IV, ii, circa 1611:

> Golden lads and girls all must
> As chimney-sweepers, come to dust.

Social commentary foreshadowing Blake, yes/no? No. Kenner recounts this startling fact:

> . . . in the mid-20th century a visitor to Shakespeare's Warwickshire met a countryman blowing the grey head off a dandelion: "We call these golden boys chimney-sweepers when they go to seed."

And the point really isn't the same at all. The text has separated off from the referents we tend to think are necessary if it is to have meaning. It is only a chance encounter that restored the referent in this case. Before which we didn't miss a thing. We had been doing perfectly well without it. How can that be? Kenner again:

> Hanmer or Theobold, with Dr. Johnson, supposed that words de-noted things. A language is simply an assortment of words, and a set of rules for combining them. Mallarmé and Valéry and Eliot felt words as part of that echoing intricacy, Language, which permeates our minds and obeys not the laws of *things* but its own laws, which has an organism's power to mutate and adapt and survive. . . . The things against which its words brush are virtually extraneous to its integrity. We may want to say that Shakespeare wrote about happen-ings in the world, the world that contains mortal men and sunlight and dandelions, and that a post-Symbolist reading converts his work into something that happens in the language, where "golden" will interact with "dust" . . . and "lads" and "girls" and "chimney-sweepers," and where "dust" rhymes with "must". . . . Thus the song seems to us especially fine when we can no longer say what the phrase "golden lads" was meant to name. (And "genuine poetry," wrote Eliot in 1929, "can communicate before it is understood.")

> (*The Pound Era,* p. 123)

Ironically, though Kenner is describing a Symbolist aesthetic, we are on our way (not chronologically, but conceptually) to the view of language that makes Perloff's account of indeterminacy in non-Symbolist poetry possible. (Indicating, perhaps, that the division between the two is not so clear after all.) But we're not quite there. Kenner moves us further along. It seems that what we respond to is *"effect"* ("an effect being something hypnotic we cannot quite understand") produced by: the "extra-semantic affinities" of words, the "molecular bonds of half-understood words," the "structure of words, where the words exchange dynamisms in the ecology of language," the "chemistry of Language [which] supersedes meaning," the "characteristic force fields" of Language. Our view of language as reference pure and simple is assailed by new possibilities of linguistic impact, what with signifieds sliding out from under signifiers and meaning rudely detached from its transitional objects.

In Shakespeare it's not too disquieting. The rumor that he knew what he was talking about has survived four centuries intact. We relax on authority and experience words splendid in their burnished opacity. In our tardy arrival at *Cymbeline*, a certain loss of literal sense may well increase our susceptibility to images and raise our sense of what the old philosophers called "secondary qualities"—sound, rhythm, texture; and, for synesthesiacs, color and even taste. ("We do not discern nonsense," says Kenner.) These qualities are ingredients of the etymological elixir that suffuses the senses, awakening one as linguistic Lazarus to the play of language in the play. Those seventeenth-century Warwickshire locals shared with Shakespeare what Wittgenstein called a "form of life"— local culture, turns of phrase, familiar flora and fauna, habits of commerce, assumptions of value and rank. . . . We also share with Shakespeare a form of life, the English language. What he made of the English language has been part of our formation as linguistic creatures. His words replenish us with their dense textures. We do not require a vernacular translation.

As we approach the modern scene, indeterminacy as historical accident becomes indeterminacy as intentional effect—a structural principle of the Symbolists, according to Kenner:

> . . . we may say that Symbolism is . . . an effort to anticipate the work of time by aiming directly at the kind of existence a poem may have when a thousand years have deprived it of its dandelions and its mythologies, an existence purely linguistic, determined by the molecular bonds of half-understood words. (130)

Eliot, Kenner says, "has withdrawn in favor of the language," calling the chapter in which he deals with this development "Words Set Free." Set free as in: "the Symbolist willingness to lift words out of 'usage,' free their affinities, permit them new combination." So the Symbolists, via the Romantics, did by choice what Time did by default. But the point is that both processes enable us to pay a new kind of attention to language; language is no longer rendered invisible by dailiness or precise reference, because of course when we "refer," we are attempting to point with language at something beyond language. The point of reference is not language, but its object.

In *The Poetics of Indeterminacy*, Marjorie Perloff locates the first appearance of intentional indeterminist devices in the *Illuminations* which Rimbaud began in 1872. She offers us this quotation:

. . . I flattered myself on inventing, some day, a poetic language accessible to all the senses. I withheld the translation.

(Rimbaud, *Une Saison en enfer* [*Délires II*])

The withholding of the translation, if we find Kenner's theory of historical indeterminacy convincing, shouldn't seem so exotic. (We are used to it, no?) But of course it does. It's one thing to come upon incomprehensible passages in poetry from other eras; it's quite another in poetry just off the press. Is the poet trying to put one over on us, we ask irritably? It is thus the burden of a poetics of indeterminacy to demonstrate that these intentional *de*constructions are indeed constructive; that the experience of indeterminacy in literature is not all frustration and disappointment; that it can nourish us with a particular kind of linguistic feast, perhaps not entirely dissimilar to the great wild game of free-playing signifiers in portions of Shakespeare. Before such a demonstration can take place, however, there is other work to do. Contexts must be differentiated.

For Perloff this means primarily a distinction between the modes and intentions of Symbolism as against those of indeterminacy. Unlike Kenner who thinks *The Waste Land* (Symbolist exemplar) presents a code not intended to be broken, bearing no more than the "teasing implication of meaning" (characteristics she would find more appropriate to John Ashbery whom she locates in the anti-Symbolist tradition), Perloff firmly identifies Symbolism with reference. This position, though not implausible, tends to move the rationale for indeterminacy toward the negative ("non-Symbolist") camp, and to deprive it of the kind of historical depth one enjoys in *The Pound Era*. Though she agrees with Kenner's description of the effects of indeterminacy in literature, these effects appear in her account to have a sudden immaculate conception in Rimbaud ("There is no real precedent for the *anti-paysage* of the *Illuminations.*") in reaction to Baudelaire. The most fruitful (positive) explanation of the genesis of indeterminacy in literature probably lies in a selective synthesis of the views of Kenner and Perloff and even of Jacques Derrida who believes indeterminacy to be an inherent property of all texts. But Perloff is unequivocal on her point:

For, unlike [Ashbery's] "These Lacustrine Cities," where tower, swan, and petal have no definable referents, *The Waste Land* has, despite its temporal and spacial dislocations and its collage form, a perfectly coherent symbolic structure. (13)

However difficult it may be to decode this complex poem, the relationship of the word to its referents, of signifier to signified, remains essentially intact. (17)

And Perloff is a crack code-breaker. Like the New Critics' star pupil, she goes at passages from *The Waste Land* with gusto, efficiently unpacking symbols like bags at the start of a month's vacation, tucking everything into its proper spot; she refers to this exercise as a "Norton Anthology reading." Its purpose is to serve as a kind of negative model. This is what we should not attempt to do, cannot succeed in doing with indeterminist poetry.

What Perloff posits are two distinct literary traditions emerging out of the revolutionary milieu of the late nineteenth and early twentieth centuries (though the historical and social context is not discussed):

. . . what we loosely call "Modernism" in Anglo-American poetry is really made up of two separate though often interwoven strands: the Symbolist mode that Lowell inherited from Eliot and Baudelaire and, beyond them, from the great Romantic poets, and the "anti-Symbolist" mode of indeterminacy or "undecidability," of literalness and free play, whose first real exemplar was the Rimbaud of the *Illuminations.* . . . we cannot really come to terms with the major poetic experiments occurring in our own time without some understanding of what we might call "the French connection"—the line that goes from Rimbaud to Stein, Pound, and Williams by way of Cubist, Dada, and early Surrealist art, a line that also includes the great French/English verbal compositions of Beckett. It is this "other tradition" (I take the phrase from the title of a poem by John Ashbery) in twentieth-century poetry that is the subject of my book. (vii)

And although our own early Modernist poets generally resisted the indeterminacy model of the *Illuminations,* the notion of enigma, of the poem as language construction in which the free play of possible significations replaces iconic representation, began to gain adherence among avant garde writers. (66)

The "other tradition" as a label is not entirely first-class; shades of the "other network," the "other woman"—things we don't quite grant legitimacy—hover round. The "other tradition" has to my knowledge had only one fully positive, though not fully satisfactory, attribution, "language-centered poetry." ("Indeterminist," though still a negation, seems less pejorative since it is non-parasitic and non-hierarchical.) It is usual to oppose "traditional" poetry to something else, like "experimental" (read "arbitrary," "unstructured," "tentative") or even "non-traditional" as though this work had no tradition other than the reactive one of defying or denying what society has baptised "traditional." A currently fashionable opposition is "modern" vs. "post-modern" which Perloff's compelling argument implies is historically misleading. The two lines to which we apply these labels have in fact been flourishing alongside one another, despite partisans who periodically enjoy pronouncing the other side defunct.

The long habit of invidious comparison, the second class status of the "non," the "other," the "anti" is due to the virtual wholesale identification of the literary establishment with Symbolism, as though "Symbolism" were the generic term for poetry. Work coming out of the "other tradition" has been much abused because of this—interpreted within the Symbolist context as some sort of high Symbolism (e.g., mystical) or as failed Symbolism, or, because non-Symbolist, rejected out of hand as non-poetry. To read an Indeterminist work looking for qualities and effects of a Symbolist epiphany poem is an injustice, not to say a waste of time. Other critical methods are demanded.

Perloff identifies and explores a number of suggestive contexts, which together provide a framework for her illuminating discussions of Rimbaud, Stein, Pound, etc.: the concept of indeterminacy itself (more implicitly than explicitly); literary genealogy (Rimbaud . . . to David Antin); extra-literary influences (visual arts, cinema, ordinary speech . . .); the Indeterminist or "non-Symbolist" stance (intentions and effects). Some crucial issues related to this last context are raised in the first chapter of the book:

> Art becomes play, endlessly frustrating our longing for certainty. . . . poetic texts like "These Lacustrine Cities" . . . derive force from their refusal to "mean" in conventional ways. . . .
>
> Contemporary poets have often commented on this situation, but no one has paid much attention, perhaps because readers seem bent on absorbing the unfamiliar into familiar patterns. From Charles

Olson's "Projective Verse" (1950), with its call for "objectivism"
. . . to John Cage's remark in *Silence* (1961) that "I'd never been
interested in symbolism . . . I preferred just taking things in themselves, not as standing for other things"; to . . . David Antin's definition, in the mid-seventies, of poetry as "the language art," a form of
discourse which, rather than "saying one thing and meaning something else," returns to the literal but with the recognition that
"phenomenological reality is itself 'discovered' and 'constructed' by
poets," the question of how to create poetry in a post-Symbolist age
has been a primary concern. (34–35)

To explore what I call "the mode of undecidability" in twentieth-
century poetry is by no means to criticize the great Symbolist movement of our period. It is, rather, to suggest that much of the poetry
now emerging has different origins and therefore makes rather different suppositions. It deserves to be read on its own terms. (44)

And this from the last chapter:

"Empty Words" is Cage's way of making us look at the world we
actually inhabit, the sights and sounds we really see. So, from the
opposite direction, Antin's talk poems force us to become aware of
our natural discourse, to become sensitive to the way we actually talk
and hence think. (338)

An interesting tacit assumption throughout much of Perloff's book is
that the world we must construct or reconstruct in reading Symbolist
poetry, the restoration of the lost half of the equation, symbol = thing,
is a world less vital and less authentic, less "in process" than the immediate
world of language which does not point beyond itself. This assumption is
a complicated one and is intimately related to developments in philosophy
of language in this century found in the work of, among others, Heidegger, Lacan, Derrida, Wittgenstein, and Dewey. It is also, not surprisingly,
a controversial assumption which deserves, at least, another book. The
inverse equation (thing = symbol) is equally offensive. Perloff quotes D.
S. Carne-Ross on this point in her chapter on Pound:

Not merely does the thing, in Pound's best verse, not point beyond
itself: *it doesn't point to us.* The green tip that pushes through the earth
in spring does not stand for or symbolize man's power of spiritual

> renewal. . . . The green thrust is itself the divine event. . . . Meant
> as literally as Pound means it, this is very hard to take. Not only does
> it offend against the ways we have been taught to read literature, it
> is an offense against the great principle of inwardness or internaliza-
> tion that has put us at the center of things and laid waste to the visible
> world. (198)

The Deconstructionists, following Lacan, would take this a step further
and say that the divine event is the word itself, which creates its own
peculiar tension-filled presence in the absence of the thing.

But the critical question remains. If the poem primarily presents us
with a charged linguistic field, charged for instance by the "tension between reference and compositional game, between a pointing system
and a self-ordering system," as Perloff describes the dynamics in one of
Gertrude Stein's poems, what is to be done with it? What form can the
act of criticism take? Clearly this is a language game for which the Symbolist rules don't work. Here are two samples of Perloff's approach to
Pound:

> I would posit that Pound's basic strategy in the *Cantos* is to create a
> flat surface, as in a Cubist or early Dada collage, upon which verbal
> elements, fragmented images, and truncated bits of narrative, drawn
> from the most disparate contexts, are brought into collision. Such
> "collage poetry," as David Antin points out, "no longer yield(s) an
> iconic representation, even of a fractured sort, though bristling with
> significations." It thus occupies a middle space between the mimetic
> on the one hand and the non-objective or "abstract" on the other; the
> referential process is not cut off but is subordinated to a concern for
> sequential or spatial arrangement. Indeed, in the case of the Malatesta
> Cantos, the text becomes a surface of linguistic distortions and contra-
> dictions that force the reader to participate in the poem's action. . . .
> Pound dislocates language so as to create new verbal landscapes.
> (181–82)

On Canto VIII:

> . . . the sonorous formality of the address is undercut by a series of
> incomplete words, meant to reproduce what is on the back of the
> envelope *("tergo")*. Here the reader has to fill in the first few letters
> of each word in order to make sense of the address. . . . The poet thus

insists on our participation; it is up to us to fill in the blanks, to play
the game. . . .
    The lines, in short, do not convey information; rather they take
certain facts and present them from different linguistic perspectives
(formal, florid Italian; broken Italian words; English translation) as if
to undercut their historicity. . . . Such linguistic indeterminacy is one
of the central devices of these Cantos. (183)

Much of the descriptive language in *The Poetics of Indeterminacy* reflects
Perloff's considerable knowledge of the visual arts, an excellent resource
for getting at formal dynamisms in the partially opaque linguistic surfaces
that characterize much of the work she is discussing. The book pushes
continually toward a positive aesthetic, one divergent from but not necessarily in competition with symbolist poetics. The pervasive negatives—
anti-Symbolist, absent whole, resistance to closure, decreation, decompo-
sition, dislocation, fragmentation, incompletion, deformation; reader described as frustrated or forced—are not an indication of contrariness on
Perloff's part. They rather reflect two things: the extent to which the
experimental swerve moves us out of the reigning metaphysic; and the
extent to which that metaphysic governs our language—our concepts of
form, structure, method, the nature of the unit, etc. Though art is never
primarily polemical, polemical terms seem always to dominate the early
critical evaluation of avant garde work. Rimbaud, Stein, Pound . . .
"early"? Yes, we are still having trouble assimilating the aftermath of
structural collisions that were the turn of the (nineteenth) century origins
of Modernism. "Early" can last a long time for the avant garde.
    Considering this persistent time lag, and the Princeton imprint, Perloff's
book is an almost pioneering contribution to the development of critical
approaches to Indeterminist poetry, heretofore confined to extremely
small circulation journals. The strengths of the book far outweigh its
infelicities, but some are annoying nonetheless—frequent (non-Steinian)
repetitions; an utter misunderstanding of Wittgenstein's notion of silence;
a surprising dismissal of Cage's chance operations as "not in themselves
the mainspring of his poetic art." The treatment of Cage, in fact, has the
feeling of a run-through, with no discussion of his musical sources. There
are also a large number of descriptions of non or anti-Symbolist work as
"dreamlike," a characterization which in our post-Freudian cultural age is
almost a contradiction in terms. But the book is overridingly a valuable

one, providing the best thing a critical work can—an informed and stimulating framework for further discussion.

The Yale Gertrude Stein happily makes accessible a large quantity of Stein's work selected from the eight-volume Yale collection of "The Unpublished Writings of Gertrude Stein," available otherwise only in expensive hardback editions. This selected edition is a long time in coming and yet has a look of haste about it. The work appears haphazardly arranged. The "Introduction" by Richard Kostelanetz, editor of the volume, is an article which first appeared in the Summer 1975 *Hollins Critic*. Though full of interesting comments on Stein's work, it is clearly appropriate to another occasion. Only two of the twenty seven selections included in *The Yale Gertrude Stein* are (briefly) mentioned, while work that does not appear (mostly better known and less problematic) is copiously cited. Kostelanetz tells us in his Preface that he intentionally chose "more experimental works" for this selected edition—examples of "extended abstraction," "abstract prose," "minimal poetry," etc. This volume deserved its own introduction. The work would have been more profitably discussed than labeled.

The appearance of carelessness (on the part of Yale University Press as well) is compounded to insult when Kostelanetz ends his "Introduction" with the "curious fact that I will let others explain (of) the absence of visible [Steinian] influence upon subsequent women writers." Since we know that virtually all subsequent experimental writing in this country (probably in the English language) has been influenced one way or another by Stein, this is tantamount to saying there are no women experimental writers, or women writers who engage in some degree of experimentation. Let me name a few of the visibly influenced: Edith Sitwell, Barbara Guest, Anne Waldman, Rochelle Owens, Judith Johnson Sherwin, Laura Chester, Lyn Hejinian, Bernadette Mayer, Tina Darragh, Diane Ward, Carla Harryman, Rae Armantrout. . . . It is curious that Kostelanetz is unaware of these writers. They are all, except for Sitwell, contemporary Americans whose work appears widely in distinguished avant garde publications. Kostelanetz, as a leading advocate and impresario of experimental writing in this country, should find their work of interest.

"Fact is," Zeno of Elea (fifth century B.C.) might have said to Epicurus (in the history of ideas riposte can precede its object), "logic shows us that your so-called swerves are out. Too bad, old man. You see, before your capricious atom can go anywhere at all, it must first go half the distance. And before it can go half the distance, it must go half of that. And before it can go that half, it must again go half of that. And before . . . you get the drift . . . toward infinity and sweet stasis. 'Infinite regress,' some snide types call it. 'At my back I always hear Time's wingèd chariot not getting any nearer.' It's quite simply impossible to move through an infinite number of points in a finite amount of time. So much for your swashbuckling swerves! Motion of any kind is out of the question. ("If that piece of reasoning isn't a swerve, I don't know what is," mutters Epicurus into the future.) But don't worry, old man, in the twentieth century A.D. not getting anywhere will become fashionable. In athletic circles it will be called jogging or cycling 'in place.' In literature it will be given the lovely paradoxical name, 'continuous present.' "

By one Gertrude Stein. Or was it two? This large mythic corpus we call Gertrude Stein seems always to produce double images—female/male, playful/pretentious, fascinating/maddening, amusing/a bore. She has enlarged our range of possibilities in prose and poetry beyond comprehension, for which we are grateful and annoyed. Her intentions, not to say her effects, are deeply disjunctive. There is for instance that complicated desire to say what she wants to say without actually saying it, to "mean names without naming them"; enough one would think to render a lesser being mute. But not Stein. She had what we like to call today chutzpah (supreme self-confidence, nerve, gall). And her spirit of adventure (or was it sometimes obsession?) never seemed to flag, though it has worn out many of the less hardy along the way.

Even her deathbed scene demonstrates the capacity for persistence— popping up for one more question—"What is the question?"—a last, finally economical repetition (of form and content) squeezed into the moment before Time's proto-period. But the last thing in any ultimate sense cannot be a question since a question implies yet another thing, an answer. Grammatically she was keeping the game open, stalling her myth at the pen-ultimate. *Mortis interruptus,* again and again and again would have been her scenario had she only been able to continue writing.

To continue writing is her indisputable objective, to "commence and re-commence," as she often said, like a perpetual procession into unending graduation exercises—steering clear of valedictory exhortations and other grand finales of "moral" or "message" or "aboutness." Stein isn't fond of endings, so they are, in her prose and poetry, like deaths, arbitrary conveniences to keep things from going on too interminably. There are none of those end points foreordained from the start—no climaxes, no epiphanies, no summings up or answers of any kind. The last sentence or line in a piece is formally indistinguishable from, and probably interchangeable with, any other except in its placement as the final item in a series of what are designed to be "continuous presents." The monumental end points, the crescendoes of implication which adorn the concluding lines or pages of Symbolist work, have been deflated to the status of a punctuation mark, generally a tidy but inconclusive period. Inconclusive, in part, because it is all-purpose, used even to punctuate questions. "What is the question." she would have put it on the page, thereby having yet another thing both ways. Part of her wasn't so open; part of her disliked the prying nature of the interrogative.

Which brings us back to that odd naming without naming business. If the implications of endings could be ignored, starting points, which for Stein were always tied up with reference, were not so easy to dismiss. She wanted, in fact, to do "portraits," to celebrate the datum, and therefore could never really entirely banish "aboutness," though she certainly did not want to engage in the (c)rude behaviour of pointing. Privacy must be protected. Her aim was to honor the referent without the intrusion of reference. Referents without reference became the poles of one of her working paradoxes, poles which appear, passionate and distinct, in these passages from the essay "Poetry and Grammar":

> (Homer, Chaucer, the Bible) . . . they were drunk with nouns, to name to know how to name earth sea and sky and all that was in them was enough to make them live and love in names, and that is what poetry is it is a state of knowing and feeling a name.

> As I say a noun is a name of a thing, and therefore slowly if you feel what is inside that thing you do not call it by the name by which it is known. Everybody knows that by the way they do when they are in love and a writer should always have that intensity of emotion about whatever is the object about which he writes. And therefore and I say it again more and more one does not use nouns.

> Was there not a way of naming things that would not invent names, but mean names without naming them.

Of course you all do know that when I speak of naming anything, I include emotions as well as things.

As you can see, the rules of the game are challenging: the writer must have intensity of emotion about her objects without divulging either her objects or her emotions. To name without naming is a semantic paradox which, along with its logical class-mates, is susceptible to resolution through a rather peculiar means—language talking about language rather than about objects; language as analogue of, rather than reference to, object; words themselves playing the role of object, flashing secondary qualities without inhibition.

Consider these lines from "Yet Dish" in *The Yale Gertrude Stein:*

> A lea ender stow sole lightly.
> Not a bet beggar.
> Nearer a true set jump hum,
> A lamp lander so seen poor lip. (55)

Here Stein has vaulted over that high tension wire strung between the poles of the paradox, defying gravity and Zeno with the best of them. The swerve into indeterminacy has produced a surface which scintillates in an imbalance of mass to energy. The weight of denotation and connotation is lightened so we are free to return to language as primary process (prior to logical structuring) like young children or foreigners, aware of crisp textures (bet beggar), gentle phonemic transformations—"stow sole lightly," where the s and o move from "stow" to "sole," and the l from "sole" to "lightly" with a symmetrical balancing of s/s to l/l. There is pleasure in this elegantly textured linguistic lunch. There is also the poignancy of language cut off from circumstance, juices still flowing: fleeting but vivid images, e.g., "lea ender stow" bringing with it a taste of things maritime; or "jump hum" evoking children's games; "beggar," "lamp," and "lip," good red-blooded nouns.

The effect is reminiscent of Middle English untranslated, full of glimpsed significations, but also studded with opacities confronting the reader primarily with tactile (phonemic or graphic) qualities. We are not in this experience of language undergoing abstraction *from*; we are being returned *to* words as objects in the process of becoming—a state of suspended arrival which engages our intellect and our senses and gives them permission to play, much as we play(ed) with language in nursery rhymes and word games. We needn't hunch over annotations to enjoy "Yet Dish" or the following Stein text:

> Age in beefsteaks age in pear shapes age in round and puzzle.
> Witness a pair of glasses. Extra win eager extra win eager.
> Piles piles of splinters piles piles of splinters.
> English or please english or please or please or please or please
> or please.

("Emp Lace")

One can easily imagine a group of children chanting this, perhaps even inventing a repertoire of movements to go with different parts, thoroughly caught up in the sheer vitality of language; not needing to worry about or defend its sense because they are so in touch with its sensations. They would be exercising themselves as linguistic creatures, just as they exercise themselves as bodily creatures when they play kickball. Adults continue to run and play tennis and other games (elevated to "sports") knowing they enhance health and prowess, and also are fun. But they (most of us) stop playing with language. What are the implications and consequences of this? Interesting question to play with. And here is another: Suppose we were to value some poets primarily for their symbolic structures and epiphanies and others for their invitations to play, to swerve, perchance even to collide—the latter lot (and many spanning both categories) sought out for their ability to let us, with them, experience language, not as a reflection or description *of* reality, but as a reality itself in which we move, jump, hum?

This is not to suggest that Stein always proffers such irresistible invitations. In "A Birthday Book," a twenty-five–page poem included in the *Yale Gertrude Stein,* Zeno's laws against motion have overtaken her. This poem should be a quintessential intertwining of "continuous" and "present" since it is written in the form of a calendar diary. It begins,

> Who was born January first.
> Who was born in January first.
> Who was born and believe me who was born and believe me,
> who was born who was born and believe me.

At that rate.
Let us sell the bell. (73)

Not an entirely inauspicious beginning, especially had she taken her own good humourous advice in the last two lines. But she goes on, clanging a duller and duller bell throughout a full calendar year:

January the twenty-fourth makes it as late, as late as that.
January the twenty-fifth ordinarily.
January the twenty-sixth as ordinarily. (75)

By this time, the third page of the poem, having rapidly flipped through the remainder to see if any relief is in sight, one realizes as Zeno's stunned runner must have, there is no way to go the distance; at least not as "reader," if that term presumes even a minimal engagement with the text. Stein herself is exercising in place. The mid-point (which we must first achieve in order to get to the end) finds her in this regressive state:

June and so forth. June the twenty-fifth, June the twenty-
fifth. June and so forth.
June the twenty-sixth her name is June and very soon. (86)

To have gotten this far one must first have read half-way, and so on and so forth. The problem is as fundamental as Zeno's—how to get from one point to the next—because Stein too has presented us with a series of discrete units (lines), rather than a continuum. Without engines of plot or semantic development to push or pull us across the gaps, there must be a current of energy running throughout to draw us on and connect other-wise isolated parts. In the absence of this current we are psychologically, if not logically, stuck; unable even like poor quaking Kierkegaard to contemplate leaps of faith, since that strenuous athleticism is also depen-dent on an unusually high degree of energy—energy that a text like the Bible, not without its own share of repetition and illogic, seems somehow able to generate, unlike "A Birthday Book." This is not to imply a direct comparison between Stein and the Old Testament psalmist, though at least one respected critic has called her a mystic, but just to say that some texts are "charged," moving readers to take a great deal of active responsibility for missing links, and others are not. We must ask in the case of "A Birthday Book" why not?

Ironically, the stolidity of the poem is exacerbated by the superficial appearance of movement. After all, we are racing through the year, are we not? But the mechanics of this incessant series of dates, the pro forma pace of the familiar unto deadeningly habitual sequence, renders one as enervated as Beckett's "Unnamable"—"you must go on, I can't go on, I'll go on," knowing the next words will be "I can't go on," and so on and on to yet another infinity of fixation. But the major reason why there is no dynamic "continuous" in "A Birthday Book" is that, in contrast to "Yet Dish" and "Emp Lace," there are no lively "presents." The reader is starved rather than fueled. Rhymes, for instance, are of the order of clang associations—June/soon, door/more, stew/do: "May and might hold me tight, might and may night and day. . . ." This facile rattling on is childish, not child-like. Mother Goose would yawn. With virtually no surprising combinations, no interesting vocabulary to savor in its rigidly structured abstract language, the poem is like an obligatory form filled out with nonvital statistics.

Movement in Indeterminist poetry is generated to a large extent by the inherent interest of individual units (ripe in their presentness, as a Zen master would say), whether they be lines, sentences, phrases, or phonemes. These must whet the appetite for more. And they must spill over with excess energy—enough to create a lively magnetic field, a charged whole raised to a power significantly greater than the mere sum of parts. There is nothing to "find out at the end," no solution to the crime or the lovers' plight, no homily to live by, no punch line. There is the process of reader interacting with text, a process which must deliver an abundance unimaginable at the start. This, in contrast to logical conclusion ("December thirty-first. So much so."), which can never outgrow its premises.

In "A Birthday Book," the paradoxes which generated abundance and inventiveness in other work have resulted in absence and evasion. Perhaps this is the phenomenon of "protective" language about which William Gass has written. Love that wants to but dares not speak its name fosters an aversion to naming; caution about desire in language short-circuits linguistic intuitions. Or, perhaps some of Stein's strategies for naming without names are just too logically efficient. Paradox, though a creature of logic, won't tolerate an excess of it without losing its dynamic tension. Of course, these perhapses are not mutually exclusive.

The most logical of strategies is to excommunicate nouns altogether, along with their cheeky adjectives. The discreet pronoun can remain. But the really dependable parts of speech are active, non-referential elements —conjunctions, verbs, and prepositions. The poetry which logically follows resembles William James's image of language as a kind of algebra— anonymous variables exercising themselves with mathematical rigor, staying thin:

> They must be always careful to just be with them
> Or they will not only be but could be thought
> To change which they will never know
> Not only only all alike
> But they will be careful . . .

> ("Stanzas in Meditation," Part II, Stanza X, 347)

The words in these five lines fade into invisibility even as we read them because they are almost pure syntax. Contrary to Stein's goal of "continuous present," the function of syntax is to move us right along. There is no syntactical present. This is why Stein in other work, along with contemporary writers attempting to achieve the effect of continuous present, has dislocated syntax or discarded it entirely. The abstract syntactical flight in "Stanzas in Meditation" not only avoids reference, it blocks resonance. Later in the poem Stein writes, "It is natural to think in numerals/ If you do not mean to think."

One must question the judgment in devoting 148 pages (well over a quarter) of the Yale volume to this work. It is of interest to Stein scholars of course but should prove daunting and dull to the non-scholarly reader with a zest for language who, admirably, just wants to play.

In delightful contrast to "Stanzas in Meditation" there is "Dates," which presents words as things replete with pith, not variables, in a deliciously humorous compositional game that with its orderly but surprising permutations (mostly noun to noun) sustains a lively momentum:

> II

> Worry.
> Wordly
> Pies and pies.
> Piles.
> Weapons.

> Weapons and weapons.
> World renown.
> World renown world renown.
>
> III
>
> Nitches.
> Nitches pencil.
> Nitches pencil plate.
> Nitches vulgar.
> Nitches vulgar pencils.
> Nitches plate.
>
> V
>
> Spaniard.
> Soiled pin.
> Soda soda.
> Soda soda.
>
> (197–98)

In section II, transformations from "worry" to "wordly" to "world"; and "pies" to "piles"; or "wordly . . . weapons" to "world renown" are pleasing in themselves, but they also give us enough semantic stimuli to conjure visions of an Achilles and the Tortoise armaments race ("worry" will never catch up with "world renown" anymore than Achilles can overtake the Tortoise in that other of Zeno's logical tales). This gives us both language as object *and* as analogue of object. In section III, crunchy nouns like nitches and plate—word salad garnished with "vulgar pencils," absurd and delightful as "soiled pin"—are of fully independent means. They do not require an "objective correlative" to support them. Nor does the phonemic unfolding of "Spaniard" into "soiled pin" and "soda"—a lighthearted, unpredictable assortment in the eclectic spirit of Dada. The words are free for the exhilaration.

The fifty-page poem, "Lifting Belly" which Kostelanetz calls a "lesbian classic," ranges high and low from the delightful to the tedious. First the former:

> I have feathers.
> Gentle fishes.
> Do you think of apricots . . .

If this language is erotic, and I think it is, it is not because it refers to sexuality, but because it shares with sexuality a tense we might call "present sensual." The words don't direct us very far beyond themselves. They are largely ornamental. As with ornamental lacquered boxes, the aesthetic object is the outside, we forget to wonder what, if anything, is inside or behind or underneath:

> Say anything a mudding made of Ceasars.
> Lobster. Baby is so good to baby.
> I correct blushes. You mean wishes.
> I collect pearls. Yes and colors.
> All colors are gods. Oh yes Bedlington.
> Now I collect songs.
> Lifting belly is so nice.
> I wrote about it to him.
> I wrote about it to her. (24)

The contrast between the pleasantly flowing and the awkward or strained, between the lush and the restrained, creates an evocative tension. Though, as in the "feathers/fishes" lines, there is some transformational development of sounds, any budding lyricism is always interrupted ("Oh yes Bedlington"). Removed from "poetic" sentimentality, the poem does not attempt to whip the reader into unearned emotional peaks. Its engagement is in its sensuality of language and its fun.

When it is not fun, when it is tedious, it may be that it has fallen into a different sort of sentimentality, verging on private language—words like pet names, cherished and exclusive, self-contained units again with no overflow. Private language used in public arenas, like books or dinner parties, reveals conflict about sharing and condemns readers or companions to boredom. In Stein's case the language may have so crackled with private meaning that the drab surface went unremarked:

> Lifting belly is a third.
> Did you say third. No I said Avila
> I would not be surprised surprised if I added that yet.
> Lifting belly to me.
> I am fondest of all of lifting belly.
> Lifting belly careful don't say anything about lifting belly.
> I did not change my mind.

> Neither did you carefully.
> Lifting belly and again lifting belly.
> I have changed my mind about the country.
> Lifting belly and action and voices and care to be taken.
> Does it make any difference if you pay for the paper or not.

Here Stein is straddling, like a dilatory Hamlet, "to name or not to name," "to open or close." The gaps have widened again, yawning vacuums interspersing remote vacuities. Of the relatively few nouns (other than "belly") most are abstract: "third," "mind," "action," "care," "difference." Tone and rhythm are unrelievedly awkward and strained, though entirely devoid of active tension, as straddling is bound to be. The minimal impact is that of a spat, *sotto voce* and yet something we are not quite meant not to overhear. We have the nagging impression that the matter at hand could be of little interest to any but the interlocutors. In such sections of the poem, language hasn't been given the substantiveness of object; neither is it transparent. We are, if not intentionally excluded, subject to sensory deprivation. (Experiment: Lock subjects in bare rooms with abstract Stein texts. How soon will they begin to hallucinate? Control group to be given portions of "Yet Dish" or "Dates.")

The concluding lines of "Lifting Belly" are in the active, resonant voice of the poem. Curiously, they reveal virtually no "information" and yet are not "private language" in Wittgenstein's sense of alienation from a shared context. They are pleasing to the communal ear, tone deafness having undergone miraculous cure. We share in the rhythmical grace of "Lifting belly enormously and with song." We are pleased by the echo of "signs" in "Pauline," the balance of "meantime listen" and "Miss Cheatham," by the openness (even graphically), the spirit of affirmation and ebullience, the amusing whimsy that brings together Miss Cheatham and Aunt Pauline and a cow. The surface is so delightful that it totally absorbs our attention:

> Lifting belly enormously and with song.
> Can you sing about a cow.
> Yes.
> And about signs.
> Yes.
> And also about Aunt Pauline.
> Yes.
> Can you sing at your work.

Yes.
In the meantime listen to Miss Cheatham.
In the midst of writing.
In the midst of writing there is merriment.

In the midst of Gertrude Stein's writing there is merriment or not, depending on the piece or the part. She is in that awkward but intriguing position of having proven both Epicurus and Zeno right. No mean feat. She can ride the currents of indeterminacy like a wonderful, mad balloonist, ornamenting an unsuspecting terminus, an otherwise ordinary field, with her colorful and regenerative improbability. She can also remain securely tethered, refusing to budge, grimly over-determined. Large enough to accommodate more opposition than most of us could bear, she is a formidable ancestor of much issue.

We are haunted by an odd bunch—Epicurus, the great paradoxical Buddha, even Pound—when we come upon John Cage's "nutshell" philosophy in *For the Birds*: "Get out of whatever cage you find yourself in." On the periphery lurk specters of prominent cage manufacturers—Western Rationalists and Academicians in whose shadow Epicurus would have entirely disappeared were it not for his reputation as a gourmet. It is the collision of currents East and West that makes Cage what he is, but though he became a student and practitioner of Eastern philosophy, he always remained with us, the quintessential American—pragmatist and experimentalist, not unlike one of his chief mentors, Buckminster Fuller. The following exchange between Daniel Charles (French philosopher and musician) and Cage in *For the Birds* tells a good deal of the story:

D.C.: What you just said about your last *Thunderclap* [composition by Cage] reminds me of McLuhan and his ideas on an electronic environment. But how has Fuller inspired you?

J.C.: But Fuller talks about that too. I remember the years 1949 and 1950 when I met him at Black Mountain. One day he told us that the wind around the earth always went from west to east. There were people who went with the wind, others against the wind. Those who went with the wind went to the East and developed the Eastern type of thought; those who went against the wind went to Europe and developed European philosophy. And he suggested

that the two tendencies met in the United States, and that their
meeting produced a movement upward, into the air.

D.C.:   What is this movement into the air? Spiritual ascension?

J.C.:   No, the invention of the airplane!

Cage, of course, has worked with another kind of aerodynamics—the
movement of sound through the air to the ear. His methods for choosing
(or not choosing) and launching these sounds have again combined East
and West: East providing a philosophy of Indeterminacy as well as a *modus
operandi,* the Chinese "Book of Changes," *I Ching;* West providing the
active technological model. American experimental pragmatism (Cage's
father was an inventor) and the sort of sunny disposition we identify with
California have generated the humor to bring these qualities together in
happy synergy. But the kind of optimism inherent in trusting to chance
as one's primary guide in certain personal and most significant aesthetic
matters could probably only have been nourished by Eastern philosophy.
It involves a profound belief in the unity and value of all things, a kind
of wholesomeness that ecologists exhort us to develop before it is too late.
Though it largely characterized the world view of the early Greeks (who
also began the process of breaking it down), it is no longer indigenous to
the West.

What is indigenous is the logic of the laboratory: the idea of isolating the
subject as a necessary purification in the search for truth, and belief in law.
Jung, in his introduction to the Bollingen *I Ching,* comments on this:

> . . . we know now that what we term natural laws are merely statistical
> truths and thus must necessarily allow for exceptions. We have not
> sufficiently taken into account as yet that we need the laboratory with
> its incisive restrictions in order to demonstrate the invariable validity
> of natural law. If we leave things to nature, we see a very different
> picture: every process is partially or totally interfered with by chance,
> so much so that under normal circumstances a course of events abso-
> lutely conforming to specific laws is almost an exception.

Hence Cage, who wishes to imitate Nature not in her appearance, but in
her manner of operation employs the chance operations of the *I Ching* for
the process of his art. Chance methods, he feels, enable us to explore the

abundance outside our laboratories and logical structures (read "strictures"); to move our music, for example, beyond classical constraints inherent in harmonic arrangements of "pure" sound. They draw us out of intolerance and isolation, not into chaos, but into collaboration with Nature's processes. Cage's wish is to free our attention from habits of narrow focus, to turn it away from the static precedence of the art object toward the world with its inimitable, unimaginable, rich flux of sound; toward joyous appreciation of events around us. Cage, his own best exemplar, says he has never heard a sound he didn't like.

Daniel Charles, the persistent interviewer in *For the Birds,* worries that this attitude may be fostering yet another restrictive habit—that of adaptation:

D.C.:   Then art as you define it is a discipline of adaptation to the real as it is. It doesn't propose to change the world, it accepts it as it presents itself. By dint of breaking our habits, it habituates us more effectively.

J.C.:   I don't think so. There is one term of the problem which you are not taking into account: precisely, the world. The real. You say: the real, the world as it is. But it is not, it becomes! It moves, it changes! It doesn't wait for us to change. . . . It is more mobile than you can imagine. You are getting closer to this reality when you say as it "presents itself"; that means that it is not there, existing as an object. The world, the real is not an object. It is a process.

D.C.:   There can be no custom or habit in a world in the process of becoming. . . . Is that your idea?

J.C.:   Yes, it is an idea of changing, like all my music, which could be defined as a *Music of Changes.* And I found that title in the *Book of Changes,* the *I Ching.*

D.C.:   I cannot help but believe that *logos,* logic, has only the slightest hold on this world as you define it.

J.C.:   It's simply that I am not a philosopher . . . at least not a Greek one! Before, we wished for logical experiences; nothing was more important to us than stability. Today, we admit instability alongside stability. What we hope for is the experience of that which is. But 'what is' is not necessarily the stable, the immutable. We do know quite clearly, in any case, that it is we who bring logic into the picture. It is not laid out before us waiting for us to discover it. 'What is' does not depend on us, we depend on it. And we have to draw nearer to it. And unfortunately for logic, everything we understand under that rubric 'logic' represents such a simplification with regard to the event and what really happens, that we must learn to keep away from it. The function of art at the present time is to preserve us from all the logical minimizations that we are at each instant tempted to apply to the flux of events. To draw us nearer to the process which is the world we live in. (80–81)

Those familiar with Cage's distinctive voice will frequently miss it in *For the Birds.* The book is a reconstructed transcript (and a translation of a translation) from a series of interviews conducted by the knowledgeable and perceptive Daniel Charles in Paris in the late Sixties. Some of the original tapes were damaged or lost or accidentally erased; others were not entirely audible. The meticulous and repeated editing of the final manuscript (by both Charles and Cage) necessitated by these mishaps leaves us with an unprecedentedly logical unfolding of Cage's theoretical frame of reference, intricacies of technique, etc. Logic emerging out of accidental and contingent events did not offend Cage, who is, above all, not dogmatic. The result is an indispensable introduction and/or companion to the many books in which Cage demonstrates, but does not explicate, his Indeterminist approaches.

The work which appears in *Themes and Variations* came, according to Cage, "out of a need for poetry." This is bound to be an interesting need in one who says, "There is poetry as soon as we realize that we possess nothing" and "I hope to let words exist, as I have tried to let sounds exist." *(For the Birds)* As with most fundamentally simple things, the complications are enormous, because we must get around heaps of cultural paraphernalia. Marjorie Perloff says "what is really 'easy,' in the context of the present, is to write little epiphany poems in free verse, detailing a 'meaningful experience.' " This creates an artifact, poem as object, remnant of a process called "writing poetry." It is not, if it conforms to the criterion of easy access, in process itself. It is finished, fixed, mimetic, mirror image of things jelled in our habits of thought and perception. The reader is pampered, protected from uncertainties, unpredictabilities—the untidiness (the unHeidiness) and excitement of process. Like most of ordinary language, this poetry is designed to smooth out irregularities, to move us from one word to the next with a minimum of resistance.

We may thus be fooled into taking the continuity of syntax for ontological necessity. Cage warns us, "We forget that we must always return to zero in order to pass from one word to the next." There is no ontological glue between words. There is no ontological glue connecting certain words with certain ideas or feelings. Process is Indeterminacy is process:

> We would not have language if we were not in process. But I don't believe normal language can *provide* us with that process. That's why I insist on the necessity of not letting ourselves be dragged along by language. Words impose feelings on us if we consider them as objects, that is, if we don't let them, too, be what they are: process.

> (*For the Birds* [151])

Themes & Variations combines "mesostics" (a variation of acrostics) with a traditional Japanese form called Renga. The mesostics are built around capitalized letters which run down the middle of the poems spelling fifteen names of men who have been influential in Cage's life and work. Words and phrases in the poems have been chosen by means of an intricate series of chance operations from a list of 110 ideas culled from five of Cage's previously published books. He developed the procedure "to find a way of writing which though coming from ideas is not about them; or is not about ideas but produces them." Here is a sample:

> we coMe
> to the sAnd
>
> no Regrets
>
> we Know
> enTertainment
> Or not
> and Backwards
>
> thE stones
> impermanentlY

> (42)

What Cage has to say about Japanese poetics in his Introduction is surprising. It turns out that haiku has a much greater element of indeterminacy built into it than we are led to believe from translations:

> A haiku in Japanese has no fixed meaning. Its words are not defined syntactically. Each is either noun, verb, adjective, or adverb. A group of Japanese of an evening can therefore entertain themselves by discovering new meanings for old haikus.

A literal translation of a Bashō haiku would go like this:

> pine mushroom
> ignorance   leaf of tree
> adhesiveness

This group of words is left syntactically, and therefore semantically, free to stimulate a meditative or imaginative response in the reader as collaborator. Writing and reading, though two very different kinds of processes, become part of an active whole. The free-floating condition of the words in the Bashō poem brings to mind a quotation, with a distinctly European point of view, that opens *The Poetics of Indeterminacy*:

> . . . modern poetry, that which stems not from Baudelaire but from Rimbaud. . . . destroyed relationships in language and reduced discourse to words as static things. . . . In it, Nature becomes a fragmented space, made of objects solitary and terrible, because the links between them are only potential. . . .
>
> (Roland Barthes)

For the optimistic Oriental and for Cage, the response is not terror, but delight, and the words are dynamic in the potential of the negative space that surrounds them.

Cage goes on to explain Renga:

> Traditionally renga is written by a group of poets finding themselves of an evening together and having nothing better to do. Successive lines are written by different poets. Each poet tries to make his line as distant in possible meanings from the preceding line as he can

take it. This is no doubt an attempt to open the minds of the poets and listeners or readers to other relationships than those ordinarily perceived. . . . Thus an intentionally irrational poem can be written with liberating effect. This is what is called purposeful purposelessness.

That old Buddhist swerve, and what Cage is referring to when he says, "Poetry is having nothing to say and saying it; we possess nothing."

Empty words. Empty words brimming with power to elicit active collaboration. That evocation from empty to full is desire in language, what we desire of language. Aristotle in one of many wise moments said happiness is activity of soul in accordance with its special capabilities. For "soul" we would today substitute "nature" as in human nature. If we take this to be a peculiar union of the sensual and intellectual, and language (that sensual/intellectual pièce de résistance) to be our special capability, then nothing should make us happier than the process of filling empty words with the process of filling empty words with the process . . . , though not all empty words stimulate this process. The difference between those that do and those that don't is the great perennial question of poetics. But one thing is certain, immediately accessible "finished" texts which leave us in a state of unadulterated passivity won't do. Cage's poetic texts, "Empty Words" and "Mureau," are both in process, evocative of process. What about *Themes & Variations?*

nEed
betteR
to be wIthout

quicK
Sound of children

A
waTer

superfIcial
aspEcts

fixEs itself

boRedom
or I
worK

Stones
And
unemploymenT

from heIght
rEgrets

What follows could be called "Notes from an Experimental Reader." They are based on a running record of my approaches to, and engagements with, the text of *Themes & Variations:*

(1) This is schematic, cool (Cage would say "empty") poetry that is formally engaging and open, so different from Stein's impacted abstractions which close the reader out. *Themes & Variations* is an inviting book. It is "cool" in the sense Marshall McLuhan described in *Understanding Media* :

> . . . a cool medium [is] of low definition, because so little is given and so much has to be filled in. . . . On the other hand, hot media do not leave so much to be filled in or completed by the audience. Hot media are, therefore, low in participation, and cool media are high in participation or completion by the audience.
>
> . . . the hot form excludes, and the cool one includes. . . .
>
> We . . . find the *avant garde* in the cool and the primitive, with its promise of depth involvement and integral expression.

(2) Looking at the graphic surface of the text, thinking of how to approach it, brings to mind Wittgenstein on "language games." *Themes & Variations* is clearly a text where familiar rules for reading won't work.

> Doesn't the analogy between language and games throw light here? We can easily imagine people amusing themselves in a field by playing with a ball so as to start various existing games, but playing many without finishing them and in between throwing the ball aimlessly into the air, chasing one another with the ball and bombarding one another for a joke and so on. And now someone says: The whole time they are playing a ball-game and following definite rules at every throw.
>
> And is there not also the case where we play and—make up the

rules as we go along? And there is even one where we alter them—
as we go along.

(*Philosophical Investigations*, 83)

(3) The rules which generated the text of the mesostics did not dictate a
finished game anymore than the rules of Renga do. In both cases, the
writing procedure ensures an open field for the reader who can in turn
make up and alter her rules as she goes, all the while staying within the
domain, the playing field, of the text.

(4) Turning the pages, I begin by looking for the names as in a "Find the
_____" puzzle, as families and friends do at the Vietnam Name Memo-
rial. Names *are* memorials—for the quick, the slow, and the dead.

(5) But these names on a vertical axis are somehow insubstantial. They are
certainly not comfortably sedentary or complacent like the horizontally
"Reclining Name." This is more like "Name Descending the Staircase"
after MARCEL DUCHAMP (one of those honored in *Themes & Variations*).
Or is it "Name Falling Down Stairs"? Or names suspended mid-Fall like
Icarus in Breughel, like Icarus in Auden and Williams. Or perhaps these
are linguistic atoms (letters) stuck in moments of collision.

(6) In Cage's poems these falling (but not fallen) names are just that—
letters colliding with other letters, forming word structures along the way.
There is both surprise and order.

(7) And humor and mnemonic resonance: names, flagrantly dangling their
letters, bond with words in ragged columns that resemble the (flattened)
helical structure of DNA. (In linguistics, they speak of "transformational
strings.")

(8) Vertebral letters: stalk of central nervous system shoots off most regen-
erate of neural impulses, words. Trunk shoots off branches and twigs
toward other electrobiological exchanges. Or, aerial view: narrow stream
of names fed by tributary words.

(9) This could (maybe does) begin to look like *Snow White and Seven Types
of Ambiguity*. Making connections is important. It's what the human brain
is designed to do. But Fairy Tales and free associations take you where
you've been before.

(10) Reading from left to right, there is no semantic tension between
horizontal and vertical axes. Is there formal tension? Capitalized letters act
as interference. Tendency is to stress them, silently or aloud. Feels/sounds

like a stutter. Stutter, like foreign accent, heightens awareness of phonemic components of words.

(11) Becoming more accustomed to capitals. They are smoothing down, rounding off into pleasant lumps, like beads, something for fondling, relaxing one's attention. Is this the experience of the rosary (or sucking stones)—freeing the mind to operate on an intuitive plane?

(12) But then, intermittently, the awkwardness returns—uppity, upper case letters like grains of sand in oysters—formative irritations. Mellowing again, overhead view again, they become small ripples in flowing water —surface tension.

(13) I have discovered that I particularly like upper case Os and Zs: hOw, nOw, hOrn, wOrd, Organ, dOors. RevOlution and harmOny are one-word blues songs. Then there's bliZzard, wiZard, gaZing. . . . Os and Zs should probably always be in upper case. Also, there is the pleasant realization (sensual, not intellectual) of the role of the conciliatory H, how it softens the t in patH.

(14) False etymology game: taking parts of words beginning with capital letters as original concepts embedded in them—Egrets in rEgrets, Ravings in engRavings, Hots in sHots, Ape in tApe, Sic in muSic, Ion in salvatIon, Ted in unexpecTed . . . words in words—telescoping words.

(15) Before I read *Themes & Variations,* egrets were in regrets and ravings were in engravings. After I read *Themes & Variations* Egrets were in rEgrets and Ravings were in engRavings.

(16) Meanwhile, there is always the peripheral sense of names flowing by: "Sweet names run softly, till I end my song." No; one is not always conscious of their presence *as* names. They submerge and re-emerge quietly like dolphins, dolphins and river swimming together downstream, toward the sea. Not an end point; an opening out.

(17) Discovery that the last word in *Themes & Variations* is "river." I trust that this may have been coincidence—tribute (tributary) to a connectedness of things that needn't be forced, *bon chance.*

(18) There are piquant juxtapositions, pleasantly recurrent words and phrases, but mostly the sense of gentle unfolding. The experience of reading Cage is similar to a summer's picnic by the edge of a stream: leaning back against a tree, letting the rhythms of events intermingle with one's own associative rhythms; every now and then being stirred into acute focus by a bird's song, a twig snapping, wind in the leaves, a fragment of a conversation taking place nearby. You go home rested and

refreshed. What could it mean, to go home to Language rested and refreshed?

(19) Interesting question. Questions counter the centripetal force of association by moving you away from self, toward the appealingly gratuitous otherness of the unknown. Excitement of exploration. Not knowing what you will find. The experimental attitude: "That's it: research. I call that 'experimental' music: the kind where you do research . . . but without knowing what the result will be," says Cage in *For the Birds*. ReSearch, QuestIon: Re Search Quest Ion. . . .

(20) Research question: where can language take us? If we know that we know only too little, and wish to explore, then we are onto indeterminate adventures: schemes and variations, swerves and collisions. . . .

"The Threading of the Year"

David Barber

In his later years Kenneth Rexroth came to assume the very appearance of a weathered Chinese sage. That drooping mustache and the incalculable crinkles round the eyes, the high forehead and the set of the square chin, something about the mixed air of gruffness and whimsy in that battered physiognomy—one feels certain, gazing at the snapshots of this doughty septuagenarian, that we have seen him countless times in the corner of an inkbrushed screen, a venerable figure dwarfed by cliffs and all but lost in swirling mists, ever watchful, scroll in hand.

And so in a way we have. Rexroth looked toward Asia every bit as purposefully as another Midwestern kid by the name of Eliot took to Britannia, and his transformation into an Oriental poet-scholar was no less convincing or complete than Eliot's reincarnation as an English don. Translations and imitations from the Chinese began appearing in Rexroth's collections of poetry during the 1940's, and his initial pair of New Directions anthologies, *One Hundred Poems from the Japanese* (1955) and *One Hundred Poems from the Chinese* (1956), became touchstone volumes as they passed through their many editions. From the start there was a refreshing candor and undisguised ardor about it all. "I have chosen only those poems whose appeal is simple and direct . . . poems that speak to me of situations in life like my own," Rexroth stated in his notes to the Chinese volume. "I have thought of my translations as, finally, expressions of myself."

That candor and ardor never slackened. As he grew older Rexroth read widely in Buddhism, and lived for a time in Kyoto, courtesy of a Fulbright. In the last decade of his life he produced or coauthored six collections of Far Eastern poetry, assemblages spanning a panoramic range of periods, styles, and sensibilities. Thanks in large part to the accessibility of the texts and the sturdiness of Rexroth's renderings, this portfolio of translated verse not only found an ample following but to a sensible degree can be said to have formed and cultivated that wider readership. Self-schooled in this enterprise as in everything else, splendidly undaunted by his lack of fluency and scholarly bona fides, he became his day's foremost popularizer of Chinese and Japanese verse,

From *Parnassus* (vol. 18, no. 2/vol. 19, no. 1, 1993).

the translator most likely to have introduced the common reader to the women court poets of Japan or the gnomic utterances of Tu Fu.

Rexroth also published two collections of original verse during his last rush of industry in the 1970's. You can now read them side by side in the single trim edition recently published by Rexroth's old camping chum James Laughlin under the title *Flower Wreath Hill: Later Poems.* And with that book in hand and a few biographical facts at your disposal you might tell an absorbing story about a stormy iconoclast from the American Heartland who reinvented himself as a contemplative imagistic poet in the Golden State, a story of how an avant garde firebrand turned his back on the dialectics of the West and the precepts of modernism to embrace the distilled quietism of the East. You would observe that a full half of *New Poems* (1974) is given over to Chinese translations or adaptations, and that most of *The Morning Star* (1979) was written in the gardens and temples of Kyoto. You would point out that in the poems from Rexroth's own hand, the line between poet and translator has blurred almost beyond recognition: One sees the same highly concentrated structures, the same containment, the same cultivation of open line and frozen image, a kindred predilection towards sequence and diary notation.

Finally, you would unfold the tantalizing dance of veils behind "The Love Poems of Marichiko," the sequence of fifty erotic lyrics that close out the book. Five of these poems first appeared in Rexroth's *One Hundred More Poems from the Japanese* (1974), and the poet was glossed in the end-notes as "the pen-name of a contemporary young woman who lives near the temple of Marishi-ben, in Tokyo." In the notes to the "Love Poems," however, one comes across a wink and a nudge. "Notice," Rexroth writes, "that the sex of the lover is ambiguous." This Marichiko, it emerges, is a fabrication, cross-cultural identification turned inside out, translation in drag. What better climax to a virtually lifelong intimacy with Far Eastern verse? Rexroth, on the final pages of his last book, speaks to us as a Japanese woman.

It is an almost irresistible story, resonant with psychobiographical reverberations and socioliterary overtones. There is no disputing or diminishing the importance of the Orient to the contrarian temperament and tempestuous career of Kenneth Rexroth. There's also no denying that the cultural tradewinds blowing out of California in the

1950's and 1960's helped sweep Rexroth along: The aura hovering over those New Directions paperbacks glimmered all the brighter as an amalgamation of Eastern mysticisms and wisdoms took on a faddishness in youth culture and as hybrid variations on open forms began to attract a growing faction of metrically disaffected poets. As a longtime resident of the state and the tribal elder of the San Francisco literary caravansary, as an evolutionary link between the California of Jeffers and the California of Snyder and Hass, as a driving force in both the countercultural and crosscultural permutations of the regional imagination, Rexroth is a natural when cast as the framing spirit of what contemporary punditry insists we call the "Pacific Rim." If he hadn't reinvented himself, it may have been necessary for us to invent him.

An arresting story, then, but one that's rather too available. A story, finally, that remains more colorful than sufficiently insightful, and one that helps explain why Rexroth, to quote poet (and former Rexroth student) Sam Hamill, is "among our best-known and least-read poets."[1] It not only encourages us to lazily stylize an irrepressibly eclectic personality, but deprives us of much incentive to grapple with a body of poetry distinctive for its robust unorthodoxy and bracing restlessness. It condescends too quickly to the presumption that Rexroth's diehard Bohemian leanings and fire-breathing disdain for Eastern Seaboard snobbery bred an animus toward his own Americanness.[2] It perpetuates the impression, this narrative line does, that Rexroth lacked the requisite quotient of modernist irony and ambiguity to himself become a fully realized poet in an age of anxiety, that he was forced to compensate for the unevenness and coarseness of his own verse by co-opting the Orient's polished refinements of sense and sensibility. It justifies his marginality and excuses his neglect. It gives his metamorphosis the cynical spin of a good career move.

Like so many others, I suspect, my first brush with Rexroth was as the name on the spine of those compact and handsomely packaged New Directions "100 Poems" paperbacks, which I regarded as standing invitations to steal a march on Milton-loving prep-school teachers everywhere. The name was not the spur. Rexroth was, as far as this Southern California schoolboy was concerned, merely the humble translator, and as such, properly shadowy. I don't think it would have much mattered to me if I'd been told at that time that Rexroth was living some 90 minutes north in Santa Barbara, ever the cantankerous poly-math and for many the dean of California poets. What mattered to me was the mystique of all that white space on the pages, the allure of those calligraphic brushstrokes, the attar of exotica that seemed to promise a hidden garden of significance. What mattered was the sensation of being spoken to directly and intimately by an alien tongue across the ages:

> Tumult, weeping, many new ghosts.
> Heartbroken, aging, alone, I sing
> To myself. Ragged mist settles
> In the spreading dusk. Snow skurries
> In the coiling wind. The wineglass
> Is spilled. The bottle is empty.
> The fire has gone out in the stove.
> Everywhere men speak in whispers.
> I brood on the uselessness of letters.
>
> ("Snow Storm" [Tu Fu])

So it was jarring, some years later and the Milton-lovers safely behind me, to discover that shadowy humility was not exactly Rexroth's forte. Threading my way through the largely embalmed Bohemian quarter of San Francisco in the dawn of the Reagan *risorgimento*, I would spin squealing postcard racks and come across the same photo time and again. It was a blurry, noirish shot of Rexroth declaiming his verse to the accompaniment of a jazz ensemble sometime in the throes of Eisen-hower America, bulldog jaw jutting into the nicotine haze, all pugnacity and bardic torque. Who was this nightclubbing Homer, this leather-lunged hipster doyen? Could he possibly be the same canny soul who had made the T'ang master Tu Fu seem my contemporary?

I indulge in this scrap of personal reminiscence because I am con-vinced that the Rexroth of initial impressions and general acquaintance is more often than not a caricature, a "figure" whose singularity is most conveniently filed away as the headstrong sum of his polarized selves. Depending on which way we want the compass needle to quiver, he can be emblematic of a certain kind of aggrieved excess, a certain brand of generational dissonance and provincial dissent, a certain mixed breed of cosmopolitan primitivism that could call itself neither redskin nor paleface, a certain fearless vigor which is also a certain endless quandary. And depending on one's own cherished notions of artistic essence, an appraisal of Rexroth's powers can lend itself instinctively to either salutary ideals or cautionary tales. As a constellation of contradictions, enthusiasms, and antagonisms, he is perhaps surpassed only by that other notable maverick from the American interior—Little Dipper to Pound's Big. In Yeatsian terms, alas, he made the fatal error of seeking perfectibility in both the life and the art, eternally falling short of reconciling a life of action and a poetry of inwardness.

"He is no writer in the sense of the word-man," wrote Williams of Rexroth. "For him words are sticks and stones to build a house—but it's a good house."[3] And true enough, the mature Rexroth did not write poems that anyone would be tempted to call, with a nod to Williams, "little word machines." Much of his writing seems to be one species or another of pedagogy—lectures and lessons, sermons and tracts. As anyone who's read across Rexroth's bully-pulpit prose knows well, his was an incorrigibly discursive and dialectical mind, a polemical intellect of nearly inexhaustible capacity, wheels within wheels. The verse, too, often seems to have been composed in the spirit of instruction and exhortation. Rexroth's pair of long poems from the 1940's, "The Phoenix and the Tortoise" and the European travelogue "The Dragon and the Unicorn," are sprawling monuments to his mania for association and assimilation, running commentaries crammed with arcana and opinion, diatribe and panegyric, cerebral pontification and encyclopedic information:

> Bath a stageset for Terence,
> One of the world's unlikely
> Cities, as freakish as Venice.
> In the midst of its colonnades
> And the swarming well-fed people,
> Bath Abbey, immense and absurd,
> Like the skeleton of a
> Whale or a dirigible,
> Built by Walpole Gothicizing,
> The most eighteenth-century
> Product of the Middle Ages.
>
> (from "The Dragon and the Unicorn")

But we do wrong by Rexroth if we overstate his didacticism and only have ears for his windier topicality. This was also a poet who all his life wrote quietly wrought and intensely intimate homages and elegies, love lyrics and pacts. It's a fetching irony, in light of the above remark by the good doctor of Paterson, that one of the most moving and telling of these is Rexroth's 1946 poem, "A Letter to William Carlos Williams," in which Rexroth lionizes Williams as "the first / Great Franciscan poet since / The Middle Ages" and praises the "wonderful quiet / You have, a way of keeping / Still about the world . . . ."

> Nowadays, when the press reels
> With chatterboxes, you keep still,
> Each year a sheaf of stillness,
> Poems that have nothing to say,
> Like the stillness of George Fox,
> Sitting still under the cloud
> Of all the world's temptation . . .

Let others celebrate William's earthiness; in Rexroth's eyes he shall be known for his saintliness, his Quaker-like gravity, a containment that verges on mysticism. The poem closes with an affectionate prophecy, the Passaic having become "the lucid Williams River" and a young woman imparting the essence of the poet to her young ones as they stroll alongside.

> ' . . . And the
> Beautiful river he saw
> Still flows in his veins, as it
> Does in ours, and flows in our eyes,
> And flows in time, and makes us
> Part of it, and part of him.
> That, children, is what is called
> A sacramental relationship.
> And that is what a poet
> Is, children, one who creates
> Sacramental relationships
> That last always.'

One might well expect that Rexroth would hold keen admiration for Williams. His own sense of measure and cadence owed something to Williams' perceptually alert line, as did his colloquial worldliness and moral allegiance to the local. His is arguably the most moving and incisive tribute we have for a poet who inspired a great many. But this Williams of stillness and sacrament, of "wonderful quiet," seems also a selective embodiment of the kind of poet Rexroth himself wished to become, a personification of the knowing reserve and meditative concentration his early verse only fitfully sustained.

Our leading story, of course, would have it that Rexroth learned to keep still about the world, at long last, by donning the robes of the Buddhists and assuming the manner of the classical poets of the East. "Sitting still under the cloud / Of all the world's temptation"—aren't we already closer here to the Yangtze than to the Passaic? But Rexroth is one of those poets who only grow more distorted the more we squint at him through the lens of artistic development; we must take care not to twist him into the lotus position quite so briskly and willfully. He is never quite the poet we expect him to be, or rather, we are obliged to revise our sense of his reach and his grasp the further we read on. To traverse the nearly 800 pages of his poetry amassed in the *Collected Shorter*, the *Collected Longer*, and *Flower Wreath Hill* is only to confirm that there are no shortcuts around the manysided soul that was Kenneth Rexroth. It's chiefly for this reason that I want for the rest of this essay neither to take the high road of eulogy nor the low road of apology but rather to locate Rexroth in a very particular clearing, a place apart from the forking paths where poets are hustled into their rightful anthologies or obscurities, a buffer zone somewhere between that squealing postcard rack and that hanging inkbrushed screen:

> All day I walk over ridges
> And beside cascades and pools
> Deep into the Spring hills.
> Mushrooms come up in the same spot
> In the abandoned clearing.
> Trillium and adder's tongue
> Are in place by the waterfall.

This is from a poem called "Hapax," and it too appears among the autumnal offerings of *Flower Wreath Hill*, early in the book under the section title "Love Is an Art of Time." Contrary to the collection's Oriental cast, the poem opens with a bow to the Christian calendar ("Holy Week. Once more the full moon / Blooms in deep heaven / Like a crystal flower of ice.") and bears the curiously exculpatory epigraph, "The Same Poem Over and Over." It's a nocturne set in an unspecified patch of Rexroth's beloved California ranges—a valedictory piece of meditation spoken at the end of a daylong ramble through the up-country so familiar to the poet that "A heron lifts from a pool / As I come near, as it has done / For forty years, and flies off / Through the same gap in the trees." The tone is reverent; the language direct and unadorned. A general atmosphere of monkish solitude prevails through-out, the poem by gradual degrees convincing us that it was intended all along as a rough-hewn prayer: "Back at my cabin / In the twilight an owl on the same / Limb moans in his ancient language. / Billions and billions of worlds / Full of beings larger than dinosaurs / And smaller than viruses, each / In its place, the ecology of infinity. / I look at the rising Easter moon. / The flowering madrone gleams in the moonlight."

"Hapax" is not by any stretch one of Rexroth's most accomplished works. In fact, it's a poem that can seem to confirm one's worst suspicions about his relative indifference to linguistic tension or pro-sodic rigor, his disdain for psychological intricacy and dramatic irony, the mulish matter-of-factness of his compositional method, his weak-ness for the scenic and susceptibility to fuzzy mysticism. A commentator disposed to unkindness could well claim that not only is the scenery distinctively Californian but so too is the poem's cosmic bathos and its over-eagerness to be "at one" with the universe. Rexroth's religiosity appears for the most part to be a matter of vibes rather than spirit, the end-product of the poem's predetermined rhetoric of transcendence. The operative phrase, "ecology of infinity," sounds as if it should be the slogan of a Silicon Valley software firm.

But it is in this vein, I would argue, that Rexroth did write some of his most transparent and transfigured poems throughout his life—poems that shuttle more surely than this one between natural pieties and elective affinities, poems at once grounded in the immediate and bent toward the beyond, poems of *en plein aire* mindfulness and loamy ongoingness that ask to be read as authentic spiritual exercises, devotional verse. "Hapax," for all its seeming offhandedness, is an Easter poem set down in good faith—which is not to say that it enunciates a Christian creed, but that it seeks an emptying of self as a condition of spiritual consolation. It is here, in abandoned clearings, in alpine retreats, in periodic monastic solitudes, that we come upon Rexroth's variants on "poems that have nothing to say," to borrow his encomium for Williams. It is here, in poems where a stripped-down declarative idiom corresponds to a greater stripping-away of pretense and ingenuity, that we find a self-made contemplative poet for whom significance has become a test of artlessness.

I daresay one can find in Rexroth's writings a précis or an ars poetica for each and every paradox his temperament was heir to. It's curious nonetheless to observe him glossing this particular reconstitution of his poetic humors as the most effortless of conversion experiences, in a little wartime poem called "Precession of the Equinoxes":

Time was, I walked in February rain,
My head full of its own rhythms like a shell,
And came home at night to write of love and death,
High philosophy, and brotherhood of man.

After intimate acquaintance with these things,
I contemplate the changes of the weather,
Flowers, birds, rabbits, mice and other small deer
Fulfilling the year's periodicity.

And the reassurances of my own pulse.

This rather sounds like the poem one would write in the autumn of one's days, disabused of youthful illusions and disencumbered of overblown ambitions. In fact, Rexroth was not yet forty, and not nearly the master of his nervous system that these lines would have us believe. As such, one can't help thinking that the poem is wise to its own wishful thinking, set down more as a prospectus than a fait accompli. Rexroth, in any event, certainly didn't become a contemplative overnight, and breaking with his past was no simple matter of losing himself in the birds and the stars. That "time was" takes us back only a year or so to the hot-blooded auguries and maledictions that fill the pages of his first book, *In What Hour* (1941), and a disposition given to spasms of rampant self-doubt. "Time was," he seems to have been teetering on the brink of jettisoning the fairest hopes of art and language and learning altogether: "What is it all for, this poetry, / This bundle of accomplishment / Put together with so much pain? / . . . What words can it spell, / This alphabet of one sensibility?"

Born a round generation behind Pound and Williams in 1905, Rexroth came of age while the Lost Generation was sowing its oats and the dashing Europe of the charter modernists was counting its dead in the trenches. We might therefore exonerate him for what might appear like grandstanding pessimism in the above passage, which can be found at the beginning of a set piece titled "August 22, 1939." Like the canonic poem of Auden's that's dated ten days later, Rexroth's is an epochal lamentation written in the throes of one of the modern era's darkest hours. And like Auden, just two years his junior, Rexroth was attempting to raise his voice against the march of armies and the sleep of reason—a "world in stupor," to borrow one of the many majestically disabused phrases from "September 1, 1939."

Poetry makes nothing happen, Auden had testified in his elegy to Yeats earlier that year, but of the two poems written at the close of that grim summer, Rexroth's is the bleaker as well as the cruder deposition on the futility of the poet. The role reversal, if you will, is perhaps more noteworthy than the synchronicity. Central casting surely would have called for the rough-and-ready Midwestern autodidact, not the urbane Oxonian, to have been "one of the faces along the bar" that "clings to their average day," and keeps alive "an affirming flame." Yet it is Rexroth rather than Auden who seems to have been rendered abject by a "low, dishonest decade," coarsely cursing the darkness where his emigré contemporary nurses sparks of luminous humanism. "August 22, 1939" ends not with a gesture of affirmation but a bray of exasperation: "What are we doing at the turn of our years / Writers and readers of the liberal weeklies?"

Certainly, this poem of clenched fists catches Rexroth at the turn of *his* years, still more the fiery lefty than the full-blown man of letters. It is not, like Auden's, a poem for the ages but a broadside on the times.

Liberals or no, the initial readers of *In What Hour* were no doubt more apt than we to recognize that the date of the poem salutes the anarchists Sacco and Vanzetti (executed August 23, 1927) and to place its unattributed quote from Marx's *Kapital* ("From each according to his ability, / Unto each according to his needs"). "August 22, 1939" is one of a number of poems in the collection that rage and grieve over the bitter harvest of partisan struggle or rail at the various avatars of the Big Lie. At times this pitch of righteous declamation and unrepentant disenchantment turns Rexroth into a cross between a soapbox Marxist and an Old Testament prophet:

> It is later than you think, fires have gone over
> Our forests, the grasshopper screamed in our corn.
> Fires have gone over the brains of our young girls,
> Hunger over young men and fear everywhere.
> The smell of gas has ascended from the streets,
> Bloomed from the cartridges, spread from wall to wall,
> Bloomed on the highways, and seeped into the corn.
> It is later than you think, there is a voice
> Preparing to speak, there are whisperings now
> And murmurings and noises made with the teeth.

(from "The Motto on the Sundial")

But *In What Hour* ran against the grain of cultural orthodoxy in calmer and more collected ways too. There is a clear-eyed as well as a wild-eyed poet at work in this Depression album of poems. As Robert Hass has suggested, we find in its pages a sensibility taking root: a Midwestern outcast remaking himself into a California citizen-poet, a fierce moral intelligence fighting the good fight at the far margins of the nation.[4] Although it's evident that Rexroth's radical disaffection from the centers of official culture made the Bay Area an appealing base of operations, it's also plain that his embrace of the California hinterlands stemmed from impulses at least as elemental as ideological. An avid and delicate alertness to his adopted region's natural history, a charged responsiveness to its open sprawl and utter scale, ground the more durable passages in *In What Hour*, revealing backcountry affinities and reflective leanings one doesn't usually associate with hardboiled anarchists:

> Autumn in California is a mild
> And anonymous season, hills and valleys
> Are colorless then, only the sooty green
> Eucalyptus, the conifers and oaks sink deep
> Into the haze; the fields are plowed, bare, waiting;
> The steep pastures are tracked deep by cattle;
> There are no flowers, the herbage is brittle.
> All night along the coast and the mountain crests
> Birds go by, murmurous, high in the warm air.

(from "Autumn in California")

Readers whose acquaintance with California isn't limited to glossy postcards of the Golden Gate or celluloid montages of Hollywood palms can attest to the rightness of that "sooty green" and that oak-devouring haze, but one needn't be a native to be impressed by the fine-spun attention Rexroth musters for a "mild / And anonymous season" that few writers in his day (and no great number in our own) would deem worthy of more than passing notice. A Currier and Ives calendar of stock seasonal footage is next to useless in coming to terms with the muted annual cycle of the Californian countryside, and Rexroth's precedence in paying homage to this *terra incognita* is a credit to both his sense of nuance and his sensible knack for "making it new." The ear must shake off the echoes of intoxicating Keatsian stanzas before it can pick up the unprepossessing stateliness of *this* ode to autumn, and that's arguably all to the good: The ruminative texture of the above passage, the chariness toward fully ripened rhyme ("Mild"—"valleys"; "green"—"deep") and verbal dazzle ("Birds go by"), seem altogether more fitting to the hazy, colorless, and anonymous character of the landscape under scrutiny than the chiming couplets, lush pentameters, and rapturous sprung rhythms that a verdant, dramatically transitory clime wrings from its laureates.

Rexroth had been a resident of San Francisco for more than a decade when *In What Hour* came off the presses. He also had some twenty years of literary industry already behind him, much of it hyperactive philosophical collage and programmatic dabblings in Objectivist serialism.

These experimental proclivities apparently withered as the breadlines formed and his political activism intensified, but what really seems to have brought Rexroth back from the brink of linguistic cubism was his growing intimacy with Northern California's coastal wilds and Sierra ranges. It is surely not a trifling biographical detail that Rexroth was periodically under the employ of the Federal Writers Project during these years, contributing unsigned descriptive sketches and touring squibs to such publications as the *WPA Guide to California* and a *Field Handbook of the Sierra Nevada.* These commissions had to be a happy circumstance for an enthusiast of the trail like Rexroth, and it's safe to say that the grit and dirt he picked up along the way was a decided blessing for his poetry. Amid such abstruse set pieces as "Dative Haruspices" ("Film and filament, no / Donor, gift without / Reciprocity, transparent / Tactile act, an imaginary / Web of structure sweeps / The periphery of being . . .") and "New Objectives, New Cadres" ("By what order must the will walk impugned, / Through spangles of landscapes, / Through umbers of sea bottom, By the casein gleam of any moon / Of postulates and wishes?") that take up considerable breathing room in his first collection, one welcomes the tempered measure that marks Rexroth's epistles from the mountains:

> Frost, the color and quality of the cloud,
> Lies over all the marsh below my campsite.
> The wiry clumps of dwarfed white bark pines
> Are smoky and indistinct in the moonlight,
> Only their shadows are really visible.
> The lake is immobile and holds the stars
> And the peaks deep in itself without a quiver.
> In the shallows the geometrical tendrils of ice
> Spread their wonderful mathematics in silence.
>
> (from "Toward an Organic Philosophy")
>
> In the long day in the hour of small shadow
> I walk on the continent's last western hill
> And lie prone among the iris in the grass

My eyes fixed on the durable stone
That speaks and hears as though it were myself.

(from "A Lesson in Geography")

Lines like these assure us that Rexroth from early on was wholly conscious of casting himself as a poet in honorable regional exile, and they also affirm the elements of style that were coalescing into trustworthy habits of composition. The "outdoors" poetry of *In What Hour*—lean and economical in its syntax and its diction, coolly observant and solemnly meditative in its essential register, its balance of trust placed in the testimony of the senses rather than the force of rhetorical address—assumes the concentrated plainspoken form that Rexroth would avail himself of increasingly in the years to come. Implicit in this streamlined prosody is a finetuned moral sensibility. Steeped in the organic rhythms and seasonal variations of the California landscape, this is verse that divines in ecology a higher ethical order that might expunge the taint of a corrupt and corrosive social ethos. More simply, the mountaintop had become for Rexroth the most reliable place to steel the conscience and clear one's head. Here is the opening of "Hiking in the Coast Range," a poem commemorating the death of two dockworking unionists:

The skirl of the kingfisher was never
More clear than now, nor the scream of the jay
As the deer shifts her covert at a footfall;
Nor the butterfly tulip ever brighter
In the white spent wheat; nor the pain
Of a wasp stab ever an omen more sure;
The blood alternately dark and brilliant
On the blue and white bandanna pattern.

What bears out the intensity and urgency of these clean-hammered lines are their scrupulous attentiveness and inherent clarity: the balance of cadences and concentration of stresses ("white spent wheat," "omen more sure"), the taut quasi-scriptural deployment of successive negations and accumulating pivots, the deft interlocking of naturalistic and emblematic detail as the passage moves from "skirl" to "scream" to "wasp stab." This is not the voluble and splenetic poet who elsewhere confounds oracular power with oratorical volume; this is not the poet whose moral imperatives are largely indistinguishable from his imperious moods. It is the difference between grandiloquence and gravity; between a short fuse and a drawn bowstring.

Even so, "Hiking the Coast Range" is still in its own way a public poem written on the barricades. The hiker has hied to the hills to galvanize his resistance to injustice in the polis and to gird his loins for renewed class warfare. What's striking as one thumbs toward the midpoint of the *Collected Shorter* is the hush that falls over Rexroth's later backcountry poetry of the 1940's and 1950's, the hue and cry of causes and the outbursts of anathema fading out like crackling radio signals.[5] In their place one hears a virtual liturgy of earthly delights and soulful gleanings, poems claiming sovereignty in what a later, blither generation of Californians would champion as the here and the now. A handful are examples of the forthright and singularly unaffected love poetry that is justly accorded a place of honor among Rexroth's more devoted readers. Initially most distinctive for an unblinkered erotic candor rarely encountered in mid-century American poetry (Rexroth was an acolyte of Sappho long before "Marichiko" was so much as a rustle in a kimono), these amatory poems retain their boldness on the far side of the sexual revolution because they are unmuddied by either sentimentality or lubricity and unblemished by Puritan and Freudian galls alike. Up where the air is clear, Eros routs Thanatos from the field, if only for the most fleeting of interludes. As demonstrated in the exemplary "Lyell's Hypothesis Again" (Charles Lyell was the preeminent geologist of the early nineteenth century and one of the forefathers of modern geological time), Rexroth's sylvan settings are vivid environments, not allegorized Gardens, and his grasp of the material world vastly exceeds that of your average passionate shepherd:

> Naked in the warm April air,
> We lie under the redwoods,
> In the sunny lee of a cliff.
> As you kneel above me I see
> Tiny red marks on your flanks
> Like bites, where the redwood cones

> Have pressed into your flesh.
> You can find just the same marks
> In the lignite in the cliff
> Over our heads. *Sequoia*
> *Langsdorfii* before the ice,
> And *sempervirens* afterwards,
> There is little difference,
> Except for all these years.

Encountering other such poems ("Floating," "Still on Water," "When We with Sappho") that twine in a double helix around the force of nature and power of desire, we are reminded of Rexroth's admiration for the eroticized, mystical pulse of D. H. Lawrence's poetry, which he praised in his rousing 1947 introduction to the first American edition of Lawrence's *Selected Poems*, for achieving its visionary authority in "the pure act of sensual communion and contemplation" and reaching its highest mastery in Lawrence's explicit love poems to Frieda composed during the couple's travels along the Rhine. This cluster of lyrics, declared Rexroth in his best Poundian manner, comprise "the greatest imagistic poems ever written," capturing the romantic union of a man and woman in so primal and natural a state that "everything stands out lit by a light not of this earth and at the same time completely of this earth . . . ."[6] That line could serve as the epigraph for Rexroth's own intermittent poetry of spiritualized Eros and conjugal grace, his Lawrentian tendency—revealed nowhere more indelibly than in these closing lines of "Floating"—to spot the fingerprints of the divine in the couplings of humankind:

> Move softly, do not move at all, but hold me,
> Deep, still, deep within you, while time slides away,
> As this river slides beyond this lily bed,
> And the thieving moments fuse and disappear
> In our mortal, timeless flesh.

Memorable though they are, Rexroth's present-tense lyrics celebrating a flesh-and-blood Other under an open sky are outnumbered by wilderness poems conceived in the absence of companionship or the aftermath of passion. Most of them take the form of soliloquies rather than direct addresses to the beloved, and they chronicle more hours spent in soulmaking than lovemaking. Much as Rexroth cherished having a mate by his side as he scaled peaks and forded brooks, the evidence of these poems lays bare an even deeper need to wrestle with body and spirit in perfect solitude. The impulse is ancient, and at this late date often wearily formulaic, yet the verse Rexroth mined on a "high plateau where / No one ever comes, beside / This lake filled with mirrored mountains" ("Time Is the Mercy of Eternity") or "On the ground beside lonely fires / Under the summer stars, and in / Cabins where the snow drifted through / The pines and over the roof" ("A Living Pearl") stands out as some of the most measured and least derivative he would ever compose. While these meditations always assume a monastic distance from the madding crowd, they seldom indulge in the presumptions of holy loneliness; while they commonly incline toward mysticism, they rarely court the thin air of worldly detachment. The rituals of purification Rexroth invokes are better described as escapes *into* the world, revolving as they do around the pleasures of the flesh and the manifestations of place, sharply specific as they are about the passage of the seasons, the changes in the weather, the fluctuation of waters and the cycles of flowerings, the comings and goings of creatures. "Nature poetry" is almost always an enfeebling appellation, but especially so for these benedictions and baptisms written at the intersection of natural history and preternatural mystery:

> Forever the thought of you,
> And the splendor of the iris,
> The crinkled iris petal,
> The gold hairs powdered with pollen,
> And the obscure cantata
> Of the tangled water, and the
> Burning, impassive snow peaks,
> Are knotted here together.
> This moment of fact and vision
> Seizes immortality,
> Becomes the person of this place.
> The responsibility

> Of love realized and beauty
> Seen burns in a burning angel
> Real beyond flower or stone.
>
> (from "Incarnation")

"This moment of fact and vision"—here, in a phrase, is Rexroth's plumbline, the unit of measure by which he set about divining the limits of knowing and the depths of being as he lit out for the timberline. Yet the poems Rexroth consecrates to such moments have precious little in them of Romantic self-exaltation and sublimity: The visionary awakenings that grip this poet on his lonely summits or beside his rushing streams are specimen reaffirmations of recurrence, of continuity, of pattern, of the habitual and the diurnal, of responsibility. The "burning angel / Real beyond flower or stone" that appears in the closing lines of "Incarnation" gains all the greater purchase on reality by virtue of the fact that we are in the hands of a poet who is inordinately attentive to flowers and stones and by virtue of the fact that we have been paced through a poem that begins not in inspiration but perspiration: "Climbing alone all day long / In the blazing waste of spring snow, I came down with the sunset's edge / To the highest meadow . . . ." The elevation of the soul and the attainment of serenity pivots not on "either/ors" but hangs in the balance between infinitely renewable "ands" and "thens."

The alpine wilderness, to be sure, was where Rexroth sought a peace surpassing all understanding, and in certain poems he enshrines his waterfalls and meadows and glades as the way stations of a pilgrim. Occasionally, they verge on ecstatic experience, glimpses behind the veil. In "The Signature of All Things" (the title poem of Rexroth's 1949 collection, named after the seminal work of the 16th-century German mystic Jacob Boehme) he lays the text aside and "gaze[s] through shade / Folded into shade of slender / Laurel trunks and leaves filled with sun" until "My own sin and trouble fall away? Like Christian's bundle." In "Time Is the Mercy of Eternity" he stares into a high-country pool upon an August evening and discerns "that the color / Of the water itself is / Due to millions of active / Green flecks of life . . . / The deep reverberation / Of my identity with / All this plentitude of life / Leaves me shaken and giddy." But for the most part, in transcribing his communions with nature, Rexroth succumbs neither to grandiosity nor to giddiness. The devotional integrity of his compactly built verse paragraphs derives from their implicit insistence that looking closely, speaking directly, and feeling deeply can (and perhaps must) merge into a steadfast and continuous sacramental habit of mind.

There is a rugged humility in Rexroth's readiness to be steadied by the cyclical and his willingness to be schooled by the commonplace. Observation, these poems intimate, incubates perception; description, revelation. "Although / I expect them, I walk by the / Stream and hear them splashing and / Discover them each year with / A start," he writes of a salmon migration in "Time Spirals." And again, in "Doubled Mirrors," tramping down a familiar road at night and descrying a "glinting / Everywhere from the dusty gravel," Rexroth hunkers down for a remedial seminar in wonder: "I suspect what it is / And kneel to see. Under each / Pebble and oak leaf is a / Spider, her eyes shining at / Me with my reflected light / Across immeasurable distance." The salmon spawn every year, it is an old story; the spiders proliferate under the leaf-fall at summer's end, there's nothing remarkable in it; and there is Rexroth, expecting and suspecting, lingering over his yoked moments of fact and vision as if they were a rosary.

Rexroth is never more firmly in possession of his tone and touch as when he seems to be simply marking time, noting the hour, fixing the night sky, taking stock of what stirs around him. His finest poems of this ilk, with their delicacy and accuracy of perception, their owlishness and gravitas, their fastidious rhythms and spare syntax literally portray a man coming to his senses. What commends them—the poems and the senses—is their exemplary composure. Time and again in this poetry of the interior Rexroth cultivates keen regard where others might have lapsed into wild rapture—dedicating himself not to leaps of faith but rather, as he articulated in one of his most lovely poems, to "pauses of fate." The poem is "We Come Back," from the 1944 collection *The Phoenix and the Tortoise*, and it follows in its entirety:

> Now, on this day of the first hundred flowers,
> Fate pauses for us in imagination,
> As it shall not ever in reality—
> As these swifts that link endless parabolas

Change guard unseen in their secret crevices.
Other anniversaries that we have walked
Along this hillcrest through the black fir forest,
Past the abandoned farm, have been just the same—
Even the fog necklaces on the fencewires
Seem to have gained or lost hardly a jewel;
The annual and diurnal patterns hold.
Even the attrition of the cypress grove
Is slow and orderly, each year one more tree
Breaks rank and lies down, decrepit in the wind.
Each year, on summer's first luminous morning,
The swallows come back, whispering and weaving
Figure eights around the sharp curves of the swifts,
Plaiting together the summer air all day,
That the bats and owls unravel in the nights.
And we come back, the signs of time upon us,
In the pause of fate, the threading of the year.

Here, I submit, is the most telling and limpid draft of "the same poem over and over" that the elder Rexroth makes reference to at the head of "Hapax." For all its classical elegance of bearing and the formal mastery of its syllabics, it is a supplicant's poem and a sacramental incantation. For all its worldliness, it seeks meaning in provisionality and in the shedding of metaphysical conceits and moral precepts. If any poem was ever a "sheaf of stillness" it is this one: In that pause of fate an orgy of motion becomes a tapestry of eternal forces and the vernal turns autumnal as our eye works down the page. Stated baldly in "Hapax," the "ecology of infinity" is a shibboleth, a buzzline. Inscribed in the "endless parabolas" of swifts and the "fog necklaces on fencewires" that "seem to have gained or lost hardly a jewel," it's a spiritual condition made manifest and a phrase redeemed.

I don't want to give the impression that this pietistic poet of the woods and rockfaces is the "true" Rexroth or a Rexroth to be extolled at the expense of all the rest there are to go around. Nor would I venture to say that this medley of work constitutes anything so commanding as a "period" or anything as coherent as a system of thought. Notwithstanding the auspiciously titled "Toward an Organic Philosophy," one of the contemplative respites among the fiery polemics of *In What Hour*, this is not a poet to whom we turn for grandly mounted summas. In the years roughly spanning Pearl Harbor and the McCarthy hearings (one instinctively reaches for political watermarks when considering a muckraker of Rexroth's caliber), Rexroth's poems cover a teeming variety of subjects in a variety of forms and registers: urbane epigrams ("Me Again"), erotic homages ("A Dialogue of Watching"), memoirs bittersweet and unrepentant ("The Bad Old Days," "A Living Pearl"), playful verse for his daughters ("A Bestiary," "Mother Goose"), outright screeds (most notoriously, "Thou Shalt Not Kill," an ostensible elegy for Dylan Thomas that some adherents of incendiary anaphora hail as an ur-"Howl"), and of course, the earliest of his floodtide of Chinese and Japanese translations. But I believe these intermittent Hapaxes hold up so well precisely because they occupy an honestly arrived-at middle ground between Rexroth's more vexed compulsions and volcanic convictions, sinning neither on the side of preachiness or aloofness. For that reason they are also some of the most humane poems from Rexroth's hand, urgent without straining after effects, serious without resorting to homiletics, thoughtful without thirsting for themes. Theirs is a versification and idiom of proportion, which in turn bears out the rectitude and the scrupulousness of the speaker's self-reflection.

What they are surely not, this group of contemplative verses occasioned by travels upcountry and downriver, are California eclogues or Sierra idylls, numbers written in honor of some idealized, half-mythical territory of honeyed light and stirring vistas.[7] Proportion presupposes equilibrium, and the landscapes that loom so large in Rexroth's field of vision are as empirical and historical as they are archetypal and sanctified. As fleshed out in poems like "We Come Back," "Time Is the Mercy of Eternity," "Time Spirals," or "Lyell's Hypothesis Again," Rexroth's California has fewer links to the legendary island that the first European mapmakers drew or the promised land that the nineteenth-century popular imagination painted than it has ancestral ties to an innately Protestant branch of debate over the conception of nature as scripture and geography as destiny. Call him Ishmael: The deeper Rexroth penetrates into the region's lonely isolation, the more inescapably he becomes entangled in uniquely American contours of imagination and realms of spirit. However much his work asks to be understood with reference to Marx or in light of Tu Fu, however boldly his personal history carries the impress of beatnik San Francisco and beatific Kyoto, his reckonings with the wilderness bear the telltale marks of Jeffersonian and Emersonian bloodlines.

Seeking expression through nature, argued Emerson in "The Poet," "is a very high sort of seeing, which does not come by study, but by the intellect being where and what it sees; by sharing the path or circuit of things through forms, and so making them translucid to others." In Rexroth's backcountry poetry, California—and the so-called American Century that he waged such a holy war against—finds a glowing ember of Transcendentalism, no longer a creed or a mission but a latent aptitude for, in Emerson's words again, "the condition of true naming . . . resigning himself to the divine aura which breathes through forms . . . ." Wherever else Rexroth's long and winding paper trail leads us, it also runs through the vicinity of Concord, and that is where, just now, this reader would like to leave him:

> Deer are stamping in the glades,
> Under the full July moon.
> There is a smell of dry grass
> In the air, and more faintly,
> The scent of a far off skunk.
> As I stand at the wood's edge,
> Watching the darkness, listening
> To the stillness, a small owl
> Comes to the branch above me,
> On wings more still than my breath.

The Virtues of the Alterable

HELEN VENDLER

Now that Knopf has given us O'Hara's *Collected Poems* they had better rapidly produce a *Selected Poems,* a book that wouldn't drown O'Hara in his own fluency. For the record, we need this new collection; for the sake of fame and poetry, we need a massively reduced version, showing O'-Hara at his best. His charms are inseparable from his overproduction—the offhand remark, the fleeting notation of a landscape, the Christmas or birthday verse, the impromptu souvenir of a party—these are his common forms, as though he roamed through life snapping Polaroid pictures, pulling them out of his camera and throwing them in a desk drawer sixty seconds later. And here they are—some overexposed, some under-developed, some blurred, some unfocused, and yet any number of them succeeding in fixing the brilliance of some long-forgotten lunch, or the curve of a body in a single gesture, or a snowstorm, or a childhood movie. If these poems are photographic in their immediacy, they remind us too of the rapid unfinished sketches done by an artist to keep his hand in, or to remind him of some perishable composition of the earth. If there were a movie equivalent to a sketch, some of these poems would be better called verbal movies—the "I-do-this, I-do-that" poems, as O'Hara himself called them.

The generic form of O'Hara's poems is conversation, the generic punc-tuation the exclamation point, the generic population O'Hara's friends, the generic landscape Manhattan and Fire Island, the generic mythology the flora and fauna of art shows, radio shows, and movie shows. Sureness and insouciance pervade this décor. But two aspects of his work tended to do O'Hara in: his radical incapacity for abstraction (like Byron, when he thinks he is a child) and his lack of a comfortable form (he veered wildly from long to short, with no particular reason in many cases for either choice). The longest poems end up simply messy, endless secre-tions, with a nugget of poetry here and there, slices of life arbitrarily beginning, and ending for no particular reason. "Dear Diary," says O'-

Review of Frank O'Hara's *The Collected Poems* from *Parnassus* (vol. 1, no. 1, 1972).

Hara, and after that anything goes. The perfect freedom any diarist enjoys
—to put anything down that happened on a certain day simply because at
the head of the page there is that hungry date saying June 13, 1960—is
what O'Hara claims for himself in the long poems. Beside these poems,
even Ginsberg looks formal. The theoretical question O'Hara forces on
us is a radical one: Why should poetry be confined in a limited or closed
form? Our minds ramble on; why not our poems? Ramblings are not, to
say the least, the native form of poets with metaphysical minds, but O'-
Hara, in his fundamental prescinding from the metaphysical, believes
neither in problems nor in solutions, nor even in the path from one to the
other. He believes in colloquies, observations, memories, impressions,
and variations—all things with no beginnings and no endings, things we
tune in on and then tune out of. Turn on the oscilloscope, attach the leads
to the tuner, take gauge readings—these are the O'Hara processes. In one
sense, there is no reason why a poem of this sort should ever stop. The
inherent limitation seems not to be a formal one within the poem, but
rather an external one—the limited attention span of the poet or his
reader. We can attend to life in this hyper-attentive way for only a short
time, and then our energy flags, so that like overexcited electrons we
subside back into our low-energy orbits. The poet's language weakens,
our response sags, and the poem loses us. And yet O'Hara was stubborn
enough to wish, like Emily in *Our Town,* that life could always be lived
on the very edge of loss, so that every instant would seem wistfully
precious. Therefore the attitude of perpetual wonder, perpetual exclamation, perpetual naïveté. O'Hara had enough of all these qualities by nature
(judging from their consistent presence from the earliest poems to the
latest) so that this poise at the brink of life was no pose, but it does make
me wonder how he would have endured that jadedness of age that, in their
different ways, all old poets confront.

Some of O'Hara's poems are already deservedly famous, for the best
reason in the world: nobody else has done anything like them in English.
One reading of "Blocks" guarantees that the stunning last half will never
be forgotten:

O boy, their childhood was like so many oatmeal cookies.
I need you, you need me, yum, yum. Anon it became suddenly

like someone always losing something and never knowing what.
Always so. They were so fond of eating bread and butter and

> sugar, they were slobs, the mice used to lick the floorboards
> after they went to bed, rolling their light tails against
> the rattling marbles of granulation. Vivo! the dextrose
> those children consumed, lavished, smoked, in their knobby
> candy bars. Such pimples! such hardons! such moody loves.
> And thus they grew like giggling fir trees. (108)

The intense appeal of these lines comes from their having suppressed nothing of adolescence: the persistence of the childish in candy bars and giggles; the startling new growth "like fir trees"; the incongruous nursery scene of the mice in the children's bedroom eating their bedtime snack while the children suddenly discover themselves having hardons and pimples; the sudden flash of the personal ("I need you, you need me") combined painfully with its psychic results ("like someone always losing something . . . such moody loves"). Almost all other poems about adolescence have concealed one or the other of these facets of the state, whether out of shame or aesthetics one scarcely knows. An aesthetic that permits the coexistence of moody loves, hardons, mice, and candy bars has a good chance of being a new source of truth.

The same capaciousness appears in the ethereal poem "First Dances," where O'Hara touches in sequence a dancer's first attempt to lift a ballerina, a high-school dance, and then, I think, his first dance ever:

> 1
> From behind he takes her waist
> and lifts her, her lavender waist
> stained with tears and her mascara
> is running, her neck is tired
> from drooping. She floats she steps
> automatically correct, then suddenly
> she is alive up there and smiles.
> How much greater triumph for him
> that she had so despaired when his
> hands encircled her like a pillar
> and lifted her into the air
> which after him will turn to rock
> like boredom, but not till after
> many hims and he will not be there.
> 2
> The punch bowl was near the cloakroom
> so the pints could be taken out of the

boys' cloaks and dumped into the punch.
                    . . .There were many
introductions but few invitations. I
found a spot of paint on my coat as
others found pimples. It is easy to
dance it is even easy to dance together
sometimes. We were very young and ugly
we knew it, everybody knew it.
3
a white hall inside a church. Nerves. (458–9)

The wholly intimate presence of the male dancer in the first section is suddenly dispensed with—"He will not be there"—and the agony and pleasure sketched so vividly in the second dance give way to a seriocomic summation ("We were very young and ugly")—and yet finally summary or dismissal is wholly scrapped and the primacy of recollection is allowed: "A white hall . . . nerves." This invalidation of judgment is both dangerous and satisfying. After all, what difference does it make what happens later on or how the picture looks in retrospect or in second-order reflection? The final equation, First Dances = Nerves, is the truest.

O'Hara distrusts spectatorship, so that even his most cinematic self-filmings are expressed from the inside out, as though they were blood-pressure readings rather than a nurse's external observations on a chart, self-generated electrical impulses which record themselves without the interposition of a watching person. An evening is improvised, in "At the Old Place," and the gay-bar scene is sketched with no retrospective frame, noted down simply as it happens. I'm not sure why this method succeeds, except that the mixture of frivolousness, bathos, high-pitched boredom, and self-satire is not one that men have allowed into poetry very often, if ever:

Joe is restless and so am I, so restless.
Button's buddy lips frame "L G T TH O P?"
across the bar. "Yes" I cry, for dancing's
my soul delight. (Feet! feet!) "Come on!"

Through the streets we skip like swallows.
Howard malingers. (Come on, Howard.) Ashes
malingers. (Come on, J. A.) Dick malingers.
(Come on, Dick.) Alvin darts ahead. (Wait up,
Alvin.) Jack, Earl and Someone don't come.

> Down the dark stairs drifts the steaming cha-
> cha-cha. Through the urine and smoke we charge
> to the floor. Wrapped in Ashes' arms I glide.
> (It's heaven!) Button lindys with me. (It's
> heaven!) Joe's two-steps, too, are incredible,
> and then a fast rhumba with Alvin, like skipping
> on toothpicks. And the interminable intermissions,
> we have them. Jack, Earl and Someone drift
> guiltily in. "I knew they were gay
> the minute I laid eyes on them!" screams John.
> How ashamed they are of us! we hope. (223–4)

The wish *not* to impute significance has rarely been stronger in lyric poetry. It happened, it went like this, it's over. Why is it worth recording? Because it happened. Why is what happened worth recording? Because what else is there to record? And why should we want to read it? Because what else is there to know except what has happened to people? Such a radical and dismissive logic flouts the whole male world and its relentless demand for ideologies, causes, and systems of significance. The anarchic elasticity of O'Hara's poetry depends entirely on his athletic effort to make the personal the poetic—the personal divested of religion, of politics, of mysticism, of patriotism, of metaphysics, even of idealism. One might be reminded in part of Forster's ethic of personal relation but Forster shored up that ethos with innumerable arabesques of myth, ranging from Pan to Brahma. O'Hara's designedly light explanation of his theory of poetry (which he winsomely named "Personism") rests on intimacy and immediacy:

> It was founded by me after lunch with LeRoi Jones on August 27,
> 1959, a day in which I was in love with someone (not Roi, by the way,
> a blond). I went back to work and wrote a poem for this person. While
> I was writing it I was realizing that if I wanted to I could use the
> telephone instead of writing the poem and so Personism was born. It's
> a very exciting movement which will undoubtedly have lots of adher-
> ents. It puts the poem squarely between the poet and the person
> . . . The poem is at last between two persons instead of two pages.
> (499)

In another statement (500), later partially disavowed (511), O'Hara made a more serious formulation:

> I don't think my experiences are clarified or made beautiful for myself
> or anyone else; they are just there in whatever form I can find them.
> . . . It may be that poetry makes life's nebulous events tangible to me
> and restores their detail; or, conversely, that poetry brings forth the
> intangible quality of incidents which are all too concrete and circum-
> stantial. Or each on specific occasions, or both all the time.

Experiences, incidents, events—O'Hara's vocabulary betrays how impatient he was of any notion which would separate novel-writing and poetry-
writing. He liked to cite Pasternak as an example of a writer who could
do both, and we may guess that O'Hara suffered from a persistent wish
for a longer form than his own poems afforded him. Without that long
form, we are offered glimpses of relation, happy and sad, but no continuous curve of a life-spiral; like Roman candles, O'Hara's poems burst into
a shower of bright particulars and then extinguish themselves, often
enough in a few modest ashes, on the page.

O'Hara in some way refused to take his poems, I would guess, as
seriously as he took life. "It's a pretty depressing day, you must admit,"
he wrote, "when you feel you relate more importantly to poetry than to
life" (511) (a feeling that underlies one of his most brilliant poems, "A
Step Away from Them"). The greatest poets would have found that
antithesis unthinkable and unsayable, and it works to the harm of O'Hara's
poetry that he thinks it is *not* life. The shadowy, if immense, privileges he
admits for art appear at their most impressive in his comic manifesto "Ave
Maria":

Mothers of America
          let your kids go the movies!
get them out of the house so they won't know what you're up to
  it's true that fresh air is good for the body
                  but what about the soul
that grows in darkness, embossed by silvery images
and when you grow old as grow old you must
                  they won't hate you
they won't criticize you they won't know
                 they'll be in some glamorous country
they first saw on a Saturday afternoon or playing hookey. (371–2)

It's typical of O'Hara that the silver screen, however glamorous its images,
can't compete with the real thing, which is of course sex. The poem

continues, in a child's experience of a wonderful *épanouissement* better than anything in the movies:

> they may even be grateful to you
> > for their first sexual experience
> which only cost you a quarter
> > and didn't upset the peaceful home
> they will know where candy bars come from
> > and gratuitous bags of popcorn
> as gratuitous as leaving the movie before it's over
> with a pleasant stranger whose apartment is in the Heaven on Earth bldg
> near the Williamsburg Bridge
> > O mothers you will have made the little tykes
> so happy because if nobody does pick them up in the movies
> they won't know the difference
> > and if somebody does it'll be sheer gravy. (372)

O'Hara's presentation of early sex as pure physical pleasure bestowed like the bribery of popcorn hovers on the edge of Romance. Would being picked up by a stranger in the movies really be that nice? Yes, maybe, sometimes, other times not, and the poem survives its loading of these particular dice only by its inveterate air of resolute comedy. O'Hara has a line in one poem about writing poetry to cheer people up, and there is an air of determined social duty about a lot of these poems, as though the balloon of group cheerfulness had to be batted back to the next player— over to you, Kenneth—and Kenneth Koch, himself equally noble in his obligations, serves a jaunty poem back, and so on through the clan, to Bill Berkson to John Ashbery, like Tinker to Evers to Chance. The important thing is to be quick on your toes, elastic and springy, especially springy.

It took O'Hara several years of writing to perfect his individuality. The reason he wasn't noticed early on is that most of his early work is his worst. John Ashbery, in his introduction to this volume, suggests a cabal of the anti-avant-garde who, ostrichlike, hid their heads against O'Hara's radiance:

> It was not surprising that [O'Hara's] work should have initially proved so puzzling to readers—it ignored the rules for modern American poetry that had been gradually drawn up from Pound and Eliot down to the academic establishment of the 1940s. (vii)

If Dylan Thomas, who sounded not at all like Pound or Eliot, could be welcomed in America, so could anyone else, and this conspiracy theory is entirely untenable. O'Hara's poems got measurably better with the publication of *Meditations in an Emergency* (1957), and by the time O'Hara published *Lunch Poems* in 1964 he was well known. The early poems are often tiresomely insistent: the last of the twelve "pastorals" entitled "Oranges" reads in its conclusion (after five pages of ramblings):

> Marine breeze!
> Golden lily!
> Foxglove!
> In these symbols lives the world of erection and destruction,
> the dainty despots of society.
> Out of the cloud come Judas Agonistes and Christopher Smell
> to tell us of their earthy woe. By direction we return to our
> fulfilling world, we are back in the poem.
> Across the windowsill lies the body of a blue girl, hair
> floating weedy in the room. Upon her cypresses dance a Black Mass,
> the moon grins between their legs, Gregorian frogs belch and
> masturbate. Around the window morning glories screech of rape
> as dreadful bees, consummately religious, force their way in the dark.
> The tin gutter's clogged by moonlight and the rain barrel fills
> with flesh. Across the river a baboon blesses cannibals.
> O my posterity! This is the miracle: that our elegant invention
> the natural world redeems by filth. (8–9)

A lot of this has been picked up from the more blasphemous French poets, and the strain is felt. The confused antagonism between art ("elegant invention") and sex ("filth") is almost buried in a welter of lurid images, and the soapbox is not far away. In the early verse exclamation points attempt over and over a rape of the reader, and even in "A City Winter," the title poem to his first volume, O'Hara sounds like bad Meredith:

> I plunge me deep within this frozen lake
> whose mirrored fastnesses fill up my heart.
> where tears drift from frivolity to art
> all white and slobbering, and by mistake
> are the sky. I'm no whale to cruise apart
> in fields impassive of my stench, my sake,
> my sign to crushing seas that fall like fake
> pillars to crash! (77)

The miracle is that even while O'Hara was writing trash like this there was growing a small pile of poems far more unassertive, self-deprecatory and self-admiring, at once combining pain and joy:

> *Autobiographia Literaria*
> When I was a child
> I played by myself in a
> corner of the schoolyard
> all alone.
>
> I hated dolls and I
> hated games, animals were
> not friendly, and birds
> flew away.
>
> If anyone was looking
> for me I hid behind a
> tree and cried out "I am
> an orphan."
>
> And here I am, the
> center of all beauty!
> writing these poems!
> Imagine! (11)

This was written in 1949 or 1950, when O'Hara was twenty-three or twenty-four, and even that early O'Hara had found the poignant way of talking to the world that he brought to perfection in "A True Account of Talking to the Sun on Fire Island," written in 1958:

> I picked up a leaf
> today from the sidewalk.
> This seems childish.
>
> Leaf! you are so big!
> How can you change your
> color, then just fall!
>
> As if there were no
> such thing as integrity!
>
> You are too relaxed
> to answer me. I am too
> frightened to insist. (21)

Breathless and marveling, as he says of himself in an early verse letter to Bunny Lang (16), O'Hara patrols the paths of the world, hoping to

unclutter himself of cynicism and false sophistication, tempted by fantasy
and yet shamed by it. One of the most finished of the early poems is a
transparent look inward to the fascination of the movies:

> The cinema is cruel
> like a miracle. We
> sit in the darkened
> room asking nothing
> of the empty white
> space but that it
> remain pure. And
> suddenly despite us
> it blackens. Not by
> the hand that holds
> the pen. There is
> no message. We our
> selves appear naked
> on the riverbank
> spreadeagled while
> the machine wings
> nearer. We scream
> chatter prance and
> wash our hair! Is
> it our prayer or
> wish that this
> occur? Oh what is
> this light that
> holds us fast? Our
> limbs quicken even
> to disgrace under
> this white eye as
> if there were real
> pleasure in loving
> a shadow and caress
> in a disguise! (35–36)

The medium of the poem is so simple that the title—"An Image of Leda"
—comes almost shockingly to reinterpret our attachment to movies. Hyp-
notized and repudiatory at once, the poem holds its double feelings in a
momentary tranced suspension, quickening from reflection to vicarious
action and then subsiding in withdrawal. These small triumphs succeed in
their pure colloquial strength, and even such random samples as these few
quotations from the early poetry demonstrate that O'Hara's native gifts

for simplicity and a fresh view, though scarcely noticeable in the bulk of less completely achieved poems, were nonetheless present from the beginning.

There is scarcely a poem lacking striking lines in this volume, and almost never a poem, no matter how bad in general, lacking some wonderful words from O'Hara's tumultuous vocabulary. Chasubles and buzz saws, zebras and tendrils, yawns and ponies, gullies and rattletraps, Afghanistan and Broadway, Prussian leather and Mack trucks, the U.S. Senate and Spenser's False Florimel—all join the proliferating herbage of O'Hara's acquisitive mind. There is everywhere a breakdown of logical categories, sometimes only in a false imitation of Dada, but later in the volume in a true attempt to synthesize all of American experience, taking even a wider field than Whitman (though Whitman, to do him credit, wanted a poetry that could have room for all the names of all the drinks served in all the taverns of America, as he said in *An American Primer*). O'Hara follows both Whitman and Williams in writing urban pastoral, but neither Whitman nor Williams took the pleasure in the city that O'Hara did:

> I love this hairy city.
> It's wrinkled like a detective story
> and noisy and getting fat and smudged
> lids hood the sharp hard black eyes. (198)
>   the country is no good for us
> there's nothing
>   to bump into
>   or fall apart glassily
> there's not enough
>   poured concrete
>   and brassy
> reflections . . .
>   New York
> greater than the Rocky Mountains (476–77)

Both Whitman and Williams suffer from a rueful attachment to the natural world (and in Williams's case to the past as well) precluding any full assent to city life. But the sun has to chide O'Hara for not looking up more:

> I know you love Manhattan, but
> you ought to look up more often. (306)

Impulsive and appetitive, O'Hara rakes in friends, paintings, and eve-
nings-out with the same impartial joy. Tedious though the in-group references (to Bill and Kenneth and Janice and Edwin and Vincent, etc., etc.)
can be, they are genuinely invoked to make the real precious, an experiment that is at least worth trying. In one of the most beautiful of many
beautiful love poems, "Having a Coke with You" (1960), there is a praise
of consummated life which always, for O'Hara, must (the highest compli-
ment) transcend art; and this consummation is here the most banal of acts,
having a Coke. Having the Coke, O'Hara can scorn to change his state
with kings (in this case Marini, Duchamp, Leonardo, or Michelangelo).
These quintessential hyperboles of love begin partly tongue-in-cheek, but
suddenly gather to a crystallization of liberated insight, and conclude in
happiness:

Having a Coke with You
is even more fun than going to San Sebastian, Irún, Hendaye, Biarritz,
　　Bayonne . . .
partly because in your orange shirt you look like a better happier St. Sebastian
partly because of my love for you, partly because of your love for yoghurt . . .
and the portrait show seems to have no faces in it at all, just paint
you suddenly wonder why in the world anyone ever did them
　　　　　　　　　　　　　　　　　　　　I look
at you and I would rather look at you than all the portraits in the world
except possibly for the *Polish Rider* occasionally and anyway it's in the Frick
which thank heavens you haven't gone to yet so we can go together the
　　first time
and the fact that you move so beautifully more or less takes care of Futurism
just as at home I never think of the *Nude Descending a Staircase* or
at a rehearsal a single drawing of Leonardo or Michelangelo that used
　　to wow me
and what good does all the research of the Impressionists do them
when they never got the right person to stand near the tree when
　　the sun sank
or for that matter Marino Marini when he didn't pick the rider as carefully
as the horse
　　　　　　it seems they were all cheated of some marvellous experience
which is not going to go wasted on me which is why I'm telling you about it. (360)

The happy marriage in this poem of the paintings, the trees, the Coke, the
past, the present, the lovers, and the artists shows how unerringly the

jumble in O'Hara's sensibility could sort itself out into shapely forms. Though the *journal intime* can be sometimes more gripping for the diarist than for us, yet in the late poems there are signs that O'Hara could take the full measure of himself, America, and the arts better than any other of his contemporaries except perhaps Lowell and Ginsberg. In his "Answer to Voznesensky and Evtushenko" (468) he forsakes the winsome, the cute, and the childish, and launches into a grand manifesto resisting the conventional picture of America transmitted by contemporary Russian poets, and reminding them in scorn of their great ancestors Mayakovsky and Pasternak:

> We are tired of your tiresome imitations of Mayakovsky
> we are tired
>   of your dreary tourist ideas of our Negro selves
> our selves are in far worse condition than the obviousness
> of your color sense
>   your general sense of Poughkeepsie is
> a gaucherie no American poet would be guilty of in Tiflis . . .
>   how many
>   of our loves have you illuminated with
> your heart your breath
>   as we poets of America have loved you
> your countrymen, our countrymen, our lives, your lives, and
> the dreary expanses of your translations
>   your idiotic manifestos.

The accomplished swings between the grand and the minute, contempt and love, keep us teetering on a bravado always just avoiding the ridiculous on the one hand and the sentimental on the other, a version of public poetry which does not abolish the private. O'Hara would like a world where nothing excluded anything else, where a conversation can coexist with a private fantasy, as it does in his almost seamless abutting of a private recollection of a movie *(Northern Pursuit)* with a search for remedies for Allen Ginsberg's stomach:

>   . . . Imagine
>   throwing away the avalanche
> so early in the movie. I am the only spy left
> in Canada,
>   but just because I'm alone in the snow
> doesn't necessarily mean I'm a Nazi.

                                        Let's see,
two aspirins a vitamin C tablet and some baking soda
should do the trick that's practically an
                                        Alka
Seltzer. Allen come out of the bathroom
                                        and take it. . . .
        Ouch. The leanto is falling over in the
firs, and there is another fatter spy here. They
didn't tell me they sent
                        him. Well, that takes care
of him, boy were those huskies hungry.
                                        Allen,
        are you feeling any better? (488)

All of these poems are demonstrations—demonstrations of what mind
is by what mind does, its remarkable double and triple tracks, so that a
question about old movie scores leads to a full-dress recollection-fantasy
even while one is collecting vitamin tablets, getting down the baking soda,
uncapping the aspirin, and hollering to Allen in the bathroom, all the
while having second-order reflections on movie-making. The number of
possible tracks is theoretically limitless and it seems as though in some
poems O'Hara pushes the possibilities beyond intelligibility. But when the
technique works, spontaneity fills the poem like helium, and the poem
takes off with pure buoyancy.

The reason O'Hara can be truly aerial is that he genuinely has no
metaphysical baggage. No religion, no politics, no ideology, no nothing.
It is only partially a joke when he calls these lines "Metaphysical Poem":

                When do you want to go
                I'm not sure I want to go there
                where do you want to go
                any place
                I think I'd fall apart any place else
                well I'll go if you really want to
                I don't particularly care
                but you'll fall apart any place else
                I can just go home
                I don't really mind going there
                but I don't want to force you to go there
                you won't be forcing me I'd just as soon
                I wouldn't be able to stay long anyway
                maybe we could go somewhere nearer

> I'm not wearing a jacket
> just like you weren't wearing a tie
> well I didn't say we had to go
> I don't care whether you're wearing one
> we don't really have to do anything
> well all right let's not
> okay I'll call you
> yes call me (434-5)

These relational intricacies are the only metaphysics O'Hara admits, and their probable transiency precludes the sublime relational metaphysics, whether deluded or not, of the Keatsian "holiness" of the heart's affections. Happiness yes, holiness only maybe. Dismay followed by elation, comfort succeeded by loneliness, getting mad giving way to a shrug, apathy followed by quickening—these are O'Hara's dimensions and out of them he creates his poetic space. There are ominous sighs in the later poems, sighs especially about America, that make us wonder whether O'Hara could have kept up the verve and bounce and amplitude of his best poems, but even a sad poem wafts up, often enough, a comic energy. An old Russian in America reminisces unhappily,

> . . . meanwhile back in my old
> country they are renaming everything so
> I can't even tell any more which ballet
> company I am remembering with so much
> pain and the same thing has started
> here in American Avenue Park Avenue South
> Avenue of Chester Conklin Binnie Barnes
> Boulevard Avenue of Toby Wing Barbara
> Nichols Street where am I what is it
> I can't even find a pond small enough
> to drown in without being ostentatious
> you are ruining your awful country and me
> it is not new to do this it is terribly
> democratic and ordinary and tired (434)

When the democratic and the ordinary get tired for O'Hara, there remains no substratum he can deck with his fantastic tinsel of reference. O'Hara was, as he said himself, "the opposite of visionary" (256), and all he asked was "grace to be born and live as variously as possible" (256). When variety in the real is the only value, the Chameleon is God, that Chameleon that, in the poem called "Etiquettes Jaunes," O'Hara had been unable to reconcile with integrity. By the time we finish the *Collected Poems* we at least know that that particular ethical problem has disappeared. Integrity, cherishing the variety of the self and the world, persists through O'Hara's mercurial poems, ebbing and flowing with "the tender governing tides of a reigning will." "Alterable noon," he says, "assumes its virtue" (261), and that virtue of the alterable adorns him too as he saunters through the world, a step away, as he truthfully notes, from the variety he records. Guessing, observing, looking, reading, comparing, reflecting, loving, writing, and talking, he takes us through life as though he were the host at a spectacular party. We may regret the equableness and charm of our guide, and wish him occasionally more Apollonian or more Dionysian (the sex poems aren't very good, though they try hard and are brave in their homosexual details), but there's no point wishing O'Hara other than he was. The scale he works in is deliberately, at least by past ideological standards, very small. Klee might be the painter who seems comparable, in his jokes, his whimsical collocations, his tenderness, his childlike naïveté, his sprightliness, his muted levels of significance, his sentiment. In O'Hara, modern life is instantly recognizable, and a modern ethos of the anarchically personal receives its best incarnation yet. If it satisfies some portion of us less than a more panoramic ambition, we are self-betrayed in recognizing the frailty of our own supports. We cannot logically repudiate ideology and then lament its absence (though Stevens made a whole poetry out of just that illogic). O'Hara puts our dilemma inescapably before us, for the first time, and is therefore, in his fine multiplicity and his utter absence of what might be called an intellectual syntax, a poet to be reckoned with, a new species.

The May King

DARRYL PINCKNEY

Resist much, obey little.

—Walt Whitman

The Revolution has been accomplished: *noble* has been changed to
no bull.

—William Carlos Williams

Prophet, seer, vatis, Redeemer, *élève,* witness, Man of America, angel in
comical form, Buddha-eye—Allen Ginsberg, born in Paterson, New Jer-
sey, in 1926, plotted at an early age his high drama of self-definition. He
wrote to Mark Van Doren while still a student at Columbia University:
"I want to be a saint, a real saint while I am still young, for there is much
work to do." This mission to find and seize the holy spirit took Ginsberg
on his legendary journey, by car, boat, and plane, from desolate railroad
yards of the Wild West to soothing enclaves in stricken India, and included
detours into drugs, radical politics. Ginsberg is no longer young and the
road from the Six Gallery in San Francisco where he first read "Howl"
to the Jack Kerouac School of Disembodied Poetics at The Naropa Insti-
tute in Boulder, Colorado is a long and winding one. Revelations and
discoveries along the way have been relentlessly recorded. The story, the
quest for the grail, is more likely to end at home on the Lower East Side
than in the apotheosis of Los consumed by flames.

Every vanguard contains the seeds of its own obsolescence. And so the

Review of Allen Ginsberg and Peter Orlofsky's *Straight Hearts' Delight: Love Poems and Selected
Letters,* Donald Allen's *Allen Ginsberg: Composed on the Tongue,* and Michael McClure's *Scratching the Beat Surface* from *Parnassus* (vol. 10, no. 1, 1984).

memoirs, the anthologies, the collected and selected works of the Beats pour forth, some posthumous, most not. Anniversary lectures or readings become features of the season; the commemorative occasions are well attended and most of the audience is young, in the way Mick Jagger now performs for stadiums of fans who weren't alive when he recorded his first hit. One might still find, on a spring day, two undergraduates at the fountain, posed like Kerouac and Lucien Carr under the all-seeing gaze of Alma Mater. Who knows what might be scribbled in the dust of dormitory window sills? Rebellion against authority, the inward voyages of peyote, the Surrealist manifestoes advocating the recovery of personal psychic forces through a "dizzying descent" into the self—these are now a kind of orthodoxy. Opposition to the war in Vietnam, in spite of the clumsy revisionism of the New Right, is a commonplace. "Be kind to yourself, because the bliss of your own/ kindness will flood the police of tomorrow," Ginsberg advised—and it is hard to recall the enthusiasms of those days, the unquestioning faith that the Word had merely to be proclaimed for it to become Flesh. For the young generation of readers the LSD, amphetamine, or marijuana-inspired visions, the confessions of the outlaw, and the homoerotic desires are not shocking, not even a big deal. The fleeting years are passing by.

But Ginsberg knows his market: the chanting of Blake songs has given way to a record, a single called "Birdbrain," in which Ginsberg, supported by a punk band, excoriates both the United States and the Soviet Union. If Ginsberg once influenced the cultural climate, he now seems to be struggling to keep up with it, needing the favor of the moment as well as that of the Fair Nine. Balzac, the Goncourts tell us, wanted to be so famous that he could fart in public and have society think it the most natural thing.

The punk band may be just the latest in a long experiment, like the harmonium he pulled out in Rapallo to chant Hare Krishna for Ezra Pound. Ginsberg has always had an interest in rhythm, sound, breathing, and he subscribes to Pound's notion that poetry erred when it departed from dance and then song. His ideas of prosody admit a variety of influences—Stein's automatic writing, Christopher Smart's use of anaphoric words, Olson's theory of projective verse, Pound's leading vowel tones, Williams' attention to direct speech, Kerouac's immediate presentation of spontaneous images, the bardic tradition, and even the libidinous sprawl of jazz improvisation. Anything can be found and used, appropriated, from a mantra to anonymous, scrawled messages like those in "Grafitti 12th Cubicle Men's Room Syracuse Airport."

Ginsberg's aesthetic, his cosmology, is inspired by a sort of gnostic All Souls. In the fervent search for mystical connections, Blake becomes a kinsman of the Zen masters, "Song of Myself" is elevated to a sacred text. The political and the sexual are cast as religious preoccupations in Ginsberg's poetry. But it is not political or sexual freedom that leads to release, to salvation: with Ginsberg the higher consciousness seems to come first; and he is the mediator, the intercessor, between wisdom and the reader —chosen, anointed, apostolic. *Rintrah roars and shakes his fists in the burdened air.*

The call came early. John Tytell discusses the visitation in *Naked Angels: the Lives and Literature of the Beat Generation.* While reading "Ah Sun-Flower" (and masturbating) Ginsberg heard a voice recite the poem and then "O Rose thou art sick." It was, Tytell writes, "a psychospiritual transportation, a departure from corporeal awareness that allowed ineffably ecstatic energies to pervade his consciousness—something between what Buddhists might call Nirvana and the 'terrible beauty' of Yeats's 'Easter 1916.' " In any case Ginsberg resolved to dedicate his work to the "tradition of magic prophecy." It took time—along with moving to the West Coast and meeting Peter Orlovsky—for Ginsberg to find his voice in the "uncharted verbal rhetorical seas." The question is whether the themes and the language of the past are still alive, vivid, possible.

The early poems of *Empty Mirror* were printed after those of *Howl.* It is hard, now, to understand why that collection was preferred; hard also to see the resemblance to Williams, even with the short, terse lines, and Williams' generosity with introductions. There is none of Williams' observant detail, his delight with things as themselves. The accumulation of perceptions in a poem like "The Bricklayer's Lunch Hour" creates a brooding, ominous atmosphere: "Meanwhile it is darkening as if to rain/ and the wind on top of the trees in the/ street comes through almost harshly." *Empty Mirror,* for the most part, is despondent, dejected, in tone, laced with the isolation and paranoid vanity of youth. If Ginsberg's early critics responded to his work in a psychoanalytic vein rather than an aesthetic one, the temptation must have been rather hard to resist. Ginsberg demonstrated a very clinical concept of cause and effect.

Tytell has argued for the significance of the 1949 poem in this volume, "Paterson." Later positions were, according to Tytell, suggested by lines such as "What do I want with these rooms papered with visions of money?" The uneasy nerve of "In Society" is another kind of prefiguring:

> I walked into the cocktail party
> room and found three or four queens
> talking together in queertalk.
> I tried to be friendly but heard
> myself talking to one in hipster talk.
> . . .
> I ate a sandwich of human flesh,
> I noticed, while chewing on it,
> it also included a dirty asshole.
> . . .
> "Why you narcissistic bitch! How
> can you decide when you don't even
> know me," I continued in a violent
> and messianic voice, inspired at
> last, dominating the whole room.

The calm, transcription-like tone of the dream is disturbed first by the shoving forward of the unpleasant "dirty asshole," and in the second stanza by the aggressive posture, by confronting the person who took an instant dislike to him. The poem has its tension in the abrupt movement from the submissive to the active. The last lines are revealing, and this will to domination, to shout down all opposition, was given full dominion in the later declamatory, "Angelic ravings," as if there were no room for doubt or reflection or complication within the poem, no room for anything that might taint or slacken the prophetic vehemence. Hence, famous defiant lines such as:

> who let themselves be fucked in the ass by saintly motorcyclists,
> and screamed with joy,
> who blew and were blown by those human seraphim, the sailors,
> caresses of Atlantic and Caribbean love,
> who balled in the morning in the evenings in rosegardens and
> the grass of public parks and cemeteries scattering their
> semen freely to whomever come who may, . . .

Ginsberg got more from Whitman than the strophe.

It must be said that Ginsberg has profited more from his identification with Whitman than Whitman has, in the same way Patti Smith later went on to insinuate herself into the company of the elusive, unwilling, long-dead Rimbaud. "I want to be Chateaubriand or nothing," Hugo shouted. In another context George Steiner has called such borrowings "subtle larceny"—and the term might not be out of place in describing Ginsberg's relation to Whitman.

Yet "A Supermarket in California" is a genuine tribute to Whitman and there is no questioning the sincerity of Ginsberg's appreciation of the "dear father, graybeard, lonely old courage-teacher." The poem, an homage, has the charming improbability and flow of surprises of, say, Ashbery's "The Instruction Manual."

> What thoughts I have of you tonight, Walt Whitman, for I walked down the sidestreets under the trees with a headache self-conscious looking at the full moon.
> In my hungry fatigue, and shopping for images, I went into the neon fruit supermarket, dreaming of your enumerations!
> What peaches and what penumbras! Whole families shopping at night! Aisles full of husbands! Wives in the avocados, babies in the toma-
> toes!—and you, Garcia Lorca, what were you doing down by the watermelons?
> I saw you, Walt Whitman, childless, lonely old grubber, poking among the meats in the refrigerator and eyeing the grocery boys.
> I heard you asking questions of each: Who killed the pork chops? What price bananas? Are you my Angel?
> I wandered in and out of the brilliant stacks of cans following you, and followed in my imagination by the store detective.
> We strode down the open corridors together in our solitary fancy tasting artichokes, possessing every frozen delicacy, and never passing the cashier.

This is tender and funny, especially with Lorca down among the watermelons. The supermarket itself is proper, the supermarket and neon being popular symbols of what Whitman's America has come to. All that fruit is, of course, a traditional erotic device, particularly "peaches" and what is implied by its juxtaposition with "penumbras." Whitman adored the "muscular classes" and it is amusing to think of him, well, cruising grocery boys by means of interrogation. The merry amorousness is sustained by "tasting artichokes, possessing every frozen delicacy."

The clause "and followed in my imagination by the store detective" together with "and never passing the cashier" are part of another feeling simultaneously at work in the poem. The lines speak of something else Whitman's homeland has become as well as of the official hostility to his "enumerations." But the fear and discomfort in the lines belong to Ginsberg, not Whitman. The density of the poem, as in all of Ginsberg's best work, comes from the compression of images. Its mood is carried by unexplained shifts of tense and place. Beginning in the present, it slides quickly into the past. The third stanza begins with an ambiguous future. "Where are we going, Walt Whitman? The doors close in an hour./ Which way does your beard point tonight?" A jarring return to the present occurs: "(I touch your book and dream of our odyssey in the supermarket and feel absurd.)" The reader wonders if Ginsberg means he has returned from the supermarket, in keeping with the first line, or if he means that he feels absurd in dreaming of the odyssey, bringing in the process, the immediacy of composition. The future is taken up again: "Will we walk all night through solitary streets?" Ginsberg provides the definite future in "we'll both be lonely" and the reader knows he has eclipsed Whitman as the subject though the poem ends with a lachrymose question to Whitman, whom Ginsberg envisions ferried to the "smoking banks" of Lethe.

Ginsberg's long search for a master, the shaman, took him from Lionel Trilling all the way to a poet like Whitman. That Ginsberg should be so attracted by Whitman is hardly surprising, given the obvious common denominator. It is hardly unusual for someone to seek consolation by reading, by excavating proof that he is not alone. Just as in writing of Peter Doyle, Whitman could say of himself that he may be "fancying what does not really exist in another, but is all the time in myself alone," so Ginsberg could write to Kerouac, "If I overreach myself for love, it is because I crave it so much, and have known so little of it." But the differences of sensibility, the radically different meaning of their work, let alone the matter of gift, are so striking as to make Ginsberg's almost dynastic ambition an act of self-congratulation.

The visionary way, the symbolic invention in it, has been, historically, most congenial to "O unspeakable, passionate love," more commonly known as "the love that dare not speak its name." Whitman's elasticity and Crane's obscurity are accommodations of this. Ginsberg's subversive intent was to renounce such accommodations. But his work has not amounted to an extension of Whitman's. It is, instead, a narrowing, a contraction of it. Robert K. Martin in his study *The Homosexual Tradition in American Poetry* asserts that Whitman viewed sexual experience as a means toward "a greater understanding of the world." The urge, with Ginsberg, however, turns in on itself, regresses, is reversed, until the sexual encounter itself becomes the "perfect religious experience."

Martin also points out the alienation present in Ginsberg's work and how that contrasts with Whitman's affirmative efforts, though given the dissimilarity between Whitman's landscape and twentieth-century America it is difficult to think of Ginsberg considering the nation in a pastoral mood. But this awareness of his separateness is a fundamental departure from Whitman's ethos.

"Love Poem On Theme By Whitman" never moves the reader beyond voyeurism to the point where he participates, as in Whitman, in what Martin calls the role of "gatherer of experience." The theme Ginsberg is alluding to comes, one assumes, from Section 21 of "Song of Myself" ("Thruster holding me tight and that I hold tight!/ We hurt each other as the bridegroom and the bride hurt each other."). But it also puts one in mind of some of the "Calamus" poems and particularly of "The Sleepers."

If the transcendence of the "I" in Whitman's poetry is something of a strategy, enabling him to present what could not be presented between two men in 1855, it is nevertheless a fortuitous one. Whitman's "I," as it wanders in its night visions, is free-ranging, all-embracing. Ginsberg's "I" is entirely personal, concentrated on the door closed against him:

> I'll go into the bedroom silently and lie down between the bride-
> groom
>   and the bride,
> those bodies fallen from heaven stretched out waiting naked and
> restless,
> arms resting over their eyes in the darkness,
> bury my face in their shoulders and breasts, breathing their skin,

But in Ginsberg there is no levity, no playful uncoverings, no sensuous ascent. The poem begins in an aroused state. Whitman often employed the

device of the woman's point of view, a device usually superseded by
metaphors of the release of orgasm itself. In Ginsberg's poem it is not a
transformation, but a simple displacement of the bride:

> and stroke and kiss neck and mouth and make back be open and
>   known,
> legs raised up crook'd to receive, cock in the darkness driven
>   tormented
>   and attacking

and there follows a description of the act, including ". . . throbbing
contraction of bellies/ till the white come flow in the swirling sheets
. . . ," which may be a feeble attempt to echo "their white bellies swell
to the sun." The use of a conjunction also brings the poem from the future
to the present:

> and I rise up from the bed replenished with the last intimate
>   gestures and
>   kisses of farewell—
> all before the mind wakes,

which seems to indicate that the speaker is so inside the fantasy that the
wish has been displaced, like the bride, by the act itself, but the phrase
"before the mind wakes" hints that the speaker realizes he did not go into
the bedroom. The last lines betray the word "replenished"—the waking
is in a "darkened house"

> where the inhabitants roam unsatisfied in the night,
> nude ghosts seeking each other out in the silence,

and that is far from Whitman's "I am satisfied." "Love Poem On Theme
By Whitman" was written in Neal Cassady's house and that may be a clue
to this ode to the realism of longing.

Ginsberg does not seem to share the ideal of "adhesiveness" so central
to Whitman's "athletic democracy." Curiously, Ginsberg's "saintly motor-
cyclists" and "human seraphim" belong to an underground elect, very
conscious of its exclusivity, not unlike the homosexual elite of Burroughs'
Wild Boys and *Cities of the Red Night* who have alarming tendencies toward

crypto-fascist behavior. The combative stance Ginsberg takes toward society is very much at odds with Whitman's ability to transform every incident into an occasion for communion. The oppositions within Whitman's poetry are not nearly as violent. Where Whitman tends toward the philosophical, Ginsberg is resolutely autobiographical. Ginsberg's poems are far-flung in their locations but Whitman's work gives a larger sense of place and feeling. Moments of being form his subject, whereas consciousness, *his* particular state of mind, is Ginsberg's true concern. Protest and deliberate obscenity come first to mind when thinking of Ginsberg. "Howl" as a whole is more impressive than its parts and what is made of language is the essential difference between the two poets. "Even a few of his phrases are enough to show us that Whitman was no sweeping rhetorician, but a poet of the greatest and oddest delicacy and originality and sensitivity," Randall Jarrell wrote in *Poetry and the Age.*

The recent collection *Straight Hearts' Delight* brings together most of Ginsberg's love poems and it is startling to look back on how much a part of his oeuvre this poetry is. The letters included in the volume between Ginsberg and Peter Orlovsky are rough going but worthwhile for those interested in their relationship as literary history. The volume also illustrates how much Ginsberg is not at home with the lyric mode. The very early "A Further Proposal" (1947) is hardly promising. The stilted couplets are not as offensive as the opening: "Come live with me and be my love,/ And we will some old pleasures prove." Marlowe's slumber is harassed. So much of Ginsberg's work is heedlessly allusive.

Neal Cassady, "secret hero" of "Howl," is the object of many of the love poems. The anguish and frustration of Ginsberg's passion is, by now, part of the tale, recounted in books like Ann Charters' biography of Kerouac. Many of the songs and ballads are scarcely memorable, hope turning into exhaustion. In "The Names" "we all go into the ancient/ void drunkard mouth" and Cassady is asked to "Stay with me Angel now in Shroud of railroad lost bet racetrack broke/ leg oblivion/ till I get the shining Word or you the cockless cock to lay in my ass hope/ mental radiance—." "Song" offers some respite, some distance:

> but we carry the weight
> wearily,
> and so must rest

in the arms of love
   at last,
must rest in the arms
   of love.

No rest
     without love,
no sleep
     without dreams
of love—
     be mad or chill
obssessed with angels
     or machines,
the final wish
     is love
—cannot be bitter,
     cannot deny,
cannot withhold
     if denied:

the weight is too heavy

The several poems written after Cassady's death reflect the struggle to find the proper tone, to unravel, to name, remember, decode: "Tender Spirit, thank you for touching me with tender hands" or "breast warmth, man palm, high school thigh,/ baseball bicept arm, asshole anneal'd to silken skin" or "Look out on Denver, Allen,/ mourn Neal no more,/ Old ghost bone loves departed,"—and one feels that these are intimate jottings to sweeten the sad grave. In his private musings Ginsberg neglects the organization of words, as if too distracted by undigested feelings, and in his extended elegies the rhetoric overwhelms and obscures the object.

Marjorie Perloff noted the puzzle in Ginsberg's eulogy for Frank O'Hara, "City Midnight Drunk Strains," included in *Straight Hearts' Delight*. O'Hara is "the gaudy poet," "chattering Frank," one of the "guys talking about paint." "Did he think me an Angel/ as angel I am still talking into earth's microphone/ willy nilly." O'Hara is presented as a "chatty prophet" "off to a date with Martinis & a blond." Perloff finds Ginsberg's tone somewhat competitive and aggressive. There does seem to be some condescension in:

```
I tried      your boys and found them ready
          sweet and amiable
            collected gentlemen
                    with large sofa apartments
          lonesome to please           for pure language;
      and you mixed with money
                because you knew enough language to be rich
```

and:

```
            Elegant insistency
                    on the honking self-prophetic Personal
```

Unfortunately, none of Ginsberg's love poems is as fine as the ones O'Hara wrote for Vincent Warren. "When I am feeling depressed and anxious sullen/ all you have to do is take your clothes off," "That's not a cross look it's a sign of life," "We hardly ever see the moon anymore/ so no wonder/ it's so beautiful when we look up suddenly"—the mere mention of first lines can scarcely do justice to the beauty of some of these poems. Perhaps the ambivalence in Ginsberg's poem about O'Hara may help explain the limitations of his love poems, as if those things—or those persons—that cannot be adapted to Ginsberg's mythology remained impenetrable.

The closest Ginsberg comes in exhilaration and vulnerability to that of, say, O'Hara's "Ave Maria" is "Malest Cornific Tuo Catullo," written after meeting Orlovsky:

> I'm happy, Kerouac, your madman Allen's
> finally made it: discovered a new young cat,
> and my imagination of an eternal boy
> walks on the streets of San Francisco,
> handsome, and meets me in cafeterias
> and loves me. Ah don't think I'm sickening.
> You're angry at me. For all of my lovers?
> It's hard to eat shit, without having visions;
> when they have eyes for me it's like Heaven.

That was 1955. Some, like Bruce Cook, author of *The Beat Generation,* found a poem like "The Change" in which Ginsberg comes to terms with the "body principle, woman" a sign of rejeuvenation. If so, the late poems indicate that this renewal did not hold.

"Che Guevara has a big cock/ Castro's balls are pink"—Ginsberg seems more comfortable when he can hurl scandalous language, taunt and rave, which may explain why he is uncomfortable with the lyric. But there is a kind of exhaustion in his endless, repetitive lists:

> Come heroic half naked young studs
> That drive automobiles through vaginal blood
> Come thin breasted boys and fat muscled kids
> With sturdy cocks you deal out green lids
> Turn over spread your strong legs like a lass
> I'll show you the thrill to be jived up the ass.

Some of the later poems are downright pathetic:

> Please master can I touch your cheek
> please master can I kneel at your feet
> please master can I loosen your blue pants.

Was it Sassoon who proclaimed that "homosexuality is a bore. The intelligentsia has captured it."? Rimbaud, who knew everything there was to know about men and never shrank from giving that knowledge expression, never gave into verbal fatigue, not even in *"Nos fesses ne sont pas les leurs"* or *"Le coeur supplice."* "Sweet Boy, Gimme Yr Ass" and "Punk Rock Your My Big Crybaby" are part of the didacticism infiltrating gay poetry, a didactic streak similar to that which corrupted black and feminist poetry. Balls and cocks and erect this and smelly that don't amount to much on the page when they are still pricks and nuts. And so anatomy becomes a tool, part of the propaganda machine for the Love That Won't Shut Up. One wonders, in the end, what quarrel "Asphodel, That Greeny Flower" has with "Lay your sleeping head, my love."

Ginsberg's political poetry has diminished over the years through the sheer redundancy of the evangelical. The intensity and rage of "Howl" dissipated as the woes of Ginsberg's office, that of one of Shelley's unacknowledged legislators, carried him on waves of phrases from campaign to cause and back again. Helen Vendler said of *Planet News* that Ginsberg took "a wrong turn in abandoning the domestic for the planetary."

And the Communists have nothing to offer but fat cheeks and eyeglasses
          and lying policemen
and the Capitalists proffer Napalm and money in green suitcases to the
Naked,
and the Communists create heavy industry but the heart is also heavy
and the beautiful engineers are all dead, the secret technicians
conspire
          for their own glamor
in the Future, in the Future, but now drink vodka and lament the
Secu-
          rity Forces,
and the Capitalists drink gin and whiskey on airplanes but let
Indian
          brown millions starve
and when Communist and Capitalist assholes tangle the Just man is
ar-
          rested or robbed or had his head cut off,

Ginsberg expanded his constituency, no longer defender of the best minds
of his generation but the guardian of Everyman. Descriptive, excessive—
"the poet is priest." Ginsberg, for all his laudable concerns, is a distress-
ingly unworldly poet. If Ginsberg prefers a sort of diabolism in his love
poetry, he is one of the cheated and baffled in the political poems—but
not quite: he can call a spade a spade for everyone's sake. "I have a
message for you all—I will denote one particularity of each," he declared
in "Sather Gate Illumination." But the particulars lost their riveting quality and a short poem like "American Change" is more convincing in its
familiarity with the national style than the longer "Wichita Vortex Sutra."
     The power of Ginsberg's most notable work rests in the recognizability
of the moral impulse. The convergence of various cultural forces lessened
the shock value of what he had to say. Ginsberg, however, was content
to state the obvious again and again. He attempted to persuade by ridicule
without taking into account that he had not necessarily convinced his
audience of the soundness of his ideas. But the landscape Ginsberg drew
on was sufficiently suggestive and a metaphor was always at hand in the
"negro streets at dawn" or the "huge karmas of broken minds in beautiful
bodies" to express the American predicament. There were times when
Ginsberg's confidence in his message of uniting mind and body in the

pursuit of enlightenment wavered. "I wanted to be a saint. But suffer for what? Illusions?" he wrote in *Indian Journals*. He went back to nature, he turned to writing the blues. Since then his pilgrimage has taken on the qualities of the burlesque, suitable to the society of spectacle. That the exhortations have not changed much over the years makes them readily available as entertainment for the youth of the leisure class—the bohemian as minstrel.

Ginsberg's political vision is an apocalyptic one, and the outside world on which he projects his imaginings has steadily become less coherent and real. Homosexuality is a political stance in Ginsberg's poetry; drugs are as well. But Ginsberg is not able to make much of the subject. There is the fatuous expansiveness of "Lysergic Acid":

> and I am on the last millionth infinite tentacle of the spider-web
> > a worrier
> lost, separated, a worm, a thought, a self
> one of the millions of skeletons of China
> one of the particular mistakes
> I allen Ginsberg a separate consciousness
> I who want to be God
> I who want to hear the infinite minutest vibration of eternal
> > harmony

Some of his voyages are circular and banal, as in "Mescaline":

> what universe do I enter
> death death death death death the cat's at rest
> are we ever free of—rotting Ginsberg

In "Consulting I Ching Smoking Pot Listening to the Fugs Sing Blake" it is "Death," not spring, that is "acommin in."

> One must see the Great Man
> > Fear not it brings blessing
> > > No harm
> > > from the invisible world
> Perserverance
> > Realms beyond
> > > Stoned

> in the deserted city
> which lies below consciousness

What to make of such platitudes? Ginsberg often takes an ironic tone
toward the contemporary situation.

> Wagner rides again! Hark
> Ye, Ministers of Power and
> ye Premiers of vast China
> and ye Dalai Lamas of
> Tibet
> Hark ye balding soldiers

And of course there is outburst against the war in Vietnam: "Vietnam War
flesh-heap grows higher." Ginsberg often spoke against the repressive
tendencies of the left in America as well as against bureaucracy, etc., but
he never seems able to find an alternative beyond *"Hari Om Namo Shivaye"*
—and it makes one think that Eastern religion is not necessarily the
kindest thing that happened to his poetry. But elsewhere Ginsberg manages to fuse the personal and the political, as in the long poem "Eco-
logue." It works because the "issues" involved are particular, closely
examined, acted out, a feature of autobiography rather than turned into
vague abstraction as in most of the sweeping diatribes and Blakeian pro-
nouncements Ginsberg usually offers.

Neurotica: The Authentic Voice of the Beat Generation 1948–1951 edited by
John Clellon Holmes and Michael McClure's *Scratching the Beat Surface* are
two recent books that reveal something of the cultural climate that
launched Ginsberg on his search for the systemless system. The Holmes
volume collects the issues of the "little magazine" devoted to a radical
critique of American life—the struggle with psychoanalysis, with orthodox sociology, with traditional aesthetics. (G. Legman's eccentric essays
on comics and the murder mystery are finds.) McClure, remembering San
Francisco in the Fifties, writes, "We hated the war and the inhumanity and
the coldness. The country had the feel of martial law. . . . We saw that the
art of poetry was essentially dead—killed by war, by academics, by neglect, by lack of love, and by disinterest. We knew we could bring it back
to life." Ginsberg has retained this sense of mission and struggle—the
yogin, the one who made the reckless choice, warning, listing every

feature of American life, the numbing ones as well as the inspiring ones, and noting his reactions at every turn in the road. "See how the World its Veterans rewards!"

By this time "Kaddish" is safely in the canon. The elegiac is most suited to Ginsberg's turn of mind, to his sense of loss, of incomprehensible vastness. Unlike the traditional anthem, death is very much in Ginsberg's hymn. His mother, Naomi, is the central subject of the poem and for once Ginsberg has met his match: her torment, as he recalls it, is so great that he cannot compete with his subject, his usual tendency, or push her out of view, even in the digressions. There is anguish and humility in the poem, and ideas that are annoying or awkward in other poems are acceptable, here, because the mourning, the reckoning tone, permits much— everything muted, subdued, measured, true.

> There, rest. No more suffering for you. I know where you've
>   gone, it's good.
> No more flowers in the summer fields of New York, no joy now,
>   no more fears of Louis,
> and no more of his sweetness and glasses, his high school decades,
>   debts, loves, frightened telephone calls, conception beds,
>   relatives, hands—

It is a condensed account of his mother's madness, a portrait of a family as well as of their time.

> But then went half mad—Hitler in her room, she saw
> his mustache in the sink—afraid of Dr. Isaac now, suspecting
> that he was in on the Newark plot—went up to Bronx to live
> near Elanor's Rheumatic Heart—

The range of feeling is extraordinary, from the wry and absurd to despair:

> Blessed be you Naomi in tears! Blessed be you Naomi in fears!
>   Blessed Blessed Blessed in sickness!
> Blessed be you Naomi in Hospitals! Blessed be you Naomi in
>   solitude!

In this *éloge* everything is remembered in a waterfall of episodes, images, that approaches the actuality of the mind stirred.

O mother
what have I left out
O mother
what have I forgotten.

Nothing, and for once Ginsberg's habitual call to the unknown is totally prepared for: "Lord Lord great Eye that stares on All and moves in a black/ cloud/ caw caw strange cry of Beings flung up into sky over the wavering trees."

Once, in 1965, Ginsberg travelled to Prague and was elected King of the May Day festivities. This displeased the authorities and, eventually, he was ejected from Czechoslovakia. "And I am the King of May, which is the power of sexual youth," he states in the poem "Kral Majales." "And *tho* I am the King of May, the Marxists have beat me upon the street, kept me up all night in the Police Station, followed me thru Springtime Prague, detained me in secret and deported me from our kingdom by airplane." There is much naïve glee in the poem, and in a sense all of Ginsberg's life has been devoted to finding followers as well as divine light. The much publicized political gestures, the orotund proclamations of the poems are offered and offered again and even if they are not accepted there is refuge in the sting of being so wonderfully misunderstood. The poems in which he, the sage, occupies center stage, pushing aside lovers, historical events, past masters, fade quickly, but that one poem in which he celebrates the one who got away, "Kaddish," seems to endure, sad and steady.

Adrienne Rich and Lesbian/Feminist Poetry

CATHARINE STIMPSON

> . . . it is the subjects, the conversations, the facts we
> shy away from, which claim us in the form of writer's
> block, as mere rhetoric, as hysteria, insomnia, and
> constriction of the throat.[1]

> Four years after . . . (Adrienne Rich) published her
> first book, I read it in almost disbelieving wonder;
> someone my age was writing down my life . . . I had
> not known till then how much I had wanted a con-
> temporary and a woman as a speaking voice of
> life. . . .[2]

"Lesbian." For many, heterosexual or homosexual, the word still con-
stricts the throat. Those "slimy" sibilants; those "nasty" nasalities.
"Lesbian" makes even "feminist" sound lissome, decent, sane. In
1975, Adrienne Rich's reputation was secure.[3] She might have eased
up and toyed with honors. Yet, she was doing nothing less than
seizing and caressing that word: "lesbian." She was working hard for
"a whole new poetry" that was to begin in two women's "limitless
desire."[4]

Few poetic things could be more difficult—even for a writer of such
fire, stone, and fern. For the "intense charge of the word *lesbian,* and
. . . all its deliquescences of meaning . . . ," (*LSS,* 202) necessarily
provoke readings that are potent, but confused, confusing, and contradictory. Some of us read Rich with disbelieving wonder. Imagine being
a mother, in court, on the stand, in the dock, during a child custody
case. Your husband's lawyer asks, with brutal repetition, "When did
you first kiss this woman?" Imagine, then, the gratitude and relief of
hearing:

> The man is walking boundaries
> measuring   He believes in what is his
> the grass the waters underneath   the air

From *Parnassus* (vol. 12, no. 2/vol. 13, no. 1, 1985).

> the air   through which child and mother
> are running   the boy singing
> the woman   eyes sharpened in the light
> heart stumbling   making for the open

(DCL, p. 59)

Yet, others read with wondrous disbelief. Alicia Ostriker, my colleague, pugnaciously declared Rich's "myth" of female sexuality "too narrow": "I find the Lesbian Imperative offensively totalitarian, and would prefer to defend human diversity as well as human liberty."[5]

To add to the mess, even some of the supporters and defenders of Rich's sexual ideology find the call for a "whole new poetry" an emblazoned naiveté. *Surely,* they whisper nervously, she must know about our post-structural awareness of the nature of the sign. *Surely,* she must realize that language is a fiction, not a transparent vehicle of truth; that signifiers are bits and bytes of an arbitrary system, not elements in a holistic union of word and idea, word and thing. *Surely,* she must now admit that this system creates the human subject, not the other way around.[6] Others grumble that Rich's theory contradicts her poetic practice. The first is new, the second old. Rhetorically, she is more like—well, Robert Lowell—than Gertrude Stein. Rich undermines her calls for action, Marjorie Perloff claims, because of her ". . . conservative rhetoric, a rhetoric indistinguishable from the Male Oppressor."[7]

This messiness is ironic—if only because Rich herself is radiantly clear. She is, of course, one of a number of outspoken lesbian poets of the last part of the American Century. She resists being laid down as the star track in what ought to be a multiple-trek tape of the language of such women as Judy Grahn, Susan Griffin, Marilyn Hacker, Audre Lorde, Susan Sherman. "To isolate what I write," she has warned, "from a context of other women writing and speaking feels like an old, painfully familiar critical strategy."[8] Yet, I want, in gratitude and relief, to spell out how she has moved from the constriction of the throat to the construction of the page.

Before the 1970s, Rich had published poems about the feelings, social relations, and mythic promise of women. "Women" (1968) sees three sisters ". . . sitting/ on rocks of black obsidian," versions of the fates. (*PSN,* 109) Deromanticizing heterosexual love, Rich had written of the strains and loneliness within marriage. Symbolically, she had put aside a

1962 poem, "For Judith, Taking Leave."[9] Here a speaker longingly memorializes another woman, Judith: ". . . a singular event . . . a beautiful thing I saw." (*PSN*, 132) The speaker praises feminist predecessors who "suffered ridicule" for them. Then, in the middle of the poem, she calls out:

> Judith! that two women
> in love to the nerves' limit

Only to add, as the line runs on to the next, "with two men—."

In the early 1970s, Rich riskily uncoiled the repressed sexual and psychological materials that she had once coiled and from which she had subsequently recoiled. She announces that release in "Re-forming the Crystal." Addressed to a man, it gives him his due, and discharge. The speaker first imagines what male sexuality, "desire/ centered in a cock," might feel like. However, she passes on, old identity gone. Voice at once tough and exultant, she states, "my photo on the license is not me. . . ." (*PSN*, 228) She will move, a key word in Rich's vocabulary of action, to ". . . the field of a poem wired with danger . . . into the cratered night of female memory. . . ." Women now live to the nerves' limit with women. Inevitably, some poems counterpoint past identity with present; tradition with radical change. "For L.G.: Unseen for Twenty Years" ruefully wonders who, and where, a male homosexual might be. He and the speaker had been boon travelling companions twenty years before, when both were turning to men.

Significantly, "Re-forming the Crystal" alternates vertical columns of "poetry" with paragraphs of "prose." For Rich was producing controversial, influential prose as well as poetry. From 1981 to 1983, she and Michelle Cliff were to edit *Sinister Wisdom*, a lesbian/feminist journal. Rich, a sophisticated student of the genetics of the text, coherently crossed autobiography with biography; polemic with scholarship; political theory with literary criticism.[10] In part, her transgressions of generic conventions are the deconstructive gestures of post-modernism—without much manic play or ludic romps. In greater part, her mingling of "subjective" and "objective" genres, advocacy and argument, demonstrates her belief in their inseparability. Her style also emblemizes the position of contemporary, educated women. No longer forced to choose between public or private lives, women can lead both—at once. No longer forced to choose between writing about public or private concerns, women can take on both—at once.[11]

Rich had consistently been "a poet of ideas,"[12] of hewn arguments as well as images. Now her ideas, doubly sited, could reinforce and annotate each other. In its totality, her work is that of a kind of conceptual artist. What is disturbing and dazzling is not the familiar notion of a conceptual artist, but the content of her ideas. Rich's lesbian/feminism reveals both the steely, stubborn logic of the geometrician (or the convert) and the sinuousness of imaginative reason. Those who insist that she is the Great Generalissima of Lesbian Poetry resist granting her her habitual gift for pragmatic self-revision and subtlety. ". . . the subject of truth," she noted in 1975. "There is nothing simple or easy about this idea. There is no 'the truth,' 'a truth'—truth is not one thing, or even a system. It is an increasing complexity." (*LSS,* 187) Yet, she consistently walks out from the cultural space in which the libraries of her father and of Harvard University had enclosed her. She announces the primacy of a woman's perspective and of women as subjects. The eye of the female writing "I" fastens on the presence of a woman. The voice of the inquiring woman asks of herself and other women: ". . . how she came to be for-herself and how she identified with and was able to use women's culture, a women's tradition; and what the presence of other women meant in her life." (*LSS,* 158)

Rich, as other feminists were doing, insists upon an idea of time as a tragic process, a fall into patriarchy. However, she promises, we can reverse that process. We can outwrestle, outwit, and feminize time. Skillfully, Rich splices two mutually enhancing narratives together that dramatize her idea of time's procession. The first is that of the self. In her prose, Rich persistently tests her generalizations against her own experiences. In her poetry, she articulates experience and discovers its meaning. Though the poetic self has a vast capacity for experiences, it reveals itself, rather than develops, in time. Indeed, a measure of development is the degree of revelation. So convinced, Rich assumes the primacy of the primal self. Appropriately, then, "Natural Resources" brilliantly extends the trope of the woman miner, as both rhetorical and historical figure. The miner excavates experience to find buried strata. In other passages, Rich is a Dickinsonian surgeon, ". . . cutting away/ dead flesh, cauterizing old scars. . . ." (*DCL,* 70) She rips away the tissue that covers old wounds, old traumas, to recover the origins of self and pain.

In her narrative, Rich is a child whom two women (one white, one black) first love before they turn her over to the father. The reality of the maternal body gives way to the "charisma" of the father's ". . . assertive mind and temperament. . . ."[13] Her reward for their rejection, and her loss, is his approval and the power of language, the conviction that ". . . language, writing, those pages of print could teach me how to live, could tell me *what was possible.*" (*LSS,* 200) She becomes a child-of-the-word, unable to see that those pages veil and erase the feminine. Rich is no fan of psychoanalysis, but its tales and that of her passage from the tender passions of the realm of the mother to the symbolic order of the domain of the father half-echo each other.

Educated, a published poet, her father's pride, Rich then rejects the father—to marry a man he despises. She bears three sons. As Rich knows, but never exploits, the sheer masculinity of her heterosexual experience (the husband, the long marriage, the sons) burnishes her credibility as a witness of, and for, lesbianism. That credibility challenges a popular perception that lesbians are maculately sterile—either because they are butches, imitation men, or femmes, who will never receive the sperm of real men.

Rich's second narrative is that of any child, female or male. For them, "The mother-child relationship is the essential human relationship." (*OWB,* 127) Binding the two are the sucking mouth, the milky nipple, the mutual gaze. Then, the father—his demands, commands, needs, and seductions—will pick at those bonds; pick up his children and possess them all in a "savagely fathered and unmothered world." (*PSN,* 237) Heterosexual institutions damage both sons and daughters, but, Rich insists, in the crucial axiom of feminist theory, they damage women far more than men. Those institutions embody sufficient psychological, economic, social, and legal power to *compel* heterosexuality.[14] That compulsion redirects women away from the first and most profound object of love, the mother. Rich writes: "Probably there is nothing in human nature more resonant with charges than the flow of energy between two biologically alike bodies, one of which has lain in amniotic bliss inside the other, one of which has labored to give birth to the other. The materials are here for the deepest mutuality and the most painful estrangement." (*OWB,* 225–26)

To redeem her past, and to begin her future, Rich must return to the mother's body, in memory or with other women. So must all women.

Their sources are their natural resources. In a 1963 poem about marriage, Rich, in one of the crazy intuitive flashes we label the cognitive gift of poetry, describes wanting husband to be mother:

> Our words misunderstand us.
> Sometimes at night
> you are my mother:
> old detailed griefs
> twitch at my dreams, and I
> crawl against you, fighting
> for shelter, making you
> my cave.[15]

Not until she becomes a lesbian is she content; not until then can desire fulfill its needs. In *Twenty-One Love Poems,* she writes of her female lover's

> . . . strong tongue and slender fingers
> reaching where I had been waiting years for you
> in my rose-wet cave—whatever happens, this is.

> (*DCL,* 32)

The fecundity of woman is such that she can also give birth to and mother herself. Her body can be her "crib"; she can be her own "midwife." She can then become a matrix that mothers others, through personality or the page. Some evidence: in 1975, Nancy Milford, the writer, read through Rich's poetry. She had a dream of the person within "Diving into the Wreck." A maternal figure was walking towards, and empowering, her: ". . . naked, swaying, bending down . . . her full breasts brushing my cheek, moving toward my mouth . . . The hands of that diving woman become our own hands, reaching out, touching, holding; not in sex but in deliverance. That is the potency of her poetry. . . ."[16]

As Rich grounds women's thoughts and feelings in their bodies, she *naturalizes* them. Her poetry harvests the earth and the elements for its metaphors: the cave; trees; plants; flowers; fields; the volcano, at once peak to ascend and crater into which to descend, breast and genitals, cervix, womb. Rich, too, has absolute competence in composing a poem, in arranging implosive patterns of rhythm and sound. Because the quality of her verbal music and choreography is so assured, a reader learns to trust the palpability of a poem; its replication of the intellectual and emotional movements of experience.

Because of the pressure and magnetism of her metaphors; because of the surprising physicality of her lines; and because of her contempt for patriarchal culture, especially in its modern and urban forms, Rich may seem to be endorsing a feminized primitivism. However, she is far too intelligent a grammarian of reality to parse it into two opposing spheres of "nature" and "culture," and clamor only for the pristine ecological purities of the first. She constructs houses on her land. Rich's dream, her imaginative vision, is of an organic, but freeing, unity among body, nature, consciousness, vision, and community. Unequivocally, lyrically, she asks women to think through their maternal flesh and their own bodies, ". . . to connect what has been so cruelly disorganized—our great mental capacities, hardly used; our highly developed tactile sense; our genius for close observation; our complicated, pain-enduring, multi-pleasured physicality." (*OWB*, 284) In a leap of faith, she wants women to become the presiding geniuses of their bodies in order to create new life—biologically and culturally. Their thoughts and visions will transform politics, ". . . alter human existence," sustain a "new relationship to the universe." (*OWB*, 285–86)

The primal bonds among mothers, sisters, and daughters are the soil from which lesbianism grows. Lesbianism does mean women's erotic passion. Indeed, the most explicitly erotic lyric in *Twenty-One Love Poems* is "(The Floating Poem, Unnumbered)," as if physical passion drifts and runs like a deep current through the seas of the connection between "I" and "you" in the sequence. However, Rich declares, in a move that lesbian/feminism, but not the culture-at-large, accepts, the lesbian cannot live only in and with love. "I want to call this, life." Rich writes, "But I can't call it life until we start to move/ beyond this secret circle of fire. . . ." (*DCL*, 9) Moreover, a lesbianism that is more than a treasured carnality is a synecdoche for any female sexuality. Rich, like Monique Wittig, projects ". . . lesbian love (a)s a paradigm of female sexuality that is neither defined by men nor exploited by a phallocentric political system."[17]

Even more than a fancily labelled metaphor, even more than a schematized paradigm, lesbianism forms a "continuum," a range of "woman-identified" activities that embraces eros, friendship, and intensity between women, resistance to gynephobia, and female strength. A woman can love men, live with men, and inhabit a point on this continuum—if she has managed some distance from patriarchal heterosexuality. For its imprisoning institutions have ripped daughters from mothers; lobotomized and slashed women's psychological, cultural, and political energies. As the brief accumulates in "Compulsory Heterosexuality," Rich mourns: "The denial of reality and visibility to women's passion for women, women's choice of women as allies, life companions, and community; the forcing of such relationships into dissimulation and their disintegration under intense pressure have meant an incalculable loss to the power of all women *to change the social relations of the sexes, to liberate ourselves and each other."* (657) "Transcendental Etude," a chiselled monument of a poem, dedicated to Michelle Cliff, elegizes "rootless, dismembered" women, whose "Birth stripped our birthright from us,/ tore us from a woman, from women, from ourselves." (*DCL,* 75)

If women are to change themselves and their social relations, if they are to liberate themselves and each other, they must revivify that lesbianism hidden or denied, feared or despised. Lesbianism is an imperative, not because Rich imposes it, but because it is a wellspring of identity that must be sprung if women are to claim any authentic identity at all. "It is the lesbian in us who is creative, for the dutiful daughter of the fathers in us is only a hack." (*LSS,* 201) I remember Rich giving us these words, quietly, tautly, in a New York hotel ballroom, in 1976, at a panel at the Modern Language Association. She leaned forward from a dais, where three other poets were also sitting: June Jordan, Audre Lorde, Honor Moore. I was on a chipped and gilded chair, between two scholar/critics: one a divorced mother, heterosexual, who called herself a lesbian out of political sympathy, a radical feminist act of the late 1960s and early 1970s; the second a married mother, about to begin a secret love affair with a woman, who rarely (if ever) spoke about lesbianism. "Right on," said the first. Enigmatically, the second looked at the husband next to her. Grinning, with the casualness of marriage, he affectionately slapped her thigh. There we were—an imperfect, blurry shadow of Rich's continuum.

Deftly, Rich's theories of female sexuality invert the accusatory slander that lesbianism is "unnatural." To Rich, what is "unnatural" is not the presence, but the absence, of women's bodies, to be "homesick . . . for a woman. . . ." (*DCL,* 75) In the 1970s, her theories were influenced by, and influences on, the cultural feminism that was a powerful strain in feminist thinking, particularly about sexuality, culture, and identity.[18] Reconstituting and eroticizing nineteenth-century ideologies of gender, with their endorsement of "female" and "male" spheres, cultural feminism tends to divide the world into female and male; to idealize female sexuality and being, and to demonize male sexuality and doing. Ironically, some of the principles of cultural feminism gravitate toward a conservative ideology that prefers divinely authorized gender roles and "female" and "male" behaviors that fit squarely into them. However, cultural feminism's preference for women's communities, its commitment to women's self-determination, and its loathing of patriarchal heterosexuality dismay, and repel, right-wing flappers in the Eagle Forum and their ilk.

To discover that female sexuality and being, women are to nurture natural, but defaced and obliterated, capacities for nurture and for nature itself. With the help of scholars and artists, they are to unearth primal images of these capacities, and of rituals with which to celebrate them. Some of Rich's most poignant, lambent poems present the poet as a priestess in a service with a lost script; in a liturgy with missing words. In "Toward the Solstice," she laments that she does not know "in what language to address/ the spirits that claim a place/ beneath these low and simple ceilings." (*DCL,* 69) She fears that she has forgotten or failed to say the "right rune"; to "perform the needed acts. . . ." (70)

Such theories were to serve neither abstract debate (a "male" activity) nor mere poetic need (a self-indulgent sport). On the contrary. They were to be designs for action and for communal life. As a result, cultural feminists have taken sides in some of the most volatile political quarrels within United States feminism: How separate from the rest of society are women's groups to be? What is the relationship of feminism to other political movements and to the New Left? What is the meaning of pornography? What, if anything, should be done to banish it? Many of Rich's poems refer immediately to those fights. The controversial "For Ethel Rosenberg," for example, speaks vocatively to "Ethel Greenglass Rosenberg":

                              would you
    have marched to take back the night
    collected signatures

    for battered women who kill[19]

"Take back the night" is a slogan and rallying cry for the anti-pornography movement that cultural feminism has conceived and organized. The words have inspired women. They flatten Rich's poem. Their presence gives some critics permission to tsk-tsk and scold Rich for letting a political agenda master a poet's imagination. She might legitimately scorn their motives and the blatancy of the division they invent between politics and poetry. However, she, too, is warily aware of any domination of her imagination. She fears the hunters, trappers, and wardens of the mind. One of her toughest poems, "North American Time," written in the gritty style of much of *A Wild Patience,* starts:

> When my dreams showed signs
> of becoming
> politically correct
> no unruly images
> escaping beyond borders
> when walking in the street I found my
> themes cut out for me
> knew what I would not report
> for fear of enemies' usage
> then I began to wonder

> *(FD,* 324)

Something hardens the difficulty of interweaving a passionate fidelity to a politics that wants to change the laws of history; to the imagination; and to the unconscious, which nourishes the imagination as mother does the child: the very terms of Rich's politics. For lesbian/feminism, the casting of the world as a duality of dominating male and damaged female carries the virus of a double threat: it reduces the world to a duality; it reduces women to a monolith. Rich distrusts the false universal, especially among women, who are to think more specifically than men. A resonant section of "Natural Resources," the 1977 revision of "Diving Into the Wreck," rejects the words "humanism" and "androgyny." They are falsely universal; therefore, universally false.

Rich has wonderfully escaped the nets she fears, the "impasse" at which some critics pin her.[20] In part, she does so because of the Jamesian (William) belief in change that has marked all her work. We must live in an

Einsteinian world of flux and chance that has neither "center nor circumference."[21] We must work and wish for a world, not as it is, but as it might be. Yet, we must respond to time present as it presents and represents itself. Because errors and lapses can stain our responses, we must abandon dreams of purity, of final cures, of a process with an end.

Logically, then, responsibly, the lesbian/feminist Rich has continued to rewrite her sense of self and politics; to question what it means to "cast my lot" in the world and to be "accountable." More and more deeply, she has engaged the structures and pain of racism. She has said that the Civil Rights Movement of the 1960s lifted her ". . . out of a sense of personal frustration and hopelessness."[22] However, the 1970s had to teach her the harsh stiffness of her own "racist blinders." Black women's response to *Of Woman Born* had to school her in her ignorance about them.[23] Rich believes that political poetry emerges from the self's encounter with the world. Her explorations of race start with her black nurse, her other mother. Necessarily, she cannot rest there. She must go on to still other structures, other pains, of domination. Racism is inseparable from still another vise and vice of modern politics: colonialism. "To understand colonization," she writes, with self-consciousness and some self-contempt, "is taking me/ years." (*WP,* 55)

Some of Rich's most ambitious lesbian/feminist poems speak for all women and mourn their suffering, affliction, and powerlessness: "From an Old House in America," "Culture and Anarchy," "For Julia in Nebraska." Like Rich's poems about her grandmothers, they offer women their history; the arts of their endurance. Because Rich fuses women with nature, especially with the land, a history of people is a pangyneric record of place as well.

However, the recognition of racism and colonialism demands that Rich issue a series of ironic, searing, yet empathetic poems about cultivated white women with the disadvantages of sex but the advantages of class and race. A tart observation, "No room for nostalgia here," opens "Turning the Wheel," an extraordinary 1981 sequence in which Rich returns to a desert landscape. (*WP,* 52–59) The wheel belongs to both a modern woman driving her car and a Native American woman creating her pottery. The speaker sees a "lesbian archaeologist," studying shards, who asks ". . . the clay all questions but her own." She imagines, too, a letter that Mary Jane Colter might have written home. Colter, an architect and

designer, planned buildings at the Grand Canyon for the Santa Fe Railroad. She both preserved and appropriated Native American culture. Two
years later, in "Education of a Novelist," Rich calls across time to another
Southern writer, Ellen Glasgow. She condemns Glasgow for not teaching
her black nurse, Lizzie Jones, to read, but confesses:

> It's not enough
> using your words to damn you, Ellen:
> they could have been my own"
>
> (*FD,* 317)

Lesbian/feminist politics remain, but Rich's perceptions expand upon
them. She thinks, not only of male domination, but of a system of iron
patterns of power that wheel and deal and work together. Pornography
violently debases and exploits women, but its nauseating "objectification"
of women also warns us against slavery—of anyone by anyone.[24]

Rich now wants, in women, both "difference and identity." Women
share the architecture of their bodies, the humiliation and mutilation of
those bodies. What "fuses my anger now . . . ," she wrote in 1978, "
. . . is that we were told we were utterly different." (*LSS,* 310) Yet, as
race proves, so obviously, so profoundly, women differ, too. With delicate
audacity, Rich pushes at the boundaries of those differences, pushes for
the specific, and particular. As she does so, she uncovers, and must enter,
still another buried part of herself: her Jewishness, the faith of father,
husband, and first woman lover. She circles back to Jerusalem, the original
City on the the Hill. *Sources,* perhaps her most fragmented but suggestive
book, exhumes that past. Rich affirms her "powerful" and "womanly"
choices; a "powerful, womanly lens"—in brief, the domain of the
mother.[25] However, *Sources* returns to the domain of the fathers, and to
their vulnerability and pain. Arnold Rich, her father, was the outwardly
successful, assimilated son of a Jewish shoe merchant from Birmingham,
Alabama. Powerful and arrogant patriarch though he was, he also bore
"the suffering of the Jew, the alien stamp." (15) Her mother carried the
cultural genes of the Christianity that would stamp Jews out.

Then, with immense dignity, Rich writes to Alfred Conrad, the husband
who committed suicide. She has had ". . . a sense of protecting your
existence, not using it merely as a theme for poetry or tragic mus-

ings." (32) Now, for the first time, she believes he might hear her. "No person," her elegy ends, "should have to be so alone. . . ." (33) She has passed through the moral and psychological process that some of her most magnificent poems—"The Phenomenology of Anger," "Integrity"—envision: that between wildness and patience, rage and pitying compassion, fire and water and tears. She has completed the hardest of swings between "Anger and tenderness: my selves." (*WP,* 9)[26]

That fusion of the moral and the psychological, the ethical and the emotional, marks Rich. Her writing inflects a stable vocabulary of the good that flows, as feminism itself does, from principles of the Enlightenment, radical democracy, and a redemptive domesticity: freedom; choice; truth; a lucidity as clear as water pouring over rocks; gentleness, an active charity, swabbing "the crusted stump." (*DCL,* 63) The last of *Twenty-One Love Poems* asserts:

> I choose to be a figure in that light. . . .
> . . .
> . . . I choose to walk here. And to draw this circle.
>
> (*DCL,* 36)

As insistently, Rich's writing asks how to reconcile the claims of autonomy (being free, having will) and the claims of connection (being together, having unity). Connections fuse within the self, between lover and beloved, with others. "Sometimes I feel," she wrote in 1982, "I have seen too long from too many disconnected angles: white, Jewish, anti-Semite, racist, anti-racist, once-married, lesbian, middle-class, feminist, exmatriate Southerner, *split at the root."*[27] She longs, then, for wholeness, for touch, a desire the hand signifies. The hand. It holds the pen, clasps the child, finds the lover, sews the quilt, cleans the pot, dusts the house. For Rich, hands hammer nails, empty kettles, catch babies leaping from the womb, work vacuum aspirators, stroke "sweated temples" (both body and sanctuary), steer boats. (*WP,* 9) The hand also knots in anger, smashes in pain. As palms are the canvas of our life-lines, so the figure of the hand backs Rich's vision.

Before the 1960s, her lesbian/feminism was, if not inconceivable, unspeakable. Yet, if her ideas are contemporary, her sense of the poet is not. For Rich refuses to sever poetry from prophecy, those morally driven, passionately uttered visions of things unseen and foreseen, and poetry from witnessing, those morally driven, passionately uttered insights into actions seen. What she said of Dickinson she might have said of herself:

"Poetic language . . . is a concretization of the poetry of the world at large, the self, and the forces within the self . . . there is a more ancient concept of the poet (as well) . . . she is endowed to speak for those who do not have the gift of language, or to see for those who—for whatever reasons—are less conscious of what they are living through." (*LSS*, 181)[28] She is painfully aware that she cannot control what might happen to her words after she chooses them, but she is accountable for that choice, and for her accuracy.

Rich's lesbian/feminism helps to sculpt her role as prophet and witness. Because patriarchal culture has been silent about lesbians and "all women who are not defined by the men in their lives,"[29] the prophet/witness must give speech to experience for the first time. This is one meaning of writing a whole new poetry. However, patriarchal culture has not been consistently silent. Sometimes, it has lied about lesbians. The prophet/witness must then speak truth to, and about, power. At other times, patriarchal culture has distorted or trivialized lesbians. The prophet/witness must then use and affirm ". . . a vocabulary that has been used negatively and pejoratively."[30] She must transvalue language.

Necessarily, the prophet/witness is a performer. She demands an audience, primarily of women. However, the ideology of lesbian/feminism is suspicious of star turns. Rich herself writes in "Transcendental Etude":

> "The longer I live the more I mistrust
> theatricality, the false glamour cast
> by performance, the more I know its poverty beside
> the truths we are salvaging from
> the splitting-open of our lives."
>
> (*DCL,* 74)

The performing Rich—unlike Walt Whitman or Jeremiah—has more stamina than flash; more intensity than ebullience. She is a laser rather than an explosion of fireworks. She will speak, but in "North American Time," a grim, colloquial meditation on the poet's responsibility, she says, self-deprecatingly:

> "Sometimes, gliding at night
> in a plane over New York City
> I have felt like some messenger
> called to enter, called to engage
> this field of light and darkness.
> A grandiose idea, born of flying."
>
> (*FD*, 327)

She will also speak, if possible, to an audience of many women. She is allusive and intricate, but rarely elusive and snobby. In part, she has the clarity of classical poetry. In part, she has the clarity of one who wishes to be heard.[31]

But what language will she speak? Clearly, Rich believes in the power of language to represent ideas, feelings, and events. Although she writes about film and photography, she is no postmodern celebrant of the visual media. She fears that mass TV induces passivity, atrophies the literacy and language we need to "take on the most complex, subtle, and drastic re-evaluation ever attempted of the condition of the species." (*LSS*, 12) Her dream of a common language is of *words,* a shared cultural frame and thread, communal and quotidian, "hewn of the commonest living substance: as well as "violent, arcane." (*PSN*, 232)

Yet, the lesbian/feminist poet cannot accept language that smoothly. What is she to do with the fact that the powerful have used language to choke and to erase her? To mystify and to disguise? Some French theoreticians of *écriture féminine* advocate stealing, and then, flying away with the oppressor's speech. That theft and that escape are acts of re-appropriation and control. Certainly, in her references to male poets—yes, even to Robert Lowell, Rich shows her authority.[32] More fervently, Rich selects female experience—the body; mothers, daughters, and granddaughters; lesbianism; women's history—as her subject. Men, too, have written such experiences up and down, but men, because they are men, have been false prophets, narcissistic and perjuring witnesses.

Sadly, that selection offers little ease. For what is Rich, who believes in poetry, to do with the fact that lesbian/feminism has naturalized female experience? That lesbian/feminism has rooted female experience less in language than in things, objects, inarticulate but pregnant silences? Rich's poetry itself shows how craftily she handles the issue. First, she reduces the physical presence of language on the page. She wipes away diacritical marks, the busyness of syntax. Then, she alternates words with blank spaces—for breathing, for gazing. As she pushes language towards silence, she does to the verbal image what Nathalie Sarraute (or, in her way, Jane Austen) does to narrative. Yet, she refuses silence. She has words, and doubts-in-words.

Read "The Images." (*WP*, 3–5) The poem is a series of six sections, each an irregular series of staggered three- or four-line sections. The eye cautions the reader against regularities, sonorities. Two women are in bed. In the "pain of the city," the speaker turns. Her hand touches her lover "before language names in the brain." The speaker chooses touch, but not this city, where both images of women, and the looks of men, string women out and crucify them.

The speaker then recognizes that she has romanticized language, music, art, "frescoes translating/ violence into patterns so powerful and pure/ we continually fail to ask are they true for us." In contrast, when she now walks among "time-battered stones," she can think of her lover. She has gone to the sea, among flowering weeds, and drawn a flower. She has been "mute/ innocent of grammar as the waves." There, feeling "free," she has had a vision of a woman's face and body. Her breasts gaze at the poet; the poet at her world. Rich writes:

> I wished to cry loose my soul
>   into her, to become
>   free of speech   at last."

"Free of speech" is, of course, a syntactical pun. For the speaker is both free from speech, and, now, free to speak. She comes home, "starving/ for images," a body in need of culture. She and her lover, as they remember each other in sleep, will "reassemble re-collect re-member" the lost images of women in the past. They will do the work of Isis, but for Isis, not Osiris. As the culture's images seek to "dismember" them, they will fight the war of the images.

The poem's last lines then recall the picture that the speaker has drawn: a thorn-leaf guarding a purple-tongued flower. Perhaps the picture represents only a flower on a beach. Perhaps not, too. For the thorn leaf can signify the lovers' vigilance in protecting the purple-tongued flower of the vulva, of their sexuality, and of their speech. The thorn is the anger that guards their tenderness, and their poetry.

Language lies. Language invents. Poetry lies. Poetry invents. Rich accepts that "truth." Writing tells stories that matter. Writing gives us images from the mind and of the body, for the relief of the body and the reconstruction of the mind. Rich accepts that "truth" as well. If some words ("lesbian") constrict the throat, say them. Open them up. Only then can we speak enough to wonder seriously if language lies, because it is language; if language invents, because it is language, or if language lies because people are liars who invent to control, rather than to dream and justly please.

Notes

1. Adrienne Rich, "It Is the Lesbian in Us . . ," *On Lies, Secrets, and Silence,* hereafter *LSS,* (New York: W. W. Norton and Co., 1979), p. 201.
2. Helen Vendler, "Ghostlier Demarcations, Keener Sounds," *Adrienne Rich's Poetry,* ed. Barbara Charlesworth Gelpi and Albert Gelpi, hereafter *ARP,* (New York: W. W. Norton and Co., Norton Critical Edition, 1975), p. 160. Vendler's essay was originally published in *Parnassus,* II, 1 (Fall/Winter 1973). As Marjorie Perloff has pointed out to me in conversation, Rich is the only living poet who is the subject of a Norton critical anthology.
3. In 1975, when *ARP* appeared, Rich also published *Poems Selected and New, 1950–1974,* hereafter *PSN,* (New York: W. W. Norton and Co.). Mark that the first poem is "Storm Warnings", the last "From an Old House in America," which ends, "Any woman's death diminishes me."
4. Adrienne Rich, *The Dream of a Common Language: Poems 1974–1977,* hereafter *DCL* (New York: W. W. Norton and Co., 1978), p. 76.
5. *Writing Like a Woman* (Ann Arbor: University of Michigan Press, 1983), p. 121.
6. Rachel Blau DuPlessis, *Writing beyond the Ending: Narrative Strategies of Twentieth-Century Women Writers* (Bloomington: Indiana University Press, 1985), pp. 138–9, expresses this position most sympathetically, in an elegant exegesis of Rich, which discusses the poetics of her lesbian/feminism.
7. Marjorie Perloff, "Private Lives/Public Images," *Michigan Quarterly Review,* 22 (January 1983), 132. My essay, "Curing: Some Comments on the Women's Movement and the Avant-Garde," compares Stein and Rich. Manuscript read at the University of Houston, March, 1985, and at the University of California/Irvine, May, 1985, forthcoming in a collection of essays

about the avant-garde, edited by Sandy Friedan and Richard Spuler, Munich: Fink (sic).

8. Adrienne Rich, " 'Comment' on Susan Stanford Friedman," *Signs: Journal of Women in Culture and Society*, 9, 4 (Summer 1984), 737. Friedman's article, " 'I go where I love': An Intertextual Study of H.D. and Adrienne Rich," appeared in *Signs*, 9, 2 (Winter 1983), 228–245. Elly Bulkin, " 'Kissing /Against the Light': A Look at Lesbian Poetry," *Lesbian Studies: Present and Future*, ed. Margaret Cruikshank (Old Westbury, New York: Feminist Press, 1982), 32–54, is a solid survey. For analyses of other genres, see Bonnie Zimmerman, "The Politics of Transliteration: Lesbian Personal Narratives," *Signs*, 9, 4 (Summer 1984), 663–682, and my "Zero Degree Deviancy: The Lesbian Novel in English," *Critical Inquiry*, Special Issue, "Writing and Sexual Difference," ed. Elizabeth Abel, 8, 2 (Winter 1981), 363–379.

9. See, too, Bulkin, 45–46.

10. Marilyn R. Farwell, "Adrienne Rich and Organic Feminist Criticism," *College English*, 39, 2 (October 1977), 191–203, analyzes Rich's literary criticism.

11. I have adapted this idea from one of the most competent studies of Rich, her development, and relationship to Anne Bradstreet and Emily Dickinson as Puritan American women writers: Wendy Martin, *An American Triptych* (Chapel Hill: University of North Carolina Press, 1984), p. 5.

12. Ostriker, *Writing Like A Woman*, p. 102.

13. Adrienne Rich, *Of Woman Born: Motherhood as Experience and Institution*, hereafter *OWB* (New York: W. W. Norton and Co., 1976), p. 219.

14. Rich writes of this most fully in "Compulsory Heterosexuality and Lesbian Existence," hereafter *CH*, *Signs: Journal of Women in Culture and Society*, 5, 4 (Summer 1980), 631–660. The founding editor of *Signs*, I had asked Rich, over a white tablecloth at lunch in a Chinese restaurant on the Upper West Side of New York City, if she would be generous enough to contribute. I respected, and feared, her intellectual purity. I hoped she would not find me an academic muddle. Yes, she said, she had an article, about heterosexuality and lesbianism. The essay was one of the most famous *Signs* published. For extended comment, read "Viewpoint," by Ann Ferguson, Jacquelyn N. Zita, and Kathryn Pyne Addelson, *Signs*, 7, 1 (Autumn 1981), 158–199.

15. "Like This Together," *The Fact of a Doorframe: Poems Selected and New 1950– 1984*, hereafter *FD* (New York: W. W. Norton and Co., 1984), pp. 62–63.

16. "This Woman's Movement," *ARP*, p. 202.

17. Martin, p. 211.

18. Alice Echols, "The New Feminism of Yin and Yang," *Powers of Desire: The Politics of Sexuality*, ed. Ann Snitow, Christine Stansell, and Sharon Thompson (New York: Monthly Review Press, 1983), pp. 439–459, gives an informed, if not throbbingly sympathetic, account of 1970s cultural femi-

nism. She has published a version in "The Taming of the Id: Feminist Sexual Politics, 1968–1983," *Pleasure and Danger: Exploring Female Sexuality,* ed. Carole S. Vance (Boston: Routledge and Kegan Paul, 1984), pp. 50–72. Together, the books represent new directions in the feminist debate about female sexuality in the 1980s, largely toward a theory of female sexuality as a source of pleasure, fantasy, delight. Elizabeth Wilson, "Forbidden Love," *Feminist Studies,* 10, 2 (Summer 1984), 213–226, is an intriguing English parallel.

19. "For Ethel Rosenberg," *A Wild Patience Has Taken Me This Far,* hereafter *WP* (New York: W. W. Norton and Co., 1981), p. 29.

20. Perloff, 136, for one.

21. Martin, p. 9.

22. "Split at the Root," *Nice Jewish Girls: A Lesbian Anthology,* ed. Evelyn Torton Beck (Watertown: Persephone Press, 1982), p. 81. Rich notes the extent of her debt to her friendship with Audre Lorde and her life with Michelle Cliff for her understanding of racism, and of "passing."

23. "Response," *Sinister Wisdom* 14 (Summer 1980), 104–05. Rich thanks Elly Bulkin, who helped open a public debate in lesbian/feminism about racism and Mary Daly's work.

24. Adrienne Rich, "Afterword," *Take Back the Night,* ed. Laura Lederer (New York: William Morrow and Co., 1980), p. 314.

25. *Sources,* hereafter *S* (Woodside, California: The Heyeck Press, 1983).

26. I suggest that Rich has refined a poetics of anger and tenderness in a line that begins with the two stresses of the spondee, or, occasionally, a trochee, and then relaxes into her controlled, but flexible, iambic feet. Look at the phrase "Anger and tenderness" itself.

27. "Split at the Root," p. 83. Rich's work is evidence for Alicia Ostriker's typology of women's poetry: ". . . the quest for autonomous self-definition; the intimate treatment of the body; the release of anger; and . . . for want of a better name, the contact imperative." The latter craves unity, mutuality, continuity, connection, touch. "The Nerves of a Midwife: Contemporary American Women's Poetry," *Parnassus,* 6, 1 (Fall/Winter 1977), 73, 82–83.

28. Albert Gelpi, "Adrienne Rich: The Poetics of Change," *ARP,* p. 148, persuasively casts Rich as prophet and scapegoat.

29. "Three Conversations," *ARP,* p. 112.

30. "An Interview: Audre Lorde and Adrienne Rich," in Audre Lorde, *Sister Outsider* (Trumansburg, New York: The Crossing Press, 1984), p. 112.

31. Several critics comment on Rich's clarity, e.g. Martin, p. 169; Suzanne Juhasz, *Naked and Fiery Forms, Modern American Poetry by Women: A New Tradition* (New York: Harper Colophon Books, 1976), pp. 178–180, 202.

In her memoir of Rich as teacher, a sort of performance, Joyce Greenberg says: ". . . there was nothing of the actress, nothing of the performer about her." "By Woman Taught," *Parnassus,* 7, 2 (Spring/Summer 1979), 91.

32.   Joanne Feit Diehl, " 'Cartographies of Silence': Rich's *Common Language* and the Woman Writer," *Feminist Studies,* 6, 3 (Fall 1980), 545, confronts the issue of Lowell and Rich. My comments about Rich and language owe much to this essay.

The Dandy at Play

Harold Beaver

John Ashbery is a dandy, a *flâneur*. His aim is not to be secretive or evasive
so much as consistently playful. In place of truth or value, he proposes
elegance, style, art. "The only criterion of an act is its elegance," proclaimed Genet; which Sartre brilliantly expounded as "the quality of
conduct which transforms the greatest quantity of being into *appearing.*"
Barthes consciously echoed Genet, transforming his camp ethics into a
camp poetics:

> It can be seen that we deal in no way with a harmony between content
> and form, but with an *elegant* absorption of one form into another. By
> *elegance* I mean the most economical use of the means employed. It
> is because of an age-old abuse that critics confuse *meaning* and *content.*
> The language is never anything but a system of forms, and the mean-
> ing is a form.

That is how John Ashbery reinvents his motifs, or rather how he takes
personal possession of them. He reinvents himself, like an actor, in multiple acts of transformation and illusion. He calls it "Punishing the Myth":

> At first it came easily, with the knowledge of the shadow line
> Picking its way through various landscapes before coming
> To stand far from you, to bless you incidentally
> In sorting out what was best for it, and most suitable,
>
> Like snow having second thoughts and coming back
> To be wary about this, to embellish that, as though life were a party
> At which work got done. So we wiggled in our separate positions
> And stayed in them for a time. After something has passed
>
> You begin to see yourself as you would look to yourself on a stage,
> Appearing to someone. But to whom? Ah, that's just it,
> To have the manners, and the look that comes from having a secret
> Isn't enough. But that "not enough" isn't to be worn like a livery,

From *Parnassus* (vol. 9, no. 2, 1981).

To be briefly noticed, yet among whom should it be seen? I haven't
Thought about these things in years; that's my luck.
In time even the rocks will grow. And if you have curled and dandled
Your innocence once too often, what attitude isn't then really yours?

There is the problem: "To have the manners, and the look that comes
from having a secret/ Isn't enough." In other words: *"You've got to show
them who you are./* Just being a person doesn't work anymore." This new
set of fifty 4 × 4 quatrain poems hardly exhausts the theme. It continually
plays with it in paradoxes and oxymorons (title of poem facing "Punishing
the Myth"). It is a continual game of Hunt the Thimble, of chasing a bar
of soap round the bath whose slippery name is here announced as "innocence." Innocence is the note resounding throughout this sequence, not
love.

This slippery ambiguity is achieved by a fidgety mixture that compounds
an intimate tone of address with a scattering of unanchored and uncharted
points of reference. Deictics, to use the linguists's word, are everywhere
but point nowhere. Each tiny drama tends to open, as here, with the
indeterminacy of an "it." That is where the guesswork begins, hardly
helped by the various landscapes and shifting weather. Any kind of emotional stress could be implied or intended, leaving "you" and the dual
"we" wiggling in their isolated positions. The actors are as self-conscious
as the poem; yet, like art itself, they long to reach beyond such self-
consciousness, such dandling of attitudes. In this they remind me of
Kleist's great parable of the marionettes.

Marionettes, before Kleist, had been viewed as tragic dolls, victims of
malignant forces that bewitched men into puppets. Ashbery will have no
such romantic dross. That is strictly for the nursery, for Andersen's "Steadfast Tin Soldier." For Ashbery, as for Kleist, art must never be guilty of
affectation. How he shies from the least hint of affectation! "I haven't/
Thought about these things in years," he insists with a wry recoil; "that's
my luck." We are not meant to believe that. Any more than that "the rocks
will grow." It is all part of a pose to undermine a pose. But the ultimate
aim, in this play of self-consciousness, must be to undermine self-consciousness itself, like Kleist's marionettes:

For affectation is seen, as you know, when the soul, or moving force,
appears at some point other than the centre of gravity of the move-

ment. Because the operator of the marionette controls, with his wire or his thread, only this centre, the attached limbs are just what they should be . . . lifeless, pure pendulums, governed only by the law of gravity. This is an excellent quality, and you'll look for it in vain in most of our dancers.

That is the kind of operator Ashbery aims to be, controlling his poems like pendulums. As he performs his quatrains, he would like us to exclaim: "Just look at Ashbery pursued by Apollo! He turns to look. At this moment his soul seems to be in the small of his back. Now, look, he is offering an apple to Venus. His soul is located (and it's a frightful thing to see) in his elbow." I paraphrase Kleist since Ashbery, in so many ways, is really an old-fashioned kind of poet. He is haunted by traditional poetry with its pretension of telling us what life is all about, while flinching from the emotionally committed, didactic attitudes to which such pretensions may lead. Each poem, then, must remain a mysteriously self-contained gesture, like a sequence of Burmese or Javanese dancing, or a formal puppet show. "The acrobat," as Wilde wrote in 1889, "is an artist. The mere fact that he never speaks to the audience shows how well he appreciates the great truth that the aim of art is not to reveal personality but to please."

John Ashbery certainly has pleased. He has captivated and tantalized a large audience. He has won a Pulitzer Prize, a National Book Award, and a National Book Critics Circle Award. The critical rafters ring to the echo, as if Ashbery had rediscovered poetry's secret in a convex mirror. For Kleist the mirror was concave in which an image, after dwindling, turns up again in front of us. So grace itself returns, Kleist concluded, when knowledge has, as it were, passed through infinity: "Grace appears most purely in that human form which either has no consciousness or an infinite consciousness; that is, in the puppet or in the god."

So much for the poetics. The state of mind this induces is paradoxically both alert and dreamlike: alert to the enfolding chain of evasions and hesitations; dreamlike in the suppression of mannered responses. "All life," in a rare moment of lucidity he recorded in *As We Know,*

> Is as a tale told to one in a dream
> In tones never totally audible
> Or understandable, and one wakes

> Wishing to hear more, asking
> For more . . .

Ashbery is a story-teller, certainly. These new poems are all skeletal tales, sometimes opening with biblical sonority: "It came about that there was no way of passing/ Between the twin partitions . . ." or "Job sat in a corner of the dump eating asparagus/ With one hand"; at other times more urbanely: "Work had been proceeding at a snail's pace/ Along the river . . ." or "All around us an extraordinary effort is being made./ Something is in the air." Yet no story will be told. Certainly nothing like a narrative or plot emerges. Not even feelings emerge exactly, more like feelings *of* feelings, gropings *after* feelings whose ultimate interpretation is doomed

> To end in failure, unless that person happens to be
> Exactly the same person as the artist who is doing
> All this to them, which of course is impossible.

So we must resign ourselves to peeping over Narcissus' shoulder into his convex mirror.

Take the last of these narrative openings (entitled "Catalpas"). Here is the poem:

> All around us an extraordinary effort is being made.
> Something is in the air. The tops of trees are trying
> To speak to this. The audience for these events is amazed,
> Can't believe them, yet is walking in its sleep,
>
> By twos and threes, on the ramparts in the moonlight.
> Understanding must be introduced now, at no matter what cost.
> Nature wants us to understand in many ways
> That the age of noyades is over, although danger still lurks
>
> In the enormous effrontery that appearances put on things,
> And will continue for some time. But all this comes as no surprise;
> You knew the plot before, and expected to arrive in this place
> At the appointed time, and now it's almost over, even
>
> As it's erupting in huge blankets of forms and solemn,
> Candy-colored ideas that you recognize as your own,
> Only they look so strange up there on the stage, like the light
> That shines through sleep. And the third day ends.

All is dreamlike, disjointed, iridescent about these apparitions, pleasing to any juvenile admirer of Walter de la Mare. Yes, this is poetry. This is poetry on the making of poetry; or rather, on the remaking of one's own image in the order of the poem. The recessive vortex of introducing rationality into this context, "at no matter what cost," is dizzying. But luckily that is only a game, a game handed over to us, the readers. That is the danger of peering over anyone's shoulder into a mirror. Ashbery himself seems quite content to remain bemused by those "Candy-colored ideas" lit up on the stage of his poem by a light "That shines through sleep." Not only the poetry's status, I repeat, or the poetic idiom, but the poetic persona in this dream-bound labyrinth is deeply traditional.

John Ashbery is the best surrealist poet in English since David Gascoigne. His is the first significant extension of stream-of-consciousness, since the Pound generation, that succeeds in harnessing the discontinuous instabilities of a story unfolding. It is the illusion of that unfolding that absorbs him and at least part of his appeal lies in the nature of the narratives chosen. These ever shifting tableaux, as often as not, derive from the tripiest of crime fiction or romantic fiction or Hollywood *kitsch*. Go back to *The Tennis Court Oath* almost twenty years ago:

> They dream only of America
> To be lost among the thirteen million pillars of grass:
> "This honey is delicious
> *Though it burns the throat.*"
>
> And hiding from darkness in barns
> They can be grownups now
> And the murderer's ash tray is more easily—
> The lake a lilac cube.
>
> He holds a key in his right hand.
> "Please," he asked willingly.
> He is thirty years old.
> That was before
>
> We could drive hundreds of miles
> At night through dandelions.
> When his headache grew worse we
> Stopped at a wire filling station . . .

I can make nothing of the wire filling station. But the vaguely Cubist fuss is welded with bits of Auden ("hiding from darkness in barns") and Whitman, of course, to what Ashbery has elsewhere called a "Forties Flick." Such is Ashbery's game of royal tennis, or *Jeu de Paume.* It is in this sense that Peter Porter has likened him to Browning for "his lucubrative, playful, inclusive style of verse." Elsewhere bits of Shakespeare, Pope, Tennyson, or Gérard de Nerval ("I am the shadowed, widower, the unconsoled") crop up. "I want to write poems that are as inexact as mathematics," he has asserted. And again: "Sometimes/ I think we are being punished for the overabundance/ Of things to enjoy. . . ."

That joy is constantly resolved to appearances, to forms and surfaces. "This poem is concerned with language on a very plain level," "Paradoxes and Oxymorons" opens, its initial oxymoron ("Look at it talking to you") resolved into a paradox ("The poem is you"). In between there emerges, in its quaint and sentimental way, an old-fashioned love poem:

> This poem is concerned with language on a very plain level.
> Look at it talking to you. You look out a window
> Or pretend to fidget. You have it but you don't have it.
> You miss it, it misses you. You miss each other.
>
> The poem is sad because it wants to be yours, and cannot.
> What's a plain level? It is that and other things,
> Bringing a system of them into play. Play?
> Well, actually, yes, but I consider play to be
>
> A deeper outside thing, a dreamed role-pattern,
> As in the division of grace these long August days
> Without proof. Open-ended. And before you know
> It gets lost in the steam and chatter of typewriters.
>
> It has been played once more. I think you exist only
> To tease me into doing it, on your level, and then you aren't there
> Or have adopted a different attitude. And the poem
> Has set me softly down beside you. The poem is you.

The focus and subject of many of these poems turns out to be a shared intimacy between two shiftless, sexless pronouns. They constitute not a testament of love but what Barthes called *Fragments d'un discours amoureux*; what R. D. Laing called *Knots.* The poet lives in repeated cycles of false discovery which need to be recycled and unravelled. "Alone with our madness and favorite flower," he had written in *As We Know,*

> We see that there really is nothing left to write about.
> Or rather, it is necessary to write about the same old things
> In the same way, repeating the same things over and over
> For love to continue and be gradually different.

In "Drunken Americans" Narcissus gazes at his reflection to disclaim something about the nature of desire. Yet "to desire it/ And not want it is to chew its name like a rag":

> Violence, how smoothly it came
> And smoothly took you with it
> To wanting what you nonetheless did not want.
> It's all over if we don't see the truth inside that meaning.

Ashbery turns out to be an ethical poet, after all, worrying away at the assertiveness of the ego in all its consequences and inconsequentialities and relationships. He is all "Paradoxes and Problems," to use Donne's phrase. Like the prisoners in Dante's *Inferno,* he yearns for what he fears. Only in solitude can he "split open/ The ripe exchanges, kisses, sighs. . . ." For the nature of that desire, between that neutral "you" and "I," is absolutely reversible, absolutely homosexual, like the glyph "69."

> I thought it was you but I couldn't tell.
> It's so hard, working with people, you want them all
> To like you and be happy, but they get in the way
> Of their own predilections, it's like a stone
>
> Blocking the mouth of a cave. And when you say, come on let's
> Be individuals reveling in our separateness, yet twined
> Together at the top by our hair, like branches, then it's OK
> To go down into the garden at night and smoke cigarettes,
>
> Except that nothing cares about the obstacles, the gravity
> You had to overcome to reach this admittedly unimpressive
> Stage in the chain of delusions leading to your freedom,
> Or is that just one more delusion? Yet I like the way

Your hair is cropped, it's important, the husky fragrance
Breaking out of your voice, when I've talked too long
On the phone, addressing the traffic from my balcony
Again, launched far out over the thin ice once it begins to smile.

Again and again Ashbery launches out on to that thin ice. Again and again he addresses himself, you, us, over the roar of society's traffic. Up on that Manhattan balcony, he stands, Orpheus on the telephone, older now, *El Desdichado,* "The Desperado," *"Le prince D'Aquitaine à la tour abolie,"* both actor and voyeur, schoolmaster and casuist,

Coaching, pruning young spring thoughts
Surprised to be here, in this air.

Double Dutch

TURNER CASSITY

If you write in lines so long that your book has to be printed sideways, it seems to me you might well reconsider your methods. However, James Dickey has always been the least succinct of poets, and here, in a grand horizontal sprawl, is *The Strength of Fields,* a collection of lyrics and of adaptations from other languages. Dickey writes with undiminished vigor, but I am not sure I can say this as praise. Intellectually, he is so seldom on secure ground that he ought perhaps to proceed with caution.

His title poem, for example, is in direct contradiction to the Warren Court. It seems to say that politicians do represent trees and stones.

        Men are not where he is
    Exactly now, but they are around him   around him like the strength
    Of fields . . .
        The stars splinter, pointed and wild. The dead lie under
    The pastures. They look on and help.

Perhaps President Carter, for whose inauguration the poem was written, needs livelier helpers. One is reminded of those unreadable Scandinavian novels about "The Land." If Dickey covets a Nobel Prize, *The Strength of Fields,* as a title, should do it. For its purposes, it is the best since *The Good Earth.*

As a matter of fact, the poet's position is not vastly different from what Mrs. Buck's used to be. He has real talent, a wide public, a geographical area delineated for him by that public, and no serious critical appeal whatever. Buckhead, even when Dickey was living there, must have borne about the same resemblance to The South as the coastal treaty ports to China, or Pasadena to the Wild West. No Wonder his Buckhead Boys feel rather out of things.

Within his limits—one cannot really call them self-imposed; that would imply a sense of focus he does not have—he can be effective. "Root-light, or The Lawyer's Daughter" is a very amusing put-down of the idea of the

Review of James Dickey's *The Strength of Fields* and *The Zodiac* from *Parnassus* (vol. 8, no. 2, 1980).

Platonic Idea. Or would be if one could rescue it from its surrounding welter of verbiage. It is the dread Southern urge to use eight words wherever one will do. Surely it will be the punishment of the garrulous to sit in Hell at the knee of Edith Wharton's mother.

> She came flying
> Down from Eugene Talmadge
> Bridge, just to long for . . .
> If you asked me how to find the Image
> Of Woman to last
> All your life, I'd say go lie
> Down underwater . . .
> Be eight years old . . .
> in the clean palmetto color
> [and] naked with bubbles,
> Head-down . . . there she is.

No Georgian, I least of all, would be willing to forsake Eugene Talmadge Bridge, but the rest of the detail in the full version adds nothing.

> That any just to long for
> The rest of my life, would come, diving like a lifetime
> Explosion in the juices
> Of palmettoes flowing
> Red in the St. Mary's River as it sets in the east
> Georgia from Florida off, makes whatever child
> I was lie still, dividing,
> Swampy states   watching
> The lawyer's daughter shocked
> With silver   and I wished for all holds
> On her like root-light. She came flying
> Down from Eugene Talmadge
> Bridge, just to long for as I burst with never
> Rising never
> Having seen her except where she worked
> For J.C. Penney in Folkston. Her regular hours
> Took fire, and God's burning bush of the morning
> Sermon was put on her; I had never seen it where
> It has to be. If you asked me how to find the Image
> Of Woman to last

> All your life, I'd say go lie
> Down underwater for nothing
> Under a bridge and hold Georgia
> And Florida from getting at each other   hold
> Like walls of wine. Be eight years old from Folkston ten
> From Kingsland twelve miles in the clean palmetto color
>   Just as it blasts
>   Down with a body   red and silver buck
>   Naked with bubbles on Sunday   root
>   light explodes
>   head-down, and there she is.

Root-light is phosphorescence, one of many spooky Southern phenomena. What has phosphorescence to do with the lawyer's daughter? Nothing. That is why I left it out. "The clean palmetto color" is of course so attractive a phrase I should like to steal it, and may.

I do not understand why he sets up the poem typographically as he does. If there is any rhythmic measure, or any non-random relationship of sentence to line, I cannot discern it. I have heard him read the poem—most engagingly—and still cannot. As a lyric it is marred by a leering resemblance to a *Playboy* cartoon, but it does represent the poet at his least pretentious.

"False Youth: Autumn: Clothes of the Age" (even his titles are long) shows him at his most pretentious, but may nevertheless be the most successful poem in the book. It is worth quoting in full, because, unlike root-light, its details are relevant to its subject, and do not paralyze the narrative.

> Three red foxes on my head, come down
> There last Christmas from Brooks Brothers
> As a joke, I wander down Harden Street
> In Columbia, South Carolina, fur-haired and bald,
> Looking for impulse in camera stores and redneck greeting cards.
>   A pole is spinning
> Colors I have little use for, but I go in
> Anyway, and take off my fox hat and jacket
> They have not seen from behind yet. The barber does what he can
> With what I have left, and I hear the end man say, as my own
>   Hair-cutter turns my face
> To the floor, Jesus, if there's anything I hate

It's a middle-aged hippie. Well, so do I, I swallow
           Back: so do I   so do I
And to hell. I get up, and somebody else says
           When're you gonna put on that hat,
Buddy? Right now. Another says softly,
           Goodbye, Fox. I arm my denim jacket
On and walk to the door, stopping for the murmur of chairs,
And there it is
                       hand-stitched by the needles of the mother
           Of my grandson   eagle riding on his claws with a banner
                 Outstretched as the wings of my shoulders,
                       Coming after me with his flag
                 Disintegrating, his one eye raveling
                       Out, filthy strings flying
           From the white feathers, one wing nearly gone:
                       Blind eagle, but flying
                 Where I walk, where I stop with my fox
Head at the glass to let the row of chairs spell it out
                 And get a lifetime look at my bird's
One word, raggedly blazing with extinction and soaring loose
In red threads burning up white until I am shot in the back
           Through my wings   or ripped apart
                       For rags:

                            Poetry

Poetry is not so badly off as all that, Mr. Dickey; it needs only to be saved
from its practitioners. One is tempted to say that Thom Gunn could have
written the poem better, but since he hasn't, there is no point in withholding praise from the actual author. The barber pole is a real inspiration.
Admittedly, I am predisposed to like any poem that savages Columbia,
South Carolina. I went through basic training there. If the following line
break is not random it is a stroke of genius, and the very last sort of effect
one ordinarily expects to find in Dickey.

                 I arm my denim jacket
           On and walk to the door

The defensiveness is gotten across with marvelous subtlety.
    "The Rain Guitar" suffers from being a sequel to or trial run for

the dueling banjos scene in *Deliverance*—that abyss—and from our suspicion that what a man of Dickey's age should really be playing is a ukulele. The guitar reappears in "Exchanges," a notably bad performance. The poet, with no hint of irony, is apparently going down a checklist of cocktail party chic: smog, offshore drilling, freeways, the quality of life, and the death of whales. All too appropriate, unfortunately, for a Phi Beta Kappa poem, "being in the form of a dead-living dialogue with Joseph Trumbull Stickney (1874–1904)—(Stickney's words are in italics)." Italicizing was not necessary. It is perfectly obvious which words are Stickney's: his are the ones that make sense. In the Dickey text nothing has anything to do with anything else. You cannot call it free association because there is no association. The narrator is sitting on a bluff above the Pacific Ocean outside Los Angeles (where else?) and playing Appalachian music to a companion while worrying about environmental pollution. "We sang and prayed for purity." A reader who will believe that will believe anything, although I should say in its defense that it is the most straightforward utterance in the poem. Compare it with this:

> Day-moon meant more
> Far from us   dazing the oil-slick with the untouched remainder
> Of the universe   spreading   contracting
> Catching fish at the living end
> In their last eye   the guitar rang moon and murder
> And Appalachian love, and sent them shimmering from the cliff

The operative phrase is living end. The girl, we learn presently, is now in Forest Lawn, and everything—astronauts have by now been added—is supposed to come together in an image of death. It doesn't. Nothing could get itself together after images like "birds black with corporations." It brings one solidly down on the side of Chevron. Well, if there is anything I hate it is a middle-aged hippie.

I take this opportunity to say I personally find offshore drilling platforms the most attractive thing in any seascape. They provide a middle distance. In the bay at Santa Barbara they are like great ideographs on the oriental haze of the islands.

It would be just as easy to hatchet "For the Death of Lombardi," a maudlin threnody for the iconic coach. It would be easy but counter-

productive. We should regret instead that someone who is uniquely qualified to give us a good poem on the world of the locker room has failed
to do so. Very few writers play football, and we should have our understanding enlarged if a poet could convey to us what it is actually like. My
interest in endangered species is in seeing that they do not disappear from
the table, but I neither hunt nor fish. I therefore owe a particular debt to
Ernest Hemingway, and come away from Dickey with a sense of waste and
frustration, his as well as mine.

"Lombardi" confirms what one has suspected for years: Dickey thinks
he is Paul Hornung (whose autobiography, incidentally, is not to be
missed; its narcissism makes poets seem self-effacing).

> Yet running in my mind
> As Paul Hornung, I made it here
> With the others, sprinting down railroad tracks,
> Hurdling bushes and backyard Cyclone
> Fences, through city after city, to stand, at last, around you

The debt to John Cheever is this side of plagiarism, but only just. The real
trouble with the poem is that its details are predictable. The statement of
them is furiously hyped, but they are themselves predictable without being
inevitable. They are exactly what I should have used in writing a poem
about locker rooms, and I never go close to locker rooms.

> Around your bed the knocked-out teeth like hail-pebbles
> Rattle down   miles of adhesive tape from hands and ankles
> Writhe in the room like vines   gallons of sweat blaze in buckets
> In the corners   the blue and yellow of bruises
> Make one vast sunset around you.

To measure their failure you have only to think of the hyena in *Green Hills
of Africa* "racing the little nickelled death inside him," or of the Kipling
galley-slaves.

> We fainted with our chins on the oars and you did not see that
> we were idle, for we still swung to and fro.

The sunset of bruises is wonderfully bad, the taste of the Easter show at
Radio City Music Hall brought to literature, and it appears *twice.*

                    the bruise-colors brighten   deepen
        On the wall   the last tooth spits itself free
    Of a line-backer's aging head

The tooth exemplifies the syntactical desperation to which Dickey has
been reduced: something, anything, to make the obvious seem "poetic."
There is no conceivable way in which a tooth can spit itself out. The
meaningless reflexive makes one see why Freshman English instructors
tell their students to avoid the passive. The writing in "Lombardi," as
writing, confronts us with what three generations of modern poets have
been unwilling to face: no amount of talent is going to help if the rest of
your mind is a mess. Common sense is as useful in poetry as it is elsewhere.

    I do not want anyone to think I underrate Dickey's talent. The best
phrase in the poem is very good indeed.

                the weekly, inescapable dance
        Of speed, deception, and pain

It is no accident that it consists of abstractions (you can be sure in any
modern poem that dance does not actually refer to dancing).

    The passage on the athletes grown middle-aged ought to work but
doesn't.

                Paul Hornung has withdrawn
        From me [sic], and I am middle-aged and gray . . .
                We stand here among
            Discarded TV commercials:
    Among beer-cans and razor-blades and hair-tonic bottles,
        Stinking with male deodorants: we stand here
                Among teeth and filthy miles
        Of unwound tapes, novocaine needles, contracts, champagne
    Mixed with shower-water . . .

I have to say, however, the champagne mixed with shower water has
exactly the unexpectedness whose absence I was deploring above. As for
the deodorants, well, surely it is better to stink with them than without
them.

    I am not familiar with the originals of the translations in *Strength of Fields,* but I conclude either that the translator likes long-winded poets or that he can make anyone seem long-winded, even an oriental.

> But I remember, and I feel the grass and the fire
> Get together in April   with you and me, and that
> Is what I want   both age-gazing living and dead

Nothing could be further from an ideograph.

More Chinese than his Po Chu-yi is Dickey's own brilliantly observed image in "The Rain Guitar."

>   eelgrass trying to go downstream with all the right motions
> But one

A bit dynamic—fluid, if you like—for the oriental taste, but you will find no haiku nearly as good. Pound's *Cathay,* much of it, is static by comparison.

>   the willows
>   have overfilled the close garden

Alfred Jarry is here (*Ubu roi*; the guitar player is still going down that checklist). Octavio Paz is represented, as is Georg Heym. In English, the best of the lot is Vicente Aleixandre. I do not know him, but assume he is fashionable, as he is in the company of Evgeny Yevtushenko. I have a feeling I am using different systems of transliteration for the first and last names, but let it pass. The swordfish in "Undersea Fragment in Colons" is strikingly rendered.

> Swordfish, I know you are tired: tired out with the sharpness of your face:
>   Exhausted with the impossibility of ever
> Piercing the shade: with feeling the tunnel-breathing streamline of your flesh
>   Enter and depart

The Art Deco quality of the fish is perfectly captured.

It would be agreeable to say that in the translations we are at least freed of Dickey as a persona, but the voice of most of them is relentlessly first person, and we never get very far away from Paul Hornung. Still . . . Dickey's egoism has generated a thousand self-perpetuating anecdotes, yet the truth is, he is less imprisoned in his psyche than most poets. Whatever his poems are, they are not claustrophobic. Extroversion is an attractive thing about them, and may well account for their popularity. The poets he translates are, compared to him, closeted.

Speaking in his own voice he is a lyricist whose gift for the dramatic moment, for the accurate, vivid observation quickly rendered, is dissipated in non-structures enormously inflated. I seem to be describing Meyerbeer, and one could say that, like Meyerbeer, he will be immortal in his lifetime and for a few months after. The identification is not capricious: Meyerbeer may be said to have invented publicity—advertising—as we know it, and publicity has made Dickey one of the better poets who has ever been really popular.

Curious, therefore, that reviewers and public alike have by and large ignored *The Zodiac,* his magnum opus, if not his masterpiece. It appeared in 1976 in a trade edition from Doubleday and in a luxury edition from Bruccoli Clark. For the latter the author wrote an introduction that obscures as much as it reveals, and which I shall have to contradict from time to time.

I want to say at once *The Zodiac* is a work not just anyone could have written (so is *Les Huguenots*), and the question of indebtedness is to that extent moot. In basing it on "another of the same title," however, he invites speculation. That other is by Hendrik Marsman, a Dutch poet killed in World War II. In the introduction to the Doubleday edition Dickey says "This poem is in no sense a translation, for the liberties I have taken with Marsman's original poem are such that the poem I publish here, with the exception of a few lines, is completely my own." Prefacing the Bruccoli he says "Some thirty years ago, as a student at Vanderbilt, I read Hendrik Marsman's original." I think he did not. I think he read A. J. Barnouw's translation of it published in *The Sewanee Review* in 1947, and I think Barnouw, not Marsman, is due the disclaimer. Everyone who compares the two will have to decide for himself the degree of Dickey's indebtedness. The main difference, to put it bluntly, is that Dickey's protagonist is more of a drunkard.

One can see what attracted Dickey. If Barnouw has represented the original dependably, it is the most American poem ever written by a European. Of his own version Dickey writes "*The Zodiac* is at the same time a vindication of the drunken, demonic poet and the desperately serious artist." Although they were drunken and demonic respectively, there was nothing American about Verlaine or Rimbaud. Verlaine was too incompetent, and Rimbaud could have come only from the French bourgeoisie of the nineteenth century. At one point he wanted to work for the *Compagnie Universelle du Canal Interocéanique.* The presence of Arthur Rimbaud is perhaps the one thing that could have made the problems of the French in Panama worse than they were.

A strength of the Marsman-Barnouw is that in spite of manifold opportunities it at no point evokes Rimbaud. "Its twelve sections are the story of a drunken and perhaps dying Dutch poet who retires to his home in Amsterdam after years of travel and tries desperately, by means of stars, to relate himself to the universe." (Dickey, in his own version.)

I can spare scholars of those months of Dickey's posthumous immortality a great deal of trouble by telling them that the division into twelve sections does not mean a one to one relationship with the signs of the Zodiac. Cancer the Crab appears, but the divisions are purely arbitrary.

The Dickey gets off to an unpromising start, by sticking too close to the Marsman-Barnouw.

> The man I'm telling you about brought himself back alive
> A couple of years ago. He's here,
>   Making no trouble
>   over the broker's peaceful
> Open-bay office at the corner of two canals
>   That square off and starfish into four streets
>   Stumbling like mine-tunnels all over town.
>
> (Dickey)

> The man of whom I tell this narrative
> Returned, some time ago, to his native land.
> He has since lived, for nearly a full year,
> Over the peaceful broker's offices
> Which, at the corner between two canals,
> Front on the square that, starfish-shaped, ejects
> Its corridors into the city's mine.
>
> (Barnouw)

The starfish is too ingenious by half, and doubly inappropriate to Amsterdam, which has neither beaches nor salt water. Nor do the tunnels improve things. Holland cannot even keep water out of its basements. Dickey had no reason to know better—except by checking his facts—but his mother lode had.

The real Amsterdam makes its appearance here:

> . . . houses whose thick basement-stones
> Turn water into cement inch by inch
> As the tide grovels down.

(Dickey)

> . . . a row of mansions
> Whose cellars stand in water masonried

(Barnouw)

One up for Dickey. It would be invidious to point out that the city is sealed off from the tide by locks, and as the canals are flushed artificially every now and then, I am prepared to give the benefit of the doubt. Most of the first section is devoted to the vagaries of the badly hungover protagonist, but the author announces his theme baldly.

> The Zodiac.
> He must solve it must believe it   learn to read it
> No, wallow in it
> As poetry.

Here he does not follow the Barnouw closely enough. It says simply

> The puzzling palimpsest of the common life
> That he must solve and read as poetry

An attack of D.T.'s—he imagines an invasion of army ants*—delays things, but soon he is drunk and writing, and the poem rises to a passage of genuine power. It is not parallelled in the original.

> Will the animals come back
> Gently, creatively open

---

*The ants are an expansion of Barnouw's "insect plague of his own thoughts."

Like they were?
            Yes.
The great, burning Beings   melt into place

A few billion-lighted inept beasts

Of God—

Embedded in the delirium is an article of faith any poet will have to respect.

            the poem is *in* there   out there
            Somewhere, the lines that will change
            Everything, like your squares and square roots
                    Creating the heavenly music.

Section II is a meditation on the nature of time, precipitated by the striking of a clock.

            The whole time-thing: after all
            There's only this rosette of a great golden stylized asshole

The level of diction in this section, throughout, is the uneasiest in the poem, and owes nothing to Barnouw. To credit its force I shall say I can never look at the rose-window of a cathedral in quite the same way again. Another onslaught of the shakes ends the meditation, and this time the poet imagines that he is attacked by a giant lobster, whom he considers elevating to Zodiacal status. The passage may or may not be a parody of Eliot's pair of ragged claws. In any event, the lobster is in the Barnouw.

Section III, the least effective in the poem—Dickey's and his model—is a reminiscence of travel.

                    That remembered Greek blue
        Is *fantastic.* That's all: no words
        But the ones anybody'd use: the ones from humanity's garbage can
        Of language.

"Anybody'd," I think, is a word practically nobody would use.

Section IV is a recovery. A poetic recovery; the narrator's liver is beyond recall. The section includes one of Dickey's more interesting conceits.

> Without that hugely mortal beast   that multi-animal animal
>   There'd be no present time:
>   Without the clock-dome, no city here,
>   Without the axis and the poet's image   God's image
> No turning stars   no Zodiac   without God's conceiving
>   Of Heaven as beast-infested   Of Heaven in terms of beasts
>   There'd be no calendar   dates   seasons
>   No Babylon   those abstractions that blitzed their numbers
>   Into the Colosseum's crazy gates   and down
>   down
>   Into the woven beads that make the rosary
>   Live   sing and swirl like stars
>   Of creatures

The train of associations, while quite free, can easily be followed. Of course, it has Barnouw to keep it on the track. "Blitzed" is a mistake. In a poem about the heavens the root meaning, lightning, will get in the way of the Panzer divisions. The fault is Dickey's. In Barnouw the verb is "struck."

We have in section V the first hint of reconciliation, of relating by means of stars to the universe. Barnouw's lines are quoted without alteration.

> The faster I sleep,
> The faster the universe sleeps

To seek in sex the meaning of the cosmos is about as intelligent as it would be to use an ephemeris as a sex manual, and I should like to dislike section VII on principle, but I cannot. I like it. The meaning could not be more clearly conveyed, and the sense of quiet at the end is very impressive.

> Don't shack up with the intellect:
> Don't put your prick in a cold womb.
> Nothing but walking snakes would come of *that*—
>
> but if you conceive with meat

Alone,
       that child, too, is doomed.
              . . .
                        Realities
Are revealed in Heaven, as clouds drift across,
Mysterious sperm-colored:
                        Yes.
There, the world is original, and the Zodiac shines anew
       After every night-cloud. New
With a nameless tiredness   a depth
       Of field I can't read   an oblivion with no bottom

The Marsman-Barnouw, in the casting of old barren Reason from the house, is downright priggish.

       Do not sleep with the intellect,
       Do not couple with a cold womb.

I incline to a view that writing is one thing and sex is another, but whatever turns you on, as they used to say in my and Mr. Dickey's early middle age.

   I do not know what to make of Section VIII, and I don't think Dickey does either. In the Barnouw it gives the impression of a lyric imported from somewhere else, from Heredia, or one of the later Parnassians (nothing American here).

              He goes along
   The dead canal that sleeps in its bronze bed
   Between the quays.

Dickey gives it the full treatment, to try to bring it in line with the rest of the poem, but nothing he does really works. First we have the Midnight Cowboy.

                        Time
   To city-drift leg after leg, looking Peace
       In its empty eyes as things are beginning
       Already to go twelve hours
   Toward the other side of the clock

He takes on the canal as if he were Teddy Roosevelt.

> He moves along the slain canal
>> Snoring in its bronze
>> Between docks

In another line he big-sticks the Parnassians on their own ground.

> The trees are motionless, helping their leaves hold back
>> Breath

I can produce no hard evidence, but I have an impression section IX owes something to *Tonio Kröger,* in German-language courses in the Netherlands often a set piece.

> . . . the bitter right his shyness granted her
> To pass him in the street with a frigid look,
> Haughtily jesting with the sinister boy
> Who once had been his idol and his friend
> And who had taken her away from him

> (Barnouw)

Again, Dickey's only response is to hype it up.

> Empty is the grave of youth

> (Barnouw)

> *The* grave of youth? HA! I told you: there's nobody *in* it.

> (Dickey)

One feels he has sat too long in creative writing classes where they tell you everything must be dramatized.

Section X is a love scene, and not at all interesting. Where a little sexiness would have helped, Dickey perversely adds none.

Section XI is the first intrusion of social life into the poem. The protagonist goes to a party. How he secured an invitation I find the most stimulating problem the work poses. Barnouw renders the arrival vividly, and Dickey wisely does not change it.

> He polar-bears through the room

But if, as Dickey claims, he completely re-worked the "original," why did he feel compelled to stick so close to it when no purpose is served? His worst enemy never said he did not know how to enjoy a party, and surely this is a scene in which we had rather have Dickey than Marsman. What, finally, did the Barnouw mean to Dickey? If it stuck in his mind for thirty years, and had enough force to make him compromise what is clearly intended as his artistic testament with the hint of plagiarism, it must have seemed to him a text brought down on stone tablets, but a text to be elaborated in art and lived out in life. I can think of no more convincing argument for keeping romantic poems out of the hands of the young, and for discharging agrarians who would put them there.

Easy to see that Dickey's idea of making something poetic is to add "intensity"—as if he went about with a hard gemlike Bunsen burner. In spite of his fondness for Appalachian stage effects (if one did not know Buckhead better, one would say he grew up waited on by White servants who sang a lot), it seldom occurs to him to use a homey image. The voltage would seem to him too low. On the rare occasion when he does use one, it is a disaster: the determination to say everything by way of images, be the image good, bad, or indifferent.

> The garden, he thinks, was here,
> Bald   a few sparse   elephant-head hairs

"Bald" is in the Barnouw, but for the elephant-head Dickey has no one but himself to blame. Nor was the bald itself necessary; I presume the Dutch word is *kaal,* which can also be translated as "bare." In the Transvaal, kaalveld is bare veldt.

The concluding section has been praised, and correctly so.

> Oh my own soul,   put me in a solar boat.
>   Come into one of these hands
>   Bringing quietness and the rare belief
> That I can steer this strange craft to the morning
> Land that sleeps   in the universe on all horizons
> . . .
> So long as the hand can hold its island
>   Of blazing paper, and bleed for its images:
>   Make what it can of what is:

So long as the spirit hurls on space
The star-beasts of intellect and madness.

If we can have an elaborate statement of a simplistic notion, *Zodiac* is the most elaborate and the most explicit example we have of the idea of poetry as the unconsidered utterance of the bardic genius aided in his unreason, if need be, by drink and drugs. If we take Whitman and Sandburg seriously, we have to consider Dickey, because he has more specific literary talent than either, and is by no means the phoniest of the three. His poems compare poorly with those of Hart Crane, but who knows what Crane would have written like in his fifties. I for one doubt that he could have written at all. Appalachia knows what to call such transports—speaking in tongues—and what to think of them: they are in the same category as the handling of snakes. In secular and more pretentious guise they are endemic to American poetic thought, and are not likely to go away. My own feeling is that if you wanted to invent a method to get the least out of the most talent, you could hardly do better.

Sibyls, Shards, and Other Semi-Precious Litter

SUSAN MITCHELL

Everything only connected by "and" and "and."

—Elizabeth Bishop, "Over 2000
Illustrations and a Complete
Concordance"

The work is not put in a place, it
is that place.

—Carl Andre, as quoted in *The
Writings of Robert Smithson*

1

Toward the end of the *Paradiso,* Dante compares the fade-out of his vision
of divine order to the melting of snow and then, more poignantly, to the
scattering of those leaves on which Virgil said the sibyl wrote the signs and
symbols of her prophecies. That second image is, of course, intended to
be more than a visual correlative for the dispersal of Dante's poetic vision:
It implies the dissolution of the classical world, the break-up and parcelling
out of its ideas and assumptions, the loss of Humanistic wholeness. When
the Roman emperor Theodosius officially closed the oracle at Delphi in
A.D. 390, more than the oracle was lost. Delphi housed the famous navel
stone, or *omphalous,* which marked the site as the center of the world. (In
fact, the navel stone had been the shrine's original deity.) Not only was
the great book of knowledge unbound, its pages thrown together in
random order, but the sense of the center was also lost.

Review of Julia Budenz's *From the Gardens of Flora Baum* and Constance Hunting's *Collected
Poems* from *Parnassus* (vol. 15, no. 1, 1989).

From the vantage point of the present, the scattering of the sibyl's leaves on the wind of her cave-shrine (as if the oracle's breathing, her inspiration, had itself become a principle of entropy and disorder) might well seem a cryptic gesture prefiguring the Postmodern with its multiplicity of styles and codes. As disconnected events uplift (or are they downfalling?) into a gravity-less universe, the Delphic palm leaves flutter with the rags and relics of Milton's Paradise of Fools to the accompaniment of Dylan's "Blowin' in the Wind." While such floating bric-a-brac would have signified disorder for Milton and Dante (the lustful are similarly blown about in the second circle of the *Inferno*), the postmodern artist is excited by the possibilities of connecting all the intriguing debris into, say, something on the order of Philip Johnson's AT&T highrise, with its Roman colonnades, neo-classical mid-section, and Chippendale pediment on top. Milton would have found appealing, I suspect, the historical eclecticism of postmodern art (*Paradise Lost* does, after all, combine classical, Hebrew, and Christian traditions, or as Milton boasted, "Things unattempted yet in prose and rhyme"). And Dante, who chose to write the *Divina Commedia* not in Latin, but in the vernacular, might have been sympathetic to a movement which allows images from high and low culture to hobnob as familiars. It's the High Modernists among us who look askance at Postmodernism's macaronic tendencies[1] and who turn out to be more conservative than the old *auctores.* Why should this be?

Modernists and Postmodernists have this much in common: Both regret the loss of cultural nuclei. In 1920, W. B. Yeats was predicting a new loss—"Things fall apart; the centre cannot hold." His forecast proved accurate, for two years later, in the conclusion to *The Waste Land,* T. S. Eliot could write as if the cataclysmic event had occurred, "These fragments I have shored against my ruins"; and by 1947, Wallace Stevens's "turbulent Schlemihl," Ludwig Richter, was not only whirled with statues, roofs, a theater, churches, and some massive sopranos, in a manner reminiscent, though on a smaller scale, of Milton's Paradise of Fools, but also had "lost the whole in which he was contained."[2] Aftershocks of the demolition continue to be felt in the Postmodern. Practically every poem by John Ashbery acknowledges, if only tacitly,[3] the absent center, which accounts to some extent for their elegiac mood and refrain of belatedness. According to Charles Jencks, there is a similar preoccupation among postmodern architects:

This return to the absent centre is one of the most recurrent figures of Post-Modernism. It is portrayed both consciously by Arata Isozaki as a comment on the decentred nature of Japanese life, and unselfconsciously by James Stirling at Stuttgart, Michael Graves at the Humana Building, Ricardo Bofill at Montpellier and just about every Post-Modern architect who makes a central plan and then doesn't know what to put in the honorific place. This paradox is both startling and revealing; a desire for a communal space, a perfectly valid celebration of what we have in common, and then the admission that there is nothing quite adequate to fill it.[4]

So far, it would seem that Modernists and Postmodernists have nothing to argue about, but this is not the case. Disagreement focuses on what is to be done with the fragments, with all the odds and ends still washing up on the contemporary scene.

Though Postmodernists, like Modernists, appear to be in a protracted period of mourning, not only deploring the emptiness at the center, but actively longing for the old Humanistic wholeness, they keep rummaging among the ruins, gluing the curved cheek of a plaster of paris doll to the Pentelic nose of a Greek Aphrodite—or, like Louise Nevelson, picking up all the driftwood on the streets of New York City and painting it gold. According to Jencks, what interests the Postmodern artist is "dissonant beauty,"[5] but since dissonance is a salient feature of modern poetry, it's important to distinguish between modern and postmodern approaches to the disharmonious whole. Though there is the same appetite for inclusiveness among poets in both groups, with the Postmodernists there is a greater willingness, even a need, to let conflicts and contradictions remain unresolved. This means that a postmodern whole is necessarily going to include loose ends. Look at what happens in this passage from "The System," one of the prose poems in Ashbery's *Three Poems* (1972), a postmodern manifesto if ever there was one:

What place is there in the continuing story for all the adventures, the wayward pleasures, the medium-size experiences that somehow don't fit in but which loom larger and more interesting as they begin to retreat into the past? There were so many things held back, kept back, because they didn't fit into the plot or because their tone wasn't in keeping with the whole. So many of these things have been discarded, and they now tower on the brink of the continuity, hemming it in like dark crags above a valley stream. One sometimes forgets that to be all one way may be preferable to eclectic diversity in the interest of verisimilitude, even for those of the opposite persuasion; the most powerful preachers are those persuaded in advance and their unalterable lessons are deeply moving just because of this rigidity, having none of the tepidness of the meandering stream of our narration with its well-chosen and typical episodes, which now seems to be trying to bury itself in the landscape. The rejected chapters have taken over. For a long time it was as though only the most patient scholar or the recording angel himself would ever interest himself in them. Now it seems as though that angel had begun to dominate the whole story: he who was supposed only to copy it all down has joined forces with the misshapen, misfit pieces that were never meant to go into it but at best to stay on the sidelines so as to point up how everything else belonged together, and the resulting mountain of data threatens us; one can almost hear the beginning of the lyric crash in which everything will be lost and pulverized, changed back into atoms ready to resume new combinations and shapes again, new wilder tendencies, as foreign to what we have carefully put in and kept out as a new chart of elements or another planet—unimaginable, in a word. And would you believe that this word could possibly be our salvation? For we are rescued by what we cannot imagine: it is what finally takes us up and shuts our story, replacing it among the millions of similar volumes that by no means menace its uniqueness but on the contrary situate it in the proper depth and perspective. At last we have that rightness that is rightfully ours. But we do not know what brought it about.

The "new spirit"[6] Ashbery describes is obviously voracious, but then so is the modernist spirit that Stevens projects onto his Canon Aspirin, whose meditations do not stop at that point "beyond which fact could not progress as fact," or even when "thought could not progress as thought."[7] What's new about the postmodern poem is that it gobbles up oppositions without bothering itself about whether or not it can reconcile or harmonize the differences. When Ashbery thinks of those who prefer homogeneity to his own eclectic system, he doesn't argue against all-of-a-pieceness; nor does he attempt to mediate between that aesthetic and his own. His poem carries the adversary position along intact. And, as if his narrative really were the meandering stream he compares it to, it sweeps along a bit of romantic imagery, those "dark crags" filched from Wordsworth. (The angel has been swiped from Stevens.) Eclecticism has room for so much, precisely because it has no time to puzzle over contradictions. Though a meandering stream is not a rushing torrent, still it is in motion, and what's more, the recording angel has been caught up in the flow. All that can stop the postmodern narrative is the unimaginable, but the moment that blank is mentioned it makes its presence felt in the poem, the way the shadow of something muffled up and indistinct in a doorway will enter a room.

While the order the Canon Aspirin contemplates seems equally expansive, Stevens pulls back from the brink of the Postmodern. The Canon has reached that point

> Beyond which thought could not progress as thought.
> He had to choose. But it was not a choice
> Between excluding things. It was not a choice
>
> Between, but of. He chose to include the things
> That in each other are included, the whole,
> The complicate, the amassing harmony.

> (from "Notes toward a Supreme Fiction")

Where Ashbery's narrative graciously accepts all the ideas and images that come its way, Stevens's Canon makes choices: The amassing harmony is to include only those things so intimately compounded that they are complicate—twisted and wrapped around each other. In Ashbery, even pulverization does not produce mixtures. Within his poems, parts retain their autonomy like Prokofiev's duck, whose familiar oboe theme can still be heard inside the wolf's stomach. What keeps the reader from paying too much attention to the scattered nature of the Ashberian whole is that it is so difficult to keep up with a totality that is in motion. Where the Canon Aspirin has time to deliberate, his meticulous grammatical distinctions practically bringing the poem to a stop, Ashbery's poems keep escaping the reader, like the meandering stream that tries to bury itself in the landscape. Even when Ashbery's poems are not made of water or cloud, they are elusive wholes, and Ashbery's image of an ice storm collapsing into "diamond rubble" and "galled glitter"[8] could describe many of his own poems which splinter as they are read, showering the reader with gorgeous fragments.

Like Ashbery, Constance Hunting and Julia Budenz write postmodern poems with appetites that trope themselves. Hunting loves the paraphernalia of the world. Her poems are plunder, heaps of broken shell, piles of sand, spoils, loot, swag, and boodle. While she realizes there is always the danger that "the mind's eye swells and boggles at such troves, / desiring to embrace the entire, may fail" ("The Heron"), she has no interest in fusions and blends. The seams and gaps show because they too are part of totality. Similarly, when Budenz's heroine and alter ego— sometimes referred to as Flora, more often as she—begins to build her poem / temple, what is stressed is the structure's diversity:

> Now she'll cut out
> A contemporary temple
> In compartments. Segments,
> Sections, cuttings, clippings
> Constitute her bricks; for instance,
> The universe is smaller than we thought.
> We thought there was a hotter fire.
> We thought of a gleam beyond the massed atoms of the stars.
>
> Post no bills,
> It said on the gray sky.
>
> Now she'll settle for a temple of bricks.
> But then a temple of marble,
> Then the showy echo of Pentelicus
> Will rise around her as she climbs the steps
> Up to the desired sidereal sheen.

> (from "The Fire Escape")

Where the classical temple was whole, Budenz's will be broken into "segments, / Sections, cuttings, clippings"; and where the classical temple was marble, Budenz's is to be made of bricks. Like the universe with its massed atoms, her poem is to be an aggregate, not only of differences (the grandeur of Greek art played off against contemporary Humble Pie), but also of mixed feelings—an obvious joy in building set side by side with the Modernist's sense of loss. Budenz's emphasis on diverse form has its counterpart in postmodern architecture which sets up stylistic collisions between different segments of the same edifice and which replaces traditional elements with brutalist materials, as in the Japan Style whose hallmark, the Tea Ceremony Room, is no longer constructed of wood, but of stained concrete. Budenz arranges stylistic collisions too, mainly between Wallace Stevens and T. S. Eliot, whose poems keep echoing in hers, but also between Stevens's self-mocking florid style of "The Comedian as the Letter C" and his sterner style of "the necessary angel." So allusive are Budenz's poems, that memory threatens to overwhelm the poet, making it difficult for her to decide where to situate her temple; but even as she poses the problem, she manages to parody the last section of Stevens's "The Auroras of Autumn," which keeps weighing different possibilities— "An unhappy people in a happy world," "A happy people in an unhappy world," "A happy people in a happy world"—as well as a memorable line from Eliot's "Burnt Norton":

> A remembered temple in a remembered sky.
> A remembered temple in an actual sky.
> An actual temple in a remembered sky.
> These are possible. But it's too cold
> For too much actuality. Either your windows
> Are streaked or your eyes water. And it's too bright,
> Too early on the eve of Advent for a hymn
> To the dews of heavens past. The sparrows
> Have just relinquished their harping. Then set
> The actual in the remembered. Ignore
> Your bricks splashed on the opposite windows.

> (from "The Fire Escape")

But Budenz's poem is not only parody, it is also a hymn to the dews of High Modernist heavens—and gardens, for the many orioles and lilacs Flora encounters among her trees and flowers are unmistakably transplanted from Stevens. Memory is problematic for Budenz because it deluges her with all the litter of the High Modernists, as well as with salvage from the classical world. Where Eliot could speak of "fragments I have shored against my ruins," Budenz is so bombarded by fragments that it seems impossible for her to be anything but a suspension fluid in which the tradition floats, its silts and sediments unmixed.

For Hunting, memory is problematic in a different way: It turns out to be a power with its own built-in contradictions, capable of making whole, but also of fragmenting. In an early poem "The Gathering," Hunting recalls what must have been a regularly recurring ceremony, her family sitting down for their evening meal. Note how the memory does not return as a picture, but as a mosaic of prominent details:

> Summer. Evening. The dark-veined honeycomb
> of glass, the colored dome to childish eyes
> a marvel is slid downward on its chain
> and sheds its colors as it comes
> to harlequin us all. Features stand out
> suddenly: an older uncle will begin to look
> like his own mother as she looked in age;
> his wife will give her maiden name away
> in her hand's shape, as if a common line
> were written in her palm,—
> a dozen like it gesture down the row.
> Light falls upon a cheek as it did years
> ago for someone else,
> and little Shelagh's got the double crown.
> We pass our plates up for the victuals,
> talking the whole time, or the grown people do,—
> interspersed others clutch soft silver spoons
> teethed over long since by their elders;
> eager in bibs, and propped, they lean
> forward and breathe, and slobber slightly,
> dazed by the noise, the smells, the light.

Memory does not reconstruct the family: It refracts them—into a cheek here, a hand there. But the scene is unstable in other ways. As the prominent features of the uncle and his wife change into those of long-dead relatives, these figures become wraith-like and remote. Instead of bringing the past closer, memory pushes it further away. Moreover, as the diners are broken into smaller pieces by the Tiffany lamp, the colorful splinters multiply, generating still more fragments. But what kind of whole do these fragments add up to? We never learn how many people are seated at the table; "interspersed others" suggests that their number will always be greater than those we can point to and count. Hunting's imagination, like the harlequining light, shatters whatever it beautifies, or beautifies what it shatters. I don't think it's sheer coincidence that the passage brings to mind Shelley's famous simile, "Life, like a dome of many-colored glass," for Hunting's poems, like Budenz's, are filled with such deliberate echoes. So, it would seem that literary tradition is also passed along as scraps and scrapings, those raspy ghost voices that haunt the poet and yet make her aware of what is left out and lost.

To the extent that Hunting and Budenz express regret for a world that is gone, even as they build something new out of its ruins, they are postmodern. In fact, the dynamics of Postmodernism frequently recalls Lewis Caroll's Carpenter who wept over the little oysters while he was eating them. This is a movement energized by its contradictions. As if to compensate for its sense of lost wholeness, it strives for inclusiveness through historical citation and literary allusion. Architect Philip Johnson writes:

> My direction is clear; eclectic tradition. This is not academic revival-
> ism. There are no Classic orders or Gothic finials. I try to pick up what
> I like throughout history. We cannot not know history.[9]

But the drive to be all-encompassing leads to a paradox. Its very eclecti-cism makes postmodern art appear fragmented while its many references to a larger tradition call attention to it as incomplete. If E. M. Forster's "connect, only connect" has become the rallying cry of Postmodernists, it was Yeats who foresaw (with horror) the stylistic solution such connec-tions would lead to—in the vision that concludes his "News for the Delphic Oracle":

> From where Pan's cavern is
> Intolerable music falls.
> Foul goat-head, brutal arm appear,
> Belly, shoulder, bum,
> Flash fishlike; nymphs and satyrs
> Copulate in the foam.

Piece by piece Yeats's vision assembles itself, with the abrupt staccatos of its music emphasizing the jounces and shocks, not only between body parts, but between different species; indeed, this copulation can only produce a form even more mixed than the satyrs. Yeats apparently found such hybrids intolerable. Perhaps it is the taboos against crossbreeding that shed such a pejorative light on macaronic styles, which as far back as the Middle Ages have always been burlesque forms—just as the word *macaronic* has always carried the disgrace of its lowly origins in *macaroni*, a coarse, jumbled fare fit for peasants. But it seems time for the term *macaronic* to step out of the cupboard; for Postmodernism, with its delight in mixed codes, eclecticism, disharmonious harmony, and fragmented wholes, is essentially a macaronic sensibility and seems the offspring of a rich variety of adventurous cross-pollinations.

2

The single white and black flower growing up straight and tall against the sky-blue cover of Julia Budenz's *From The Gardens Of Flora Baum* is misleading. It fails to suggest the polychromatic riches of Flora Baum's horticulture or the complexity and range of this ambitious first book. As its two intricately-related meditative-narratives, "The Fire Escape" and "The Sheen," reach back into the classical world of Homer's epics and Ovid's *Metamorphoses*, their heroine, Flora Urania Baum (to give her full name), embarks on a journey reminiscent of the old Quest Romance. But where the crisis of the Quest Romance hero, at least before Wordsworth, was religious or philosophical, Budenz's heroine is in search of answers to aesthetic questions. Is it possible for Flora to reconcile, or at least enfold, in a single poem the contradictions passed down by our diverse cultural heritage? More specifically, what should Flora do with her love of classical beauty, if, as Budenz suspects,

> Beauty has faded with the gods
> And must no longer be invoked
> Or even named (if merely a mouthing
> Of the appellation makes us blush. . . .
>
> (from "The Sheen")

And how should she handle her desire for the sublime, her passion for ascents and infatuation with the heavens in an era of Postmodernism when, as Marjorie Perloff has observed, the romantic lyric and its offspring, the modern crisis poem, with their rapid movement toward ecstasy and epiphanic insight, are extinct?[10] Can Flora, aesthetically speaking, have it all—a sequence of intense, emotive lyrics Mallarmé would have adored along with mock heroic, parody, and a rich variety of burlesque forms whose yeasty fertility would have delighted Thomas Nashe? A postmodern poetics of "both . . . and"?[11] A macaronics even?

These opposing aesthetics are crucial to Budenz for two reasons. First, Budenz cannot simply reject the romantic tradition. Her fascination with the way mind connects and assembles inner and outer realities evolves from a Wordsworthian interest in making subjective experience the subject of the poem. Secondly, recent developments in quantum physics suggest a paradoxical universe in which light is understood to be both matter and energy; given such blatant inconsistency in the macrocosm, shouldn't artistic form be equally complex and contradictory—"Like something almost possessed, / Restful and never at rest" ("The Sheen")? Shouldn't poetry aspire to a new, more inclusive wholeness? Marjorie Perloff has argued that

> Postmodernism in poetry . . . begins in the urge to return the material
> so rigidly excluded—political, ethical, historical, philosophical—to
> the domain of poetry, which is to say that the Romantic lyric, the
> poem as expression of a moment of absolute insight, of emotion
> crystallized into a timeless patterns [sic!], gives way to a poetry that
> can, once again, accommodate narrative and didacticism, the serious
> and the comic, verse and prose. . . . Minor poets continue to write
> neo-Romantic lyric; in this context, the attack on television and the
> media as the enemy can be seen to be a kind of defensive nostalgia.
> At the same time a new poetry is emerging that wants to open the
> field.[12]

Opening the field is important to Budenz because she is both a romantic and an anti-romantic, and of course, her fence-sitting provides one more reason for her to welcome an aesthetics that can embrace contradictions. Usually, Budenz sloughs off onto Flora her romantic tendencies, in the way that Wallace Stevens gave to Crispin his own attraction to the florid and Flaubert yielded to Emma Bovary his languor and lyrical outbursts. Charles Jencks has noted that Postmodernism's detractors equate the movement with parody and pastiche,[13] but in doing so, they miss the double stance of many Postmodernists. For unlike Flaubert and Stevens, Budenz does not reject her own romantic leanings; instead, her poems allow her conflicted feelings to co-exist unresolved. Such wavering, which is due to the loss of a unifying center, is reflected in a wobbly tone. But isn't that tone the true center for a macaronic sensibility?

Perloff remarks that in postmodern poetry "the lyric voice gives way to multiple voices or voice fragments,"[14] and it's interesting to consider in this light that the title of *The Waste Land*, before Eliot bowed to Pound's aesthetic wisdom, was *He Do The Police In Different Voices*, which of course calls attention to the narrator as multiple. In suggesting its present title, Pound substituted for the narrator's fragmentation the High Modernist's response to shattered wholeness—malaise and enervation—and in a way, transformed a poem well on the road to being postmodern into one that was modern. Budenz's contradictory stance leads to the breakdown of her own narrator who occasionally speaks in the first person singular, but more often narrates her poems with Flora or *she* or even *you* as the protagonist. Just how she maintains her contradictory attitude toward her romantic leanings can be seen in this passage from "The Sheen" where the narrator splits into a a *she* and a *you*:

> Because it was quite enough
> Or because it was not quite enough,
> The intersection of tree and sky
> Seemed the clearest clear, the truest
> Gold, the happiest blue. And wading out
> From the bright strand into the bright
> Azure she began to feel
> On ankles, on thighs, on shoulders the eternal
> Swirl, the eternal pull.
> Is there a tide in the sky?
> Is there an undertow in the sky?
>
> No, you can't say these things.
> You can't say any of these things.

You can't say any of these things because romantic yearnings for oceanic mergers have become embarrassingly passé. But by the time the reader reaches the two-line disclaimer, which sounds like the poet's own critical response to what was rapidly becoming a neo-romantic lyric, these things have been said. What's more, the entire passage keeps asserting Budenz's desire to have everything at least two ways. So instead of merging, critic and poet co-exist in what Ashbery might call the "cooperative new climate,"[15] a postmodern consciousness restlessly aware of multiple facets. This sensibility is, in fact, shared by Hunting. In "Subsistence Level," her speaker asserts, "my vision's / cut to facets," while in "Lives of the Poet," the narrator compares the eye of the owl to "a single agate / cut in two / by a frugal crafter,"—that owl eye also the poet's, since the poem is broken down into glints and nuggets that flash sharp, autonomous perceptions. In Budenz's passage, too, the style reflects the poet's split vision. On the one hand, its many doublings, especially those hammered down by the mono-rhymes—"quite enough / quite enough," "sky, / sky," and "these things / these things"—make everything seem *un peu trop*, as if mocking the romantic heroine's yearnings for intensity. Surely, if "eternal swirl" is quite enough, "eternal pull" must be quite, quite enough. And when Budenz specifies where her heroine feels that pull—on her ankles, her thighs, her shoulders—the enumeration of body parts slyly implies she is about to drown in her old-fashioned desires, which are made to seem all the more old-hat by the intentionally romantic diction. *azure* (for sky), *truest gold*, *happiest blue*, and *strand*. But on the other hand, the doubling of so many phrases seems to be a desperate attempt to ward off the extinction of the romantic lyric, a charm which says everything twice to ensure its preservation.[16] Perhaps, the postmodern urgency "to embrace the entire" is a similarly magical gesture, an effort to stop up the hole created when the center was lost.

If all this seems to prove that you can't tell a book by its cover, the back of the book jacket in this case is a better guide to the poet's encyclopedic sweep, informing the reader that Budenz, a former instructor of classics, was, at least at the time of publication, with the history of science department at Harvard. She is now with that university's English department. But who exactly is Flora Baum? What are her gardens? And how do they grow?

Though Flora's identity is hinted at in the first poem, "The Fire Escape," it is not until "The Sheen" that she is formally introduced.

> My name is Flora Urania Baum. My home,
> which I seek, is Ithaca Island, on which stands
> A mountain rich in trees and rainbow flowers
> With summits rising far above the gray
> Of rains and mists and clouds into the great

Blue binding of our black-cased world. I seek tall oaks
And polychromatic flowerets—gold crepe, crimson
Silk, peach satin, velvet prussian blue,
And lace of burnt sienna. I must read,
Then, the candid letters on the spine.

As her three names indicate, Flora Urania Baum is a linguistic and cultural
hybrid. Flora was, of course, the ancient Roman goddess of flowers, and
from her Latin name comes, not only *Florida*, a place of flourishing
blooms, as Flora Baum duly notes—"Florida, said Flora, is the land of
flowers" ("The Fire Escape")—but also *florid*, a word which designates
flushed complexions (and yes, Flora's romantic tendencies do make Budenz blush at times), as well as flowery, overblown styles of writing (to
which Flora, like Crispin's third daughter, the "pearly poetess," is frequently attracted). Her middle name, Urania, alludes to the muse who
presides over astrology and whose name, in Greek, means *heavenly* or
celestial. In *Paradise Lost*, Milton calls Urania the sister of Wisdom and
makes her the spirit of loftiest poetry. So, like Flora, Urania is also associated with a style of writing. Finally, Flora's cognomen, *Baum*, is the
German word for *tree*. Unlike the colorful flowers whose ambrosial scents
carry on the breeze, trees root deep in the soil. At the same time, their
branches reach up to the sky. Trees were even the models for the classical
columns of Greek temples,[17] particularly the Ionic column, and on several
occasions in "The Sheen," Budenz suggests the close relationship between
the two forms: "stone gray columns of royal palm," "The Ionian white
and gold / Of the birches lined the portico," and "The elm, though
American, not Ionic, / Combined Ionicity of line / And curve with its
barbarous exuberance." As proto-column, the tree has a prominent place
in Budenz's temple, serving as a link between two realms, earth and
heaven, and two styles of writing, down-to-earth and lofty.

Flora Urania Baum is then a composite, rather like those peculiar portraits that Arcimboldo (1527–93) painted for Maximilian, anamorphic
faces which take on greater and greater complexity as the viewer looks at
them: the *Cook*, with a turnip for a nose, onions for cheeks, carrot for an
ear, serving dish for a hat; as well as his *Summer* and *Autumn*, allegories
of the seasons, which are not only heads, but heaps of vegetables, like the
Cook, and also visual puns. Roland Barthes has pointed out that the portraits even introduce verbal puns and so are made up of words as well as

images: At least in French, writes Barthes, "the botanic *prunella* becomes
the ocular *prunelle*, our word for eyeball."[18] Similarly, Flora Baum is not
only a woman, the poet's alter-ego, but also a cluster of natural elements
(flower, sky, tree), and therefore an emblem for gardens. It is even possible to think of her names as words and of her identity as language itself.
For Flora's gardens include not only trees, but also etymologies of tree
names—in particular, the Malaysian cajeput and the American elm. Given
Flora's patronymic, *Baum / Tree*, these etymologies have to be read as her
lineages or family trees—that is, as witty jokes alerting the reader to
Flora's multiple identities; she is woman, things, *and words*. That she is to
be understood as language itself is further suggested by her appetite for
unusual words—*euonymus*, *deodar*, *callistemon*, *anatids*, *orpiment*, *viridity*,
gephyrism, *monoecious*, *lithospermum*, *aoede*, *ananthous*, *tormentil*, *alate*, *aureo-
lation*, and *niello*—to mention just a few not likely to be on the tip of the
reader's tongue. In other respects, too, Flora's identity is closely allied
with the dictionary and the thesaurus, for she has collected clichés, and
even composes one section of "The Fire Escape" entirely from them, a
brilliant *tour de force*. But because her three names are related to styles of
writing—florid, lofty, and earthy—she is both language and style, or that
part of the poet's sensibility that can be sublimated into text and carried
along as part of our linguistic and literary tradition.

If Flora is such a complex hybrid, then what are her gardens? While the
flowers and trees sometimes appear to be drawn from Budenz's personal
experience, more often the floriculture is bookish or literary. When Flora
identifies herself and gives her homeland, the tall oaks and flowerets she
seeks seem to be growing on the lavishly ornamented cover of a rare book,
for she speaks of gold *crepe*, crimson *silk*, peach *satin*, *velvet* prussian blue,
and *lace* of burnt sienna; or perhaps in the lush illuminations of a richly
illustrated Book of Hours, such as the one that adorned the library of Jean,
Duc de Berry. Flora's homeland is not so much the world, but the book
as symbol of the world. Given that her gardens tend to grow styles as
variegated as her flowers—along with the echoes of Eliot and Stevens
previously mentioned, there are parodies of Yeats and Homer, and even
rich burlesque styles imitative of medieval macaronic verse which interspersed Latin with the vernaculars or twisted English words to fit the
grammar of Latin—they can be thought of as *anthologies,* a word which in
Greek means *collections of flowers*. Her collections of flowers are actually
bouquets clipped from vaster literary gardens. Compendious as Flora's

gardens are, they are only a fragment of a much larger landscape, the literary tradition, as that *From* in the title of Budenz's book emphasizes.

Perhaps because they are so literary, after a while the gardens begin to resemble stage sets—the backdrops and props change continually. Royal palms and banyans replace northern elms; egrets fill in for orioles; an urban scene of falling snow follows a cerulean summer sky. Sometimes the reader looks through dirty city windows at a single oak, sometimes through the plastic and glass of an airplane to skies that are themselves gardens: "A painted sky. Skies like trees / Blunt in paintings" ("The Fire Escape"). The lighting changes, even the atmosphere shifts from misty to dazzling. Every mood and ambience necessary for the drama is meticulously controlled, just as Budenz promised.

> A blue background. That will do for a while.
> Branching in a December dusk,
> On late azure, on early rose.
> That will do. A sudden shift
> To greenest Florida or greenest June
> With brightest flittings. That will serve.
> We suppose—superpose—the same sky,
> Turning the lights up or down,
> Filling or clearing the stage.
>
> (from "The Fire Escape")

But what exactly is the drama? Ashbery predicted that the cultural tradition would finally be converted into "ingenious shifts in scenery, a sort of 'English garden' effect."[19] In Budenz's poems, the stage sets are almost the whole show—but not quite. The poems are peopled, though primarily with fictional characters, pop-culture versions of Homer's men and women: Helen of Troy, playing the gracious hostess, stubs out her cigarette; Circe sends for a silvery Cadillac; Calypso is a bitch; Odysseus wears a soft gray suit that plays up his electric gray eyes. To some extent, the contemporizing attributes struck me as gratuitous. (Why is Helen a smoker, and not Circe? Why does Circe drive a Cadillac and not a Mercedes?) But even these fictional recreations don't seem to interest Budenz as much as beautiful forms—sky, weather, tree, whatever is simultaneously at rest and in motion. And Budenz makes sure the reader doesn't miss the point that the natural world is her stage par excellence:

Watching, to the cicadas' orchestration,
Past the goldenrod and Queen Anne's lace,
The stage where action glimmered among the columns of the trees.
There's something there.
But under the klieg afternoon
All the birds stopped playing their parts.

(from "The Sheen")

Where Ashbery's poems melt as one reads them, Budenz's stage sets move like a "slow kaleidoscope" of beautiful forms. The moving eye of the reader is enough to jostle the bits and pieces, shifting the pattern. A reader who hopes for a drama of passions will be frustrated. Instead, there is an aesthetic rhythm that progresses from Flora's yearnings for the heights to a falling away from rapturous moments of dazzling beauty. This is, of course, the rhythm Keats immortalized in the nightingale ode: the music caught at the zenith, followed by the poet's futile efforts to hold to the feverish pitch. Budenz's most impassioned thinking is concerned with beauty, the pleasures of the eye, the surface gorgeousness of the world, "De profundis surfaces" ("The Sheen"). On these she meditates, as in this passage from "The Fire Escape":

She saw the single, multitudinous elm.

The trunk with its primary branches
Is firm, is still. A motion inheres
In that stillness: all the growing, the upholding,
The struggle recorded in a stance—
Antaeus kept from the earth,
The discus almost hurled,
A slain god just arisen.

The moving branchlets with their moving
Leaves are at rest, are not uneasy,
Are at ease, are resting as unresisting,
As swans rest on the stirring stream,
As eagles rest on the warm drafts of late morning.

Here is a solitary being, self-contained
And self-directed; here two hug and kiss;
Here is the generous outreach, proffering

Of gifts; then follow revel, bacchanal
Of lifted arms, green brands alight,
Frisson of verdure; ladies come
With fans and trailing gowns.

A form, a formulation, an assertion
Builds as clauses rise, and phrases dangle
Into a green flutter of interjections
Among which cluster golden promises,
Promising the post-autumnal blank.

Buds supply the wintry punctuation.

Like so much else in Flora's gardens, the elm isn't only a tree, but an emblem. Single and multitudinous, still and in motion, self-contained and yet reaching out, it is the natural expression of all those paradoxes Budenz hopes to formalize in her poems. The earnest reader who thinks through each simile and metaphor will discover that Budenz's comparisons hold up to close examination, though even someone steeped in classical myth will move slowly toward the realization that a tree, in so far as it renews its strength through contact with the earth, is like the giant Antaeus who was nourished by keeping his feet firmly planted on his goddess-mother, the Earth. Other similes are just as chewy; the thinking they compress and concretize is as elaborate as a metaphysical conceit. In fact, the description made me think of Stanley Kunitz's early metaphysical poem, "Very Tree," which also takes organic form as a paradigm: "Here is a timeless structure wrought / Like the candelabrum of pure thought."[20] But where Kunitz's tree, with its "alliterative leaves," is utterly still, Budenz's elm, with its "green flutter of interjections," is both at rest and in motion. While the many syntactical repetitions anchor the description in a pavane performed so slowly, its movements are as controlled as the tree's almost imperceptible growth, the visual imagination is as nervous as a rabbit escaped from a magician's hat. By the third stanza, images are projected in such rapid succession that the slides jam, super-imposed: The picture of ladies with fans and trailing gowns partly collages onto the picture of the tree, with its heavy branches sweeping the ground. Even words from different linguistic traditions arrive so fast they produce a verbal logjam, with the elegant French of *verdure* and *frisson* almost slammed against Anglo-Saxon *brands* and *gowns*, the Latin *bacchanal* wedged against the French *revel*. But isn't the tree's essence precisely its contradictions (sturdy yet graceful, tough yet elegant) and the rich counterpoint of its various motions? *Frisson* provides the key not only to the elm's complicated dance, but also to the dance of Budenz's intellect. The visual imagination that sets the tree in motion sends a surge of energy through the entire passage until the shudder of leaves is the thrill of delight the reader feels.

Budenz obviously loves to slap on the tropes. Sometimes this produces passages so lushly beautiful I don't care whether they are neo-romantic or lyrical-extinct. I simply want to luxuriate in

> Remember the sky as solid,
> Motionless, metallic. Remember
> The sky of moving parts, the machine
> In full operation, the ragged clouds
> Like hares, the smoother clouds behind
> Like tortoises, the leisured moon,
> The wandering stars on their old grand tour,
> And the fixed stars, stuck,
> Unstuck, and stuck again
> Without clogging the parade. I mix
> my metaphors. The sky,
> Like fire, like frost, transforms
> Its tropes as one applies them, slapping
> Ferns and palms and hills and stars
> Around like paint. Remember
> The pigmentation, blue, as cold
> As frost, ablaze like flame,
>
> (from "The Sheen")

Budenz is always compelling when she can find a natural pattern to express her aesthetic. But sometimes her parade of forms does become clogged. The busyness of the last pages of "The Sheen" made me feel as if I had entered a clock shop, all the machines whirring at once. If forms are to be appreciated, there needs to be enough space for the reader to move around in. "The Fire Escape" is more successful than "The Sheen" because it has found its structure, the circle described by the uroborus: Through a play on words the solid fire escape on which the poet spreads her red blanket in the opening sections is finally transformed into an escape from a fire, seemingly ignited by the intensity of the poet's vision. Like the mythical snake that takes its own tail into its mouth, the poem concludes by consuming itself. I would have preferred a kenosis at the end of "The Sheen," an emptying out that would have left me filled. Despite the fact that "The Sheen" can't quite bring itself to end, Budenz's book is no less stunning and commanding of attention than a marble Aphrodite missing a nose or an arm. It's still worth making the grand tour.

3

Where Budenz favors multilayered words unstable as radioactive elements, words whose permutations set off chain reactions of new meanings, Hunting's ideal words have the hard, annealed beauty of broken glass, shards, splinters of ice. Hunting loves words that have the tactile magic, the self-containment of talismanic objects: words like *glint*, *daz*, *hexad*, *glit*, *obelisk*, *mosques*, *phalanx*, *quirks*, *phials*, *quoise*, words that invite the reader to pronounce them, say them aloud, take them into the mouth, surround them with the lips, bite and polish them. Hunting loves words that glisten with the refractive light of emerald and diamond, and I suspect she would agree with André Breton's assertion:

> There could be no higher artistic teaching than that of the crystal. The work of art, just like any fragment of human life considered in its deepest meaning, seems to me devoid of value if it does not offer the hardness . . . the luster on every interior and exterior facet, of crystal.[21]

Hunting's love of the obdurate makes her prefer analogy to metaphor. Even when things resemble one another in her poems, they do not lose their shape, do not melt like mist and cloud. Consequently, her poems appear to have disengaged from some mysterious landscape of ice. Aloof, insular, they float past the reader or the reader voyages past them, admiring their cool, fractile beauty, their gleaming facets, the art that carved and polished them. Each one gives the impression of a self-contained world, an experiment not likely to be repeated, that challenges the reader to tease out connections.

Hunting's aesthetic finds its fullest expression in her most recent work, particularly in "Dream Cities," which shares with conceptual artist Robert Smithson's own dream cities a fascination with the remote, the marginal. "Consider," wrote Smithson,

> a 'City of Ice' in the Arctic, that would contain frigid labyrinths, glacial pyramids, and towers of snow, all built according to strict abstract systems. Or an amorphous 'City of Sand' that would be nothing but artificial dunes and shallow sand pits.[22]

According to Smithson, "All language becomes an alphabet of sites,"[23] and Hunting's "Dream Cities," especially her "City of Glass," seem to be precisely such linguistic sites, the words turning up as glossy debris broken off from slag heaps or vast mineral deposits:

towrs	the traveller's eye	goal	chalce	thyst		
false	dime	paque	spark	clear	struck	
ester	sili	lime	actual	mark	awns	spun
wares	heap	ice	rosy	rads	let	cabbages ruta
merle	transpar	window	finned	scales	early	
breakrs	play	salt	live	shine	jasp	pearl

What is the reader to do with such a trove? Examined one by one, each word seems a rare find on the shelf of a mineral shop, though careful inspection shows that some words are chipped. *Thyst* has broken off from *amethyst*; *breakrs* has lost an *e*; and *rads*, *let*, and *ruta* are no longer whole *radishes*, *lettuce*, and *rutabago*. While some words cluster because of similar sounds (*window* and *finned*, *chalce* and *thyst*), others congregate because they *shine* (*shine*, *jasp*, *pearl*) or because they are iridescent (*finned*, *scales*). How connections are to be made will depend on whether a reader's bent is metaphoric or narrative. Perhaps "City of Glass" is a metaphor for the ocean. Given the words *breakrs*, *salt*, *shine*, *pearl*, *finned*, *scales*, *spark*, *clear*, *ice*, and *towrs*, that seems like a good direction to take. At times, the sea does appear frozen, and besides, Hunting's own bent is to make the fluid and continually changing solid, even if solidification means fragmentation. Or perhaps a traveler's eye is taking in a magical city, its towers of jasper and pearl, its market *wares*; its vegetables, petrified as mineral wood, *transparent* as *windows*, which shatter when touched. Or is the "City of Glass" a center where language is transformed into poetry, a demonstration of how words pressure one another to connect and take on meanings, a sea that keeps churning out stories and metaphors. Because Hunting gives no syntactical directions, her verbal scree becomes a seemingly inexhaustible source, though the reader will discover that it's nearly impossible to make all the words fit one story. The reader keeps completing the jigsaw puzzle only to find that there is always a piece left over. As Perloff has observed about Ashbery's poetry, the images do not coalesce "into a symbolic network. There is no whole to which these parts may be said to belong."[24] Consequently, despite the verbal profusion, the reader is left with a sense of incompleteness.

If one compares Hunting's recent word-huddles with earlier, more traditional poems, a first impression may take in only the vast difference in styles, as, for example, in this opening passage of "Year-Round":

> With what deceptive
> gradualness the summer guests
> depart,
> bearing the various trophies
> of their stay, shells, driftwood
> antlers, a seabird's skull,
> leaving
> for our instruction shards
> of the season's visit: sand on the stairs,
> odd sneakers, a torn sweater, a child's ball,
> and on the dressing table an unmailed letter.

But even in this poem from her first book, *After The Stravinsky Concert* (1969), Hunting seems unusually interested in what she calls "shards," objects left over from a larger story, here a summer vacation by the sea. Implicit in this passage is the aesthetic of debris, just as implicit in Budenz's unpeopled stage sets there is what Jean Baudrillard calls "the aesthetics of ruins."[25] What is it that makes such an aesthetic attractive to Hunting? If the reader can trust as genuine autobiography Hunting's poems concerned with family, her aesthetic would appear to have had its origins in such childhood experiences as this one in "Cimmerian," the poem that gave the title to her second book. Here the poet's mother has "rummaged" a square of black

velvet from another of her ages, summoned
me to the open casement window where we leaned
to spread the black patch to catch flakes,
each, she said, perfect, and no two alike,
perfection in the plan and in the execution,
she said, becoming excited with morality
while I saw only changes in the air to earth
the frozen pitch, star-shot
without sound, feather-soft down
from the breast of the owl gray sky
(four o'clock in the afternoon),
plume bristles from the flight of the Arctic fox,
shards of the great icefloe, and ashes
of the fire of sped virtues' light—
I stuck my private tongue out to receive
a flake quick and cool as a wafer
to my topmost earthern root,
but her hair blew in my mouth with the wind,
we were close, her strong
arm rosy with the challenge held
the lovely litter of silence on a shred of night.

In this sumptuous scene, mother, child, and poet remembering back attempt to make palpable and permanent what is tantalizingly ephemeral:
the mother by attempting to capture momentarily the snowflakes, each
with its distinct, crystalline shape; the child by attempting to consume the
beauty that ravishes her, which she takes as communion. Now the poet
thinks back to the time when she and her mother lived like the Cimmeri-
ans, those mythical people who dwelt in a remote realm of mist and gloom,
and wants to give form not only to the snow crystals, those needles,
hexagons, drums, and stars her mother trapped on velvet, but also to what
she describes as "changes in the air to earth" and even to feelings unexpressed at the time: the rare closeness she felt with her mother, that near
merger of the two in which, nevertheless, she felt them both distinct,
separate. Where the mother caught the snow crystals on a patch of velvet,
the poet holds them through the repetition of sounds in *black*, *patch*, *catch*,
and *flake*, and, at the same time, sustains a mood as likely to melt away
as the snowflakes. Even the silence of the "feather-soft-down" is sounded,

becomes, in fact, a shaped sound as Hunting rhymes *down* with *sound* and then with *owl* in the next line, thus drawing out the music of the inaudible the way the damper pedal on a piano will allow a note to linger. From something just tangible enough to be heard, the silence becomes more and more sensuously present as the snowflakes are imaged first as "feather-soft-down," next as "plume bristles," then as "shards of ice," and finally as "lovely litter of silence." The gradation of size or thickness, as the speaker mentions *down*, *bristle*, *shard*, then *litter*, is what makes the images graspable. While the mother attempts to fix the beauty of the scene in moral plan and execution, a schema the child rejects, the poet succeeds in keeping before the reader a rapture that threatens to disperse in the wind, as Dante's vision did, by situating it in the same sensuous reality the child took into her mouth. While the snowflakes must finally have melted on the velvet, the tableau the poet has described stays with the reader, a moment of beauty made indestructible.

The desire to make the fluid, the transient, even the immaterial tangibly real asserts itself in many of Hunting's poems and is the other side of the postmodern need to make a poem so in tune with instability and flux that it melts or changes as it is read. Hunting wants to snatch some souvenir from the flood—a pebble, a nuggety word, a *daz*. And "The Gathering" shows her again shaping the immaterial. As the speaker climbs downstairs in the early morning, silence, as well as the past, become forms so solid an artisan could punch holes in them:

> Long ago
> this morning,
> flattening myself
> against my spine, I try
> the top stair.
> It makes no outcry, so I test
> the next, and it receives me too.
> The third step creaks
> loudly; it makes a hole
> in silence. I draw my foot back just in time

Because of the power of the present tense, an experience of long ago is sucked forward, the past flattened against the here-and-now like the speaker against her spine. What happened then to the speaker, as child, is happening to her now, this morning. But just as the past is made to creak loudly in the present, silence is not allowed to remain an absence. Since the speaker can make a hole in it, silence is substantial, a stuff to be contended with; it is what organizes sound, structuring its tones and pitches. "One should feel as if one is playing the silence,"[26] says David Soyer, cellist for the Guarneri Quartet. And Hunting, whose musical sensibility was trained at the New England Conservatory of Music, continues to play the silence in this poem when the child discovers her grandmother in the kitchen:

> Oh, it's you!
> she says, and, Good: you can pit cherries.
> But I don't know
> how, I whine. She
> shows me how my thumb can pop
> the pit out neat as an eyeball. Charmed,
> I set to work, we set to work.
> "Juice makes a cherry," says the woman wisely,
> sticking in stalks
> pendent with bloom. "I wouldn't give a fig
> for a cherry without juice."

Though Hunting never explicitly states the connection between the child's making a hole in silence as she descends the stairs and the grandmother's popping holes in cherries, the reader senses the analogy and suddenly feels the pit of silence pop out neat as an eyeball, too. And of course, those short, hard words whose staccatos tap out a rhythm that keeps time with the pitting of the cherries are also punching holes in the silence. Juice may make the cherry, but words that hammer and rap have struck this poem from the silence.

As early as "The Gathering," Hunting is already assembling her scenes from fragments, a strategy she will perfect in her later poems. In the earlier poems the fragments are memorable scenes broken away from a larger past, like the clutter of summer houses. In "Beyond The Summerhouse," a poem from her second book, Hunting has started to use words as fragments, as in this visit to a cave where her language achieves a hard-edged mineral presence:

Echo echo *ecce*
wrenched and infinitely injured
voices ricochet
from shelves and corners mock

and hoot mimick
birds at aurorean carol
animals at dusk
snufflings (if we have met walls

fingers come wet away) and human
susurrations
in the interstices
hum

silence
the silence
the silence runs
like water in the dark

over the rock of itself
within this rough dome of this dark
I stumble
something is thrust

at me instantly he lends
he is lending
bending towards me in the avocal silence
he lendeth me

his stick
which I strike
against a stalactite like a bell
hollow the knell redounds

from that inverted steeple
bleak and deep the toll
recoil
fooled foiled again I reel

Here the wrenched rhythms appear to be feeling their way, word by word,
like a spelunker groping in the darkness of a cave. But the poet as spelunker is feeling for rhythms and new sounds, striking *hoot* and *echo* from
rock with bare hands, and "fingers come wet away" as if these noises were

so primordial they were watery as birth. Blind, not knowing where she is going, the poet rings with the weird music of every unknown she stumbles against. Since this scene is part of a much longer poem in which the narrator is searching for a way back to her childhood, trying to distinguish false memory from true memory, her confusion in the cave acts out a deeper psychological confusion. Even when, in an earlier section, she sees after long absence the house where she grew up, it clashes with what she remembers:

> —but stop!
> He is taking me wrong
> the wrong way around
> away from the facade
>
> the facade is what I want

Her repetition of the word *facade* suggests that what she wants is the false memory. However, since reality and illusion are never sorted out in this poem (a task that would be as difficult as distinguishing between sound and echo in the cave), the reader is also left with fragments, never certain how much of the story coincides with lived reality or how much is derived from the world of the imagination; a complex mixture of childhood games, scenes remembered from prints, and panoramas recalled from novels and films.

One thing is certain, the world of childhood was as thrillingly fluid as the avocal silence that runs "like water in the dark / over the rock of itself." The child's identity consisted of discontinuities, her many selves no different from the doll's many selves—as here:

> I am spying
> my roots like willow
> my branches in disguise
> the childish stream of prattle
>
> enters my leaves: "Your name
> what is your name today?"
> "My name today is Ben. . . ."
> Amused: "What does Ben do
>
> today?"
> "Fetches stick and growls!"

And to the other the same:
"What is your name today?"

"My name is Bet I am the doll—"
"Ben must take Bet
by the throat and shake her so—"
"To hurt her?" "Just a bit . . .

She must get down and beg
for mercy. . . . Oh
well done!" A slight clapping
as at chamber music

and then the snap of steel:
"What is my name forever?"
Syllables on the stream
sighing the ripples of.

If one child, who takes the name Ben, pretends to be a dog, then is another child playing at being Bet, the doll? The children's identities are simultaneously fluid and fragmented, "syllables on the stream," and this fugue of voices seems a model for Hunting's book, itself rich in voices and personas, splinters of personality that shiver into life. No one, it would seem, has any name forever, and Hunting's many selves keep sighing the ripples of something larger, elusive.

In her most recent work, Hunting has become even more daring in her experiments with fragmented vision, though still using her syntactic scree and verbal talus to convey emotional dislocation. In "Notes From the Voyage," the last poem in her collection, a cruise ship called the *Leviathan*, not only appears to allude to a ship by that name, sunk during World War II, but also, on account of its posh ambience, to the *Titanic*; while these allusions set the reader up to expect catastrophe, nothing cataclysmic occurs during the voyage, though the poem's narrator notes "how on every voyage there is one sensing / the iceberg's breath at the salt-glazed window." Certainly, on this crossing, *that one* is the reader. The result? "Notes From the Voyage," despite its allusiveness, remains elusive, becomes its own imaginary place, and the fragments of description and dialogue contribute to the reader's sense of dislocation and alienation:

Informal sitting lady from Buffalo in vermeil
silent spouse the siren with a Stetsoned male

> in her eyes echoes of cocaine that radiance
> a German expert in cement
> firm in Florida reverts to Prussian when the waiter
> mistakes his order of tomato soup for juice
> of lamb for ham raps out questions: "Oh, I am
> supposed to apologize? I was in the wrong?"
> Buffalo croon, "It was only natural . . ."
> the wife sealed in gray waiter considers
> jumping overboard our fragile raft trembles
> under star-seeded skies in the red saloon.

With the exception of the questions asked by the German expert in cement, the passage is an aggregate of sentence fragments, which allow for quick takes, even faster impressions, the verbs stowed away in the hold. This is a cinematic view of shipboard dining, composed of the briefest phrases Hunting can tap out without being misunderstood. Is this a Jamesian plot burlesqued? A quick sketch of a scene for a film? With all the clues pointing in different directions, one or two pieces get left out of the completed puzzle; and consequently, whatever whole the reader comes up with always feels incomplete. Still, the scene is fired to a hard glaze, as if finish or polish meant the same as finished. A similar game is played with those delicious rhymes, *soup / juice* and *lamb / ham*. Traditionally, rhymes are the binding force, the strings of sound around which a poem crystallizes. But in this scene, it is the similar sounds of certain words that confuse the waiter and lead to friction at the dinner table. What makes for order in the poem makes for chaos in reality. Moreover, even though the poem seems to match (or rhyme with) certain literary plots and historical situations, it invariably turns out that the poem only resembles them in part. Wherever the reader looks long and hard, there are fracture lines and cracks.

There are two reasons for Hunting's attraction to fragments. She has an artisan's appreciation of her materials, the rich variety of word textures. Like the carpenter who narrates a section of "Easter in New England," Hunting seems to say, "Just run your thumb along one side." Her poems aspire to the solidified brilliance of *glass songs*, *phials*, *quoise*, to the mineral presence of her dream cities, where "the yellow stone dish of the sun / the white stone cup of the moon" ("City of Stone") appear to have been carved by a folk artist. In "Notes From the Voyage," whole passages approach abstract art—not paintings, but installation pieces whose rough, conglomerate beauty seems slicked over with varnish, as in this passage which comes toward the end of the poem:

> Rouge ruffles Patagonian decor
> papier-mâché glyptodonts rocks thoroacuses
> guanacoes manadoroes Sultans mandarins
> Mrs Foshee traces of weeping mascara
> mermaid siren in green scales twists
> with male orca coruscating fin dorsal
> beneath incongrous chandeliers in the Grand Concourse
> the band pumps pumps pumps
> under the din for your leisure and pleasure
> fin de siècle finesse of the body
> corporeal cells ages raging to dance
> disguised degaussed de gustibus dance!

At this linguistic bash, words congregate like barnacles cemented to the ship's hull, spiny oysters embedded in coral, and yet the glitzy textures slyly intimate the appearance of the ship's passengers: crustaceoned like those kitsch pocketbooks, coruscating mermaids and sea monsters, on sale, no doubt, in the ship's many shops. As the band pumps pumps pumps, the reader can almost hear the thumping hearts in this geriatric ballroom where the elderly dancers appear blown up like party balloons. In their garish attires, they could be sultans and Chinese mandarins at a costume ball that also has room for a few bizarre animals: *glyptodonts*, extinct armadillos whose carapaces hint at the thick plates of make-up covering the faces of the (equally obsolete?) women; South American *guanacoes*, odd, camel-like mammals without the hump, whose name sounds like something a lot more unpleasant, *guano*, the excrement of sea birds found along some parts of the South American coast this cruise may be visiting. The most delightfully catty comment is made by the word *mandarins*, which brings to mind not only spiny citrus trees bearing orange, loose-skinned fruit, but also grotesque seated figures in Chinese costume with heads and hands so fixed as to continue nodding once set in motion. Both meanings take nasty swipes at the passengers, suggesting slack-skinned faces oranged by make-up, as well as the uncontrollable tremors of these octogenarians. The last line sums up the dreadful scene. The dancers look so freakish they seem *disguised.* What's more, they are *degaussed.* Commonly referring to ships made non-magnetic so that they will not detonate mines, here the word suggests that the passengers have lost their animal magnetism or power to attract. But the sound of the word insinuates something differ-ent—that the pumped-up dancers have been *de-gassed* and suddenly lost all their air, fizzing out with exhaustion like so many deflated balloons. And if the air has been let out of them, then surely another kind of detonation has been prevented. However, *degaussed* is a word that also teases, one of the poem's clues that mislead the reader into thinking that this ship may be the *Leviathan* that was blown up in another way entirely when it hit a mine during World War II. Finally, *de gustibus* (from the Latin *degusto,* meaning *to taste* and *to lick*) compresses two opposite impressions: the gusto of the dancers, obviously relishing the evening's entertainment, and the equally powerful distaste of the speaker, which communicates itself through an excremental vision Swift would have appreciated. Besides the *guanacoes / guano* and *degaussed / de-gassed* associations, there is *thoroacuses,* a farrago Hunting hashes up by mixing *thorax* (the part of the body which contains the pumping heart and lungs) with *cloaca* (with its own unsavory connotations). But besides their dictionary meanings, *disguised, degaussed,* and *de gustibus* all sound as if the speaker were shouting above the night club din—*disgusting!* Indeed, her words pile up into a witty, yet disturbing, scene of lavishly decorated waste. Hunting has a talent for constructing scenarios, characters, even her narrators, out of significant parts, and sometimes, as here, out of the material world that is their habitat, an environment that appears to have rubbed off on its inhabitants through long and frequent association.

Of course, to the extent that some words, like *glyptodont, thoroacuses,* and *orca,* make the mouth work so much that they feel lumpy and therefore graspable, they give the poet something to hold onto in a world that is continually slipping away. Though solid, they remain faithful to Hunting's sense of things as splintered, fractured, a pyramid of shards. Hunting's speakers, like their world, often seem unravelled, unable to construct a unified self-image:

> my two eyes thus
> my nose my mouth I imagine
> my image in the mirror

except for the mark the blemish
where I have placed
my finger on my lips

(from "Objects Of Vision")

Is the speaker looking at her reflection in a mirror? Or is she imagining her nose and mouth, imagining even the mirror? With the syntax so ambiguous, the description annuls itself, decomposes, leaving the reader vaguely uneasy. But since the speaker would appear to be a whole greater than her reflection, she is actually creating herself through concealment, the finger on the lips, like that gesture which means "Shush! Be quiet!", implying that there is more to be said. But there are other ways in which objects do not match their reflections in this poem:

Leaning over the edge
looking down into the well
one sees an eye
magnified by water

surrounded by stone
one's eye reflected
a welling of darkness
one could drown in that eye

The eye, a fragment, appears greater than the body and threatens to swallow it up. In a sense, the world does drown in the poet's eye, particularly the hungry eye of the postmodern poet, sucking up every stump and quark for safe keeping. But as viewed here, the poet's eye is alien and grotesque: It is not *her* eye, but *an* eye, looking up from the depths it has taken in and yet is part of. This poem is rich with confusions between wholes and parts, objects and images, the cratered moon and the "sensational coin" it becomes inside the brain of an old man who, like Hunting, is a hoarder, fragmenting the world even as he attempts to collect its motes and leaves.

In "Emergent Occasions," Hunting brings about a different kind of dislocation. The poem is made up of passages culled from Mary Shelley's *Journals,* as a note on the credits page informs. But where the *Journals* suggest that Mary Shelley was attempting to locate herself more deeply in the cultures of the countries she was visiting (in Italy, she read Dante,

Virgil, and Livy), Hunting disorients Mary Shelley's impressions by leaving out the larger context, as in this short passage from a section titled "Italy".

> Go to the Opera in the evening; we do not know
> the name of it and cannot make out the story.
> The singers are very good.

In Mary Shelley's *Journals*[27] these observations are part of a slightly larger entry which records that the day has been spent walking around the town of Turin. These additional facts make the comments on the opera much less disquieting. Besides, we know who the speaker is and from previous entries we can surmise that she went to the opera with her husband, possibly with Byron and his daughter. Excerpted by Hunting, the observations remain sharp, precise, clear. But who is the speaker? An ingenue? A chaperone? And who is accompanying her? Philistine tourists? We no longer know, and even the clarity of the record becomes unsettling when so much else is uncertain. Had Hunting wanted the reader to know the speaker was Mary Shelley, wouldn't she have referred to her in the poem's title? Or at least in an epigraph, as poets usually do when they want to make background material part of the poem? Hunting has gone out of her way to make the passage mysterious, to uproot it and make it part of "a floating present" that stymies the reader. Many of Hunting's poems, in fact, refuse to be pinned down to any specific time and place: They might be set in a Jamesian Europe or a Jamesian New England; or perhaps they record as lived experience scenes from paintings, book illustrations, posters. "We imagine gone, / what we are not sure existed even once," says the speaker of "Revenant," after describing a group of Victorian panel paintings.

Because Hunting frequently plays a postmodern style off against intentionally old-fashioned images (belvederes, white umbrellas, and plump girls with aprons smelling of starch) and intentionally old-fashioned diction (*prattle, domestic flurry, debouches,* and *daughter of the estate*), her poems are patently artificial. Yet, there is something funky about such oddly assembled poems, as if a girl with a slicked punk hairdo had suddenly appeared in prim Victorian lace purchased at a thrift shop. Poems that strive for the crystalline solidity of semi-precious litter are, of course, calling attention to themselves as fabricated: Even mineral fragments are almost *objets d'art*. But I suspect that these poems strive so hard to be noticed as assemblages of *splinters, sound, sand, glass birds, quirks,* and *fountains* because Hunting intends them to be an art of linguistic rubble, as well as an art of what survives the wreckage of personal and historical memory, the many broken-off pieces fused with a perdurable glaze that purposely lets the cracks and sharp cleavages show through.

Notes

1. See, for example, Dore Ashton's recent attack on Postmodernism, "Post-Modern Postures," *Art International* (Summer 1988), pp. 30–35. Ashton thinks of the movement as a monster out of a sci-fi film: "As this protoplasmic thing called Post-Modernism slowly crawls over our intellectual horizon . . . ." (p. 30). For a penetrating critique (from a conservative) of an earlier stage of Postmodernism, see Gerald Graff, "The Myth of the Postmodernist Breakthrough," *TriQuarterly* 26 (1973), pp. 383–417.
2. Wallace Stevens, "Chaos in Motion and Not in Motion," *The Collected Poems* (New York: Alfred A. Knopf, 1954), p. 357.
3. For explicit acknowledgement of the absent center, see, of course, his "As You Came From The Holy Land," *Self-Portrait in a Convex Mirror* (New York: The Viking Press, 1975), p. 6, which sets up a dialogue with Yeats's "The Second Coming." For another dialogue between a Postmodernist and a Modernist, see William Bronk's "There Is Ignorant Silence in the Center of Things," *Life Supports: New And Collected Poems* (San Francisco: North Point Press, 1982), which rejects Robert Frost's solution in "Directive" as too easy. For other poems concerned with the absent center, see May Swenson's "Banyon," in *In Other Words* (New York: Alfred A. Knopf, 1987), p. 95; and Pablo Neruda's "Everybody," *The American Poetry Review* (Sept / Oct 1988), p. 29. And for a poem which situates itself in fragmentation, see Carolyn Forché's, "In The Garden Of Shukkei-En," *Provincetown Arts* (1988), p. 99.
4. Charles Jencks, "The New Classicism and its Emergent Rules," *Architectural Design,* vol. 58, no. 1 / 2 (1988), p. 30.
5. Ibid., p. 26.
6. "The New Spirit" is the title of the first poem in Ashbery's *Three Poems.*
7. Wallace Stevens, "Notes Toward A Supreme Fiction," *The Collected Poems,* p. 402 & p. 403.
8. John Ashbery, "The Ice Storm," *April Galleons* (New York: Penguin Books, 1988), p. 91.

9. As quoted in Charles Jencks, *The Language of Post-Modern Architecture,* 3rd ed., (New York: Rizzoli, 1981), p. 82.

10. Marjorie Perloff, *The Dance of the Intellect: Studies in the Poetry of the Pound Tradition* (Cambridge: Cambridge University Press, 1985), pp. 175–76. But as the entire chapter is relevant, see "Postmodernism and the Impasse of the Lyric," pp. 172–200.

11. Jencks, "The New Classicism and its Emergent Rules," p. 28. But Jencks borrows this phrase from August Strindberg. See James McFarlane, "The Mind of Modernism," *Modernism 1890–1930,* eds. Malcolm Bradbury & James McFarlane (Harmondsworth: Penguin Books, 1976), p. 88.

12. Perloff, *The Dance of the Intellect,* pp. 180–81.

13. Jencks, "The New Classicism and its Emergent Rules," p. 28.

14. Perloff, *The Dance of the Intellect,* p. 183.

15. John Ashbery, "The System," *Three Poems,* p. 63.

16. On doubling as a psychological device to ensure preservation, see Sigmund Freud, "The 'Uncanny'," *Studies in Parapsychology,* ed. Philip Rieff (New York: Collier Books, 1963), p. 40. Freud's essay was first published in 1919. See also Freud's *The Interpretation of Dreams* (New York: Avon, 1963), p. 392, published in its present revised and enlarged form in 1930.

17. See Jess M. Gellrich, *The Idea of the Book in the Middle Ages: Language Theory, Mythology, and Fiction* (Ithaca: Cornell University Press, 1985), pp. 53–54; Sigfried Giedion, *The Eternal Present,* vol. 2 (New York: Bollingen Foundation, 1964), p. 287; Vincent Scully, *The Earth, The Temple and the Gods: Greek Sacred Architecture* (New Haven: Yale University Press, 1962), pp. 128, 103–105.

18. Roland Barthes, "Arcimboldo, Or Magician and Rhetoriqueur," in *The Responsibility of Forms: Critical Essays on Music, Art, and Representation* trans. Richard Howard, (New York: Hill and Wang, 1985), p. 130.

19. John Ashbery, "The New Spirit," *Three Poems,* p. 27. See also Catherine Francblin's "An Interview with Jean Baudrillard," in *FlashArt* (Oct / Nov 1986), pp. 54–55, which quotes Baudrillard: "Everyone seems to be saying 'I am setting up a new stage, but in this space, in this new light, no one will ever move, there will be no play.' That is rather the way I see the environment of Buren at the Palais Royal: a stage set in another set. That always seems to me to be a part of the aesthetics of ruins. The actors have disappeared; only the backstage and parts of the stage-sets remain!"

20. Stanley Kunitz, "Very Tree," *The Poems of Stanley Kunitz: 1928–1978* (Boston: Little, Brown and Company, 1979), p. 207.

21. André Breton, *Mad Love,* trans. Mary Ann Caws (Lincoln: University of Nebraska Press, 1987), p. 11.

22. Robert Smithson, "Towards the Development of an Air Terminal Site," *The*

Writings of Robert Smithson, ed. Nancy Holt (New York: New York University Press, 1979), p. 44.

23. Ibid.

24. Marjorie Perloff, *The Poetics of Indeterminacy: Rimbaud To Cage* (Evanston: Northwestern University Press, 1983), p. 10.

25. Catherine Francblin, "An Interview With Jean Baudrillard," *FlashArt,* p. 55.

26. *The Art of Quartet Playing: The Guarneri Quartet in Conversation with David Blum* (New York: Alfred A. Knopf, 1986), p. 13. What Soyer was referring to specifically were those long rests or silences in Beethoven's Opus 18, No. 1.

27. *Mary Shelley's Journal,* ed. Frederick L. Jones (Norman: University of Oklahoma Press, 1947), p. 95. Even Mary Shelley's slightly more specific "The two principal singers are very good." makes the speaker sound less alienated.

"Either I'm Nobody, or I'm a Nation"

RITA DOVE

1. Why a Collected? Why this essay?

A celebrated poet reaches a point in his career where there needs to be a retrospective consideration of the work. Several choices can be made. A *Selected Poems* demands rigorous excerpting from previous books. A *New and Selected Poems* is a way of assuring the public that one is not yet an institution. A *Collected Poems* is like tossing in one's lot with the gods.

Derek Walcott's massive *Collected Poems 1948–1984* has an edge of defiance, as if to say, "Dismiss me if you can." But who would want to dismiss him? Walcott's poems stand out from the wash of contemporary American poetry (so much of it so *mild,* like half-whispered, devious apologies) because they are so boldly eloquent. The writing is some of the most exquisite in the English language, resembling the Caribbean in its many voices—sometimes crisp, sometimes tough, sometimes sweetly lyrical, or clear and treacherous as water in a stream. The syntax is often elaborate, frustrating yet seductive in the way it both reveals and obscures. When a Walcott poem fails, the writing is rarely at fault.

A true Renaissance man, Walcott has consistently resisted being cubbyholed. He has rejected neither his Caribbean heritage nor his British education. Although in recent years he divides his time between Trinidad and Boston, for a while he lived exclusively in the West Indies as director of the Trinidad Theatre Workshop. Although St. Lucia, his birthplace, forms his primary subject matter, he has also written about Manhattan and Mandelstam. In the eyes of the public, however, his unique position as the first English-speaking Caribbean poet of international renown threatens to make him ". . . a man no more / but the fervour and intelligence / of a whole country" *(Another Life).* And so the girth of this *Collected Poems* is

Review of Derek Walcott's *Collected Poems 1948–1984* from *Parnassus* (vol. 14, no. 1, 1987).

also a demand to consider the whole man—not just his skin or age or prosody or heart or mind.

2. Two Early Poems—Precocity's *ars poetica*

> "... the writers of my generation were natural assimilators. We knew the literature of Empires, Greek, Roman, British, through their essential classics; and both the patois of the street and the language of the classroom hid the elation of discovery. If there was nothing, there was everything to be made. With this prodigious ambition one began."
>
> —Derek Walcott,
> "What the Twilight Says: An Overture"

In the very first poem—titled, significantly, "Prelude"—the young poet looks down on his island from a distance and puts it into geographical and historical perspective:

> I, with legs crossed along the daylight, watch
> The variegated fists of clouds that gather over
> The uncouth features of this, my prone island.
>
> Meanwhile the steamers which divide horizons prove
> Us lost;
> Found only
> In tourist booklets, behind ardent binoculars;
> Found in the blue reflection of eyes
> That have known cities and think us here happy.

Although he enjoys a giant's viewpoint, the "variegated fists of clouds" constitute a larger, more threatening entity which has beaten the island into submission. The poet recognizes his place in a line of bullies.

He then vows not to make his life "public" "[u]ntil I have learnt to suffer / In accurate iambics." This statement of aesthetics is an act of survival as well: coming from a marginal culture, Walcott realizes how quickly colonial attitudes would label the personal confessions of a West

Indian impulsive, lecherous, and non-intellectual. Any of the contradictions and ambivalent urgings common to all human beings would be invisible to such a prejudiced observer; the poet's only chance to be heard is to beat the masters at their own game. With the practiced duplicity of a guerrilla, he plans to

> Make a holiday of situations,
> Straighten my tie and fix important jaws,
> And note the living images
> Of flesh that saunter through the eye.
>
> Until from all I turn to think how,
> In the middle of the journey through my life,
> O how I came upon you, my
> reluctant leopard of the slow eyes.

Beneath the surface politeness, he is a cool customer whose detached observations register human beings as subjects—not merely objects but "living images of flesh," a double removal. Still, these images "saunter," and the casual iambics of the next lines, plus the tripping syllables of "In the middle of the journey through my life," are lulling. The incantatory "O" brings us up short, approximating the sudden intake of breath the poet makes when he stumbles upon that which changes his life.

Dante's *Divine Comedy* also begins in the middle of a life. Is Walcott suggesting that he is at the same point—at age twenty-eight a precocious notion—or is he saying that once "boyhood has gone over" the remaining years constitute a struggle to recapture that beatific state? ("Never such faith again, never such innocence!" he exclaims, twenty-five years later, in *Another Life*.) The image of the leopard, moreover, is "reluctant," like a shy lover or a Muse . . ." I think "Prelude," finally, welcomes passion—both sensual and communal—while warning against the pampering of personality that can lead to self-indulgent writing. Above all, it is the poet's vow to admit paradox and conflict into his intellectual makeup.

"Origins," the fifth poem in the book, was originally published in *Selected Poems* (1964). It is like a quilt of West Indian history, introduced with an epigram from Aimé Césaire; the roll of surrealistic images imitates the roll of the surf and is reminiscent of Césaire's *Return to My Native Land*. To begin, the slate is wiped clean. Tradition, history, culture, and identity are erased:

> The flowering breaker detonates its surf.
> White bees hiss in the coral skull.
> Nameless I came among olives of algae,
> Foetus of plankton, I remember nothing.

Walcott's admiration for the Hart Crane of "Voyages" and "O Carib Isle" accounts for the acoustical flamboyance here. The "flowering breaker" bombards the shoreline through the use of explosive consonants and that masterful word "detonates," with its echoing vowels. The sonic boom of the first two lines gives way to the quieter chains of nouns. The neutral material (coral skull, algae) provides a fruitful bed for the bees, the "I" with neither identity nor history. On this ground, then, one can plant. Nothingness, for Walcott, does not imply negation but rather a *tabula rasa* from which one can start afresh.

Western civilization intervenes, and the poet struggles to unite conflicting traditions in himself. His first efforts at assimilation apply the Western myths to oral African traditions:

> Between the Greek and African pantheon,
> Lost animist, I rechristened trees:
> Caduceus of Hermes: the constrictor round the mangrove. . . .

Sections III and VI are italicized homages to island patois, the linguistical result of assimilation. Here the debt to Césaire is evident in the undulating string of images laid out for our delectation—the "clear, brown tongue of the sun-warmed, sun-wooded Troumassee / of laundresses and old leaves"—images which, however, become more jarring, near-surrealistic in the juxtaposition of sensations, such as the "cracked cobalt" of the "starched, linen seas," a rising agitation that subsides with the exclamation *"Ah, mon enfance!"* Part VI most resembles the Césaire of *Cahier d'un Retour au Pays Natal (Notebook of the Return to My Native Land)* with its associative progression of images through history: "their alphabet of alkali and aloe . . . their bitter olive" have scoured the "sweet, faded savour of rivers" until we find a "twin soul, spirit of river, spirit of sea." This, however, is a positive process, a multiplication of strengths rather than a division.

Walcott's concerns, reflected in these two early poems, have not changed substantially over the years. Even when he evokes violent emotions—fury, love, grief—the writing is controlled, trenchant. In the midst of the most relentless self-scrutiny is the panning, photographic eye, returning to us flailed beachhead, yellowing coconut, the "padded cavalry of the mouse."

The primary vigor of patois informs poems like "The Liberator," "Parang," "The Schooner *Flight,*" and "Pocomania," where the cadences of dialect syncopate the iambic line and patois words are liberally sprinkled without obliterating sense. In "Sainte Lucie," in the middle of a bilingual cataloguing of indigenous fruit, he cries, "Come back to me, / my language"; later in the same poem appear the lyrics of a native Creole song he once heard on the back of an open truck; he provides an English translation in the next section.

Walcott is a poet of circling and deepening; even the framing dates for this volume—1948 to 1984—hint that everything comes full circle. A prodigy and a black, he saw his dilemma early; a poet, he knew that the iambic line, with its thumbholds of word and image, was his thread out of the labyrinth.

3. Santa Lucia: The Raw Material

> "If your daily life seems poor, do not blame it; blame yourself, tell yourself that you are not good enough to call forth its riches. For anyone who creates there is no poverty and no poor, indifferent place."
>
> —Rilke, *Letters to a Young Poet*

I had to go away to college to discover that I was supposed to be ashamed of my hometown—for wasn't Akron, with its brick factories and sooty clapboard houses, deplorable? Didn't the smell of rubber make me sick? Wasn't it true that the only river had been forced underground? (The gorge remains, choked with dogwood, oak, hickory; in summer it wafts sickeningly with the floral bouquet of rotting garbage.)

Tourists love the Caribbean for its white beaches and opal seas, its glossy vegetation trailing across restaurant lattices. How delightful to snack on pomegranates, tucking a nameless exotic flower behind your ear! How could anyone regret all this!

Derek Walcott was born in Castries, St. Lucia, a small volcanic island between St. Vincent and Martinique. Then a part of Her Majesty's Empire, St. Lucia "enjoyed" a British imprint—Christianity, white manor houses. But behind the Great House sprawled the squalor of the poor blacks. All that a writer from St. Lucia could offer, in lieu of Thomas Hardy's cool and lonely heath, were bleached shores and, puffing toward them, steamers which "prove us lost: / Found only / In tourist booklets, behind ardent binoculars."

To get a hint of the complexity of the West Indian identity crisis, first look at the map. Register the distances between islands—"little turtles from Tortuga to Tobago"—and imagine the small towns trying to imitate suburban America, the capital cities wishing they were Washington or at least Havana; imagine the tiny communities separated by distances we find insignificant but they experience as absolute. Then look at a history book: the waves of conquests from Spain, the Netherlands, France, Great Britain; the African slave trade, the influx of cheap peasant labor from India and China. Imagine the Babel of languages, the frictions arising from different religions, eating habits, body gestures. Above all, imagine the northwestern hemisphere leaning its weight on the rest of the world, telling them that their ways are primitive, shameful, wrong, and must be changed.

Colonialism imposes on its subjects many indignities, but the most insidious one is a spiritual and cultural schizophrenia. (Walcott's dilemma is also biological, as one of his grandfathers was British. In the oft-quoted "A Far Cry from Africa" he asks: "I who am poisoned with the blood of both, / Where shall I turn, divided to the vein?"). Until Walcott realizes that assimilation means embracing every culture around one, his early lyrics are often stilted and hollow. The sonnets reprinted from *In a Green Night* (1962) are technically skilled but lifeless. This description of a Caribbean harbor could have been written by a tourist rather than by someone who grew up with the fishermen and listened to their stories:

> The fishermen rowing homeward in the dusk
> Do not consider the stillness through which they move,
> So I, since feelings drown, should no more ask

> For the safe twilight which your calm hands gave.
>
> ("The Harbour")

Yet he is learning; in an elevated manner reminiscent of Crane's shorter lyrics, Walcott applies his talents to the landscape and people, faithfully recording; by the time *Selected Poems* is published (1964), the improvement is startling. "Parang" not only re-creates the language of the people but succeeds in catching the ironical humor—*laughin' just to keep from cryin'*—any member of a suppressed group well better practice for survival. "Tales of the Islands," a sequence of ten sonnets, compiles snatches of gossip, folkloric rituals—some devoutly believed, some performed for visiting anthropologists—saloon talk, and scenic views, resulting in a batch of mock-satirical "postcards."

In the struggle to prove Akron worthy of poetry, the lines of battle are at least clearly drawn. Walcott's task is complicated by that very postcard image of the West Indies. Every time he mentions the sea, we tend to sigh with envy. And so he gives us sea and shore and salt air in spades: blinding heat, stunned water, the smells of sweating humanity, the omnipresent galvanized roofs, the stars nailed into the sky, the rain like knives—he rams the scenery down our throats until we stop being thrilled and start to listen.

4. History Lesson

> "When there is no history
> there is no metaphor . . .
>
> —Michael S. Harper

> "[T]here is too much nothing here."
>
> —Derek Walcott, "Air"

Derek Walcott claims time and again that the West Indies have no history, that without history a new race is rising from these tourist-ridden islands. He plays the devil's advocate by adopting the Official Version of Events; his bitter jibes at his countrymen for not making an impact on this record is his duplicitous way of attacking the foundations of Western civilization. Arguing negatively, he is permitted, through remorse and abuse, to lavish his attention on people, communities, and landscapes that aren't historically "important."

Michael Harper's history is a matrix of memory and responsibility. He rejects the Official Version, for it has no vision or morality. It is not, humanely speaking, truthful. I can imagine Walcott replying to Harper: "Without history, there is no memory." Or conversely: "Without memory, there is no history." The Middle Passage obliterated family ties, tribal connections, and the religious and communal rites that give sense to natural law. West Indian history is a how-to manual for the brutal destruction of whole races' systems for sustaining memory.

The amnesia of the people is reflected in the island vegetation whose rapid proliferation obliterates paths and manors alike. Human accomplishment disappears with time, sun, and rain. Uncontrolled growth is emblematic of the process of forgetting:

> when the axe spoke, weeds ran up to the knee
> like bastard children, hiding in their names,
>
> whole generations died, unchristened,
> growths hidden in green darkness, forests
> of history thickening with amnesia . . .
>
> *(Another Life)*

Walcott's primary metaphor is the sea. The sea is History or, more precisely, a history book, her pages steadily turning, writing and erasing themselves. Sometimes the sea is a book of poems, left lying face down by an absent reader; more often, the sea is quintessential Nothingness. The islands take their lessons from the sea. As he points out in "The Sea Is History" (from *The Star-Apple Kingdom*), any event not recognized for its true essence does not exist. To the question "Where are your monuments, your battles, martyrs?" the West Indian replies: "Sirs, / in that grey vault. The sea. The sea / has locked them up." A list of humiliations follows—slave trade, imported peasant labor, conquerors and exploiters— to which the narrator blithely assigns biblical metaphors: the slave trade is Exodus, poverty is Lamentations, the sun setting is the New Testament. Only with the break-up of the British Empire does the clock start to tick:

> then came the bullfrog bellowing for a vote,
>
> fireflies with bright ideas
> and bats like jetting ambassadors
> and the mantis, like khaki police . . .

"This," Walcott claims wryly, is the "rumour without any echo / of History, really beginning." In other words, History begins with self-determination, no matter how corrupt the struggle to prevail, which, after all, is the last thing any empire that "sneers at all thoughts in the future tense" wishes. More suitable to the colonial game plan is the scenario of "Return to D'Ennery; Rain":

> So azure and indifferent was this air,
> So murmurous of oblivion the sea,
> That any human action seemed a waste,
> The place seemed born for being buried there.

5. Portrait of the Artist as a Young Man

> The dream
> of reason had produced its monster:
> a prodigy of the wrong age and colour.
>
> —Derek Walcott, *Another Life*

I first met Derek Walcott in the basement of the Performing Arts Building at my undergraduate university. He was in town to give a poetry reading that I would miss because of the dress rehearsal of my first play, a one-act incorporating pantomine, dream, and song into a forty-five-minute recounting of the last thirty years of Afro-American history. It was spring 1973, the year Walcott's phenomenal narrative poem, *Another Life,* was published. We shook hands and I croaked a hello; I had read *Dream on Monkey Mountain* the previous summer and couldn't believe that the author of that great play was standing outside the auditorium where my diluted imitation was struggling through missed cues and uncertain direction.

I did not read *Another Life* until much later. When I finally did, out of graduate school and on my way to Europe for the third or fourth time,

I recognized its major themes as chords in my own life: loss of innocence, the search for a heritage; the schizophrenia of assimilation, the writer as exile to his homeland and to his own life.

Another Life's 4,000-plus lines are divided into four parts, which are then divided into twenty-three chapters. The narrative operates on many levels, often shifting times and perspectives in mid-line; it is a lyric *Bildungsroman,* Walcott's *Buddenbrooks* or *A la Recherche du Temps Perdu.* His usual rhetorical reticence disappears, and the telling is made more haunting by its elasticity; he cajoles, proclaims, rages, and whispers. There are straight descriptive passages, dramatic monologues, self-interviews, brief spurts of song. Walcott's experience as playwright and theater director finds a second life here, in poetry.

Part One, *The Divided Child,* recounts the first artistic stirrings. His ambition to become a great painter is undermined by the very literary metaphor that sets the opening scene:

> Verandahs, where the pages of the sea
> are a book left open by an absent master
> in the middle of another life—
> I begin here again . . .

The absent master refers equally to the dead father, the drawing teacher Harold Simmons, God (who is either indifferent or dead), and the absence of racial memory. The image of the sea as a book occurs again and again, charting Walcott's deepening relationship to literature.

> And from a new book,
> bound in sea-green linen, whose lines
> matched the exhilaration which their reader,
> rowing the air around him now, conveyed,
> another life it seemed would start again . . .

By Chapter 3, the narration is firmly in the hands of dramatic literature; the "town's characters, its cast of thousands" are presented in alphabetical order, from Ajax the "lion-coloured stallion" to Zandoli, rodent exterminator. "These dead, these derelicts," claims Walcott, ". . . were the stars of my mythology." He involves this cast in a mini-drama, but by Chapter 7, the narrator withdraws with an ironic commentary on his own creation:

> Provincialism loves the pseudo-epic,
> so if these heroes have been given a stature
> disproportionate to their cramped lives,
> remember I beheld them at knee-height . . .

Is this sly disavowal prompted by embarrassment, or has Walcott anticipated our condescension? The ruse is Shakespearean, a clue that we will have to watch ourselves, a warning to avoid the easy judgment. Look at Julius Caesar, Macbeth, King Lear—what are heroes but plunderers, murderers, and vengeful, foolish men?

Part Two, "Homage to Gregorias," recalls Walcott's boyhood friend Dunstan St. Omer and their years together as apprentices of the artist Harry Simmons. Dunstan's name is changed to Gregorias because "it echoes the blest thunders of the surf . . . / because it sounds explosive, / a black Greek's!"; it also suggests that St. Lucia, with its misted mountains and wilderness of ocean, has affinities to ancient Greece.

Soon realizing he does not have the gift for painting, the narrator envies "mad, divine Gregorias / imprisoned in his choice." But there is literature and the growing compulsion to articulate the dreams of his people who were "dazed, ignorant, / waiting to be named." Of Gregorias he says "He had his madness," then: "mine was our history." But where was this history to be found? Not in the school headmaster, "a lonely Englishman who loved parades, / sailing, and Conrad's prose," nor in the pupil's red-jacketed *History of the British Empire.* Not in the tapestry of Waterloo hanging in the house of one of his mother's sewing clients, not even in daydreams of Montparnasse in the twenties. (When I was ten I read an article in *Jet* about Dorothy Dandridge losing out to Elizabeth Taylor for the role of Cleopatra. Right then I knew that History didn't include me.) Taking a cue from Gregorias, the poet turns to his immediate environment for inspiration and sees "vowels curl from the tongue of the carpenter's plane." The two drink, talk through the night, criticize and praise each other's work, and make a vow:

> But drunkenly, or secretly, we swore,
> disciples of that astigmatic saint,
> that we would never leave the island
> until we had put down, in paint, in words,
> as palmists learn the network of a hand,

all of its sunken, leaf-choked ravines,
every neglected, self-pitying inlet
muttering in brackish dialect, the ropes of mangroves
from which old soldier crabs slipped
surrendering to slush,
each ochre track seeking some hilltop and
losing itself in an unfinished phrase . . .

The youthful fantasies accelerate, almost reveling in the squalor which they plan to extol—the endless sentence, so customary of Walcott, rolls through intricate couplings of landscape and language, finally slithering to a pause with the soldier crabs falling into slush . . . those crabs being a foreshadowing of the disillusioned older poet who, looking back on those days, would exclaim: "Yet, Gregorias, lit, / we were the light of the world!"

That pun, with its cocky tenderness, erupts in Part Three into the purging, catalytic nature of fire. A conflagration devastates the town of Castries. Now the world of their youth is gone: ". . . with the fierce rush of a furnace door / suddenly opened, history was here." Castries' resurrection as "a cement phoenix" is paralleled by the poet's discovery of sex and the possibility of education abroad:

Tea with the British Council Representative,
tannin, calfskin, gilt, and thank you vellum much . . .
I am hoisted on silvery chords upward,
eager for the dropped names like sugar cubes.
Eliot. Plop. Benjamin Britten. Clunk. Elgar. Slurp.
Mrs. Winters's cheeks gleaming. Polished cherries.
Lawns. Elegance. Remembering elms. England, then. When?
Down on her speckled forearm. More tea.
Thank you, my mind burrowing her soft scented crotch.
First intimations of immortality.
Other men's wives.

First love also sparks with the appearance of Anna, "gold and white . . . light / of another epoch." He makes her his lover and then, imitating literature, idealizes her until she dissolves into all the literary Annas he has adored: Anna Christie, Anna Karenina, Anna Akhmatova. Finally, inevitably, she loses out to Art: "The hand she held already had betrayed / them by its longing for describing her."

He leaves for study abroad, praying that nothing will change—a futile wish, for though he returns many times, he carries the guilt of the prodigal son. In Part Four, "The Estranging Sea," Walcott—"One life, one marriage later"—encounters Gregorias and finds him

> unable to hold down a job, painting so badly
> that those who swore his genius vindicated
> everything once, now saw it as a promise never kept.
> Viciously, near tears, I wished him dead.

This self-punishing rage rapidly turns outward: news of the suicide of his mentor, Harold Simmons, prompts a scathing denunciation of "the syntactical apologists of the Third World," those ill-wishers who condemn their promising artists before they have even begun. He envisions them prodding Harry to his grave while exclaiming "from such a man / what would you expect, / but a couple of paintings / and a dog's life?"

Finally it is the sea which opens the way to hope. If the sea is a book, then the most natural action is to pick up that book and start to read; the next step is to write the book oneself:

> for what else is there
> but books, books and the sea,
> verandahs and the pages of the sea,
> to write of the wind and the memory of wind-whipped hair
> in the sun, the colour of fire?

His fury spent, Walcott assesses his present position—"I was eighteen then, now I am forty-one"—and accepts what he has been and become. The next visit home he is able to see that it "is not bitter, it is harder / to be a prodigal than a stranger." He decides to visit neither Harry's grave nor Anna; instead, he asks forgiveness of the island for his desertion. Upon those who stayed so that he might leave—Anna, Gregorias, Simmons—he wishes rest. His only desire now is "to grow white-haired / as the wave, with a wrinkled / brown rock's face . . . an old poet, / facing the wind."

6. Childhood's Aftermath

> "It is summer-gone that I see, it is summer-gone."
>
> —Gwendolyn Brooks,
> "A Sunset of the City"

Another Life took seven years to write, years in which America exploded with student demonstrations and race riots. It is typical of Walcott's contrariness that he chose "to row, but backward"; to present an introspective exploration of his personal past at the very moment so many Afro-American writers were writing "for the people." Walcott insists that only through the particular fate can a universal one be posited; his response to the call for Black Pride is to contribute his version of a life, another life, in all its ambiguities.

Sea Grapes (1976) is the calm after the storm, a resignation borne of equal parts serenity and loss. These poems are *triste*—elegant, spare constructions, almost classical:

> Desolate lemons, hold
> tight, in your bowl of earth,
> the light to your bitter flesh . . .
>
> ("Sunday Lemons")

If the green of the sea is the signature color of *Another Life, Sea Grapes's* prevailing hue is gold—lemons, Valencia oranges, the goldsmith of Benares, "oaks yellowing October, / everything turning money." I am reminded of Yeats's "Sailing to Byzantium," where a similar yearning becomes the wish to escape the body into a form of "hammered gold and gold enameling." Gold, the color of fervor and denouement, of the fire and its embers.

Which is not to imply that Walcott has given up—on the contrary, there is a sweetness to this dignity that, rather than softening the effect of his rigorous attention to craft, makes these poems all the more troubling, their severe forms filled with mutable living tissue. The youthful paradise is gone; one cannot return home. Hence the Adam poems—Adam heartbroken by Eve's betrayal ("Adam's Song"), Adam's comprehension of labor and profit in "New World." Concomitant with the construction of a New World in these poems is the proliferation of bitter fruit—lemons, olives, limes, sour apples, green grapes.

The labor begins here, outside the walls. Where a lesser poet would fall silent or imitate earlier successes, Walcott rolls up his sleeves. His unique experience as unlikely prodigy, apprentice painter, literature student, poet, dramatist, and theater director; his cognizance of the bogus glories of "fame" and "world citizenship"—all this has prepared him for a new lesson: reconciliation with the irrevocable. As he says in "Dark August":

> . . . I am learning slowly
>
> to love the dark days, the steaming hills,
> the air with gossiping mosquitoes,
> and to sip the medicine of bitterness . . .
> . . .
>
> I would have learnt to love black days like bright ones,
> the black rain, the white hills, when once
> I loved only my happiness and you.

7. The Star-Apple Kingdom

> "Shabine sang to you from the depths of the sea."

The Star-Apple Kingdom is a lyrical celebration, an explosion of breathtaking imagery. The duality Walcott described in an essay titled "What the Twilight Says: An Overture" as "two lives: the interior life of poetry, the outward life of action and dialect" reaches a reconciliation in two major works: the title poem and "The Schooner *Flight.*"

The volume opens with "The Schooner *Flight,*" a rare persona poem. Shabine, whose name is "the patois for / any red nigger," leaves the "dreamless face" of his lover Maria Concepcion and boards the schooner *Flight.* The names are not accidental: Shabine's ordeal is the allegory of Everyman, and his flight becomes a quest. Like Odysseus, he encounters terrors and defeats them; unlike Odysseus, he is running away rather than trying to return, although his ambitions are loftier:

You ever look up from some lonely beach
and see a far schooner? Well, when I write
this poem, each phrase go be soaked in salt;
I go draw and knot every line as tight
as ropes in this rigging; in simple speech
my common language go be the wind,
my pages the sails of the schooner *Flight*.

The similarity between Shabine's aesthetic and Walcott's (a much earlier poem "Islands" states: "I seek . . . to write / Verse crisp as sand, clear
as sunlight, / Cold as the curled wave, ordinary / As a tumbler of island
water . . .") is intriguing; more important, however, are the differences
between the two men: Shabine, never having left the islands, still belongs;
the cab driver addresses him familiarly, and he suffers no agonizing sense
of estrangement from the spirit of his community. Perhaps Shabine is the
man Walcott might have become if he had stayed on St. Lucia; perhaps
he is simply himself, one man in a nation of individuals. In any case, he
embodies the universal in the particular. To those who would consider
him exotic and look upon his culture with a vague nostalgia, Shabine is
quick to call their bluff: "either I'm nobody," he says, "or I'm a nation."
    Shabine has escaped a web of corruption and betrayal—now, on the
high seas, he "had no nation . . . but the imagination." A willing castaway,
he is the privileged witness to miracles. God speaks through a harpooned
grouper, and one dawn the ship enters the Middle Passage:

where the horizon was one silver haze,
the fog swirl and swell into sails, so close
that I saw it was sails, my hair grip my skull,
it was horrors, but it was beautiful.

The vision includes the ghosts of great admirals as well as slave ships, "our
fathers below deck too deep . . . to hear us shouting." Here is contemplation rendered palpable; Shabine is not as painfully self-conscious as Walcott and so is able to travel backward, over the troubled waters, to become
whole. Later, during a life-threatening storm, what sustains him is the
memory of those slave ships, superimposed on a church episode from
childhood "when the whale-bell / sang service" and

> proud with despair, we sang how our race
> survive the sea's maw, our history, our peril,
> and now I was ready for whatever death will.

His last vision is of Maria Concepcion in the wake of the storm, marrying the sea and drifting away. "I wanted nothing after that day," Shabine states:

> I stop talking now. I work, then I read,
> cotching under a lantern hooked to the mast.
> I try to forget what happiness was,
> and when that don't work, I study the stars.

All the selections from *The Star-Apple Kingdom* are vintage Walcott: the hypnotic limbo of "Sabbaths, W.I.," the grimly brilliant "The Sea Is History." "Koenig of the River," a weirdly poignant negative of Shabine's journey, depicts Koenig, the last surviving crew member of a missionary group sent to inspect a camp in the swamp, as he succumbs to fever and delirium. But the real *tour de force* is the title poem, which Walcott rightly saves for last.

The protagonist of "The Star-Apple Kingdom" is more politically astute than Shabine, his introspection more bitter and cerebral. Hence his judgments are harsher, his visions more brutal, and revelation, when it comes, is more suspect. The poem begins with him perusing an old photo album; sepia snapshots from the Victorian era afford glimpses of "lily-like parasols" floating across a landscape dubbed "Herefords at Sunset in the Valley of the Wye." As dusk falls, he looks out over Kingston, imagining a silent scream from the oppressed—all those who were not included in the photographs—rising over the landscape. He falls asleep, finally, only to plunge into a nightmare procession of images from Caribbean history: the submerged cathedral of Port Royal, a "crab climbing the steeple"; Christianity contriving so that "the slave pardoned his whip." *La Revolución* comes in the form of a woman, "a black umbrella blown inside out," who is simultaneously "raped wife, empty mother, Aztec virgin / transfixed by arrows from a thousand guitars." Refusing the bleakness of her vision, he cries out for

. . . a history without any memory,
streets without statues,
and a geography without myth. . . . no armies
but those regiments of bananas, thick lances of canes . . .

Still within the dream, he awakens to a vision of the partitioning of the
West Indian republic: seven prime ministers who buy up the sea—

one thousand miles of aquamarine with lace trimmings,
one million yards of lime-coloured silk,
one mile of violet, leagues of cerulean satin—

and resell it at a profit to conglomerates. He then plunges into a deep
sleep, one "that wipes out history." When he wakens—for real this time,
his jaw still aching from the silent scream—he is able, finally, to cry out.
The only person who hears him is an old woman scrubbing the steps of
the cathedral; she hears his scream "as a dog hears, as all the underdogs /
of the world hear." The acknowledged scream imposes on the world a
silence lasting "for half an hour / in that single second"—and though we
cannot be sure if the old woman's cracked and wrinkled face conceals a
smile, the poem assures us that the smile, if it exists, is "the same smile
with which he now / cracked the day open and began his egg."

This is virtuoso writing: the roll of fierce images, dense with conso-
nance, imitates the roar of the sea; the relentless dactylics of the last nine
lines attain the grandeur of an Old Testament prophecy. Still, there is no
resolution of conflicting energies; the outlook is nearly as bleak as at the
outset. For though the anguished consciousness has found a kindred spirit,
she is mute and ultimately inaccessible; the old woman is not about to join
him for breakfast. Where does the torn soul go from here?

8. The Prodigy Turns Prodigal

I know the dark delight of being strange,
The penalty of difference in the crowd,
The loneliness of wisdom among fools . . .

—Claude McKay, "My House"

The fate of any member of a minority who "makes it" is double-edged. As a model, he or she must be perfect; no slip-ups or "you've let us down." As a special case, he or she is envied, even reviled. Move away from the home court and you're accused of being "dicty"; return and you're a prodigal. Write about home and you blaspheme; choose other topics and you're a traitor.

In "The Spoiler's Return," a scathing portrayal of corruption, "the Spoiler" comes back to Laventille. He claims to have been to hell and back after leaving the West Indies with "no will / but my own conscience and rum-eaten wit." With Popian rancor he describes the Caribbean "scene": "Is crab climbing crab-back, in a crab-quarrel, / and going round and round in the same barrel . . ."

(In August 1963, my parents dragged us to Washington, D.C. We stayed with relatives, great-aunts and uncles with scores of children and sub-children. The day before the March, Aunt Louise organized a crab bake: more terrifying than the claws scratching against the galvanized tub was the sight of them whole, boiled as bright a red as white people the second sunny day of summer, brilliant corpses we were supposed to dismantle and devour. Aunt Helen held no truck with my squeamishness; she pulled me over to the tub and pointed. "Look at that," she said, chuckling. "Niggers just like that—like crabs in a bucket, not a one get out 'cause the other pull him back."

I was impressed at the sight, and the curiously affectionate way she had used a word forbidden among the Negro bourgeoisie up North. The expression, I thought, she had made up herself. Now, more than twenty years later, I find it again, at the source.)

Everyone wants a prodigy to fail; it makes our mediocrity more bearable. Even before leaving for study abroad, Walcott felt the first twinges of the Prodigal Syndrome: envy from the outside, insecurity and guilt from within. It doesn't matter if the prodigal returns in shame or glory— the time away from "home" will always be suspect and interpreted as rejection. Frustration with this double bind can erupt into hate. "Laventille" depicts a funeral in a poor section of town; the narrator is impatient and grieved at the backwardness he witnesses:

> The black, fawning verger,
> his bow tie akimbo, grinning, the clown-gloved
> fashionable wear of those I deeply loved

once, made me look on with hopelessness and rage
at their new, apish habits, their excess
and fear . . .

Perhaps because he is confiding in a soulmate (the poem is dedicated to
V. S. Naipaul, whose novels are grim studies of the squalor of the East
Indian community in the Caribbean), Walcott allows hidden thoughts to
burst through.

But that's not the end of the prodigy's tightrope act. There is the
problem of being accepted on one's own terms in the larger world, where
reactions can fluctuate from patronizing praise ("The best black writer
since Ralph Ellison!") to outright disdain. Those "accurate iambics" are
meant to legitimize Walcott's subject matter and to command respect both
for his craft and his conclusions. The prosody can also help him contain
his uneasiness with the dichotomy of mind and body—mind meaning
English education and body referring to sensuality, connectedness. The
traits of the body, however desirable, render one vulnerable. The attempt
to dissociate mind from body is in Walcott's case complicated by the fact
that Western civilization assigns the characteristics of the body—perceived
as "feminine" and "inferior"—to the black race as well.

Walcott's struggle, internalized by his own mixed racial heritage, appears rather programmatically in the overquoted "I who have cursed /
The drunken officer of British rule, how choose / Between this Africa and
the English tongue I love?" When the body is denied, creative expression
is diminished: "to be aware / of the divine union the soul detaches /
itself from created things," he states in "The Gulf"; later, in *Another Life,*
he laments: "my sign was Janus, / I saw with twin heads, / and everything
I say is contradicted." The wish for a separation of mind and body finds
apt metaphors: mind becomes a "ripe brain rotting like a yellow nut"; an
Indian trundles his wheelbarrow of "hacked, beheaded coconuts"; "the
lopped head of the coconut rolls to gasp in the sand." Bodies on the
subway ("A Village Life") are seen "each in its private hell, / each
plumped, prime bulk still swinging by its arm / upon a hook." Marc
Antony, stretched out next to a sleeping Cleopatra ("quick fox with her /
sweet stench"), feels "dismembered, // his head / is in Egypt, his feet /
in Rome, his groin a desert / trench with its dead soldier." In the last
poem from *Midsummer,* wood lice become seraphim, "all heads, with, at
each ear, a gauzy wing."

Even the "civilized" desire to relieve stress by a "vacation in the sun" can become an existential nightmare:

> We came here for the cure
> Of quiet in the whelk's centre . . .
> To let a salt sun scour
> The brain as harsh as coral,
> To bathe like stones in wind,
> To be, like beast or natural object, pure.

> ("Crusoe's Island")

If you want to be "like beast or natural object, pure" you will also have to assume their negative qualities—to be a beast means to be less than human, less than reasonable; natural objects do not possess history, they do not have a sense of time—which, for man, is tantamount to oblivion.

The self-consciousness which comes from seeing yourself as unsuspecting others see you *and* knowing exactly what you're thinking at that moment becomes a technical innovation in Walcott's work, as he switches pronouns from "he" to "I" to "you" when discussing the self:

> for once, like them,
> you wanted no career
> but this sheer light, this clear,
> infinite, boring, paradisal sea,
> but hoped it would mean something to declare
> today, I am your poet, yours . . .

> ("Homecoming: Anse La Raye")

To change pronouns in mid-sentence not only shakes our complacency, our sense of knowing where we stand, but creates an intricate layering of remorse. Poem XI of *Midsummer* begins with the very traditional, almost clichéd, moment of self-confrontation in the mirror. What elevates a predictable moment to a dialectic is the matter-of-fact way Walcott calls this reflection his double, and then gives him a life independent of the real "other"—one of menial action, snipping hairs and shaving—while the other is condemned to remember "empty cupboards where her dresses / shone"—the small but "fatal" sadnesses born of introspection.

Walcott explores his reactions from all angles: from a distance, in "Prelude," as if watching a rare insect ("I go, of course, through all the isolated acts, / . . . Straighten my tie and fix important jaws"), or from deep in the belly of the whale, as in "Mass Man," when he rages, half to himself and half to the laughing, dancing carnival celebrants:

> Upon your penitential morning,
> some skull must rub its memory with ashes,
> some mind must squat down howling in your dust,
> some hand crawl and recollect your rubbish,
> someone must write your poems.

9. Names on the Sand

> Craftsman and castaway,
> All heaven in his head . . .
>
> —Derek Walcott,
> "Crusoe's Island"

A recurrent figure in Walcott's work is that of Robinson Crusoe, castaway: the man forced, as the sole survivor of a race, to become a God. The epigram to "Crusoe's Journal" invites us to see home as "a place I had lived in but was come out of." A repository of British education, this Crusoe returns to his island to find himself shipwrecked among familiar surroundings; he discovers that intellect can establish the distance helpful for accurate description, but only at the expense of emotion:

> the intellect appraises
> objects surely, even the bare necessities
> of style are turned to use,
> like those plain iron tools he salvages
> from shipwreck, hewing a prose
> as odorous as raw wood to the adze . . .

The fate of being the West Indies' first internationally acclaimed poet bears with it the pressure of assuming the role of creator. As the first to "make it out," Walcott also has the dubious privilege of finding language that can "startle itself / with poetry's surprise / in a green world, one without metaphors. . . ." The Adamic mission of naming is both an invigorating and a lonely enterprise, typically masculine in its separation of the human animal from the environment. Although he never quite escapes the alienation such a role provokes, Walcott, from his marginal perspective, is capable of seeing the irony in this:

> Being men, they could not live
> except they first presumed
> the right of every thing to be a noun.
> The African acquiesced,
> repeated, and changed them.

("Names")

Still, the star witness for the defense—the native West Indian who has stayed home, who has not experienced alienation—is mute. And so it is only one step farther to see Crusoe in any exile, from John writing *Revelations* on the isle of Patmos to a hungover poet suspended over Love Field in a Boeing 747.

In "Crusoe's Island," the privilege of naming swings rapidly around to the dark side:

> Craftsman and castaway,
> All heaven in his head,
> He watched his shadow pray
> Not for God's love but human love instead.

To become a god is to relinquish human ties, to lose the father and the Father. The freedom of being the sole spokesman is fraught with the burden of total failure with nothing to hang on to:

> I have lost sight of hell,
> Of heaven, of human will,
> My skill
> Is not enough,
> I am struck by this bell
> To the root.
> Crazed by a racking sun,

I stand at my life's noon,
On parched, delirious sand
My shadow lengthens.

No matter how many times the prodigal returns home physically, he cannot obtain the purity of the stone or the crab. He cannot dissolve into the landscape that has yielded to the pressure of his observation. He cannot, in fact, touch the very people who are his legacy. At the poem's end he notices "Black little girls in pink / Organdy, crinolines" walking on the shore; in a brilliant recognition he dubs them "Friday's progeny, / The brood of Crusoe's slave." Thus Walcott becomes both Crusoe and Friday, "Crusoe's slave." The West Indian who loves those girls is a slave to the artist who stands outside their lives:

And nothing I can learn
From art or loneliness
Can bless them as the bell's
Transfiguring tongue can bless.

10. In the Air

"I don't know the language
Of this cool country
And its pace is not mine."

—Else Lasker-Schüler,
"Homesick"

As Walcott's list of publications and achievements lengthens, so does the amount of time spent away from the islands. "We're in the air," a Texan remarks upon takeoff in "The Gulf." The rootlessness of the islander is augmented by the homelessness of the traveler. The idea of being the artist in the air begins to take precedence over the concept of Crusoe, firmly rooted—however lonely—on his island.

The Fortunate Traveller (1981) is generously represented in the *Collected Poems.* Although it is natural to favor one's most recent work, in this case I'm sorry the poet gave in to temptation, for many of these poems suffer from superficiality and a touch of the maudlin. Walcott is spending more and more time in the United States, and his adopted country has seduced him. He admits, in "Upstate," to falling in love with America (Kate Smith, move over!), and decides he must become a student again:

> I must put the cold small pebbles from the spring
> upon my tongue to learn her language,
> to talk like birch or aspen confidently.

But what a meek, eager-to-please student we have here! Wistfully he says, "Sometimes I feel sometimes / the Muse is leaving, the Muse is leaving America." And yet here comes the Muse by poem's end, arrayed in her traditional garb—virgin land smelling of just-baked bread.

Okay, one can't remain an angry young man forever—but I wish some of that indignant righteousness and impatience remained. The traveler seems weary, and several poems appear to have no *raison d'être* other than the fact that a writer should keep writing. Cruel? Perhaps, but it springs from disappointment; after *Another Life, Sea Grapes,* and *The Star-Apple Kingdom,* I will not be satisfied with imitation Lowell. And though there are gems ("Map of the New World," or the vivid personae in "The Liberator" and "The Spoiler's Return"), there are far more embarrassments, such as the bland "Easter" and "Early Pompeian," where the attempt to describe a stillbirth results in overwriting ("your sorrows were robing / you with the readiness of woman") and festooned clichés ("the lamp that was struggling with darkness was blown out / by the foul breeze off the amniotic sea"). Powerful oratory fizzles to rhetoric; I can only wince when, in "The Hotel Normandie Pool," a raindrop "punctuates the startled paper" and Walcott muses, as the pool surface wrinkles with rain, ". . . all reflection gets no easier."

The title *The Fortunate Traveller* is meant to be ironic—perhaps more than its author realized.

11. Questions of Travel

> CORPORAL: We cannot go back. History is in motion. The law is in motion. Forward, forward.
>
> SOURIS: Where? The world is a circle, Corporal. Remember that.
>
> —Derek Walcott, *Dream on Monkey Mountain*

With *Midsummer,* a sequence of poems published in 1981, Walcott returns to the West Indies for inspiration; or, more precisely, the West Indies return to him. No matter where he finds himself—be it Rome, Argentina, or Van Gogh's orchards—he carries his island inside. Emblematic of midsummer is scorching heat that dries up vegetation and a glare that flattens perspectives. "Midsummer's furnace casts everything in bronze"; similarly, each poem paints itself and stiffens into elegy. One would think Walcott were bronzing memories like baby shoes. The language is appropriately baroque, with weariness and repetition built into the composition, and there is a sense of *just keep moving and everything will be all right.*

But what is he running from that always pulls him back into its gravitational field? Here and there, through the lush linguistic scenery, we're given glimpses: "[t]he hills have no echoes" in poem VII and by XXI, "the cloud waits in emptiness for the apostles." In the islands "noon jerks towards its rigid, inert centre." *Echoless, empty, inert*—modifiers for Death (dare we whisper its name?), the Great Negator. (In Western tradition, a "living death" is synonymous with a destroyed ego.) Wherever Walcott travels, whenever he lets his rhetorical guard down, the Void is waiting with its shining, blank face.

He fights back the only way he knows . . . by writing: "My palms have been sliced by the twine / of the craft I have pulled at for more than forty years." This compulsion can sometimes lead to bad writing, such as metaphors extended far beyond their initial freshness. "Here the wetback crab and the mullusc are citizens," he writes in poem XXVII, "and the leaves have green cards." Or, musing on the Holocaust, these lines, more suited for a John Belushi monologue:

> Brown pigeons goose-step, squirrels pile up acorns like little shoes,
> and moss, voiceless as smoke, hushes the peeled bodies
> like abandoned kindling. In the clear pools, fat
> trout rising to lures bubble in umlauts.

(XLI)

When the compass swings north and Walcott attempts to re-create tropical stasis in Northern cities, inertia comes off as jadedness. Efforts to fuse literature and landscape often misfire: Boston city blocks become "long as paragraphs" and ". . . boulevards open like novels / waiting to be written. Clouds like the beginnings of stories." There are, however, moments of originality and rightness that make up for these lapses.

After self-imposed exile in cities like Boston and a Chicago "white as Poland," after returning to England, land of his "bastard ancestor" (significantly, it is the grandfather who is the bastard, not Walcott himself), he finally writes himself out of the Hole. Here is the conclusion of the fiftieth poem:

> These poems I heaved aren't linked to any tradition
> like a mossed cairn; each goes down like a stone
> to the seabed, settling, but let them, with luck, lie
> where stones are deep, in the sea's memory.
> Let them be, in water, as my father, who did watercolours,
> entered his work. He became one of his shadows,
> wavering and faint in the midsummer sunlight.
> His name was Warwick Walcott. I sometimes believe
> that his father, in love or bitter benediction,
> named him for Warwickshire. Ironies
> are moving. Now, when I rewrite a line,
> or sketch on the fast-drying paper the coconut fronds
> that he did so faintly, my daughters' hands move in mine.
> Conches move over the sea-floor. I used to move
> my father's grave from the blackened Anglican headstones
> in Castries to where I could love both at once—
> the sea and his absence. Youth is stronger than fiction.

What impression does Derek Walcott want to leave us with? His insistence on the particular and personal precludes any suggestion that he'd like to be seen as statesman-poet in the tradition of Neruda. More likely, his intent is to frustrate all efforts at portraiture so that, closing the book, we can explain nothing except by referring to individual poems. With its wise artistry this collection also resists the presentation of a slick surface, shelf upon shelf of well-wrought urns polished to blinding perfection. "All the lines I love have their knots left in," Walcott writes, and this edition allows us a glimpse into the workshop. The early sonnet "A City's Death by Fire," for example, is a stilted portrayal of the Castries fire that is easily upstaged by "A Simple Flame" in *Another Life.* Certain images are recycled—an easel rifled across shoulders, a "galvanized roof with its nail holes of stars," the gull as a hinge in the sky, the pages of the sea. The last section of "Tales of the Islands" is incorporated verbatim at the end of "A Simple Flame."

Repetition and embellishment—these are also the devices of the storyteller. Walcott's rhetorical insistence works because we can hear him talking *to* us; we hear the words being strung on a breath. The story line—and I use "line" in a concrete sense, a thread running through fabric or a labyrinth—is held together by the authenticity of the storyteller's voice. Though we know we are seeing the world filtered through the teller, though we know he is weaving a spell, we trust him to tell the truth in his own way. "You have / a grace upon your words, and there is sound sense within them," said Alkinoos in praise of Odysseus, another castaway.

After reading the bulk of Derek Walcott's poetry, I am a little saddened, for I find the recent work a slight diminishment of his power, the flame turned a little lower. Still, he has surprised us before, and *Midsummer* augurs a fresh outburst. A *Collected Poems* forces a writer to start again with Nothing. *Tabula rasa.* And as the seasoned traveler knows, one of the most dangerous, and intoxicating, moments of any trip is takeoff.

Part II

The Eye

RONALD JOHNSON

The human eye, a sphere of waters and tissue, absorbs an energy that has come ninety-three million miles from another sphere, the sun. The eye may be said to be sun in other form.

It is part of a spectrum of receptors, and if we could only "see" more widely the night sky would be "brighter" than the moon. Matter smaller than the shortest wave-length of light cannot be seen.

Pressure on the surface of an eye makes vision, though what these same pressures focus to the radial inwardness of a dragonfly in flight is unimaginable. Through pressure also, the head-over-heels is crossed right-side-up, in eye as camera. (It is possible to take a cow's eyeball and thin the rear wall of it with a knife, fit it front forward in a tube, and the tube pointed at an elm will image an upside-down elm.)

The front of the eye is a convex glass, alive, and light bent through its curve strikes a lens. This lens is behind an iris—pushing it into the shape of a volcano. In light, the iris appears as a rayed core of color, its center hole dilating dark to day, transformed instantly into what man's twinned inner hemispheres call *sight*.

The retina is its bowl-shaped back—the cones at retinal center growing through intersections with rods, toward rods at the rim. Through this mesh, ray seizes ray to see. In the rods there is a two-part molecule that is unlinked by light. One quantum of light unlinks one molecule, and five rods are needed to perceive the difference. Some stars are at this threshold, and can only be seen by the sides of the eyes. The eye can see a wire .01 inch in diameter at a distance of one hundred yards. The retina, however, seeks equilibrium.

Though to look at the sun directly causes blindness, sight is an intricately precise tip of branched energy that has made it possible to measure the charge of solar storm, or to calculate nova. The universe, one imagines, is of a similar form.

Our eyes are blue for the same reason sky is, a scattering of reflectors: human eyes have only brown pigment.

In the embryo two stalks push from the brain, through a series of infoldings, to form optic cups. Where the optic cup reaches surface, the surface turns in and proliferates in the shape of an ingrowing mushroom. The last cells to form are those farthest from light.

If I sit at my table and look at the shaft of light which enters a glass filled

From *Parnassus* (vol. 1, no. 1, 1972).

with water—and exits rainbow—then move my head to the left, the shaft and glass move right, and the window behind them, left. If I stand up and step to the table, the glass at its edge moves downward, while the far end of the table, and the window with it, rise straight up in the air. Also if we stare steadily at a waterfall, then shift our gaze to the cliff face at its side, the rocks at once flow upward.

The eye is unsleeping, and all men are lidless Visionaries through the night.

Mind and eye are a logarithmic spiral coiled from periphery. This is called a 'spiral sweep'—a biological form which combines, as galaxies, economy with beauty. (We define beauty from symmetrical perceptions).

Subjects observing a flickered pulsation of light have seen something like a Catherine-wheel reversing rotation, with a center of fine detail. Men have found cells sensitive to light in the hearts of snails.

The human lens grows flatter for looking across a prairie, and the sparrow is able to see the seed beneath its bill—and in the same instant, the hawk descending. A cat watches the-sparrow-at-the-end-of-the-world in a furred luminosity of infrareds, enormous purples.

After a long time of light, there began to be Eyes, and light began looking with itself. At the exact moment of death the pupils open full width.

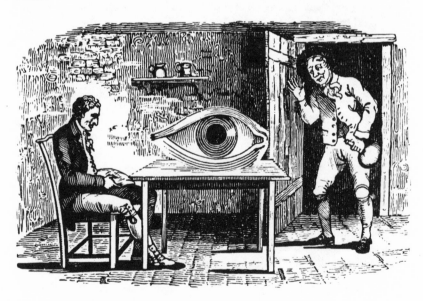

The Ear

Sound is sea: pattern lapping pattern. If we erase the air and slow the sound of a struck tuning-fork in it, it would make two sets of waves interlocking the invisibility in opposite directions.

As the prong of the fork moved one way, it compresses the air at its front, which layer in turn relieves its compression by expanding the layer in front, and so back and back. As it started the other direction it leaves the air in front (opposite) immediately rarefied. The air beyond this expands to the rarefaction—itself becoming rarefied—forth and forth.

Compression rarefaction compression rarefaction: these alternate equidistant forces travel at the rate of 1,180 feet per second through the elasticity of air, four times that through water (whale to singing whale) and fifteen times as fast through pure steel. Men have put ear to earth to hear in advance of air.

Pattern laps pattern, and as they joined, Charles Ives heard the nineteenth century in one ear, and the twentieth out the other, then commenced to make a single music of them. The final chord of the second Symphony is a Reveille of all notes at once, and *The Fourth Of July* ends with a fireworks of thirteen rhythmic patterns zigzaging through the winds and brasses, seven percussion lines criss-crossing these—the strings divided in twenty-fours going up and down every-which-way—and all in FFFF.

Both tuning fork and *Fourth* are heard by perturbations of molecules, through ever more subtle stumbling blocks, in spiral ricochet, to charged branches treeing a brain. Instantaneously.

The outer earshell leads to a membrane drum—and what pressure needed to sound this drum is equal to the intensity of light and heat received from a fifty-watt electric bulb at a distance of three thousand miles in empty space. (Though sound cannot travel, as light, through the void.) At the threshold of hearing the eardrum may be misplaced as little as a diameter of the smallest atom, hydrogen.

This starts a "hammer" to strike an "anvil" which nudges a "stirrup" —all bones—against a drum known as The Oval Window. Shut to air, this window vibrates another windowed membrane, tuning a compressed fluid between. *Here also, in curious loops, is seated our sense of the vertical.*

A resonance is set up in a spiral shell-shape receptor turned with yet another, also spiral, membrane. This is the ear's core, and as sound waves

277

themselves it trembles two directions at once—crosswise and lengthwise.

The mind begins early to select from the buzz and humdrum, till most men end hearing nothing, when the earth speaks, but their own voices. Henry David Thoreau seems to have been the first man to relearn to hear the musics of the actual: the Greeks may have strung their lyre to the planets, but Thoreau heard his stretched from first dark sparrow to last dog baying a moon.

That men may listen differently, and with wider closer ear, the poet writes.

William Carlos Williams wrote of eyeglasses lying now fifty years ago on a table, their gold earpieces folded down—"tranquilly Titicaca". Where sight and sound make crisper focus is song. The rule of perceptions is they sharpen.

While a bat uses its ears to see, its optics overtones, the fly hears only in frequencies of its own (and other) fly-wings. I once set out to learn to see and identify birds, but found instead I learned to hear—the ear better unwinds the simultaneous warblers in a summer beech-tree.

I know the housefinch singing outside the window just now heard its own song with slower and lower ears than mine, but I do not know what this means, or how it rings in finch-skull. Though all animals have an auditory range which includes hearing what they can eat, and what can eat them.

Inside, between ribs and gristle, the composer John Cage first "understood" music. When he entered an experimental room made to be without sound or echo, he has remarked, he heard two sounds "one high one low". The first his nervous system, the second the circulation of blood. "Music is perpetual," Thoreau wrote, "and only hearing is intermittent"

The physicists tell us that all sounding bodies are in a state of stationary vibration. And that when the word *Scheherazade* last shook the atoms, its boundary was an ever slighter pulse of heart, and hesitation of heat.

Matter delights in music, and became Bach. Its dreams are the abyss and empyrean, and to that end, may move, in time, the stones themselves to sing.

Brainstem Sonata: A Profile
of the Comprehensive Muse

DIANE ACKERMAN

I

For certain critical terms such as "romantic," there is, if not a law, at least
a history of diminishing returns. As long ago as 1923, the philosopher and
historian of ideas, Arthur O. Lovejoy, informed the Modern Language
Association of America that "romanticism" had "ceased to perform the
function of a verbal sign." Since then the term has gone downhill even
further, acquiring resonance as it has lost meaning, until now it ranks
somewhere between the provisional *see also* of an asterisk and an ena-
melled arm-ornament made for the Emperor Barbarossa. The history of
the word "romanticism" may even seem to be an anonymous "found
poem" evincing the phenomenological muddle that being human is, and
we are perhaps habituated to living dangerously whenever we use the
term. Like some of the unemployed, it is overqualified.

No such hazard, fortunately, attaches to the term "metaphysical." A
good deal of brisk and gratifying literary business has been done on its
behalf, and it is far from being played out. "Romantic elements in the
poems of Ponge" means much less than "metaphysical elements in the
work of Ponge"; we know, in the latter instance, roughly what we are
looking for, whereas, in the former, the main thing we can conclude is that
a booby-trap is somewhere on the premises.

If only, though, "metaphysical" were quite as simple as that. The term
is as mind-provoking as the poetry it denotes, in a sense closing before it
has opened fully, and pinning down some of the mannerisms of a certain
mental set without quite contacting the core. Emphasizing *devices,* it's a
better term for describing Donne's imitators than describing Donne himself or Herbert. It is as if anxious moderns, haunted by Aristotle's suggestion that there is "an art which imitates by language alone" which is a
"form of imitation without a name," had decided that "metaphysical" writing
would describe anything that strays from the usual categories. I will return
to that entrancing enigma of Aristotle's farther on; what matters here is
to suggest that most definitions of "metaphysical" leave something out:

From *Parnassus* (vol. 8, no. 1, 1979).

the bouquet as distinct from the taste, the vision as distinct from mere seeing.

We need the term "metaphysical" for certain poems of our own day, not so much to deprive Donne and Herbert (to name the best) of an adequate label as to rid them of one that seems inadequate, only to restore it to them amplified by what these two have in common with their successors in the present century. I have in mind not verbal gait, rhetorical strategy and tactics, not even the argument with one's self (which famously leads to poetry as surely as vinegar curdles milk), but rather an ability to register a thing's essence in the widest conceivable context: the figure in the ground of all-that-isn't-figure; not so much a trick of mind as one of mind's hungers, requiring of the poet both elasticity and something of the physician's disabused wisdom.

Before going any further though, I must return to the vicissitudes of the term itself. Eliot's formulation is well known and remains appetizing: "When a poet's mind is perfectly equipped for its work, it is constantly amalgamating disparate experience; the ordinary man's experience is chaotic, irregular, fragmentary. The latter falls in love, or reads Spinoza, and these two experiences have nothing to do with each other, or with the noise of the typewriter or the smell of cooking; in the mind of the poet these experiences are always forming new wholes." Notice, he talks of a mind that is *"perfectly"* equipped (a rare event), and when he says "work" he means work of a special kind: the work of being metaphysical. Notice, too, the implication that the poet can connect anything with anything. This is the type of poet for whom the whole of experience is fair game, and who might say to himself or herself: the universe is all that interests me, and *all* of it interests me, the only snag being that the All is unknowable. Therefore I restate my position to say: spellbound by the hypothesis of an All that is knowable only through its epitomes, I can afford to neglect nothing.

It is an amazing stance. It implies that a candle seen in the context of a star is that much more a candle, but also that the star seen in the context of a candle is that much more a star. Its augmental reciprocity wakes us up to the physics linking the two over and above the frail and sketchy nature of their names. To wake up to that physics is to become what Eliot defined as a sensibility which can "devour any kind of experience." He himself qualified over and over again in *Four Quartets* by extrapolating the swarm of phenomena to an omega point at which his mind almost failed:

a beyond which remains ineffable just past the beyonds that he can spell out as a quiver in his blood or a lurch in the stars. Eliot proposed the macrocosmic as the poet's vocation, with nothing excluded, and his shift of mind between 1921 and 1947 dealt only with what caused "dissociation of sensibility" (not Milton's fault, not Dryden's, but history's perhaps). His notion of the perfect poet's horizons remained the same, as well it might when one is a quarter of a century nearer to death and the ensuing dispersal, back into the general fund, of one's 10^{16} cells.

From that sublimity to A. Alvarez' version of metaphysical in *The School of Donne,* it is far from ridiculous to go; indeed, there is even a certain poetic justice to doing so, inasmuch as Alvarez borrowed his title from a book Eliot himself intended to write. But there is a mild descent from the view of an intermittently mystical poet, drenched in the towering loneliness-before-the-universe that is peculiar to American poets, to the view of an English critic who comes out of the crisp, no-nonsense, skeptical frame of mind which produced "Movement" poetry: cautious, dry, almost the poetic counterpart of the stiff upper lip. Alvarez is articulate, responsible, and sensitive, yet his version of Donne (as of the poetry Donne pioneered) is curbed.

A little more of the universe leaks into Donne's doings than one might think: or, to put it humdrumly, of physics and chemistry, of the unknown that was going to be known after 1905, and of the unknown that remains unknown even now. I think Donne dealt with this macrocosmic seepage more reverently than if it were some patch of impetigo on the ear. It is right to say, as Alvarez does, that "ideas, learning, dialectic and tough, sceptical rationality were *emotionally important* to" Donne (italics not mine), but it should also be said that Donne's emotions were conceptually important to him as well, and that means in the full awareness of his vulnerable status as an entity dependent on his planet. It is puzzling to find a primary case being made for Donne as a *mensch,* and only a secondary one for him as someone capable of ecstasy (being "thrown out" of one's self), misery to suicide point, and agnostic exaltation. The altogether social, hard-headed Donne, the exemplar of intelligent talk in verse, reminds us of Helen C. White's remark that "The seventeenth century was . . . very hard upon the unevenness of human energy." Donne was hard on Donne for being unstable and changeable. Picking up on that, Alvarez seems more interested in the Donne who puts a good face on things (a kind of Cavalier stoic) than in the Donne who, ever on the edge of losing his emotional poise, loses it only as a clergyman, addressing the eager audience of his sermons ("a speechless sin, a whispering sin, which nobody hears, but our own conscience"). The Donne of the hour sermon is dramatic and complete. A maestro of conjectural, exploratory wit merges with a synthesist of disparate phenomena; the man of the world merges with the man who puts his ear to the universe.

I am talking about an emphasis here, trying to rescue a point of view from its better-known rhetorical techniques, and if this entails slightly demoting Donne the polished wit in favor of Donne the death-haunted, dumbstruck muddler, then so be it. To be as intellectually in control as Donne is a fine and public thing, of course, and it must seem a superior feat of mind contrasted with what underlies it: not mysticism (he was too sociable and too much aware of himself for that), but an idiosyncratic sense of the universe, a sense which damnation and penitence and an almost flamboyant recoil from early sin flesh out, but don't quite embody. In the end, what impresses me most about Donne is not his control, but the side of his mind that threatens it. His poise has a meniscus like a full glass threatening to spill.

Enough of Donne. I stress him because he broke the ground. Among those in his wake, only Herbert in his wholly different way is unique, offering mellow decorum instead of angularity, an easy breathing yet intense tactfulness whose reverence is sensuously complete perhaps because he, much more than Donne, exploited the rhythms of prayer. Herbert's praise of God is every bit as fully documented—as thoroughly and voluptuously thought-out—as Donne's. Of course, Herbert would never have thought the sun "unruly," but his concern for mildly dependable orders of things, whether of the universe or courtly conduct at home and abroad, is far from the quaint and simplistic stance that some have thought it. What he brings to the perdurably metaphysical is agitated humility, which Vaughan manages to convey as an almost physical affliction less to be thought about (or *out*) than to be blurted almost impersonally. It is Crashaw, though, who extends what I am calling capacity or openness to include the *trouvaille,* the thing you leave in because it sounds or feels good, never mind where it came from. What is irrelevant, or seemingly so, remains in his works as a sample of itself, an instance of *what can happen to any poem*: open the mind wide enough, and the whole firmament may topple into it. Crashaw anticipates Mallarmé and Valéry and is the least British of the poets I am talking about; his is the *morning* of the fawn, in which the lapidary and the broad wash consort on the neatly cropped lawn of Seventeenth Century piety. He is his own "brisk Cherub" who "something sippes"; he is always briskly ingenious and sips just about anything within reach (the out-of-reach he improvises into his neighborhood until he can resist it no longer). To call him baroque is not enough; he is a baroque paradoxologist who heeds the rigor of Donne and Herbert, and his perversity is uncanny, enabling him to rise to the offhand metamorphosis of clothing the naked body of Christ in a suit of blood. His ability to turn one thing into another, not in the abstract but for the senses, is something a modern metaphysical can't really do without.

What have we so far? From Donne, a disabused and mortified openness that almost exceeds his enviable intellectual poise. From Herbert, the agitated humility that never boils over as it almost does in Vaughan. From Crashaw, a forceful way of interrupting the identity of a thing until everything verges on becoming everything else (the baroque One). It is almost enough, but I would be improvident not to gather up (perhaps in the spirit of Autolycus) Herbert of Cherbury's knack for worrying any given thing to death, like some aloof ferret; Cowley's weird and dual ability to sustain an argument in spite of his evidence and to remain interested in what is irrelevant without pretending to use it (he is the expert on "invisible connexions," which abound in the universe more than in his poems). All I want from Cleveland is the precedent for free association; he is an ingenious serendipitist lost in his own daydreams, given (as Alvarez says) "all the pleasures of metaphysics and only five and twenty per cent. of the danger." Marvell, who brings up the rear, merely rearranges tropes already sanctified, and his closed mind writes "begotten by despair/ Upon Impossibility" almost without probing either despair or impossibility, but rather implying, as a man among men, "*You* know; I needn't go into all *that.*" Something haughty spoils Marvell, a politician who knows too well what verse is for to be able to do anything rich with it. Five-finger exercises such as his lead to the Eighteenth Century rather than to the heart of things, which most of these other poets, in ways ranging from wholesale assault to demure sipping, try to reach and hold. Each, according to the rules of his own astute chatter, reaches and overreaches the point at which the mortal microcosm forgives the seeming immortality of the macrocosm. No small feat, that, entailing as it does the subordination of self to something too big to mourn, but big enough to survive the praises, the curses, it receives.

II

Historical conspectus can take us far enough to give an idea of what I want to retrieve from the Metaphysicals or the School of Donne, and what I want to set aside. Clearly, we have to investigate the mannerisms with which a certain attitude has been involved (and, in this instance, possibly submerged), and then ask: to what extent are the mannerisms and the attitude fused? Can the former be shed? Can the latter evolve into new mannerisms? Is the means indispensable to the matter?

It would seem almost axiomatic that a mind captivated by the All, and willing to entertain what Donne himself describes in the spirited, suave poem, "Variety," thrives on the miscellaneous, on contrarieties, on the phenomenological jumble that chance and necessity together produce. Donne himself asks

> . . . why should I
> Abjure my so much loved variety . . . ?

And in Herbert harmony arrives only when the perceiver has accommodated his senses and mind to life's complex abundance (what Charles Darwin usefully summed up as "panmixis"). The question this raises is trickier: does openness to experience require the exact mode of the Metaphysicals, with which they are definitely linked? I mean incongruous or incongruous-seeming juxtapositions, elaborated or perverse conceits, and abrupt snaps in tone. In one sense, a poem full of surprises teaches you how to read it as you advance, at once bracing you with the implication *Anything can happen next, not only in the poem but in the world,* and fortifying you with the idea that, having advanced thus far you are better able to take the next surprise. Yet the product of such a proposal would be a poetry of mere collocation, a catalogue of the Many rather than an adumbration of the One. Poets of almost unbelievable poise can give us a chaos that unnerves: Dante. Poets of no poise at all can give us only the blithe continuum of their minds, like unmade beds: Jean Arp (the running title across the page-top falls into his junk-heap of a poem, Kaspar is Dead, since there is no criterion to keep it out). If you want to be witty and *épatant,* it's no use writing like John Bunyan; but if you want to communicate what I have come to think of as a private (i.e. personal), broad, and expressible sense of the universe, you can write in whatever mode you want. Such a remark damages the Metaphysicals enormously, but only on a superficial plane. Their mannerisms clatter into the box reserved for eccentricities of intonation over the ages, while their vision—what Alvarez calls their "realism"—comes into the open as, at its best, a hyperattuned and ravenous attentiveness, a rage for dimension and complex weave. It is not mysticism or pantheism, but an appetite for the everythingness of anything. An atheist can have it. So can a devout theist. It is the humble invadedness of Traherne's "You never enjoy the world aright, till the sea itself floweth in your veins, till you are clothed with the heavens, and crowned with the stars: and perceive yourself to be the sole heir of the whole world." A compulsive stargazer afflicted with sea-fever is on the way toward it, even if he or she never says a word about it. But my concern here is with the articulated version in British and American poetry and with, in part, the disinclination of most poets (not to mention novelists and dramatists) to develop it, simple as its premise might be: call it *observant awe,* or borrow from Gabriel Marcel's *Essay in Autobiography* (1947) the following stately voluntary about

> . . . the metaphysical concern to discover the intimate at the heart of the remote, a concern, that is to say, not to overcome distance by speed, but to wrest from it the spiritual secret which destroys its power as a barrier. I think I have never felt attracted to speed for its own sake; what mattered to me was to discover an *elsewhere* which should be essentially a *here.* The world seemed to me then, as now, an indeterminate place in which to extend as much as possible the region where one is at home and to decrease that which is vaguely imagined or known only by hearsay, in an abstract and lifeless manner.

Marcel here transforms Traherne's invadedness into a feat of initiative, and his notion of "extend[ing] as much as possible the region where one is at home" is as close to a definition of "metaphysical" as I am going to come. But just flopping down anywhere, as it were, isn't enough, as he insists: you can only settle down in the universe by finding things out and by ridding yourself of superstitions, two things which the school of Donne practiced as best it could. In other words, it is an aspiration of the educated mind, a reconciliation to the way things are, predicated on the astonishing thought that, full as the universe is of juxtapositions as bizarre as any in Cowley or Cleveland, they only come about—the star-nosed mole, the

Horsehead Nebula in Orion, *pseudomonas radiodurans* (which feeds on the neutron flux in nuclear reactors), the mating habits of the bee, litmus, mercury, walnuts, eyes—because the physics and the chemistry is everywhere the same. The "invisible connexions" of which Cowley spoke form this grid along which the knowable and the unknowable are alike deployed, as if the universe itself were a demiurgic feat of pre-Elizabethan bravery in response to the puzzle: how many differing forms can you make out of a few given materials? Linnaeus thought he was going to find the answer to that with his Latin or Latin-form names for roughly 4,400 species of animals and 7,700 species of plants! Staggering, of course (especially from someone the exact contemporary of the poet Christopher Smart and a bit of a poet himself), but only half as staggering as the neat device, 10^{84}, which expresses the total of the elementary particles in the universe, give or take a few.

This quantitative view, clinched by a silent *Wow,* has implications beyond the mind's being swamped by an unthinkable number that so tiny a sign can state; the so-called qualitative response, to something so enigmatic and indefinable as "beauty," say, may well fall by the wayside, simply because it's possible for the metaphysical mind to reach a point at which everything knowable is beautiful. The created is sacred, I suppose that means, and we ought not to go about taking sides, favoring the rose petal over the tumor cell. The metaphysical mind may easily lapse into a state of opinionless gape; but that is the crude version, when words have failed and style no longer affords freedom of action. A subtler and more plausible view of the metaphysical mind would say that it may end up finding the whole of Creation beautiful while still preferring A and Z to B and Y. "Beauty," after all, derives from *deu²*, as the dictionary of Indo-European roots expresses it, and is cognate with the Greek verb *dunasthai,* meaning "to be able." The beauty of things may well consist in their ability *to be,* then, in their plain, miraculous presence.

Understandably, we feel less at the mercy of the raw, the undifferentiated, if we can interpose between phenomena and ourselves a tissue of the conceptual, and to this sense or illusion of mastery we cling, idiomatically saying *"per se,"* using a phrase to indicate that we can still go *behind* the word to the thing it signifies. In other words, when we (rather glibly perhaps) say *"Per se, gasket"*—or "in its own right, *gasket"* or *"gasket qua gasket"*—we are reliving a mental adventure latent in the word as well as confronting the thing again.

If we look up *gasket,* remotely remembering that the word provokes a giggle, we find the following: "seal or packing used between matched machine parts or around pipe joints to prevent the escape of a gas or fluid." The etymology is quite startling: *garcette,* we find, means "a little girl," presumably sealed or intact, and from whom nothing escapes and into whom nothing can enter. There is a virgin in every gasket, and behind *garcette* there is *garce* (a girl), behind which is *gars* (a boy), behind which is an unattested Frankish word *wrakjo,* meaning "one pursued, an exile." Can it be that, in the minds of distant times, a virgin was excluded or excepted until she (or indeed he) had been successfully pursued and rendered viable? Or is it the fluid that, escaping, exiles itself from its proper conduit and has to be gone after? Such resonances enrich the mind of the educated reader who, staring at a single word as both history and metaphor, discovers an ancestor in the act of coining a simile or metaphor which, in gaining his word, we lose. The word itself—*gas-ket*—sounds like something leaking with a whisper or a hiss, and it also yields an etymological ricochet through *gas,* the word coined by J. B. van Helmont (1577–1644), a Belgian chemist, to denote an occult principle supposed to be present in all bodies. The word van Helmont purloined was actually the Greek *khaos,* meaning "chaos."

It would be rash to ask all readers to enter the etymological present (some bits of etymology would get in the way of the word's modern usage), but it would be just as rash to erase the word's ancestry: to do so would be to pass up an instance of the human imagination's adapting itself to phenomena at the same time it takes mental control of them. The question raised is this: if you are dealing in language at all sensitively, how good a reason have you for discarding any aspect of a word's activity? What matters just as much as accurate definition is what a word reveals, never mind how backhandedly, about how the mind behaves. Indeed the history of such a word as *indri,* for example, is rather more entrancing than the fact that the word has stuck to a large lemur notable for silky fur and a short tail. The French naturalist Pierre Sonnerat, hearing the Malagasy word *indri!* (look!) mistakenly assumed it was the animals' name. How astonishing it would be if *indri* actually embodied some qualities of that animal: a fluke, of course, like the gas in gasket, but in the end it is part of our heritage and all we have to work with when dealing with gaskets and indris.

If, as Borges says, each single thing implies the whole universe, then each thing amounts to an inexhaustible object of contemplation, and Cowley's "invisible connexions" are with us again. Even misnomers, then, have their place not only in the epistemological gropings of the race, but also in our notion of the universe itself. Indeed, the history of misnomers tells us as much about humanity as all the wrong hypotheses in the history of science. What I call the metaphysical mind finds nothing alien to it, least of all perhaps the concept *alien* itself, and reading etymologically is just one of the ways of making contact: we put the word back together from its parts; we thicken our notion of a gasket or an indri by sampling what has accreted around it; and, in the act of rediscovering all the relationships that come to bear upon the gap where the word is going to be, we relive the role of Adam who, in James Dickey's words, "closed his eyes and saw that the world was still there, inside his head."

A chimpanzee staring at a hibiscus may feel something of this, even while preparing to eat the stem. A biologist peering at a specimen of E-coli, with the specter of recombinant DNA facing him, is open to rebuke if he or she does not feel it. And a poet dabbing a finger at an elusive blob of mercury may well feel oppressed, swamped even, by relationships and interactions that are part of the mental field in which the blob quivers. One need only read Santayana to develop a passion for the essence of something; but to wheel Heisenberg up to him, in a spirit of mischief, is to recognize—to be obliged to recognize—that the more you know what the blob is like, the less you know what works upon it. There does indeed seem to be an indeterminacy beyond the one having to do with speed *vis-à-vis* position: not only do we not quite know where something is, the more we know its position, and vice versa; the more we fix on what appear to be the intrinsic qualities of a daffodil, a fingernail, the hub of the Milky Way, the more we cheat ourselves about the quality of their membership in the universe. It is as if knowledge were *action,* and knowing were a feat of constantly agile reconnaissance. The more we put our head down, the more we should lift it up; and, even if we soothe ourselves by positing both steady gaze and alert reconnaissance in a private mental flux that needs no rubbernecking from the senses, the fact remains that even the most disciplined scrutiny is almost a Platonic ideal. We aspire to it, no doubt, but we cannot quite achieve it. And we talk about it, we set it up as an ideal for poets and esthetes, more to keep alive a needed attitude (in Arnold's phrase) than to bring about anything definite.

No thing is an island, then, though many things seem peninsulas. A criterion begins to emerge, by which second-class perceiving equates itself with seeing things in a limited way. I mean there is a second-class view of a ball-point pen (it ignores the astonishing tenacity of the component atoms within a certain pattern, until we drop the pen into the fire or a bottle of concentrated acid). The metaphysical mind, I suggest, is haunted by the perpetual possibility not only of seeing something intricately enmeshed in its context, but also of seeing it in other contexts. The pen melts or dissolves. Aristotle's ancient knife vanishes before our very eyes: we replace the blade, then the handle, and the knife has gone. Where has it gone? The idea of it has gone. The substance has gone. Yet nothing goes. In just such a way we might typify an attitude haunted by the flux that fixities are and to which they forever return. You can cry out with Pater for something fixed where all is moving, but there is no such thing, and the mature view of nature is one that is *processive*. Words themselves are slithering away from us even as we scrutinize them; etymology, which reassuringly fixes things, also opens up side-doors into metaphor and long-buried vagaries in sensibility such as only a psychometric anthropologist could pin down. As Claude Lévi-Strauss claims, certain clans in Latin America "stand in a joking relationship to each other." They have discovered the relativism of linguistic process:

> . . . among the Luapula: the Leopard and Goat clans because the leopards eat goats, the Mushroom and Anthill clans because mushrooms grow on anthills, the Mush and Goat clans because men like meat in their mush, the Elephant and Clay clans because women in the old days used to carve out elephant's footprints from the ground and use these natural shapes as receptacles instead of fashioning pots.

Against such a phenomenon, drawn from a primitive level, Francis Ponge's gratitude to Malherbe, expressed in an interview with Serge Gavronsky ("on February 7th, 1972, at five o'clock, in Francis Ponge's living room"!), seems almost a voice in the wilderness. From the time of Malherbe, says Ponge, "classical writers used words properly, their meanings emerged from their Latin roots." The trouble is, of course, that the human race almost always uses language improperly; it pleases itself, and no international polyglot academy of correct usage is going to put things right.

It is impossibly hard to deal with a thing intrinsically: with a thing or with its word. We can get so far and then we begin to overlap with another thing or another word, and then with the natural processes that sponsor both: photosynthesis, say, or imagination. The daffodil hoods a bee. The ancient word for *spring* invades the springbok. Even more daunting, one of the marks of a nimble intelligence is the capacity for wordplay, in which one thing via its word becomes another at dizzying speed, almost as if intelligence itself were always on the run, bent on thriving by sheer preposterous tangential accumulation, on asserting its presence in (or at) the world by flushing out as many rabbits as possible with the fewest phonemes. There must be, of course, somewhere, stranded in a kennel on an Alp, say, a homespun intellect capable of looking at a feather for years without *construing* it, which is the physical equivalent, I suppose, of looking at an old proverb such as *homo homini lupus,* recognizing that *homini* is a noun in the dative case but without spotting this inflected form's relationship to *homo* and *lupus*: in other words, getting not "man a wolf to man" but merely "man-man-wolf."

The difference, oddly enough, is that the physical universe is rather like the words in a Latin poem: word order matters little, except for meter, because the words can fit together in only one way for one meaning; the syntactic integrity is supposed to be unique, incapable of being used against itself. The verbal universe, on the other hand, provides no guarantees; sea-changes abound, as do libertine decipherings that end up definitive, and would-be definitive ones that end up going by the board altogether, labeled *"Obsolete"* in the grim code of the lexicographer. So the metaphysical mind has to play a double role: both relishing nature's integrity, the One's lustrous hold on the Many, even while trying to view bits of the Many as if the One were in temporary abeyance, and examining words for what in their history is discrete rather than amorphous or lost, preferring perhaps the "sprinkle" element in *spring* (it is the locution of millions of humans dead and gone) over, say, Cummings' "mud-luscious," which, appetizing as it may be, amounts to an intrusive neologism, a Johnny-come-lately to the verbal canon.

No doubt of it, nature and language have evolved differently; in the former, certain characteristics are "selected for" (as the jargon has it), whereas in the latter, things that might well have been ironed out have come to stay (*indri* we tolerate out of mere laziness) while things we need (a verb, not beginning with the letter *l*, which means to put the body horizontal!) have disappeared. Dig into the moon as we may (a later version of crying for it), the moon remains much the same, whereas the tradition of moon imagery is constantly changing, since, in one sense, it is not obliged to be accurate. The metaphysical mind tries to be accurate, initially within limits, then about context, and sees the virtue of applying just such a procedure to language itself in order to find the spoor, the trace, of early humans trying to do much the same thing with animistic equipment. *Per se* is a discipline, then, hard to sustain among the swarm of phenomena and the constant associative growth of words, but essential if we are not to have a vague, slovenly view of nature or of the nature of language itself.

III

As might be obvious, I am no longer able to keep the discussion from toppling over, naturally enough, into metaphor and metamorphosis, the latter of which I see as the consummate, irreversible version of the former (a supreme metaphor creates a metamorphosis). Occupied as I often am with the question, to what extent anything can be fully described in terms of itself, I find the answer coming to me with teasing regularity on page two of every student response to the assignment "Describe an object." Without fail they break into metaphor as if into the language of home after a strained excursion into alien terrain.

Metaphor, of course, is a transfer of meaning. Semantic analysts have called it "deviant discourse" and some have suggested that metaphorical statements cannot be verified and so are not genuinely meaningful, whereas Ernst Cassirer has argued for the existence of primitive metaphorical thinking as the source of myth and poetry. It is not hard to believe Cassirer in this, or the French poet Pierre Reverdy who notes that "Insofar as the juxtaposition of entities be separated by the greater distance, and yet be just, the metaphor will be thereby stronger." Or Max Ernst, who in relating how an illustrated catalogue stimulated his capacity for *collage* talks the idiom of metaphor itself: "I found here united elements such poles apart that the very incongruousness of the assembly started off a sudden intensification of my visionary faculties and a dreamlike succession of contradictory images. . . ." And T. S. Eliot, in his essay on Philip Massinger, observes that certain lines by Tourneur and Middleton "exhibit that perpetual slight alteration of language, words perpetually juxtaposed in new and sudden combinations, meanings perpetually *einge-schachtelt* into meanings, which evidences a very high development of the senses. . . ." Eliot is talking here about style in general, but the metaphorical yield from juxtapositions ("new and sudden combinations") forms part of what he commends. Look where we will, we find metaphor, as well as abundant tribute to it, and what mainly concerns me here is metaphor's emotional role or, if you like, the psychology of the thing, not what's suspect in it.

Why do we enjoy it? At its barest it links zones of experience not linked in nature. In "The Lord is my shepherd," for example, what's startling is not so much the apparition of the deity as a proven presence, or even the dubious idea that someone or some entity can "shepherd" a human being, as the combination of an abstraction with shepherding. Indeed, a quizzical reader may well object that the metaphor cannot even begin to work until the reader, or listener, has fed in a bit of personal anthropomorphism. I mean that "Lord" is not going to work here if it amounts only to something as abstract as universal energy or first cause or continuous creation. Of course the metaphor addresses itself to the persuaded, for whom the *shepherding* is less a surprise than for a non-vitalist, say, for whom the combination has two surprises. First, there is the association of any human at all with the deity, and, second, with that specific activity that includes watching and guiding sheep, crooking them up out of gullies and bogs, keeping off predators, and the like.

The metaphor presupposes part of itself; and, if you find the first part hard to swallow, you may find the metaphor all the more daring because now it means, perhaps, *Continuous creation is my shepherd,* and that implies a shepherd who keeps on creating new pastures to fill the wide open spaces the expanding universe creates. Of course, that's a forceful reading, a pleasurable recognition the psalmist David could not have had in mind. And yet, who knows what sense of the universe's awesome and abstract grandeur didn't get smoothed out into the *Elōhim* David used? It is worth noting that *Elōhim* is the plural of *Elōah*: Gods from God; so clearly the idea settled down from being several ideas (Strong's *Hebrew and Chaldee Dictionary* ends its entry with ". . . sometimes as a superlative:—angels, x exceeding. God (gods) (=dess, =ly), x (very) great, judges, x mighty." Quite a multiplication for a herdsman to be. So, the non-believer has to do all this theological work for him- or herself, according to very few rules.

(Christine Brooke-Rose has devised *A Grammar of Metaphor,* but essentially there is no such thing, any more than there is a "grammar" for twiddling your thumbs, whistling in the dark, or even staring at the sky.) The only "grammar" is nature's.

This renews my point. Metaphor permits links or fusions not so much forbidden as just unavailable in certain forms. For instance, it blurs at least on the verbal plane certain old dualisms: mind and body, in William Carlos Williams' words "the people and the stones." It may even relate jargon to the majesty and mystery of Creation, or the thing more intimately to its word, or the word to the mouth uttering it, or steadfastness with Gibraltar. James Dickey has it straight in his lecture *Metaphor As Pure Adventure:*

> . . . the natural order of things *is* the natural order. A river is not a stone, and a tree is not a star; nor is a woman a tigress (that is, not *literally*). But poets believe, with a high secret glee, that precisely because God made these things as they are (the star, the tree, the woman), because He made them so much themselves that they can be nothing *but* themselves, someone else—someone like a poet, say —can come along and compare a star to a woman, or to a tree, and accomplish something valuable by it. Poets believe that the things of this world are capable of making connections between each other that not God but men see, and they say so.

The sad ghost of Coleridge beckons from the shadows. Dickey says nothing about congruity and seems to imply that anything can become anything else. I doubt very much that a potato peeler can become a sponge, or an elf a sanitary napkin or the Eagle Nebula something to type on. A surrealist poem by David Gascoyne asserts that the sun is a bag of nails, but it is hardly ever likely to be that, even if you push as hard as you can for the needling sensation as ultraviolet hits and pierces the skin. All very well for the Dada or Surrealist poet to combine things at random, indiscriminately (like Jean Arp in "Kaspar is Dead," a poem already mentioned) finding idyllic deer in a petrified paper box, addressing ships as *"parapluie"* and the winds as "keeper of the bees ozone spindle your highness." It nearly works; almost anything *nearly* works since it's almost impossible to write *total* gibberish; but, in the end, even such an image as "the black bowling alley thunders behind the sun," while exemplifying a blinkered view of celestial mechanics or a parochial view of the solar system, doesn't work because it displays an unobservant eye, an incurious mind.

Now an alternative world or a heterocosm is not in itself deplorable; it's a useful way of venting spleen or making readers laugh or redemonstrating Coleridge's idea of Fancy. But it puts all the emphasis on the supervising mind and downgrades phenomena to mere bagatelle. For the believer *The Lord is my shepherd* is congruous in the extreme, for the unbeliever epistemologically it could almost be so; but *The Lord is my bowling alley* is facetious only, *The Lord is my umbrella* is possibly correct but only in an unresonant way, and *The Lord is my Manhattan collection of fatted zebras* is close to saying nothing at all. What is it that's inherent in things? Is the principle of congruity akin to that which the taxonomy of Linnaeus implies after all? Are we really much more hidebound than we think?

Metaphors multiply, but they also reduce. When Poe writes "That wilderness of glass," meaning the sea, he extends three ideas—wilderness, glass, and sea—but he also assimilates them one to another and in so doing reduces the sense one always has of experience as clutter. Wilderness, glass, and sea come together and don't come apart, whereas if I say of the sea "that menagerie of parquet," the unhappy couple will soon come apart and the sea will have nothing to do with them. So: for sheer surprise, almost any contraption will serve; any haphazard pair or group, like ice cream on fried liver, or toothpaste on apple pie. But an initial surprise that lingers on as a melody intensifying two components almost to the point of redefinition—"our little life/ Is rounded with a sleep"—demands analytical and profound discernment of a high order, an almost purposeful noticing which, for all I know, reflects the teleology that keeps the world together and a squirrel's head from forming on a lark. In short, there is a propriety in things which only nature, functioning or malfunctioning, seems entitled to break, and we are that propriety's proprietors. To write nonsensical combinations is to set down a world we don't inhabit and ignore the one we do. Poetry seems to be pragmatic after all, and obligated to its world.

If this looks like a refusal to let poetry be original, it is not. I am trying to distinguish between, on the one hand, the yoking together by violence (whim, carelessness, or the plain desire to be outrageous) words whose only relationship remains verbal, and, on the other juxtapositions that take us to the heart of things much as Lewis Thomas does when he writes:

My mitochondria comprise a very large proportion of me. I cannot do the calculation, but I suppose there is almost as much of them in sheer dry bulk as there is the rest of me. Looked at in this way, I could be taken for a very large, motile colony of respiring bacteria, operating a complex system of nuclei, microtubules, and neurons for the pleasure and sustenance of their familes, and running, at the moment, a typewriter.

Two *verys* in one paragraph evince a high degree of astonishment, I suppose, but they precede the grand-slam finale of the typewriter, which reminds us of Eliot's notion of what an *un*dissociated sensibility is like. Thomas takes his vision or epiphany further and recognizes that

> . . . the same creatures, precisely the same, are out there in the cells of sea gulls, and whales, and dune grass, and seaweed, and hermit crabs, and further inland in the family of skunks beneath the back fence, and even in that fly in the window. Through them, I am connected; I have close relatives, once removed, all over the place.

That is moving not least because it can be extended even to having a sugar-cube of material from a neutron star come drilling through everything as if everything were so much lard, like a visit from the aristocracy of matter, except that, in our physics, the neutron star is allowed for too and so is part of the nature we inhabit. It is, tangentially, part of us. Preposterous? Not half as preposterous as the story by Julio Cortázar in which a young man keeps on vomiting up baby rabbits: an entertaining, frisky story, I think, but one devised to exhibit a mentality special to its narrator rather than to conduct us into the workings of nature.

I am not arguing against fun, the free play of the mind, the corruption of the staid by the antic, the creation of what cannot be; playful writers from Aristophanes to Italo Calvino have rarely felt constrained by natural categories. Indeed, I believe that everything that is imagined belongs to the sum of created things, is "as real a fact as the sun," as Emerson says, and thus modifies the part of nature we carry in our heads.

The vast realm of natural entelechy is virtually unknowable, but we already have on the books more information than any poet can use. The odd thing is that so little of it has shown up in poetry, as if poets had been content to paint landscape without pondering the entelechy of soil, or to notice and celebrate the seasons without pondering entelechy there. It is as if knowledge, or at least knowing beyond a certain point, had been decreed unpoetic according to some unwritten principle of decorum. A finer instance of sensibility (or mentality) dissociated or split up, indeed divided and cankered, it would be hard to find. Defying its *own* entelechy, here is, and here has been, sensibility over the centuries (since the Restoration critics froze out metaphysical poetry without saying why it erred), making a part of itself do duty for the whole. It may well be that philosophy (i.e., science) can clip an angel's wings; but not an eagle's, a bat's, or those of the X-15 experimental aircraft; it is likelier that a genuine decorum—what is "fitting" according to nature in the round—cannot be breached at all, and that a true metaphysical view will find nothing unpoetic(!) in the fact of the planet Venus as a boiling hell of gas and acid wrapped in a lethal cloud. It is astonishing to find how superstition and vacuous social usage have kept poetry away from its natural dimension, which is not the cute, the pretty, the innocuous, but the *knowable.* What has happened to poetry is akin to what was thought of electricity in the Eighteenth Century: a quaint entertaining thing, just right for picking up flakes of paper with a charged comb. Our view of electricity has advanced, but in a sense our view of poetry has not, even though those forebears in the Seventeenth Century had much of the necessary equipment and, some of them, minds incapable of being shocked by an idea. Oddly enough, so that science could advance, the Royal Society and its followers, insisting on plain and literal language, lowered the boom on precisely the sensibility that could have relished and celebrated their aims. Bacon, Hobbes, and Sprat in fact threw out the baby of an integrated poetry along with the bathwater of baroque and clever excess. What those long-dead anti-individualists failed to recognize was a simple, self-evident truth: the more you delve into the entelechy of nature, the solider—the more seriously, the more consequentially founded—your individual style is going to be. Indeed, a thoroughgoing expressionist, twisting and mutilating at every turn, but twisting and mutilating what has come initially from nature, is a lot closer to the human mainstream than some plain-minded soul apostrophizing his mistress' face as cherries, peaches, cream, and crystal.

None of this is quite as far as it may seem from the metaphysical mind. It's just as well that we have shed part of our susperstitious heritage: we now have to deal with nature on its own terms, and this means our substituting awareness for magic, a capacious sense of the All for a spurious set of reach-me-down divinities. Conceivably, as a result, we may redefine our notion of harmony as the condition in which everything *belongs,* which amounts to an accommodation of our minds to nature, to what Lewis Thomas calls "a chancy kind of order, always on the verge of descending into chaos, held taut against probability by the unremitting, constant surge of energy from the sun." He goes on, after some rapt allusions to "the descants of whales" and "the tympani of gorilla breasts," to wonder if such a process has a musical equivalent beyond (his first notion) the Brandenburg Concertos, and comes up with a "grand canonical ensemble," a term borrowed by thermodynamics from music via mathematics, and clearly on its way back to music but "refreshed" after contact with such a concept as that of H. J. Morowitz, who contends that a steady flow of energy over our planet cannot but bring about the deployment of matter into an increasingly orderly state. Such is what Thomas calls "the music of *this* sphere." That is quite a thing for the head of a cancer hospital to produce, quite a harmony to present.

If we are clearer now about the nature of matter, then perhaps we are clearer, too, about the nature of language; if we know how fragile and yet how firm the forms of nature are, then we know too how fragile-firm our sign-systems are as well. We can do in words what nature cannot, and we can also do in words all that nature can—at least we can reproduce it without overt and misleading personifications, without skidding from reverence into myth. In other words, our making with words can include the unmade and the made, the only proviso being that, with the former, we know *now* that the creation happens only on the verbal level. What an extraordinary privilege, to be both reportorial and to be able to indulge in disabused mythmaking, no longer wondering if Prometheus was the first pyromaniac felon, if dragon's teeth planted really do come up as men, if there ever was a golden age. It should be clear now that I am contemplating the opportunity for an unsuperstitious poetry which, at first glance harnessed to the microtome and the stained slide, can roam farther and wider than its atavistic forebear did. It's merely a matter of allowing knowledge as much scope as we've allowed mumbo-jumbo (and then, if one so wishes, putting the myths about things into a truer context: Prometheus next to nuclear fusion or the linear accelerator; a dinosaur tooth into a copy of the primeval broth cooked up in laboratories; gold into the neighborhood of time-ceasium or the concept of the half-life). Such maneuvers can hardly bring about an extra vagueness in imagery and they almost surely enhance the idea of precision itself. Philosophy, in Keats's sense of "science," has not so much clipped the poet's wings as provided an airline instead. The astonishing thing is that so few poets have responded to the universe's invitation; the short-sighted, the merely social, seems to be the preferred mode, and so long after Emerson's ravishing, definitive proclamation in a time that had much less knowledge than ours:

> The poet, by an ulterior intellectual perception . . . puts eyes and a tongue into every dumb and inanimate object. . . . As the eyes of Lyncaeus were said to see through the earth, so the poet turns the world to glass, and shows us all things in their right series and procession. For through that better perception he stands one step nearer to things, and sees the flowing or metamorphosis. . . .

One step nearer! Whoever collects enough pop-bottles may eventually find the holy grail; and, even if there's no holy grail to be found, the collector will have a grand array of pop-bottles. I don't see how that formulation of Emerson's could be bettered, even if, along the soaring curve of the unknown, there are to be as-yet unthinkable revelations. What he offers is an entelechy of knowledge for a world turned increasingly to glass. The boldest, most comprehensive metamorphosis of all is that of givens into knowledge. What is "out there" but as yet unknown isn't knowledge, even if it affects us non-stop. Knowledge is what the mind invents in self-serving catalysis, and it is surely reckless—on the part of poets, painters, composers, suburban novelists concerned with demure changes of heart among well-to-do collectors of antiques—not to regard the known as part of the pillageable main. If I stand on my lawn and shoot an arrow south, I am aiming at the heart of the Milky Way, and I think it possible, without being in the least fetishistically automatic about it, thus to frame every mental act, every perception, every meal, every breath. Emerson's "ulterior intellectual perception" is no solecism, no fatheaded chimera, but a full stretch that rebukes all poets crouching over restricted material. *Habeas porpoise,* one says to the merely anthropocentric poet interested only in the generic, the vague, the typed. One might say other things as well, but Emerson does it better.

All things are ripe for poetry, as Rilke said, and I am proposing no exclusions, but rather something ecumenical and alchemical, way beyond the old poetic-versus-unpoetic (the pylon poetry of the 1930s for example) or even the delusive notion of Beauty, slain by Eliot during his Charles Eliot

Norton castigation of Matthew Arnold: "the essential advantage for a poet is not to have a beautiful world with which to deal; it is to be able *to see beneath both beauty and ugliness*; to see the boredom, and the horror, and the glory" (italics mine). Unfortunately the human mind likes its beauty smoothed out, made formulaic. It abhors chaos, which its hippic and reptilian cortices keep on creating even while something as yet unexplained in its transmitter chemicals regrets the fact. Hence the appeal of the Linnean taxonomy, for example, or of Plato's divided line in Book VI of *The Republic,* or indeed of Manicheanism, Marxism, or Master-Racism. Whether a genuine order matching one in nature itself or a bogus one imposed, the order the mind craves suggests a passion for pattern, almost as if neatness could serve as a substitute for teleology. We remember, we form our traditions from, those who have grouped and/or construed phenomena, and not those who have stopped short at observation. We favor seasonal time over mere chronicity, interpretation over a bewildered acceptance of enigma, and even—at our most defenseless—a hypothetical "omega point" toward which all Creation moves, according to Teilhard de Chardin, over a directionless flux. For the sake of sheer manageability, we prefer (after Isaiah Berlin's version of Archilochus) the hedgehog (who knows one big thing) to the fox (who knows many things). We ask which way is the world going, not which ways. And, in literature, those who assimilate the commotion of phenomena to some central idea or mood (say Virgil, Milton, Wordsworth, Shelley) offer more solace than those masters of contrariety and clash who assimilate the commotion without modifying it too much (say Propertius, Donne, Shakespeare, Byron). It is not, I think, a matter of a value judgment, but rather one of atavistic easiness (of being-at-ease-in-the-world: Heidegger, whom I am echoing here, saw in National Socialism something of the purposefulness he'd seen in the city states of Ancient Greece). Some writers, in Beckett's phrase, provide a form "which will accommodate the mess," whereas others, like Whitman, mold the mess into form, and present it essentially mediated.

But meaning is almost as much of an unknown quantity as beauty; the Victorian optimist who cries out with homesickness: "Is there not a heart even such as mine behind the vain show of things?" is shadow-boxing to much the same extent as Odon of Cluny, who finds intestines ugly through and through. One unappealing way of settling the matter is to attribute both meaning and beauty to efficiency in performing an assigned function.

Another way is to put the whole question aside and consider something smaller, such as life's assimilability. What with urbanity we like to call Mind abhors chaos, and is obliged to take in so much so fast, in all its haphazard multiplicity, that it fears becoming just as fragmented as what it perceives. So, lest it smother, it resorts to simplifications, psycho-pastorals, which create a category where both belong, or evolve a harmonious relationship between the two, and so on.

Reduction, puzzling-out, integration are the goals, all toward a second-best, which is the homogeneous instead of the heterogeneous, rather than best-best, which is harmony. And harmony, as suggested earlier, is a condition in which everything congruously belongs. The only problem is in figuring out the congruity, which amounts to adapting our minds to the ways of nature, or at least to those ways we haven't been able to modify to fit what we'd prefer. It follows then that our harmony will derive from two harmonies: the unmitigated ready-made one, and the made-over one from which cancer, like tuberculosis, has been erased. Even that isn't homogeneous, since nature looks unlikely to remain altogether itself or to become wholly custom-made according to the heart's desire. It is hard to tell what will come of weather-control, the control of dyslexia by antihistamines, half a century's experimentation with recombinant DNA, but it would be rash, I think, to envision a world, a nature, from which incongruity has been *removed.* We are almost certain to have to go on adjusting to things that don't harmonize with other things. Never quite gymnasts of inertia, we will never become "connoisseurs of chaos" either. A middle road suggests being ambulatory without being pedestrian, of remaining vigilant while settling down among familiar concepts.

Part of the trouble, of course, is in the mind, not "out there" at all. We free-associate, some of us more than others, but everyone has a private version of what Eliot saw as "experiences . . . always forming new wholes" and exemplified in the Conclusion to *The Use of Poetry and The Use of Criticism* as "certain images" that recur, "charged with emotion." It is worth noting that Eliot prefers to speak of "saturation" rather than of "associations," as if arguing something integral and structural rather than random. His own well-known sample goes as follows:

> The song of one bird, the leap of one fish, at a particular place and time, the scent of one flower, an old woman on a German mountain path, six ruffians seen through an open window playing cards at night

at a small French railway junction where there was a water-mill: such memories may have symbolic value, but of what we cannot tell, for they come to represent the depths of feeling into which we cannot peer.

One might easily produce several pages of commentary on this; let it suffice to point out the example's gradual crescendo of specificity, as if gathering toward an unmade point, which he then makes as a point in the abstract (the poetry is in the inscrutability) and to wonder what bearing regression under hypnosis might have on such images. What Eliot is telling us (and in a deliberately relaxed idiom that must have struck his hearers at Harvard as an excursion into inadvertent poetry) is that our heads fill up with all sorts of stuff we find hard to fathom or to control, and that it is as natural for our heads to behave this way as for flowers to attract bees. The mind is not only an instrument, but also a source, a pool, a vat, a useful oubliette, which sounds Proustian until we remember that Proust's involuntary memory cannot be cajoled or coerced and that, essentially, Proust is the master of analysis rather than the master of memory (it, if anything, masters him). Besides, the question here, as Eliot insists, is not one of either free or hindered association, but of chronic intensity leading to saturation; the image resists all overt figuring out and so is all the more useful, in the context of my own argument at any rate, as a sample of enigmatic mental flux having something in common with the vast, bombinating, proliferating growth of nature itself. Phenomena just add up, to no sum except the one the mind had reached when it was halted in mid-tally. Saliences such as these amount to what Thomas de Quincey called *involutes*—unforgettable but indecipherable. In *Suspiria de Profundis* he puts it thus:

> . . . far more of our deepest thoughts and feelings pass to us through perplexed combinations of *concrete* objects, pass to us as *involutes* (if I may coin that word) in compound experiences incapable of being disentangled, than ever reach us *directly,* and in their own abstract shapes.

An untidy, almost ungainly sentence, it nonetheless sums up a large amount of literature otherwise surrendered to analysis and anticipates formulations from writers as ostensibly far apart as André Breton and Samuel Beckett. The former's version appears in *Nadja* evoked in "facts which may belong to an order of pure observation, but which on each occasion present all the appearances of a signal, without our being able to say precisely which signal, and of what. . . ." Breton sees certain juxtapositions or combinations that surpass our understanding, and even the categories of beautiful/useful/accurate/unique, and can conclude only that life needs to be deciphered like a cryptogram, if at all. We are not far here from Beckett's reference in *Watt* to

> incidents that is to say of great formal brilliance and indeterminable purport

or the fuller version in *Molloy*:

> There are things from time to time, in spite of everything, that impose themselves on the understanding with the force of axioms, for un-known reasons.

How far, I am wondering, can we go beyond merely grooming our *trouvailles*? The metaphysical mind thrives on such things, which epito-mize the raw disconcertingness of the everyday rather than the mellow congruities of daydream. I have in mind certain keen lines of Propertius or Donne or Gottfried Benn which are just as raw as unmediated experi-ence, starting as many problems as they solve. In contrast, certain lines of Sophocles or Milton or Shelley suggest a manipulative zeal to ease the mind. The one gets you wincing a bit, the other settling back as if the poem had cooed. Take for instance this, from a macabre elegy by Pro-pertius:

> her eyes the same; her dress scorched down one side;
> the fire had eaten at her favorite beryl ring

which is by no means one of his most elliptical or startling glimpses, but which is *unobliging* or lacks the conciliatory glaze of the following from *Oedipus at Colonus*:

> Think of some shore in the north
> Concussive waves make stream
> This way and that in the gales of winter:
> It is like that with him. . . .

The Propertius makes no attempt to provide an adjustment, the other does; the Propertius has no decorum in mind, the Sophocles does, and even the difference between non-dramatic and dramatic poetry can't explain the fact away. If you take the matter further, you end up with an *impertinent* quality which reminds you not only of the world-view cultivated by the School of Donne but also of the noises their poetry made. Relish this awkward, ugly thing, they say. Hear it squawk or taste the grating sound of this indecorous comparison. The sound effects of that School, their conceits and perversities, may not have been the essential thing about them, but they showed which way the wind was blowing in their minds. You can't become a metaphysical just through tricks or trappings, but certain of both of these will come more naturally to such a poet than to poets of other kinds. Something in experience that's jarring, puzzling, raw, sharp, or vertiginously heady (like Kierkegaard's "glad over seventy thousand fathoms") afflicts the metaphysical mind, which has the feeblest response of all to life's icing, its cushions, its conventions, and reminds us of Santayana's little fit of cerebral climatics: "There are brains like a South American jungle, as there are others like an Arabian desert, strewn with nothing but bones. While a passionate sultriness prevails in the mind there is no end to its luxuriance." Shocking the bourgeoisie is all very well as a literary policy, but the metaphysical willy-nilly scandalizes him- or herself, too, as if addicted to impediment, reared on grit in a swoon, and somehow imbued with a drive that forces language to denature itself: that is, to seem less of a token than is usual and more like the nonverbal things it states.

How awkward for the poet, and how much more awkward for the poet's readers. It's like filling teeth with a superbly conducting metal, say copper; but it's the metaphysical poet who listens best to the constant shifts in epistemological perspective that flood us in the age of knowledge: who else is likely to relish the fact that a neutrino, like a vampire, has no mirror image (right-polarized neutrinos do exist, but left-polarized do not!). That, to the kind of mind I am trying to describe, seems both to test and to vindicate a certain cast of the literary mind that keeps on hoping for more of the same, with J.B.S. Haldane: "the universe is not only queerer than we suppose but queerer than we *can* suppose." It's all a matter of augmenting the sense of wonder in the context of how people behave and respond, dream and grow. There is nothing clinical in this, nothing that's incompatible with all those other things the non-metaphysical poet attends to. This extra dimension, for which it isn't hard to assemble a worthy and impressive body of recommendations, is something only a minority of poets have ever actually used with any degree of consistency. John Crowe Ransom in *The World's Body* speaks well of the poet's "desperate ontological or metaphysical maneuver":

> The poet perpetuates in his poem an order of existence which in actual life is constantly crumbling beneath his touch. His poem celebrates the object which is real, individual, and qualitatively infinite.

Of course. To eat a banana is almost to lose in dental and appetitive busyness that "qualitatively infinite" dimension it has; and to write a poem is, often enough, to bury the object beneath its own useability, to circumscribe it for specific purposes instead of apprehending it in the round. Is it an innate cast of mind, then, denied to many quite gifted poets? Is it something you can acquire by reading about it or even, since so-called "creative writing" gets itself taught, get instruction in? Do you find it as you find religion, or witch water, or prospect for uranium? I lay no claim to answers. My purpose is to recognize the dimension, to ask (quite literally) what on Earth are we doing when we absent ourselves from it or shunt it off into some no-man's-land of abstraction? One objection is that if you attend to something as fully as possible, you will never be able to use it or write about it; but such an objection, surely, belongs to the everyday world of practical living that Husserl called "naive." Case in point: the back support of my desk chair fell off in the middle of the last sentence, just before "surely," and I had to hunt around for the two bolts and nuts to fix the swivel bracket with. While doing so, and actually locating them in the two holes, and tightening up the nuts, my main thought was to get back to my interrupted sentence; I had no thought for the metal's texture, what the metal was, how it had been smelted, machined, finished. What was the thread like? (The single helix?) What would the taste be? Was it what's called white metal? Why did the bolt not fall apart? Or the nut? The metal aroma is on my hands, but, in one sense, I have just betrayed my own cause, I have failed to glory in my faculties' capacity for increased apprehension. If I reach across my desk, I find a quotation from Henry Baker's venerable and crisp primer, *Micros-*

copy Made Easy (1742), which rebukes me for generic inattention. Microscopy, he says,

> will raise our Reflections from a Mite to a Whale, from a Grain of
> Sand to the Globe whereon we live, thence to the Suns and Planets;
> and, perhaps, onwards still to the fixt Stars and the revolving Orbs
> they enlighten, where we shall be lost amongst Suns and Worlds in
> the Immensity and Magnificence of Nature.

By not pausing to take a scraping and tip it on to a slide, in other words by not converting an interruption into an epiphany, I to some extent let down "the Immensity and Magnificence of Nature."

But, argues common sense, that is no way to live; to live successfully entails all kinds of different degrees of inattentiveness, otherwise you walk under a bus or drive into the Susquehanna. Of course; but the poet is playing a risky game when he or she applies such a standard to the act of writing. I am being old-fashioned, echoing both Emerson and Wordsworth, the one's "Few adult persons can see nature" and "I embrace the common, I explore and sit at the feet of the familiar, the low," the other's craving (as paraphrased by M. H. Abrams) for "a poetry so authentic that it is life itself." After Dr. Johnson, I am hypothesizing "a mind of large general powers" which is as much deflected from the particular by the general as deflected from the general by the particular. The result of that? Perhaps a logjam of intellect, perhaps an expanded moment of preternatural poise in which both complementary and contradictory ideas come fruitfully together, conferring not merely double vision, but triple, a spectrum of indefinable multiples. If nature is a flowing chorale—amid which we wash and brush, read Spinoza and buy rosebushes, find or do not find the mate of our choice and apply tar to the roof of our house— we should at least try to overhear its choreographer, whose tenure seems invulnerable, whose score Lucretius guessed at and we moderns with increasing confidence call Unified Field Theory. Those who don't feel at home in this major league—invidiously I think of Dryden, Crabbe, Pope, or Hart Crane, Williams, Pound—do very neat and agile work, but in the end they don't ask enough, thematically, of their art. This doesn't dismiss their poetry, but it diminishes the ultimate force of it. This may be only another way of saying that, even for an atheist or an agnostic, art is religious; in addressing itself as widely as possible to phenomena, it notices the universe and by that token is universal itself. The old joke, caricaturing an examination question (Define *universe.* Give *two* examples.), directs our attention to the only one we have, to ignore or overlook which is to assume that eyes exist merely to plug up a couple of unsightly gaps in the brow. And if, as I suspect, this is watered-down Coleridge I am talking, I can only say that I prefer him concentrated; the "esemplastic" power owes dues to the object of its contemplation, of which it is an irrefragable echo.

IV

To go afield, never mind how briefly, reminds me how Precolumbian terracottas achieve an extraordinary detail or realism compared to prehistoric European art; drenched with religion as these objects are, the Colima "Prisoner in Chains" or the Jalisco "Copulating Couple" or the "Seated God of Rain" from Tierra Blanca reveal an inexhaustible delight with specificity, in comparison with which the prehistoric European things have a couple of lines here, a squiggle there, *to stand for* what the artist couldn't be bothered to depict. The difference is that between depiction and allusion. It may be that Roger Fry is right when he links humane societies with practical art and "hideous religiosity" with (oddly enough) "a certain freedom" for "the imaginative artist." The logic might be that, once what is Caesar's has been rendered unto him, anything else can have its head. In other words, benign societies yield prosaic art because they think the art is theirs and reflects their virtues, whereas tyrannies push the artist back on his or her own resources, and into the deep recesses where the macrocosmic invites the microcosmic in to dine. A better argument would be that any kind of society will drive the artist to the limit: the humdrum righteousness of the mild type, the ferocious demands of the other. It may well be that human evolution has its vague phases and its specific ones as well, for reasons unknown; I mean phases in which the artist's eye isn't quite keen enough, and phases in which it achieves an astounding hunger for precision. In the long run I am happier attributing such phases to less-than-apocalyptic causes, in the main to the effect of a group of self-confirming artists who develop a certain practice, a mediocre way out, and make it stick for a generation or two. It is easier, it is always easier, to withdraw from the challenge of the metaphysical mind than to go the limit with it, so there will always be a predominance of poets who are cautious, reluctant, and short-sighted, who collect bouillon cubes and keep them dry, thinking they are gunpowder.

Whoever did those Precolumbian terracottas had my ideal in abundance, hardly knowing where to stop, chasing the human into the divine and back again, with the weight of specificity all the time increasing: humanized gods, divinized humans, humanized jaguars, baby-faced bats, and so forth. The fusion of disparate zones, of heavily accreted images, is astonishing and adds up to an enhanced but unexaggerated regard for creative metamorphosis. And when Franco Monti in his primer on this subject speaks of the "decadent period," his choice of terms is instructive: "less elegant," "rougher and less precise," "stylization . . . even more pronounced." The eye has lapsed, the mind's eye has gone to sleep.

Beyond this, parallels multiply until no paragraph, no chapter, can hold them. Esteem for width of vision, for multiplicity fused, tempts me, though, to invoke Cubism only to say that it's not enough, and somewhat mechanical (a development, an extrapolation), whereas Abstract Expressionism is closer to what I mean, especially when it transcends a single focus of attention and attends to what's peripheral, thus fracturing the focus. The gain is in simultaneous richness, the loss is in there being no one view in which everything is in focus; the net gain, I think, is in the implication that visual analogues help us to feel at home within the confines of our own extended vision and so too in the universe, which doesn't exist aesthetically until it's evoked. Similarly, out of the corner of one's ear, so to speak, the dense exaltations of Olivier Messiaen can sometimes do the opposite of what, ostensibly, they attempt. *The Ascension* (1933), for instance, which is divided into four spells of devotional crescendo (1. "Majesty of Christ asking glory from his Father"; 2. "Serene Hallelujahs of a Soul desiring Heaven"; 3. "Hallelujah on the Trumpet, Hallelujah on the Cymbal"; 4. "Christ's prayer rising to his Father") echoes melodies from a different dimension entirely (unless my ears betray me, an old favorite of my mother's, "When I Grow Too Old to Dream," appears), the effect of which is festively pagan.

Realms colliding in this way fit my notion of the metaphysical: not something merely outrageous, or two things gratuitously linked, or *four* (which is what a metaphor properly is: *the ship plows on* links *furrows* and *waves* too); or the American composer LaMonte Young's 1964 stage spectacle entitled *The Tortoise Recalling the Drone of the Holy Numbers as They*

Were Revealed in the Dreams of the Whirlwind and the Obsidian Gong, Illuminated by the Sawmill, the Green Sawtooth Ocelot, and the High-Tension Line Stepdown Transformer. You can't go supermarketing for the metaphysical, not on this planet anyway. My own sense of wonder is altogether more humdrum and, if anything, less contrived. The Coleridgean Fancy can produce entertaining sideshows that make us blink or exclaim, but nothing such as the miniature wondered at by the Fourteenth Century hermit Mother Julian of Norwich: "He showed me a little thing, the quantity of an hazelnut, in the palm of my hand, and it was as round as a ball. I looked thereupon with eye of my understanding, and thought: What may this be? And it was answered generally thus: it is all that is made." In that sense, even though one cannot force the metaphysical mind into being, or even the right conditions in which it comes about, one can only receive as much as one gives: another idea of Coleridge, of course, although I can't quite endorse his idea that nature would have no life at all without us, the point being that nature *could* exist without humans to perceive it, and did. But a nature minus, say, earthworms, predators, plankton, or any one of a thousand other interdependent forms, would have trouble indeed in holding together.

In short, although one of the luxuries of human consciousness is the opportunity to lament a world that has no humans in it, the lament paradoxically refers us only to a world that has! There may indeed be elegies for life-forms that never came into existence, but they remain hypothetical, and Coleridge's famous lines in *Dejection: An Ode:*

> . . . we receive but what we give,
> And in our life alone does nature live

in a fashion uncharacteristic of the metaphysical mind (which the astute, seminal Coleridge had, although in an over-anthropocentric version) blur the distinction between perceivership and fact. Elsewhere, in his *Philosophical Lectures,* he offers a less chauvinist view, oddly enough dubbing the metaphysical cast of mind "genius":

> To have a genius is to live in the universal, to know no self but that which is reflected not only from the faces of all around us, our fellow creatures, but reflected from the flowers, the trees, the beasts, yea from the very surface of the [waters and the] sands of the desert. A

man of genius finds a reflex to himself, were it only in the mystery
of being.

Primary imagination, as is well known, is what the secondary helps us to
tap, but surely our view of the two has to change with the advance of
knowledge. Now that we know the universe (the so-far knowable part of
it anyway) *is* queerer than we can suppose or can imagine, the relationship
between creator and Creator seems bound to undergo some strain. If we
assume that the metaphysical mind finds some "reflex to" itself in the
"mystery of being," isn't it going to have to come up with some extraordinary performances, not so much to keep on level-pegging as merely to
keep up analogical appearances?

For instance, what's "out there" may not be out there at all, even if once
it was: the star Arcturus is 38 light years away, so if we look at it in 1978,
we see it as it was in 1940, and if we want to know if it existed in 1978,
we have to wait until 2016. Yet the mind-benders of astronomy pale
somewhat next to the mind-benders of particle physics, which is both here
and "out there." Werner Heisenberg himself seems to have become
entranced by certain enigmas in the physical matrix, twice in *Across the
Frontiers* (1974) drawing attention to the same phenomenon:

> If two elementary particles collide with extremely high energy, they
> actually fall to pieces, as a rule, and often into many pieces, but the
> pieces are no smaller than the particles that were split.

> The high energy of motion of the elementary particles shot at one
> another is transformed into matter, that is, new elementary particles
> arise out of the collision, but these are apt to be in no way smaller than
> the particles that were made to collide.

What, I wonder, can the secondary imagination accomplish that even
comes close? Use the phenomenon as a metaphor? Yes, but that's about
all the feasible open to us, and nature has come a long way from living
only in *our* life. Indeed, nature was no doubt always, or mostly, so, and
we are only just catching up with the "mystery of being." Just as René
Dubos, in *The Dreams of Reason,* reaffirms Coleridge's idea that to imagine
enables a human to be a bit godlike, nature takes a decisive lead and zooms
beyond us; our knowing about nature had nothing to do with nature,
which was always the same, atomically at any rate. And the fact that we

can interfere, with such a thing as the ozone layer or with the nuclei of cells, is not the same as our endowing nature with life itself. If, according to Berkeley, the quadrangle doesn't exist when there is no one in it, or rather continues then to exist only because it is an idea in the mind of God, the firmament itself would seem a much tougher thing to sustain in existence by the mere power of our attention. The new and imminent chore for the metaphysical mind, rather, is to become more and more open to one's own depths in the context of a physical universe which, expressed thus, sounds separate and discrete, but is here at hand, flowing through me with the quantum motion that Max Planck identified in 1900.

One poem by Ben Jonson, "The Hourglass," seems a splendid example of the mode; for sensitive, unceremonious complexity and understated audacity, it can hardly be bettered in its own time:

> Do but consider this small dust,
> Here running in the glass,
> By atoms moved;
> Could you believe that this,
> The body ever was
> Of one that loved?
> And in his mistress' flame, playing like a fly,
> Turned to cinders by her eye?
> Yes; and in death, as life, unblest,
> To have't expressed,
> Even ashes of lovers find no rest.

That recognition in the third line could be the motto for what's metaphysical. Not that in our own time we have not gone far beyond the line's implied vision: we have. What is metaphysical is the incessant presence in certain writers' heads of the devout point that Jonson makes with such incredulous finality, as if astonished that it could be "expressed" at all.

The Serinette Principle:
The Lyric in Contemporary
Poetry

EAVAN BOLAND

1

The title of this essay is taken from something that happened to me. That, of course, is an awkward way to put it; and deliberately so. Perception itself, even revelation, can be an awkward business. There are intersections of circumstance and image where light seems imminent and there is, so to speak, the sudden, exhilarating noise of a blind going up. This essay begins with such a moment.

One summer morning, I flew to Manchester to record some of my own poems for the BBC. It was a short flight out of Dublin. The program itself was not long. And then I was left with one of those cumbersome units of time: too short to do anything substantive with, too long to spend all of it at the airport waiting for an afternoon flight back to Dublin. I went to an art museum. I spent an unsatisfactory hour or so looking from Pre-Raphaelite paintings to my watch and back again. Then I browsed in the museum bookshop, bought one or two catalogues and a pamphlet, and went to the airport early, after all.

Airports are not easy places to inhabit. There is only so much steel, so much plastic, there are only so many rotating wheels and passing luggage carts you can ponder. A coffee, a sandwich wrapped in plastic and seemingly composed of it, another coffee. And then you are ready for something more.

So I reached down and took out a pamphlet from my traveling bag. I hardly knew why I had chosen it. I must have thought it fitted the bill. Its subject was musical boxes at the Victoria and Albert Museum in London, and it was a bright publication: glossy, distracting, garrulous. Here were the cylinder musical boxes of the wealthy, fashioned out of pear wood and cast steel with glass lids. Here was a description of a thirteenth-century water clock, a marvel of falcons and chimes and hydraulically operated musicians. And here, wonder of wonders, was the eighteenth-century

From *Parnassus* (vol. 15, no. 2, 1989).

music box of the Sultan of Mysore in the shape of a carved tiger well
settled at the throat—obviously music to the eyes as well as to the ears—of
a gurkha in Britain.

And then I found something else. In black and white, modestly photographed and with a brief note, was the serinette. Even in monochrome it
was an elaborate affair. A beechwood box, veneered with satinwood,
standing on ormolu feet and inlaid with a blond scroll of songbirds and
branches. "Small domestic barrel organs known as serinettes," said the
note, "were made in France during the eighteenth century for the express
purpose of teaching caged birds to sing."

Picture yourself in an eighteenth-century drawing room. The ceiling is
a whirl of plaster roses and cherubs. The fireplace is intricately chiseled
out of marble. Everything is inlaid, decorated, improved upon. The gate
legs of the dining table are the only reminder—and an emblematic one—
of the broad-leaved trees and the forest that were once the natural element
of this linnet in the corner, which now has to put up with a dome of stale
air and brass bars. That and the lid of the satinwood box, which now and
again is opened to allow a heartbreaking reminder of freedom.

I will not be oblique about the connection I wish to make. This imagery
allows me to argue that the lyric impulse has something in common with
the serinette: that it reaches out to a perceptive area that has fallen silent.
For the sake of this argument, let us call perception the bird and time the
cage; but not just any kind of time or any kind of perception. It must be
a real sense of healed possibility, enclosed and entrapped. Time, after all,
is a linear configuration. It proceeds from birth to death, or appears to.
It encloses us in the inevitability and claustrophobias of mortality. No
wonder, then, that a particular perceptive area may fall mute within it. The
bird does not sing, because he cannot fly. It is tempting to think that the
first is a commentary on the second, that we are lured back into knowing
an internal power within us by hearing its external imitation. Or, to quote
Odysseus Elytis, "poetry begins where death is robbed of the last word."

But this is only part of my argument. It is not just the serinette principle
that concerns me here, but the way in which the lyric achieves it. The lyric,
after all—there will be more of this later—has a considerable history. It
has proved itself to be endlessly adaptable to new environments and
changing circumstances. We are looking at a form that has fitted itself, on
different occasions, to the lyre, to the lute, to the harp; to the small

kingdom and the lost tribe. We could find it, if we searched, on the Pyramid texts in Egypt; under the battlements in Picardy; on the back roads of Ireland in a defeated language. It does not always occur in the same shape, and rarely in the same words. But it is recognizably the same creature we glimpse, as if we could deduce a mythical beast by its print in the snow of high places.

My interest here is in the contemporary lyric. I am particularly struck by developments in some American poems of the last decade or so that seem to show a strengthening of the lyric impulse with an easing of its traditional interpretation. The lyric, after all, has usually been considered as a melodic, and therefore metrical, unit of expression. It has an age-old relation with song and dance. It has availed itself of folk cadences and prophetic ritual. This is the lyric as we know it and, as such, has been one of the richest forms in the canon. But isn't there a danger in continuing to interpret a permanent impulse in art according to the impermanent features it deploys? Because a form has organized itself on one principle, it should not therefore be restricted to it. The expressive features of a form may change; the impulse behind it, while remaining unchanged, may in fact be refreshed.

The lyric is flourishing today in American poetry. It carries the recognizable old lyric impulse—to charm and heal our sense of time and terror— but has reshaped lyric constraints. At the same time it has retained the power of those constraints to touch areas of perception whose accesses are commonly thought to depend on music. In other words, we have a new lyric.

This is difficult to argue, and may well be presumptuous. I can only make a case from my own observations and experience, and these, after all, have been shaped by another country and another poetic culture. Part of my case will involve taking a fairly close look at two recent American poems. And the rest may involve some whistling and a fair bit of darkness. The new lyric may have the old effect, but requires a different mode of analysis and fresh terms of reference. And I have a bit of scene-shifting to do, as well. The serinette is still here. But the eighteenth-century drawing room, stuffed with porcelain and damask, is gone. Now we are in the bleak spaces and unfurnished warehouses of our own century. The cage is colder, smaller. The imprisonment seems more final. Can anything remind us how to sing?

2

I want to begin with an American poem I admire by Jorie Graham. It is called "Reading Plato." But I could as easily have chosen examples from the work of Louise Glück or Edward Hirsch. ("Mock Orange" and "Dawn Walk," respectively, would have served.) Equally, I could have argued from the fierce energies of Sharon Olds or even from some of the bleak scenarios of Stephen Dobyns. All these poets commend to me the view that there is a new lyric sophistication abroad in American poetry, an energy and abundance that could only come from exploring the lyric mode—those intersections of music and time—without the old lyric agenda.

Jorie Graham's poem "Reading Plato" must be quoted in its entirety:

> This is the story
>   of a beautiful
> lie, what slips
>   through my fingers,
> your fingers. It's winter,
>   it's far
>
> in the lifespan
>   of man.
> Bare-headed, in a soiled
>   shirt,
> speechless, my friend
>   is making
>
> lures, his hobby. Flies
>   so small
> he works with tweezers and
>   a magnifying glass.
> They must be
>   so believable
>
> they're true—feelers,
>   antennae
> quick and frantic
>   as something
> drowning. His heart
>   beats wildly

in his hands. It is
     blinding
and who will forgive him
     in his tiny
garden? He makes them
     out of hair,

deer hair, because it's hollow
     and floats.
Past death, past sight,
     this is
his good idea, what drives
     the silly days

together. Better than memory. Better
     than love.
Then they are done, a hook
     under each pair
of wings, and it's Spring,
     and the men

wade out into the riverbed
     at dawn. Above,
the stars still connect-up
     their hungry animals.
Soon they'll be satisfied
     and go. Meanwhile,

upriver, downriver, imagine, quick
     in the air,
in flesh, in a blue
     swarm of
flies, our knowledge of
     the graceful

deer skips easily across
     the surface.
Dismembered, remembered,
     it's finally
alive. Imagine
     the body

they were all once
     a part of,

> these men along the lush
>   green banks
> trying to slip in
>   and pass
>
> for the natural world.

The title of the poem, a promise of its wit and ambition, echoes the old and flawed theories of mimesis that Plato advanced. "And the tragic poet," Socrates is asked in Plato's *Republic,* "is an imitator, and therefore, like all imitators, he is thrice removed from the king and from the truth?" "That appears to be so," is Socrates' answer.

"Reading Plato" addresses itself to the irony and hubris of imitation. It does so in a wonderful spiral of ambiguity: Here is a man making flies to catch fish. He makes them out of deer hair "because it's hollow / and floats." To do this, he must set himself to the painstaking task of illusion. "He works with tweezers and / a magnifying glass." He is putting together lures. He is abstracting and distorting the protective coat of one creature to catch another. But when it is done, when the men go out at dawn under the stars, when they cast their flies, it is not a mere abstraction of the deer that floats on the surface. No, it is something more disturbing. In the very act of deception, by an eloquent paradox, these lures reintroduce us to the truth of what they imitate. They bring alive the substance they have used in the service of their "beautiful / lie":

> upriver, downriver, imagine, quick
>   in the air,
> in flesh, in a blue
>   swarm of
> flies, our knowledge of
>   the graceful
>
> deer skips easily across
>   the surface.
> Dismembered, remembered,
>   it's finally
> alive. . . .

Helen Vendler, in praising Graham's *Erosion,* the book from which this poem is taken, said of her method: "Graham continues, with her haunting, indwelling musicality, to make a pattern that constructs us as we read it." This in itself could be a description of the principle of the serinette. As "Reading Plato" proceeds, as it gathers resonance and sets up one image against another, we begin to find the correlative in ourselves. This is a poem which gains much of its effect from what Eliot calls "the music of imagery." In his essay *The Music of Poetry,* given as the third W. P. Ker memorial lecture in 1942, he stated that "it is time for a reminder that the music of verse is not a line-by-line matter, but a question of the whole poem. Only with this in mind can we approach the vexed question of formal pattern and free verse. In the plays of Shakespeare a musical design can be discovered in particular scenes and in his more perfect plays as wholes. It is a music of imagery as well as sound."

"Music of imagery" is a suggestive phrase. It evokes that rich, shifting language of symbolism, "so special, so fleeting, so vague," as Edmund Wilson called it, which Eliot canvasses again in his essay "The Auditory Imagination": "What I call the auditory imagination is the feeling for syllable and rhythm, penetrating far below the conscious levels of thought and feeling, invigorating every word; sinking to the most primitive and forgotten, returning to the origin and bringing something back, seeking the beginning and the end. It works through meanings certainly, or not without meanings in the ordinary sense, and fuses the old and obliterated and the trite, the current and the new and surprising, the most ancient and the most civilized mentality."

These are elusive matters. Yet if, for the sake of my argument, it is this auditory imagination to which the serinette sings—if this mysterious responsive level, where past and future are spliced and sundered, can respond to music—then I think the imagination will respond to the new lyric as to the old, and to the music of imagery as to the music of meter, because both have their common source in its distinctive vision of time.

But what about that music? What exactly is it? I could call it a sequence of images whose structure and effect are prompted more by the laws of instinct than the dictates of logic, by melodic allusion rather than clear thinking. But this is far from precise. In the same essay Eliot comments that "there are possibilities for verse which bear some analogy to the development of a theme by different groups of instruments; there are possibilities of transitions in a poem which are comparable to the different movements of a symphony or a quartet."

If I were to elaborate on Eliot's suggestion, I would say that the music of the metrical lyric is like that of the concerto, with fixed points of melody and theme. The music of a poem like "Reading Plato" is closer to a jazz improvisation on the saxophone in a smoky cellar after midnight: an exciting, free, and appropriate infrastructure.

Take, for instance, the recurring images of imitation and time that make up the musical imagery of "Reading Plato." The poem opens with the assertion that it is about to tell the story of "a beautiful / lie, what slips / through my fingers, / your fingers." We are told, almost as an after-thought, that "it's winter, / it's far in the lifespan / of man." The lie then becomes the dexterous, difficult work of making lures, a practical emblem of what slips through the fingers. "His heart / beats wildly / in his hands." It is this "good idea" that "drives / the silly days together." And now it's spring. The men wade out to fish with these constructs they have toiled over in a cold season, while above them, in one of the loveliest suggestions of the poem, the stars may be doing something similar.

> . . . and it's Spring,
>   and the men
>
> wade out into the riverbed
>   at dawn. Above,
> the stars still connect-up
>   their hungry animals.
> Soon they'll be satisfied
>   and go. . . .

Now the music of imagery comes to completion. The image of the stars at once encloses the other images and opens new possibilities for them: The animals the stars connect-up are also imitations and constructs. As bridges between dawn and dark, they also drive "the silly days / to-gether." Among them, however, the hungry animals—man, deer, fish— are more easily satisfied. And now the lure made from deer hair "skips easily across / the surface." The idea, although its source is paradoxically in death and dismembering, is "finally / alive." And as the men move along the riverbanks, now lush with new growth, the poem ends with a wonderful short circuit. The men also, it is suggested, are lures that have been put together—connected-up—by some force. In a final, luminous irony, they themselves reenact the arts of imitation, the "beautiful lie" with which the poem began.

```
. . . Imagine
    the body
```

```
they were all once
    a part of,
these men along the lush
    green banks
trying to slip in
    and pass
```

```
for the natural world.
```

3

The lyric as a dialect of time: It is a tempting thought. Perhaps in Ireland it is a more familiar one than in the United States. The Irish, like other European nations, have marched and wept and kept their faith and their counsel to the beat of lyrics. William Yeats even floated the idea that the Irish sensibility was better suited to the lyric than the English one. In *A General Introduction to My Work* he commented about his own early decision to write short poems: "Contemporary lyric poems, even those that moved me, seemed too long, but an Irish preference for a swift current might be mere indolence, yet Burns may have felt the same when he read Thomson and Cowper. The English mind is meditative, rich, deliberate; it may remember the Thames valley. I planned to write short lyrics or poetic drama and I did so with more confidence because young English poets were at that time writing out of emotion at the moment of crisis, though their old slow-moving meditation returned almost at once."

As an Irish poet I am not sure how much or how clearly I can see into American poetry. It may well be that I have displaced some of what Yeats calls our "preference for a swift current" onto contemporary American poems. I would like to think the reverse might also be true, that my familiarity as an Irish poet with that current allows me to see its force and vivacity in American writing now.

It may do no harm to give a name to that current, to call it the American lyric or the new lyric or whatever, despite the fact that poetic labels are neither comprehensive nor accurate. Poetry is always an alloy. It is never pure or reducible. The reason it seems to me worth naming the component parts of the alloy at all is that lyric writing, in the American critical discourse, is not accorded quite the same honor that it is in Ireland or other European countries. The reasons for this are outside my terms of reference. It may have to do with the fact that American poetry is not so heavily indebted as European cultures to an oral past. Therefore, if lyric writing is successful in American poetry—if it is risky, ingenious, and stirring—there is a danger that it will not be recognized as lyric writing at all, precisely because the lyric has become associated with muted ambitions and a predictable symmetry.

The lyric has always had its detractors. "Nothing is capable of being well set to music that is not nonsense," wrote Joseph Addison, the Augustan critic. And today, when the lyric is only sporadically set to music, his skepticism persists. Critics have needed little encouragement—especially if, like Addison, they suffer from a surfeit of reason—to take a reductive view of the lyric; to regard it as a pretty and prettified segment of poetic expression; as a fossil of times and occasions when the poem was the expressive equivalent of the sweetmeat. Such a view proceeds, quickly enough, to the conclusion that the lyric, especially considering the poetic events and discoveries of this century, has outlived its usefulness. As a formal procedure, these critics argue, it has been bypassed by modernist and postmodernist poetic strategies. And these outstrippings and outmodings, they assert, were necessary and desirable, considering the internal limitations of the lyric form.

We do not have to go far into the recent past to find these assumptions elegantly dressed and presented, sometimes by distinguished critics who are themselves practitioners. Take, for instance, Randall Jarrell's comments in *Poetry and the Age* on Richard Wilbur's 1950 volume of poetry, *Ceremony.* "Richard Wilbur," Jarrell begins ominously, "is a delicate, charming and skillful poet." He then proceeds, as only Jarrell can, to masterly faint praise: "somebody said about Christopher Fry—and almost anybody must have felt it—'I don't think real poetry is ever as *poetic* as this.' " From here, he deduces what Wilbur's poetry is, but largely from what it is not. "Mr. Wilbur seems to be a naturally lyric or descriptive poet. His book is rather like a picture gallery—he often mentions painters—and his people are usually not much more than portions of landscapes or still lifes. The poems are all scenes, none of them dramatic." Then comes the clincher. "Most of his poetry consents too easily to its own unnecessary limitations. An unusually reflective half-back told me that as a run develops there is sometimes a moment when you can 'settle for six or eight yards, or else take a chance and get stopped cold or, if you're lucky, go the whole way.' Mr. Wilbur almost always settles for six or eight yards."

Jarrell is a wonderful critic. He is, to borrow Helen Vendler's phrase, "a man delighted by poetry." He probably represents, fairly enough, many of the enthusiasms and also, no doubt, some of the critical obstinacies of his time. He was a good poet in a generation of excited and exciting American poets—a generation influenced by modernism, expressed by the New Criticism, but also, it now appears, beckoned by the demotic sparkle of a poet like William Carlos Williams. Under this dispensation there may not have been a knee-jerk reflex against lyricism; that would be going too far. But there was a definite feeling among writers like Jarrell that the lyric needed to be kept in its place, that on the new map of American poetry it should be little more than an unmarked road. For those who, like Eliot, saw the formal breakup in poetry as a "revolt against dead form," the lyric could be seen as an invitation to side with the ancien régime. By the lights of a poet as progressive as Jarrell, Wilbur was using not a form, but a formalism. And this formalism, in turn, was the product of a lyric impulse which doomed the poet and the poem to inbuilt restrictions.

In Jarrell's terms, it seems to me that the poet is discussed, almost exclusively, in terms of the mode he uses: He uses the lyric. The lyric is a form that employs constraints. It leads to "unnecessary limitations." Therefore, the poet is judged on a principle of guilt-by-association: He uses the lyric; the lyric is constrained; he is constrained by his use of the lyric.

I do not mean to caricature serious critical methods. I admire Jarrell both as poet and critic. I also greatly admire Richard Wilbur. But Jarrell's comments originate in his conviction that the lyric is a metrical form with a game plan. As such, he implies, it might snare reality in a skillful or pretty way; that will be the limit of its acquaintance with the dangers of the natural world. Jarrell is not the only critic of contemporary poetry who appears to have a pre-existing definition of the lyric mode: how it behaves, what it can achieve. But the lyric is a powerful form. Even the most rudimentary backward glance will show a volatile past and a future full of possibility.

4

The lyric originated in antiquity. It came into existence with that mixture of topical purpose and timeless power that characterizes both man and the forms he creates. It has complained and chanted and celebrated through endless changes of time and circumstance. But its early history remains its formative influence. It began in association with song. Its shape comes, as all such shapes must, from a historic poise between the internal forces that propel an art form into existence and the external factors that lie in wait, ready to shape and restrain.

Already, in antiquity, the lyric has emerged as a distinct form, upwardly mobile from its old neighborhood of song and dance. "The extraordinary variety of Greek lyric metres and their ability to take new forms undoubtedly owe much to dancing and music," wrote C. M. Bowra in *The Greek Experience.* "The word 'foot,' which we still use of metrical units and in so doing follow Greek precedent, indicates some kind of dance. In action such steps were matched by a music which marked and fitted their character, and from this combination Greek lyric metres were born." It seems important to take heed of this aspect of the lyric: to make a note of how human, animal, and visceral is that code of music carried by it into our own time. Far from being an empty formalism or a predictable symmetry, the lyric, as Bowra said, originates quite literally in the music of time.

Perhaps I can add a personal footnote to this. Years ago, having resigned from lecturing in English at Trinity College in Dublin, I went back to study Greek. It was a lost cause, really. I had entered the university with working Latin. But like many young women in that educational system, I had never learned Greek. So I had never had, and would never have, that essential head start in the mercurial syntax and runaway verbs that you need to master the language. I did, however, get far enough to read the language, although haltingly and with an uncertain sense of idiom and nuance. With my hand-to-mouth, newly acquired knowledge I turned, naturally enough, to Sappho. I deciphered the text, admired the sapphics, and for a while my mind sparkled with rumors of Aphrodite and the North African moonrise. But in conversation with a true scholar I came quickly to earth. I was pointing out some personal statement in a stanza. No, he said, be careful here. These poets of Mitylene—Sappho and her contemporary, Alcaeus—inherited a potent mix of drinking songs, war chants, and religious hymns. Therefore, the line between convention and private statement is not always clear in their work. By the time Sappho was composing, there were established lyric tropes and off-the-peg conventions. Some of these she used, some she reinvented. It needed a sharp eye to see which was which. I bring this in to suggest that even as long ago as the 6th century B.C. there could be fresh and tense negotiations between the solitary practitioner and the lyric tradition. Sappho was able to harness that tradition to her own private statement. Poets are still doing so.

And there is something else: A historical dimension to the lyric may reach back into the cloudy origins of language itself. *The Princeton Dictionary of Poetry and Poetics*, in its entry on the form, notes:

> It is logical to suppose that the first "lyrical" poems came into being when men discovered the pleasure that arises from combining words in a coherent, meaningful sequence with the almost physical process of uttering rhythmical and tonal sounds to convey feelings. The instinctive human tendency to croon or hum or intone as an expression of emotional mood is evidenced in the child's babbling; and the socialization of this tendency in primitive cultures by the chanting or singing of nonsense syllables to emphasize tribal rites is a well documented phenomenon. At that remote point in time when the syllables ceased to be nonsense and became syntactically and connotatively meaningful, the first lyric was composed.

It is a profound destiny for any form: to be a document of the line between language and its negation, to be a venerable witness. This gives the lyric the dignity of having been one of the first theaters of meaning. The first lyrics articulated, among other things, man's need for self-expression under the stress of his struggle for existence. We have no record of that need. Whatever record there might be is inscribed, not in a book or a chronicle, but in that part of our psyches that corresponds to the listening memory of the caged linnet. One thing, however, seems certain: Such an origin has left the lyric with the wonderful age-old power to be a narrative of language itself. It is something the more ornamental varieties of lyric— those which do not take Verlaine's advice to "wring the neck of rhetoric"—may have overlooked. Equally, it is a resource which, in a new age of stress for man and his meaning, the contemporary lyric poet can use to dazzling effect.

5

"Meditation at Lagunitas" is by Robert Hass. It comes from his second book, *Praise*, published in 1979. Once again, I shall quote it in full.

All the new thinking is about loss.
In this it resembles all the old thinking.
The idea, for example, that each particular erases
the luminous clarity of a general idea. That the clown-
faced woodpecker probing the dead sculpted trunk
of that black birch is, by his presence,
some tragic falling off from a first world
of undivided light. Or the other notion that,
because there is in this world no one thing
to which the bramble of *blackberry* corresponds,
a word is elegy to what it signifies.
We talked about it late last night and in the voice
of my friend, there was a thin wire of grief, a tone
almost querulous. After a while I understood that,
talking this way, everything dissolves: *justice,*
pine, hair, woman, you and *I.* There was a woman
I made love to and I remembered how, holding
her small shoulders in my hands sometimes,
I felt a violent wonder at her presence
like a thirst for salt, for my childhood river
with its island willows, silly music from the pleasure boat,
muddy places where we caught the little orange-silver fish
called *pumpkinseed.* It hardly had to do with her.
Longing, we say, because desire is full
of endless distances. I must have been the same to her.
But I remember so much, the way her hands dismantled bread,
the thing her father said that hurt her, what
she dreamed. There are moments when the body is as numinous
as words, days that are the good flesh continuing.
Such tenderness, those afternoons and evenings,
saying *blackberry, blackberry, blackberry.*

I owe my acquaintance with this poem to an American friend, a woman poet, who showed it to me one winter afternoon in upstate New York. In her company, with a snowy light shifting through the windows, and in the glow of her enthusiasm, it seemed to me I was looking at a wonderful departure in the American lyric; a poem that refined and liberated the impulse and, at the same time, restored it to its most primitive origin.

"Meditation at Lagunitas" tells on the pulse what the scholarly *Princeton Dictionary* describes in cool words. It shows language welling up from the source, drawing itself away from chant and music; dramatizes its approach to the responsibility of meaning; and infers how it attaches the mind to those meanings while leaving it with a deep yearning for a lost region of music. In short, the poem is a portrait of incantation. When it opens, however, we hear a note of deceptive stoicism:

> All the new thinking is about loss.
> In this it resembles all the old thinking.

But this is only the quiet before the storm. The sequence of thought, feeling, assertion—and the relation of all these to the metaphor—will move at a shutter speed we hardly knew existed. It is worth looking at the passage again:

> All the new thinking is about loss.
> In this it resembles all the old thinking.
> The idea, for example, that each particular erases
> the luminous clarity of a general idea. That the clown-
> faced woodpecker probing the dead sculpted trunk
> of that black birch is, by his presence,
> some tragic falling off from a first world
> of undivided light. Or the other notion that,
> because there is in this world no one thing
> to which the bramble of *blackberry* corresponds,
> a word is elegy to what it signifies.
> We talked about it late last night and in the voice
> of my friend, there was a thin wire of grief, a tone
> almost querulous. . . .

The poem is written in a surprising off-key tone. We keep getting ready to hear a piece of information or to be told a direction to the corner shop. But this is a poem of narrative tone and lyric purpose; a wonderful blend. The tone disguises and enhances the passionate intent of the argument. Look, the poem tells us, language represents the whole human adventure.

Both are at terrible risk. And the risk increases the more we rely on abstract thought. If we try to think our way through things—through words, grief, life—we only keep hitting off a series of estrangements. What we see, what we say will seem a cruel compromise of what is represented. The "clown- / faced woodpecker" will not appear to us as a lovely and intricate creature. On the contrary, it will look like a garish reminder that we have lost our "first world / of undivided light." And since—and these are some of the loveliest and most telling lines in the poem—we won't find the exact correspondence for a word, the word can only be a small funeral:

> because there is in this world no one thing
> to which the bramble of *blackberry* corresponds,
> a word is elegy to what it signifies.

"Meditation at Lagunitas" is a poem about going back to the source of the lyric. It is not a clear origin; far from it. It has the murkiness of deep water. But it is a source worth finding because within it is the reason not only for our return, but for our need to return. And in the beautiful line "a word is elegy to what it signifies," the poem tells us we must keep going back. Otherwise we may never find out whether things can be healed; whether we can ever rejoin the word to its meaning, the gesture to its source. Certainly we won't get to that source, recover that sense of healing, simply by rational analysis. That can only lead us, finally, to a reductio ad absurdum.

> . . . After a while I understood that,
> talking this way, everything dissolves: *justice,*
> *pine, hair, woman, you* and *I.* . . .

But language can, the poem promises, be restored to its function. It need not remain as just an index of our grief and estrangement from the mortal world. The theme of the poem, you might say, is our obligation and our gift, as human beings, to feel our way back into words. Feelings of love, of loss, of sexuality begin to draw language into their orbit. They restore intensity to words; they uncover wit, paradox, meaning.

> . . . There was a woman
> I made love to and I remembered how, holding
> her small shoulders in my hands sometimes
> I felt a violent wonder at her presence
> like a thirst for salt, for my childhood river
> with its island willows, silly music from the pleasure boat,
> muddy places where we caught the little orange-silver fish
> called *pumpkinseed*. . . .

Before our eyes now the poem is becoming a weave of reference, repetition, and music. It is not exactly the music of imagery. It is more an imagery wafted on the music of ideas, like seed pods on a spring wind. At one point the poem recalls to us the wit and grief of words: "Longing, we say, because desire is full / of endless distances." At another it tells us that "a word is elegy to what it signifies." Of course the poignancy of this lies in the fact that the poem is a tapestry made from these elegies and yet is not an elegy. In fact, anything but. If anything, the poem is an affirmation, taking language and moving it steadily toward healing and resolution. By the end of the poem we know we are in a place where language and the flesh have reached an angle of repose. Each shines through the other. By the end of the poem, words have healed and we are healed with them. This is the true lyric moment. We no longer hear the serinette. What we are listening to is our own song.

> . . . There are moments when the body is as numinous
> as words, days that are the good flesh continuing.
> Such tenderness, those afternoons and evenings,
> saying *blackberry, blackberry, blackberry.*

What is exciting and stirring about "Meditation at Lagunitas" is that Robert Hass has encoded the story of the lyric—its incantation, its source in ritual—within his own daring lyric experiment. And it is the old story he tells. A narrative of language that dramatizes its power and its risk: the power, on the one hand, to be itself an experience; the risk, on the other, that it will actually divide us from the experience. That possibility, that danger must have attended the very first incantations: those sounds and syllables that led the race through music toward meaning. For all that,

"Meditation at Lagunitas" is no excursion into history or aesthetics. It is a love poem, a poem of place, a wonderful anti-elegy.

6

In 1931, the British poet and art critic Herbert Read published a book, *The Meaning of Art*, in which he makes an eloquent distinction between form and expression. The book is about painting, but his distinction applies equally to poetry. "The art of a period is a standard," he writes, "only so long as we learn to distinguish between the elements of form which are universal and the elements of expression which are temporal . . . . Frankly I do not know how we are to judge form except by the instinct that creates it."

Contemporary poetry has become a complex of forces. There are revisions, histories, and aftermaths to consider. And in the process it is easy enough to overlook a simple truth, that no matter what else changes, poetry remains a venerable transaction between a private gift and a powerful accumulation. The transaction is not static. While it is happening, things change. What Read calls the elements of expression may wax and wane. And so it has been with the lyric. In "Vers Libre," Eliot puts a historical interpretation on parts of this transaction: "The decay of intricate formal patterns," he states, "has nothing to do with vers libre. It had set in long before. Only in a closely-knit, homogeneous society, where many men are at work on the same problems, such a society as those which produced the Greek chorus, the Elizabethan lyric and the Troubadour canzone, will the development of such forms ever be carried to perfection."

Eliot's words point up the danger of expecting a literary structure to remain static. It is, after all, a short step from expectation to prediction. A form like the lyric can easily be labeled, tagged, and stored in a museum of poetic reference. Yet such a critique overlooks the fact that the lyric is indeed a form, to use Read's distinction, not just a unit of predictable expression. And a form will recur while a feature of expression, to paraphrase Eliot, may decline with the occasion that gave rise to it. There are plenty of inferences to suggest that the lyric is inscribed on the history of the race and the origin of language. It is not likely to disappear now. Nor must we look for it to appear all the time in its old guise. Other poets of the same generation as Jorie Graham and Robert Hass, such as Marilyn Hacker, have made wonderful use of the lyric shapes we know. But the choice for one poet must not be made the rule for another.

Rules for experiment and expansion cannot be decreed. The new lyric will be plastic in the hands of gifted practitioners. And they are writing in America now. The two marvelous poems I used to illustrate my argument seem to me to draw on all the vitality of the traditional lyric. They display its magical ease in narrating the zone between meaning and music. But they also explore new possibilities for irony and paradox, new departures in style and tone.

Let me finish with my first question. Can there be such a thing as the serinette principle? Is there really an area of perception that the lyric can touch and prompt into articulate memory? Of course the serinette, as used by me here, is no more than a fiction. It is a construct I have made in the hopes that it might suggest the elusive transaction between a lyric poem and its reader. For all that, it might not be such a contentious proposal as it seems. Poetry lies deep within us. Its first tentative sounds must be stored in us somewhere. "What came over people," wrote Odysseus Elytis, "to make them combine words to say what we don't usually say? And why didn't they go to the end of the page but stopped and started at the next line?"

We keep asking that question. And some of us, in every generation, reenact the answer by stopping and starting at the next line. The reasons are almost unfathomable. I must be one of many poets who feels that if I do not write the poem it is not that I fail to express the experience; it is that I fail to experience it. Poetry is our way of remaking. And the remaking of time seems to be at the heart of it. In the writing and reading of poetry we seem to draw near, in Bacon's luminous phrase, to "the inseparable propriety of time which is ever more and more to disclose truth." But there is also real time. And real time has a way of making its demands, imposing its schedules, enforcing our silence within it. We need the lyric for this very reason. We are trapped in real time. We may resist it, we may subvert it, but, in the nature of things, we will concede to it in the end. And in the end I put down my pamphlet, closed my traveling bag, and went to catch my plane.

Part III

Poetry in Translation: Literary Imperialism or, Defending the Musk Ox

TESS GALLAGHER

With so much poetry now available in translation, it is not surprising that those of us who have little or no knowledge of other languages are having a hard time deciding what a good translation is. A few years back, a colleague of mine at the University of Montana suggested to me that perhaps "the moron's point of view," as she put it, ought to be represented.

Perhaps it's only right then, in the high spirit of adventure afoot in the field of translation in America now, that I should attempt to speak about translation, having at hand only the one language I was born to—a longshoreman's variant of English on my father's side and my mother's Missouri Ozark inflection on the other.

Poetry is the only second language I'm ever likely to have or that will have me in the full way a language possesses its native speaker. And there is the sense, in speaking of translation, in which all poems are a form of translation, the carrying of a secret inner cargo into visible harbors for the use, comfort, and sometimes mystification of those far-away islanders one is not permitted to meet face to face—but upon whom one may nevertheless have a lasting and often nourishing effect. In the making of the poem, the poet's inner language finds an external form. Or very often, the opposite is true: the poet's external world (I make the distinction faithlessly for the point) is translated into emotional or internal terms.

But in its most matter-of-fact sense, the word "translation" indicates the carrying over of words in one language into the facsimile of meaning in a second language. In the translation of poetry it's obvious that there is an extreme violence inherent in this act since poetry depends so much on sound and rhythms for its impact, not to say "meanings." A comprehensive discussion of this dilemma by Charles Tomlinson appears in his Introduction for *The New Oxford Book of Verse in English Translation* (1980). He begins by quoting Rossetti's dictum that at the very least "a good poem shall not be turned into a bad one." This ambition seems worthy and,

From *Parnassus* (vol. 9, no. 1, 1981).

indeed, those of us who can't compare the original to the translation with any sense of accuracy *do* depend on the translated poem to be a good poem in and of itself in the English it has come to. So wherever the poem started, what an English-only-reader wants is a good poem in English.

What more should the translator do? There seems to be a consensus of opinion among the poet-translators Tomlinson quotes that the translator is there to preserve the "flame" of the poet's intent and not the "ashes" of the original form—these images are taken from Dryden's criticism of those translators who stick too closely to the text and his corresponding applause for those who honor the spirit of the text:

> They but preserve the Ashes, thou the Flame,
> True to his sense, but truer to his fame.

Tomlinson also cites Sir John Denham's belief that an irreplaceable loss would take place unless the translator could add a new spirit to the emerging text. Dryden, whom Tomlinson identifies as the greatest translator of all times, favors keeping the sense of the words, and this sense could be "amplified, but not altered." Donald Davie approves translation which "takes more liberties than the 'trot,' but denies itself the liberties of the imitation and of other relations more tenuous still."

These "other relations" to the word "translation" give evidence of the variety of approaches various poets and translators have taken toward bringing the poem over into the new language. I made a brief list from Tomlinson's Introduction of the terms used to indicate these alternate routes: "adaptation," "imitation," "paraphrase," "translation with latitude," and "creative translation." From a collection of papers delivered by translators at the Conference on Literary Translation held in New York in May 1970, I compiled another list which gives clues to the ambitions of various translators: "recreating," "transmitting," "renovation," "bringing up to date," "evocation," and even a call for "connivance and complicity" in translating.

The latitude evidenced in these lists suggests that translation aspires to telepathy on the one hand and the stance of a benevolent dictator on the other. It is hard for a monolingual reader to know what to trust in a translation when one realizes that the poet-translator has been working from a paraphrased version ("trot") of the text which has been written out by a native speaker for the translator from a language the translator does not know. What the reader gets in this case is a translation of a translation. Perhaps this is not as strong an argument against accuracy as it may seem when we realize that during World War II the head of the American Cryptoanalytic Section of the Army Intelligence decoded the Japanese diplomatic code without knowing Japanese. Hayden Carruth has commented on this briefly:

> This (the decoding of a message without knowledge of the originating language) is regarded by the uninformed as an impossible feat. But the code is itself a language, with referents that can be (approximately, very approximately) identified with particular elements of reality which exist in both Japan and the U.S.A. The same with a poem. Except that a poem, being imagined, may be somewhat more untranslatable, or difficult to assimilate to cultural preconceptions, than a military message (or a work of prose fiction).

Accordingly, if the poet does not know the language the poem has been translated from, all may yet go well if the poet is intuitively attuned to the unknown language and able to decode it in this manner. As Carruth seems to admit, this may be possible for translating messages, but for poetry or fiction in which the texture of the language is more than informational, this decoding without knowledge of the originating language would result in the barest of scaffolds.

The translator, then, can be any or all combinations of pirate, cannibal, smuggler, extortionist, and lover. He's even a kind of blind bureaucrat of the soul. Stanley Kunitz says translating is like reconstructing a ruined city, and this seems to have heroic overtones. If we go a step further and call translating a form of urban renewal, we are, however, reminded of the terrible cost in terms of the character of once highly individualized neighborhoods—the homogenization, the sometimes misdirected efforts at making an area "presentable." Similarly, one suspects that much is lost in the move to make the translation "presentable" in the new language. The danger, then—and often the certainty—is that the translator has had to over-civilize the poem. There's the opposite danger, of course, of the translator who knows the language with such intimacy that he's likely to turn the poem into an artifact of ruthless exactitude. Or he may present some incredible amputee by forgetting to whisper a few sweet-nothings. He may even produce, God forbid, an outerspace mutant, so rich in possibility that it waddles through the doorway on fourteen legs, wearing a head like a fire hydrant.

The most convincing way of avoiding the mutant effect of translation may be Pound's suggestion that the translator be able to integrate the qualities and combinations of energy rather than merely the words themselves. The translator must find a way of arranging his substituted words, says Tomlinson, so that *"the electric current flows and that there is no current wasted."* This idea of maintaining the current of energy in the translation appeals to me, but how is someone who doesn't know both languages to know whether this current has been maintained or not? Simple, says a friend of mine teaching in the French department: get someone who knows the language to read the poem in the language it was translated from and tell you. This would be fine, if I could find this willing translator, and if he or she had expertise in poetry. All too often, the poem appears only in English (acknowledging a lack of interest in the original version?), so an original of the poem must be sought first. Also, if I want to read an anthology of translations conscientiously, I must assemble my own United Nations.

Elsa Gress in "The Art of Translating" says that it takes "both literary and linguistic know-how to evaluate the essential qualities in a translation to see whether a tone has been rendered or not, and whether tricky problems have been solved or left unsolved." Thus, it is not enough to find someone who has a working knowledge of the language; this translator-friend must also be able to assess tone. Perhaps it would not hurt if this translator were also a poet. The range of those qualified begins to narrow.

All this does not inspire confidence that the reader with only English at his disposal will be able to recognize the superior or even the good translation. Perhaps the only recourse such a reader has is to read the arguments for and against the various translations as they are reviewed— if indeed they are reviewed. Aside from this, one may line up various translations of the same poem by various translators and try to see which translation prevails as a good poem in English while it *seems* to carry a quality of the original which may only be guessed at from those elements that remain the same in the various translations. This is somewhat like trying to pin the tail on the non-existent donkey, but it is perhaps the best one can do with the limited resources of one language. Another method I have tried in order to gain a sense of tone and rhythm is to have someone who reads in the original language read the poem aloud to me several times. Then I try to carry the sense of that energy and tonality into my judgment of the poem translated into English.

One thing these amateur methods of judging the translation can't deliver is the loss of whole concepts which may not be carried intact from one language to another. I'm thinking of some things I learned about the nature of the old Irish language during my stay in Belfast. Irish speakers have no word for "no" and this has caused them to have to sit around drinking, telling stories, singing songs, having fun, and generally wasting their lives. (Even the advent of English has been unable to change this language-grown pattern.) The Irish speakers also have no word for "yes" and this causes all kinds of elaborate insecurities. Think of all those Irishmen waiting mournfully in pubs for their sweethearts to just "drop in" because there has been no way to be sure she'd turn up if they made a date. And her insulating herself with a crowd of women friends so she won't have to sit alone in the pub if he doesn't stop by.

When a language threatens to disappear through lack of usage, it threatens to take with it a whole range of emotions and attitudes. For instance, Irish is a language that has preserved a communal sense to the point that the idea of ownership doesn't exist. The idea of wife or husband or belonging or "mine" doesn't exist—only "she/he who is *with* me, who has come *along* with me."

So it is hard to tell whether or not the translator has gotten in touch with the cultural ideas and concepts of the country, its times and customs. If he hasn't, the translated poem may become a kind of awkward refugee in the new language, but only the culturally expert reader will know. The poem itself arrives as best it can, often having braved the flooded arroyo to stand dripping great embarrassing pools on the bourgeois carpet, impossibly wearing a sombrero.

When one considers that the craft of translating is at best approximate, and that American readers seldom know the language in which the poem originates, one wonders why we as readers and writers are so excited to be the purveyors and recipients of so much work in translation. After all, we do live with an entire country of writers who are working first and best in the language we were born to—English. Even Tomlinson speaks at the close of his introduction of the "inevitable but in some ways depressing translation boom of recent years."

Perhaps one of the first reasons for our attraction to poems in translation could be that we've been looking for spiritual qualities in foreign authors that often seem to be missing in our own contemporaries. I know that as a woman writer I had been unconsciously searching for a poet-heroine who was passionate, capable of supreme acts of the spirit; one who possessed intellect and personal dignity without disappearing over the horizon into the other-worldly. In my own poetic past I had Emily Dickinson who lived with her mother and father—Emily with her reclusive long-distance battles with God and a bodily death. I had Marianne Moore who lived with her mother and pirated from their conversations, and also those famed probings of the encyclopedia. In more recent times there has been a spectrum of man-haters, sexual and spiritual martyrs, suicides, placid say-no-evils, mild-mannered girl reporters, and faithful red riding hoods—Plath and Sexton, who courted their deaths, whether they intended it or not, popularized taking one's life as the ultimate manifesto against social and personal forces they no longer had the stamina to argue with. It's no wonder that the Russian poet, Akhmatova, in those first translations by Stanley Kunitz, struck me as heroic, but at the same time as more humanly approachable. Here was a woman who could speak for a country and a time. A woman who had the dignity of a witness, a survivor. Her son had been imprisoned, her husband had been executed. She herself had been haunted and spied upon, and forbidden to publish anything for ten years. Her poems were sensual without being indulgent. They carried the fullness of one who lived boldly the risks of the spirit, the heart, and the body through a time which could openly honor none of these. In short, someone to aspire to. I know I'm not the only contemporary woman poet deeply affected by these poems. Jane Kenyon is now working, with the help of a Russian translator who knew Akhmatova, on a book of Akhmatova's poems not translated elsewhere. It is hard to quote the poems singly and give the sense of what Kunitz accomplished in these translations, but here is a sampling.

> How can you look at the Neva,
> how can you stand on the bridges? . . .
> No wonder people think I grieve:
> his image will not let me go.
> Black angels' wings can cut one down,
> I count the days till Judgment Day.
> The streets are stained with lurid fires,
> bonfires of roses in the snow.
>
> ("How Can You Look At The Neva")

Before these translations of Akhmatova appeared, Louise Bogan in *Blue Estuaries* had set the high mark for what I'd considered poetic excellence. Bogan's poems seemed to have been hammered in bronze, the voice possessed of a reticence and wisdom. Yet at times I read her without comfort like the duped chimpanzee hugging the wire surrogate. Bogan's stony pride got in my way. I was yearning for a largeness of being that could be inclusive in its strengths, that took up the struggle without giving way to its most degrading aspects. In my heart of hearts I recognized Akhmatova. I had been on the waiting end of the Viet Nam war, had lived in the spirit-death of the returned pilot-husband in whose silence the destroyed terrain with its ghosted villages and mountains reappeared. Until that meeting with Akhmatova in the Kunitz translations it had seemed impossible to speak with authority; and even as I finally wrote, addressing myself to her as in a letter meant to reach us both beyond our lives, I felt humbled, unequal to the events of her life.

Stepping Outside

for Akhmatova

Hearing of you, I never lost a brother
though I have, never saw a husband to war,
though I have, never kept with my father
the emptiness of his hands, my mother
the dying of her womb.

Return: husbands, sons, fathers return.
Many with both arms, with dreams
broken in both eyes.
They try, they try
but they cannot tell us
what comes back with them.

One more has planted his hoe
in my heart like an ax, my farmer uncle
slain by thieves
in the night, burned down
with his house, buried, dug up
to prove he was no dog.
He was no dog.

You, who lived in your pain until it grew
its own face, would have left all this
like a monument in a field. Your words
would have made a feast of what ate you.

Sit with me.
No one has left; no one returns.

The ambiguity of our own political, emotional, psychic, and spiritual energies has certainly played a part in our attraction to poems in translation. There are unspoken but obvious benefits for the poets who read in translation. That at the heart of some readers' voraciousness for translations are practical considerations like the need to steal from somebody who won't find you out, a kind of secret literary imperialism. After all, it hardly seems like stealing when it is already stamped with the approval of successive fingerprints. Also, the particular cozy use of the ego in American poetry in which the "I" seems often in exact co-incidence with the poet in divulging the family secrets has brought on in some a state of near psychic bankruptcy. Frequent vacations to exotic lands has become a necessary and welcome relief.

The plunder we have brought back in the form of new subject matter from these excursions into the exotic lands of translations has perhaps been the most recognizable gain. That is, one could tell the prized remnant was intended to be a crocheted Brazilian hammock, but because it had to be thrown overboard to drag in one of the drunk passengers on the long ocean voyage over, it had shrunk incredibly and now resembled a pygmy slingshot.

I must admit that the whole panorama of literary adventure via translation has caused me to feel at times a mixture of amusement, excitment, and real question about the reasons behind it. If my tone is somewhat ironic, it's because I'm drawn and repelled at the same time. Maybe it's the story of the woman with a spoon who meets the woman with a Mix-master. Whatever it is, this abundance of poems in translation, we want it. It's new: it's different.

New subject matter. Where would we be without the voluptuous Spanish love of bones and death, the murders of passion, the particular irrational brand of surrealism that freed us from the calculated French version. What a relief whenever one slashed a wineskin to see your brother's blood "jump out," suddenly to have license to practice a kind of spastic surrealism. But also, for an American reader, there is the delight at finding a much-needed sense of humor in the Spanish attitude toward death as seen in "The Least Corpse" by Angel Gonzalez translated by Robert Mezey. The poem, for an American reader, reverses the current dictum that one should live as long as possible no matter what state of decay and biological collapse the body undergoes. Here the friends of the corpse are anxious to get on with their mourning. "Die some more," they say. The corpse is in a state of embarrassment since he seems to retain several life signs (emotions, sneezing, coughing, talking), which make us feel that perhaps the dead may not be as removed from the living as we imagine.

When the corpse flicks the worm from its sleeve, then apologizes and puts it back on the sleeve, the invitation is both funny and pathetic. The corpse gives over his body to the worm's banquet, agrees to his transformation into feast. This agreement with one's death in its most corporeal sense seems alien to prevailing attitudes in America which urge life-extension as a matter of human rights regardless of the quality of that life once it has been extended. The corpse in the poem is an ironically familiar character to us in a time when medical technology is able to sustain the body's vital signs to the extent that the death-moment has now become ambiguous and hard to define.

> He had died only a few inches:
> a tiny death that had its effect
> on three rotten molars and one toenail
> on his so-called left foot and, surprise!
> a few hairs here and there.
> They mumbled the usual prayers:
> "O Lord, forgive those three molars
> their iniquity, their sinful
> chewing. Godless teeth,
> but your own creatures, after all."
> He was there himself,
> solemn before
> what there was of his mortal remains:
> a filthy prosthesis and some hair.
> Friends had come to comfort him
> but they only deepened his sadness.

"This is impossible, it can't go on
this way. Or maybe we should say:
This ought to be speeded up.
Die some more. Die once and for all."
Dressed in mourning, he shook their hands
with that phony regret
you see at the worst funerals.
                              "I swear"
—overcome, he burst into tears—
"I want to extinguish my feelings,
I want to turn my life into stone,
my love into earth, my desire to ashes,
but I can't help it, I talk sometimes,
I move a bit, I even catch cold,
and naturally those who see me
deduce that I'm alive,
but it's not so:
you ought to know this, my friends,
even if I sneeze,
I'm a corpse, I couldn't be more dead,"
Despondently he let fall his arms,
flicked a worm from his sleeve,
said, "Pardon me," and picked up the worm.
After all it was only a scrap
of all he was looking forward to.

(from *Roots and Wings,*
ed. Hardie St. Martin)

Vital subject matter. The Russians with all those troikas that could possibly put romance back into transportation. The Russians, looking at the Neva, poems smuggled out in babushkas, severity, interminable train rides through the Urals. The Russians. Snow, snow, snow. Weariness. Inexpressible sadness. Partings. And of course, the prison camps.

There is a certain mythic credibility which these writers do attain through suffering, deprivation, and torture. American writers are responding to this. And why shouldn't they? American poets have had to be resourceful, going to a lot of trouble killing and punishing themselves, going crazy—all because poetry and being a poet does not have the same political status in a country which ignores what you say. Democracy is the worst possible condition for flamboyant, heroic gestures from a poet. If a poet writes a poem against General Motors—who cares? If a poet denounces nuclear power plants and Kentucky Fried Chicken or clearcut logging or supertankers or Bell Telephone—so what? No wonder Marianne Moore settled for defending the fast disappearing Musk Ox.

The worst that could happen to a poet in this country who found a worthy approach to a cause would be that he'd be published, not banned for years like Akhmatova or Mandelstam. The stories of the persecution of Russian poets became important in supplying a sense of consequence imaginatively to our own free status. Mandelstam's poems gained power with us through a combination of restraint and lyric necessity, and his poem "Tristia" in translations by Kunitz, W. S. Merwin and Clarence Brown, and David McDuff has become familiar to us all. Here in a translation of Mandelstam by McDuff is another small poem about the final moments before fleeing.

The poignancy of these last moments of the "we" in the home they must escape is expressed through the placement and naming of objects and through the hasty preparations they must make. The stillness in this poem is similar to that in Tomas Tranströmer's "4 a.m.: Track," a poem which has become a classic favorite with many poets who read liberally in translation.

Perhaps it is the silence in this Mandelstam poem and in the Tranströmer poem which attracts American readers. A pianist I recently heard speak commented that music is really *made of silence.* He said that the quality of his audience's silence joins the piece of music as it is played. Poetry also communicates qualities of silence through the very sound it makes, even to the reader alone with the page. Reading Mandelstam in translation is an education in these silences. American poems often proceed with a headlong velocity and we can learn much from the pacing of poems like the following:

> We shall sit together in the kitchen for a while.
> The white kerosene smells sweet.
>
> Sharp knife, a loaf of bread . . .
> If you like, burn the primus at full wick,

and if not then gather string
to tie the basket in before the dawn,

so we can leave here for the station,
Where we must hope no one will find us out.

(Osip Mandelstam,
translated by David McDuff)

Heroes and subject matter with consequence. Lorca shot. Rafael Alberti in exile in Argentina with his "Sleep Walking Angels," his "Moldy Angels," his "Memories of Heaven." I was studying with Mark Strand at the time he was translating the Alberti poems and I remember vividly the excitement of being shown one of these from the book he was compiling, *The Owl's Insomnia.* It was entitled, unforgettably, "That Burning Horse in the Lost Forests." It used a relentless cataloguing of seemingly unrelated yet causal events which appealed to my own wish to somehow out-leap the reasoned linearity of most narrative structures. The poem also made use of a predictive voice that is rare in American contemporary verse. A passage will give some idea of the compelling intersections of fate with the incidental. The poem brings violently into view the sense of time as at once stopped and going on.

And that this was somebody buried with a silver watch in his
      lower vest pocket,
which meant that at one the islands would vanish,
and at two the heads of the blackest bulls would turn white,
and at three a lead bullet would pierce the lonely host left
      out in the reliquary of a church lost at the crossing of
      two paths: one going to a whorehouse, the other to a
      health resort
      (and the watch on the dead man),
which meant that at four the swollen river carrying the
      skeleton of a fish hooked to the pantleg of a foreign
      sailor would flow past a reed,
and at five a toad lost among vegetables in a garden would be
      cut in two by the unexpected entry of a wheel from a cart
      capsized in a ditch,
and at six some unhappy cows would hurl themselves against
      the caboose of an express train,
and at seven some men on a street corner would stab a drunken

girl stepping outside her door to throw clamshells and
olive pits into the street
(and the watch on the dead man)

(Rafael Alberti,
translated by Mark Strand)

There is a coercion of happenings in the poem. The reader is forced to apply meaning and connection to disparate events by the insertion of the phrase "which meant" since it is used as a verbal hinge between catalogues.

Another unusual quality of this poem is what I'll call its x-ray vision. There is the sense that all matter is penetrable and accessible to the mind, to the eye of the mind. In the poem we receive events which are ordinarily withheld, either because of the small scale of the happening (the toad sliced in two) or by the unseen nature of the experience itself (the skeleton of a fish in the river which is hooked to a sailor's pants leg). The miraculous slips by as entirely possible in such a world so that we hardly blink when we're told of islands that vanish and black bulls that turn white. In this way the miraculous does more than coexist with "the real." The miraculous becomes actual.

The Italians. Cesare Pavese, one of the poets in the mid-Thirties who was committed to the political left wing and imprisoned by the fascist authorities when they discovered that workers were reading his poems, had stopped writing about the old classical subjects and instead wrote about beggars, whores, and workers. He managed to outlive his exile and killed himself at forty-two in 1950. In the early Seventies the poets I knew were searching the secondhand bookstores for his autobiography, *The Burning Brand,* which they tended to keep on their nightstands. In 1976 William Arrowsmith's translations, *Hard Labor,* came out in hardback only. It didn't matter. We could afford it.

Perhaps our feeling for Pavese's poems has something to do with the recent cross-fertilization between prose and poetry in American writing. There is a prosaic flatness in Pavese that is attached, in my own mind, to the romantic vision pushed to its farthest extreme so that it denies its passion on one level while reinstating it by its very absence and restraint. The matter-of-factness of the speaker's attitude toward the death in this poem causes it to become a natural event, as remarkable and unremarkable as the little cloud that "no one even notices".

Prison: Poggio Reale

A small window on the sky
calms the heart; someone died here, at peace.
Outside are trees and clouds and earth
and sky. Up here only a whisper comes:
and blurred sounds of all of life.

The empty window
doesn't show the hills beneath the trees
and the river winding clearly in the distance.
The water is as clear as the breath of wind,
but nobody notices.

A cloud appears,
compact and white, and lingers in the square of sky.
It sees stunned hills and houses, everything
shining in the transparent air, sees lost birds
sailing in the sky. People pass quietly
along the river and no one even notices
the little cloud.

In the small window
the blue is empty now: into it falls the cry
of a bird, breaking the whisper. Maybe
that cloud is touching the tree or sinking into the river.
The man lying in the meadow ought to feel it
in the breathing of the grass. But he doesn't move his eyes,
only the grass moves. He must be dead.

(Cesare Pavese,
translated by William Arrowsmith)

Pavese is aware of the negative space in a way that reminds us continually that our view, like that of the prisoner, is partial—as when "the empty
window/ doesn't show the hills beneath the trees. . . ." There is also that
silence which comes to us when we feel the world's largeness and lack of
need for us, as in the imagining of our deaths, as when the man in the
meadow of this poem "ought" to feel the disappearance of the cloud "in
the breathing of the grass." But the man becomes object-like, resists
motion, and this causes the grass which does not move to seem more alive
than the man. This poem restores the perspective of man as a creature

who, in the end and for all his elaborate, yet limited understanding, will come to the fact of his bodily disappearance, his eventual transparency in the world.

More hardships and heroes. The Hungarians who started a revolution with poetry. The Greek poet Yannis Ritsos, his father insane, his sisters insane, for political reasons was unable to publish for sixteen years. He was imprisoned in 1948, endured physical and psychological torture, spent four years in concentration camps. Arrested again in 1967, a year and a half in prisons, exile again. Perhaps it is his metaphorical extravagance that attracted us, lines like "a shriek remains nailed in the dark corridor like a big fishbone in the throat of an unknown guest." A construction so extended and awkward that no American writer could really get away with it.

The Turkish poet, Nazim Hikmet, also came into our lives with *Things I Didn't Know I Loved,* translated by Randy Blasing and Mutlu Konuk. We wouldn't have known or cared whether these translations were bad. They touched us, these poems, many of them written from prison. His book came to our shelves and stayed there. We could feel the indominability of the human spirit in these poems. We could feel the abundance of the world we had begun to take so for granted.

There is a spilling forth of love-energy in this poem: love for rain, for hills, for rivers, sparks flying from an engine of a train plunging through darkness. There is an exuberance in the tone, the sense of amazement that we are blessed with these natural miracles all of the time, yet are blind to them until much of our life is often past. Not since Whitman have we heard in America a voice so freshly and convincingly reclaiming the world. Hikmet's prison life ironically returns him to a world of amplified richness.

and here I've loved the river all this time
whether motionless like this it curls skirting the hills
European hills topped off with chateaus
or whether it stretches out flat as far as the eye can see
I know you can't wash in the same river even once
I know the river will bring new lights that you will not see
I know we live slightly longer than a horse and not nearly as long as a crow
I know this has troubled people before and will trouble those after me
I know all this has been said a thousand times before and will be said after me
. . .
moonlight the most false languid the most petitbourgeois

strikes me
I like it
I didn't know I liked rain
whether it falls like a fine net or splatters against the glass
my heart leaves me tangled up in a net or trapped inside a drop
and takes off for uncharted countries I didn't know I loved
rain but why did I suddenly discover all these passions sitting
by the window on the Prague-Berlin train
is it because I lit my sixth cigarette
one alone is enough to kill me
is it because I'm almost dead from thinking about someone back in Moscow
her hair straw-blond eyelashes blue
the train plunges in through the pitch-black night
I never knew I liked the night pitch-black
sparks fly from the engine
I didn't know I loved sparks
I didn't know I loved so many things and I had to wait until I
was sixty to find it out sitting by the window on the Prague-
Berlin train watching the world disappear as if on a journey
from which one does not return

19 April 1962 Moscow

> (Nazim Hikmet,
> translated by Randy Blasing
> and Mutlu Konuk)

Another translation classic that we all shared was *An Anthology of Twentieth-Century Brazilian Poetry,* edited by Elizabeth Bishop. There are enough fine poems in this collection to suggest that we have hardly scratched the surface of all the good poetry being written by Brazilian poets. It was my first encounter with the poems of Carlos Drummond de Andrade. His poem, "Don't Kill Yourself," is a caustic, unromantic exhortation to a heartsick lover:

> Carlos, keep calm, love
> is what you're seeing now:
> today a kiss, tomorrow no kiss,
> day after tomorrow's Sunday
> and nobody knows what will happen
> Monday.

It's useless to resist
or to commit suicide.
Don't kill yourself. Don't kill yourself!
Keep all of yourself for the nuptials
coming nobody knows when,
that is, if they ever come.

Love, Carlos, tellurian,
spent the night with you,
and now your insides are raising
an ineffable racket,
prayers,
victrolas,
saints crossing themselves,
ads for better soap,
a racket of which nobody
knows the why or wherefor.

In the meantime, you go on your way
vertical, melancholy.
You're the palm tree, you're the cry
nobody heard in the theatre
and all the lights went out.
Love in the dark, no love
in the daylight, is always sad,
sad, Carlos, my boy,
but tell it to nobody,
nobody knows nor shall know.

(Carlos Drummond de Andrade,
translated by Elizabeth Bishop)

The private pain of the lover which is so often the very stuff of poems
becomes in this poem a kind of false currency. We become aware of the
lover's own aggrandizement of his pain, so much so that it hardly seems
worth all that fuss. The oracular public voice in this poem is also an oddity
to American readers who haven't heard anything approaching it since
Auden in poems like "As I Walked Out One Evening."

Certainly the one thing we feel, reading all these translations from the
Portuguese, is that several somebodies went to a lot of trouble inoculating
those koala bears, getting passports, building elaborate cages, and ship-
ping them all at great expense. It has to be worth it. And these must be

the best, RARE in fact, the most cuddly, sociable ones to have been so chosen. Even if they eventually escape, they are of such good character and high breeding that they could only improve any ordinary brown bear they should happen to bump into.

Reading some translations, we get nostalgic for those early school days when everything was simpler. You had moved from the Squirrels to the Blue Bird reading group. That was progress—exchanging your bushy tail for wings. Dick and Jane had fed Spot the eternal bone. A sentence had a subject, a verb, and an object, mostly in that order. The verbs were often transitive. "Spot chases the ball. The car hits Spot, Dick, and Jane." There was a lot of listing and action. Roller-skating to the store to buy bread, eggs, peanut butter, and milk. Poetry in translation is sometimes like this. And because so many poets are reading in translation—as much as or more than they are reading poems of British or American origin—there has recently been the charge that translationese has begun to affect the diction, the rhythms, and the syntax of the English of contemporary poets in an adverse way.

Reading poetry in translation has the deceptive effect of making you feel that anyone could write poetry and get away with it. There is a certain colorful abandonment in some translations that American poetry wants to imitate.

Then too, we've gotten emotionally flat-footed in American poetry. All that restraint when we really wanted to bellyache and be sentimental and effusive! We forgive the relative who arrives from the old country with all those quaint expressions, queer ways, but (and don't you forget it) "real character." We can talk soppily about the heart again, and tears and sorrows and pain. The spirit can sing, can soar, can be tender without apology, as in Vinicius de Moraes' "Song":

> Never take her away,
> The daughter whom you gave me,
> The gentle, moist, untroubled
> Small daughter whom you gave me;
> O let her heavenly babbling
> Beset me and enslave me.
> Don't take her; let her stay.
> Beset my heart, and win me,
> That I may put away

The firstborn child within me,
That cold, petrific, dry
Daughter whom death once gave,
Whose life is a long cry
For milk she may not have,
And who, in the night-time, calls me
In the saddest voice that can be
Father, Father, and tells me
Of the love she feels for me.
Don't let her go away,
Her whom you gave—my daughter—
Lest I should come to favor
That wilder one, that other
Who does not leave me ever.

(Vinicius de Moraes,
translated by Richard Wilbur)

I have not mentioned those other standbys of this rich time—Cavafy, Li-Po, Neruda, Lorca, Octavio Paz. Though we often can't tell how much fidelity the translations we read bear to their originals, we do know a good poem in English, and this seems to be the deciding factor in the translations that win us. The fact that there are more good poets translating has meant that the quality of the poems in the English has risen considerably, and this is a factor in drawing a large readership to these new voices entering our literature. If it's a mixed blessing, as it seems it is, the blessing is in our favor in the search for what is new and unforeseen. All the same, it is well to ask these questions as to the quality and use being made of this influx of poetry in translation. What do these poems provide that we've been missing? How, if at all, are they affecting the language and attitudes of our own poems? In asking this last question we should remember the all-too-visible culprits in the erosion of English as it's written today —the communications media, the insistence on accessibility and literal clarity, the very pace at which we live.

Certainly one strong aspect of reading poetry in translation for one who does not speak or read other languages is the chance to enter the sense of a world literature as it tries on your language. It is the chance for a congregation of voices, and if it does not bring us into angel-hood, it will at least remind us of what we share with other poets in the way of subject matter and emotion, and more important what our differences are. The reasons poets go to poems in translation may not be altogether noble or pure, but the poetic current which Tomlinson asks for is alive there in the best efforts of poet-translators. There is a vitality, as I've suggested, mainly of spirit; and it is a resource we are going to need more than any earth-bound fuel. So if there is going to be imperialism, let it be literary and shamelessly beholding, a fading of the boundaries between *theirs* and *ours,* there in the poems where our words overlap and imperfectly meet.

Voice

Zbigniew Herbert

". . . che sola agli occhi miei fu lume e speglio"

The good soul Guido Noia had sent a letter again. Petrarch kept up this strange friendship begun in the remote past when they studied law together in Bologna, but for a long time they had nothing important to tell each other. Well, he was not Atticus! Guido remained faithful, devoted, and hopelessly banal; he wrote lengthy letters with no concern for style, informing Petrarch about the smallest details of the difficulties with his numerous family, about minor professional triumphs, lawsuits, successful appeals, and what was worst—no doubt to be worthy of his great correspondent—he densely quoted from ancient authors, pitilessly distorting their immortal stanzas and sentences. Poor Guido, Petrarch often thought, he made the worst use of the study of law. Namely, he became a lawyer.

But this time the letter lying on his table filled him with anxiety and a feeling of confusion. Guido reported:

"Two weeks ago our unforgettable preceptor Donna Novella passed from this world. I write you this *cum lacrimis.* Certainly you remember her lectures. She always spoke from behind a veil because her unusual beauty, it was universally agreed, would distract the students' attention. How funny it was. No one saw her, but all of us—and you too, Francesco—were desperately in love with her. We were ready to do battle for this incarnate creature, and die with her sweet name on our lips. I think we must have been lunatics, Francesco, but I would not exchange this madness of our youth for anything.

"Even today I still hear her voice. Melodious, sonorous, similar to music, and with a range that seemed to encompass the *totum.* A voice sometimes low, decided, almost masculine, but sometimes very feminine and seductive, especially when she would say, warningly, that law is *ars boni et aequi.* She pronounced the word *'aequi'* tenderly, like a confession of love.

"You are a poet, Francesco, and communicate with the great spirits of the past. And I, a wretched servant of the law, although recently I received a letter from the podesta praising my efforts at restoring our municipal finances to health—I won't conceal it is a great distinction; by virtue of my profession I encounter evil and lawlessness. But believe me, until today

From *Parnassus* (vol. 14, no. 1, 1987), translated by John Carpenter and Bogdana Carpenter.

I had no idea how great human wickedness is, how shameful, how immeasurable. I wanted to write you about it.

"Donna Novella, or rather her earthly remains, lay in the church of St. Laurence before the funeral, on a high catafalque lit by candles. The entire body was covered in a black cape embroidered with silver lilies and the emblem of our university. Well, imagine that at night some scoundrel slipped inside and exposed the face of the deceased. The following day the whole city knew what the true countenance of Donna Novella was like.

"Her face showed the traces of smallpox she probably had in childhood. Her skin—swarthy as that of a common peasant—was covered with a net of wrinkles. On the left side of her face a great scar ran from the temple across the cheek and down to the chin.

"Because she lived alone and died suddenly, no one had closed her eyelids. The scoundrel—I should say, destroyer of what is holy—noticed a cataract on the left eye. The mouth, through which so many years ago the sweet honey of knowledge trickled into our hearts and minds, was open as if in a shout of horror. In addition, and this is the worst, someone in their hurry forgot to cover her head with a bonnet, and only imagine this, dear friend—Donna Novella was completely bald.

"The whole city resounded with gossip. Everyone took part in this tournament of meanness, adding new details describing the monstrous ugliness of the deceased. Yet only recently everyone was praising her unearthly beauty to the skies.

"The funeral was held quickly, almost secretly, without observing due reverence for this extraordinary being.

"This is how our youth, and our love, were reviled.

"I weep, Francesco. Weep with me."

Petrarch replied immediately, in a cool, matter-of-fact manner, and taking great care that the haste of his answer did not betray his emotions in any way:

"In your last letter you reported that Donna Novella has died. Perhaps this will surprise you—though, in fact, it shouldn't—but I don't remember her at all. Neither her voice nor even her name. Dear Guido, it is a product of your imagination that I was in love with her. I always considered you to be a sober and levelheaded person, so indeed I don't understand where these absurd suppositions and allegations come from.

"Surely you have confused me with someone else. Perhaps the victim of these boyish infatuations was Agapito Collonna, Guido Settimo, or the charming hotheaded Tommaso Caloria? Or simply my dear brother Gerardo, who lives now in the quiet of a monastery, beyond the reach of worldly matters.

"As you know, the law school I attended at my father's request was an indescribable torture for me. I lost irrevocably seven precious years of my youth. Perhaps this is why everything that happened around me at the time has been erased from my memory. At any opportunity I would escape from those deadly, boring lectures to my beloved authors: Cicero, Virgil, and Horace. No earthly voice or the most enchanting woman's face could have changed my only true passion and faithful attachment.

"Forgive me that I write briefly. Yesterday I received a codex from a certain monastery library—actually I tricked them out of it—that contained a series of badly sewn together, uninteresting writings. But among them was a true treasure: the *Bucolics.* A rapid first reading led me to believe that I had in my hands a text less spoiled by copyists' mistakes than any of the others known to me. I have plunged into uninterrupted work."

He did not return to the reading of Virgil. He was overtaken by panic, by terror devastating him of all thought and feeling. Guido's letter was a sudden blow, one more attempt at the holy secret of his soul. Now—of this he was certain—the intricate architecture of beautiful fabrication that had been patiently built up over the years was finally crumbling into rubble.

In reality, throughout his life Petrarch loved only one woman, Donna Novella. He loved her in a way only boys are capable of: with a great love, ridiculously elevated, shameful, and tortured. It was total devotion not demanding reciprocity or reward, a feeling outside of time, of place, and therefore eternal.

He invented Laura in Avignon. He never met a lady with this name, which was suited for erotic puns and plays on words like no other. Two luminous syllables expressed the multiplicity of things, their metamorphoses, objects and echoes of objects: light hair, the gentle blowing of wind, shimmering, breathing of the air, laurel, a green and golden tree. *"L'aura che'l verde lauro e l'aureo crine . . ."*

Simone Martini, the superb Sienese master who worked at that time in Avignon, could not understand why his young friend begged him with such insistent enthusiasm to paint the portrait of a Laura whom he had never seen with his eyes. How could he have guessed that he was being drawn into a conspiracy, and was to become an instrument of incarnation. That is, without his consent and knowledge a mission was entrusted to him to bring a being without form onto earth, and out of a thousand different possibilities to endow it with a single, concrete, sensual form.

Finally he yielded to persuasion and produced several sketches. Petrarch immediately selected one, saying with indescribable enthusiasm that the portrait—conceived after all in the imagination—conformed exactly to the original like a face and the reflection of the face in a mirror. The same eyes with sweetly lowered upper lids: the exact arrangement of light hair: the same small childish mouth, lofty neck, the pious and tender palms of the hands. Showered with praise, Simone promised to put Laura in the fresco he was painting on a wall of the Papal Palace. And so it happened.

A communion occurred between a living voice and an invented name and figure. Laura became a shield protecting Petrarch's one defenseless love. The rest was only a matter of poetry.

But malicious tongues did not leave the poet in peace. (The human passion to destroy everything beautiful or pure is truly limitless.) The skeptical Giacomo Colonna, a classmate at the university and witness of Petrarch's youth, particularly excelled in this by his stubbornness, zeal, and poorly concealed pleasure. At every occasion he let it be understood that Laura was a product of fantasy; and what was worse, he dared to write the poet about it. Petrarch was stung to the quick—he experienced a feeling that the air and solid ground were being taken away from him— and replied with a vehemence he did not want or know how to tame.

"What do you tell me? That I invented the graceful name Laura only to have someone to talk about, and so people in return would speak a lot about me? That actually in my soul Laura is nothing, or only a poetic laurel I long for, and everything of that living Laura whose form supposedly bewitched me is only art, invented songs, counterfeit sighs?

"If your joke only went this far! If it was only a matter of imitation and not madness! Believe me, no one can pretend something for a long time without immense exertion. But to force oneself to appear to be a madman, that is truly the summit of madness. Let us suppose that when we are healthy we are able to imitate sickness. But true disease, this we cannot imitate. You are familiar with my suffering, my weakness. Watch out, then, you don't insult my sickness with this Socratic joke of yours."

The sober Boccaccio was not a friend of the poet's youth because of their difference in age; therefore his opinions do not have the force of proof. But he, too, took part in this peculiar trial of a voice, a name, and a body. His verdict rang categorically and dryly: "I myself am convinced Laura must be explained allegorically."

Meanwhile, in the course of years Petrarch was laboriously building his labyrinth. Inside, where he alone had access (was he not simultaneously Daedalus and Minotaur?), reigned the nonexistent Laura. He had invented everything: birth from nothingness, the color of her hair, the shine of the eyes, elusive life. Now he had to invent a date for her premature assumption.

It is probably no accident that in the most precious book of his library, the parchment codex of Virgil's works with a commentary by the Roman grammarian Servius, Petrarch inscribed these words: "With bitter sweetness, in painful memory of the event.

"Laurea, renowned for her virtues and for a long time celebrated in my songs, appeared before my eyes for the first time in the dawn of her youth in the Year of Our Lord 1327, the morning of the sixth day of April, in the church of Santa Clara in Avignon. And in the same city in the Year 1348, also in April and also on the sixth day of this month—also in the early hours—that light passed from the world when I was, by chance, in Verona, O unaware of my fate."

A farewell inscription. A bit exaggeratedly literary, as if appealing to the tender hearts of future generations. Glued to the cover of the poet's beloved book, this epitaph is longer than the fragment quoted above and goes on to speak of the most beautiful and pure body of Laura, about the soul, God, Scipio Africanus, Seneca, the flight from Babylon, et cetera . . . But already the first two sentences, referring to concrete events and invoking as witnesses people, places, and times, give rise, it seems, to well-founded doubts.

Well, it is disquieting that he attempted to geometrize the events of this unreciprocated love, giving it the form of a circle and therefore a figure symbolizing perfection. From the birth of the emotion to the death of the beloved, the hand of the magic clock describes a full circle: it comes to a stop after twenty-one years, on the same day, at the same hour.

It is not clear why Petrarch baptized the object of his adoration with the name "Laurea" the first time he saw her, and not Laura or Lauretta, as she appears in the sonnets. Could it be that the hand of the superb philologist, trained in copying the most difficult and illegible texts, was shaking so from emotion that it could no longer control correct orthography?

Today there is no church of Santa Clara in Avignon. Nor can its ruins or foundations be located. Would it be the fault of time alone that the decorations of the drama have crumbled?

Lastly, what is most surprising. We know from experience that memory carefully, faithfully preserves the most important dates of our life. Certainly just such a date was the day, blessed for poetry, when the eyes of Francesco and Laura met for the first time.

There exists an apparently small but essential contradiction between the poet's two confessions touching on this meeting that is fraught with consequences. In the epitaph cited above, inscribed on the cover of the Virgilian codex, Petrarch speaks of the sixth day of April. But in one of the sonnets devoted to the birth of his great love we clearly read:

> *Era il giorno ch'al sol si scolorara*
> *per la pieta del suo fattore i rai . . .*

This unmistakably indicates the first meeting took place on Good Friday, the day of the Passion of Christ, when the Evangelists testified that the sun was in eclipse. We can check without difficulty in the historical calendar that April 6, 1327, was not Good Friday but Good Monday. If we take into consideration the enormous role played by the rhythm of important religious holidays in the life of the people of the time, it is difficult, truly, to understand this thoughtless and gross negligence in his recollections.

Thus we have waded into a marshy expanse full of unsteady, lurching tracks and indiscreet conjecture. The criminological-literary method that attempts to establish irrefutably the place, time, and victim of the love-crime, and to investigate meticulously the reliability of witnesses, attempts to make the triumphant announcement: There was no Laura. But all this is honeycombed with self-complacent nihilism, pedantically dry, and sterile.

Equally doubtful are the efforts of the gossips of the story, possessed by hunger for the concrete, who swear that the heroine of Petrarch's poetry was a woman of flesh and blood, one of thousands of girls in Avignon. Supposedly her name was Laura de Noves, and at an early age she married a ruddy Provençal marquis, Ugo de Sade, upon whom she bestowed eleven children. A few months after her death the bereaved marquis married again. A story that might be taken straight from a naturalistic romance.

Let us not look for Laura. Let her rest in the alabaster tomb of the three hundred sonnets. The events of this invented and indispensable love move in different circles from the revolutions of earthly matters. The essence of the problem is this: to be able to intuit, to apprehend from unreliable reports and buried sources, the peculiar manner of existence of Laura.

Petrarch, let us repeat it once again, loved only one woman, Donna Novella, with a hopeless, blind love. For how else can one love a creature without lips, with eyes of an unknown color, without hands, whose whole being was—her voice. It was a real emotion, but it was too great, that is, it was beyond the limits of form.

Then he began to write poems devoted to the Voice on the Other Side of the Veil. Poems that were fatally awkward, without any beginning or ending or even a middle, pulsing with pain, full of empty exclamations and boring repetitions, poems whose meager emptiness he vainly tried to cover with the loud summoning of ancient heroines and gods. If these creations have any value, then surely it is only because they exactly reflect this passion without shores or name.

At this time Petrarch made a great, that is, simple, discovery. He realized he must invent a double of his love that would be born from his rib like Eve from the rib of Adam, that would be a creation of his own royal imagination, therefore obedient to all license and, above all, worthy of an art that is ruled by cool passion and disciplined madness.

This is why he defended the sacred pseudonym of love with such obstinate fury. He knew that as long as he lived he must invent proofs of the existence of what was unreal, for after his death her fate would become identified with his poems—and then, until the last conflagration of the world, Laura would be untouchable, sharp, unchanging, and clearly etched, like Penelope, Dido, Isolde, and Beatrice.

Giacomo Leopardi

R. W. FLINT

Giacomo Leopardi was one of three small, short men of the highest genius born between 1756 and 1798 who, both at home and in the United States, were fated to endure long terms of condescension and factitious pity for their real or presumed misfortunes. The other two are Mozart and Keats. All three—need it still be said?—were known from the beginning, in life as well as art, to be capable of the utmost geniality and insinuating charm. For Keats and Mozart the condescension has pretty well died out. Their work is a good deal more accessible than Leopardi's, their temperaments noticeably more sanguine, and they had the advantage, in a democratic age, of fairly low birth as such things were measured in their time.

Leopardi, on the other hand, was a provincial nobleman who had to make his reputation during the ugly backwash of Napoleon's fall, and in the normally obscurantist Papal Marches of central Italy. John Heath-Stubbs, one of his best advocates and translators, has written: "To some, Leopardi's aristocratic humanism will seem sterile and reactionary; but to others he will appear the most essentially modern and clear-sighted as well as one of the greatest poets of his time." This review will operate on the second hypothesis, at least in respect to his stature as a poet.

Known if at all in the United States either in the Indiana paperback of translations edited by Angel Flores, in the Iris Origo/Heath-Stubbs collection issued by Oxford and the New American Library, or a very few lyrics in other collections, usually *L'infinito, A Silvia,* and *A se stesso,* he hardly rivals Rimbaud, Heine, Rilke, Lorca, or Neruda as an active presence in the modernist constellation. Rimbaud acted out his rebellion, made a popular romance out of it, in ways impossible for Leopardi. Rilke has drawn great profit from our neglect of most of Goethe's and Schiller's poetry. Heine was promoted by Ezra Pound. Lorca and Neruda are to

Review of Giacomo Leopardi's *A Leopardi Reader* and *Pensieri* from *Parnassus* (vol. 10, no. 1, 1982).

most American amateurs as pristine evangels of the Spanish language as
Rilke and Heine are of German. But Leopardi's poetry returns us to a
Mediterranean austerity and essentiality that has as its chief antagonist in
the struggle for our limited powers of attention no other than Dante
himself.

It is easy to forget that Dante's second or twentieth-century wave of
popularity over here, as an obligatory ancestor, as a fixed chore, however
eagerly embraced, in the standard tour of great ideas and famous literature, began during the Twenties under the prompting of Eliot and Pound.
He thereby became Italy's chief ambassador to various new cults of plain
speaking and intellectual courage, a vital ingredient in whatever loose
agglomeration one may still wish to call modernism. To have been no less
than—or only—Italy's second best poet, as Leopardi arguably was, or
third, fourth, or fifth, is no safe ticket to renown in our endlessly distracted
literary economy.

To be sure, he often predicted and sometimes welcomed his own quick
oblivion. He was flamboyantly skeptical about literary fame. In a long,
seldom-read essay, "Parini: Of Glory" in his prose book of *Operette morali,*
he wrote: "In truth, I am persuaded that loftiness of esteem and reverence
towards the greatest writers commonly originates, even among those who
read and think about them, more from habit blindly embraced than from
individual judgment or the ability to recognize merit for itself." This and
several like remarks scattered through his writings are evidence of a
contempt for the darling rituals of literary glamour far stronger than the
mere *sprezzatura* that critics usually credit him with; it is an emotion akin
to that of Dante when the haughty Florentine met the damned souls just
outside the gates of Limbo who lived *senza infamia e senza lodo.* People miss
this in Leopardi because he casts his native drama of destitution and
dereliction in the first person, as himself an inhabitant of Limbo who treats
his own misfortune with a Dantean hauteur. Accepting so savage an
indictment not from one but from two great Italians—Leopardi's being in
the final reckoning considerably the harsher, at least as regards the literary
profession—is an act that few Americans hasten to perform. In our pros-
perity, or illusion of possessing it, we cultivate a Deer Park state of mind
regarding the authors of lyric verse, and the clinical sympathy to be
extended to them, that clashes head on with Leopardi, himself an unsur-
passed lyric poet and devout believer, like Poe, in the modern supremacy
of the short lyric.

Bitterly as he complained of his fate as man and writer—for he was the classic complainer of polite letters, second only to Job—and often as he may have deceived himself into thinking that a secure literary job was waiting for him in one of the larger cities—his mind, after all, was as capacious, curious, passionate, and well stocked as Coleridge's—he looked for no kind of demeaning sympathy. Rather, his complaints gained force and breadth as his self-assurance increased; they became generic and, in the best sense, philosophic. When he spoke as a poet he was defending his race's capacity for surrender to generous illusions. As an anatomist of illusion he knew himself to be bitter medicine, even embraced the role's slightly satanic features. "I consider love the most beautiful thing on earth, and find nourishment in illusion. . . . I do not think that illusions are entirely vain, but rather that, to a degree, they are substantial and innate in us all—and they form the whole of our life."

For dire premonitions, appallingly vivid images of private and public defeat, Leopardi held his own with any contemporary, was a sibling and forerunner (by a few years) of Poe and Baudelaire. But for every deliberately indulged negation there is a stronger instinctive, temperamental, poetically effective positive; he was the best analyst in modern times of the peculiar pleasure to be had in a handsomely executed act of denial, a vastation or successful embodiment of the *nulla* at the heart of life, of the *noia* (boredom, spleen) afflicting those with the largest capacity for hope and intelligent pleasure. When, that is, the writing is clear, simple, and spontaneous—essential conditions for him. Grimness of imagination and beauty of expression become close allies, and the whole stands as unambiguously under the signs of beauty and genius, vitality and versatility, as Mozart or Keats.

This is the poet whom Matthew Arnold considered the equal of Goethe, Byron, and Wordsworth, whom Nietzsche hailed as one of the century's four best *prosateurs.* Enough; no point in calling the roll of his illustrious enthusiasts, particularly in England. Our interesting problem lies at home. Must some of the best lyric poetry in existence be forever ignored by Americans because its author had the bad manners to express opinions diabolically designed, it often seems, to rub us raw? Baudelaire is a teddy bear in comparison.

In the General Introduction to his sturdy new anthology of selected poetry and prose, translated by himself, Professor Ottavio Mark Casale opines that "The question of how to accommodate Leopardi's melancholy is especially important to Anglo-American readers habituated for centuries to aggressively optimistic writing." Habituated, yes, but not exclusively so. If melancholy were the nub of the difficulty it could easily be overcome. Leopardi appears briefly in Melville's strange long poem *Clarel,* as a famous atheist and pessimist. W. D. Howells gives him some space (as he could scarcely have failed to do) in *Modern Italian Poets,* but his mostly sunny midwestern spirit predictably rebels at nearly everything he finds, and he puts the much-celebrated Recanati near Florence rather than in the Papal Marches where it so very obviously and crucially belongs.

Leopardi died in 1837 at the age of thirty-nine. Sainte-Beuve published a remarkably good appraisal in 1844, followed in 1850 by ringing praise for his art, though not for his thought, from the great Gladstone himself —surely a respectable endorsement. Yet no mention of him by Poe, Emerson, Thoreau, Whitman, or Hawthorne has so far been found. He was overlooked by the flourishing, erudite Dante Society in Cambridge whose membership included Longfellow, Lowell, and Norton.

A queer business altogether. The solution—apart from Dante's overpowering presence—must lie less in the poet's temperament or even in the final (and normal) untranslatability of his poetry than in the philosophic manners alluded to already, in a body of work that reaches us in a uniquely unmediated state. Professor W. S. Di Piero, a fine poet and acute critic of things Italian, is helpful here:

> Anyone who makes himself a student (and therefore a critic) of illusions and of human possibilities must be willing to follow wherever his explorations lead and willing to call things by their right names. Illusions must be made to yield to the power of one's will-to-speculate. In Leopardi, as later in Nietzsche, this will was absolute, and it was necessarily joined to great courage of mind and sentiment. The results, as we might expect, are not at all genteel.

Melancholy can be easily enough absorbed when suitably masked in comedy, farce, melodrama, the many popular forms drawn upon by Melville, Poe, Hawthorne, and Twain. In music we positively dote on it. But the conventions in and through which it is presented are all-important. In the Italy of the 1820s there were almost no popular formal resources to be exploited, after, that is, Leopardi had completed an early cycle of *odicanzoni* too reminiscent of Pindar, Alfieri, and Foscolo to be continued.

His splendid idylls and later philosophic lyrics, formally bold and full of subtle, original verbal music, crept up on the Italian consciousness after more than a century of post-Trentine stagnation. True, Vico's philosophy had prefigured Rousseau and Ossian, the Harolds, Renés, Manfreds, and Werthers. Leopardi knew him—and them—quite well. Marino, Metastasio, and Monti had been satirists, librettists, gaudy entertainers in fairly rigid, unpopular forms. Alfieri's largely unplayable neo-classic tragedies had at least fired the susceptible with patriotism. Ugo Foscolo had had his short moment of high lyric rebellion during the equally brief existence of Napoleon's Italian Kingdom at Milan. But the poets among them drew on the past with nothing like Leopardi's passionate selectivity or enthusiasm. None distantly imagined the possibility of accomplishing so much in so little compass and so short a time, nothing less than the second considerable revolution of plain speaking in the best poetry. So that however energetically and skillfully Leopardi may have defended his practice in scattered entries of the *Zibaldone,* his seven-volume daybook, it still appeared on the scene uniquely self-generated and self-referential. How much easier a time of it Wordsworth and Coleridge had with their *Lyrical Ballads!* For Leopardi's audacity was not mediated by popular forms like the sermon, the hymn, the ballad, the folk song, the political pamphlet, the lecture, or the stage. Except for the opera, the single popular form to which eighteenth-century Italy had given serious new life, none of these were available. He was contemporary with Vincenzo Bellini, a composer with a gift for melody much like his own, but one finds no indication that Leopardi was influenced by another art. To music and painting, Italy's currently hot items of export or tourist appeal, he seemed deaf and blind.

What would Coleridge's *Ancient Mariner* have been without the popular ballad? what Wordsworth's odes and sonnets without the sermon? what Emily Dickinson without the hymn? These are the extremes. Leopardi's extreme was a need for self-composition so urgent that it summoned up a courage like Newton's or Darwin's, and all the psychic and physical ills that go with the exercise of that sort of courage; a self-scrutinizing honesty so spacious that it left him mostly unread and misunderstood at home (Francesco De Sanctis, who actually met him at Naples, being the honorable exception) and vulnerable to idealist/positivist bigots like Benedetto Croce who, half a century after Gladstone, displayed no better comprehension of his great compatriot than the Prime Minister had. Decent biographies began to appear in the Nineties, but only after Croce's death did the now copious Italian critical bibliography begin to measure up. Today his peculiarly independent version of classic and modern material- ism is giving Italian Marxists almost as many headaches as it gave Glad- stone and Croce.

Not that the French wits on whose collective authority he leaned in writing his fanciful prose dialogues of the *Operette morali,* the above-men- tioned *Zibaldone,* or the concise *Pensieri* (Thoughts) were less honest than he. But their honesty was more programmatic, ran in straight lines like perspectives at Versailles. They did not scruple to make hecatombs of entire millenia, eras, and churches, for the sake of a *mot.* Leopardi's antagonist, on the other hand, was no less than the "world" as originally defined by Jesus Christ, later by Pascal; a world whose attractions he felt very keenly but which he knew to be his enemy. (His erotic propensities were exceptionally strong, though he may never have put them to the test.) When the fit was on him—usually in prose—he attacked the whole human race, or its wicked majority as described in the decisive first *Pen- siero*: "I say that the world is a league of scoundrels against men of generosity, of base men against men of good will." Being first and last a lyric poet, he eventually came to advise radical doubt in all things except poetry. His poetic certainties were simpler than those of any professional wit, any reformer of philosophy or politics. But their deployment through- out the reflective and polemical stuff of everyday existence was anything but simple. The crisis came in 1823 when he decided that man, loving himself absolutely, could never satisfy his appetite for happiness or make a truce with Nature. Life, he decided, was nothing but the consciousness of permanently imposed contradictions. But as J. H. Whitefield discovered in another connection, it was in his repudiation of Rousseau's benign Nature that he entered the claims of man. "For if into this sort of universe there were intruded the unnatural ideas of peace and stability, it was man who brought them."

Magnanimity, charity, love, generosity, the classic heroic virtues—all these at different times he treated as illusions, countering them with the devastating strength of modern *noia.* But the imagination of these things was what he lived for. "The lyric can be called the height, the perfection, the summit of poetry, which itself is the summit of human discourse."

The contrast with Dante's luck in having that rugged theological endo- and exoskeleton ready to hand is dramatic enough. Like Dante, Leopardi had a sovereign appetite for eroticizing his thought within the bounds of a high-born temperance—the very act of thinking. In a difficult but ambitious, important poem, *Il pensiero dominante* (Commanding Thought), unaccountably shirked by the Casale and Heath-Stubbs though not the Flores collection, he manages to combine and confound love and thinking so thoroughly that few critics are willing to say exactly what does dominate him, the fair female image or its effect on his mind.

> *Che mondo mai, che nova*
> *Immensità, che paradiso è quello*
> *Là dove spesso il tuo stupendo incanto*
> *Parmi innalzar! dov'io*
> *Sott'altra luce che l'usata errando,*
> *Il mio terreno stato*
> *E tutto il ver pongo in obblio!*
> *Tali son, credo, i sogni*
> *Degl' immortali . . .*

("What a world, what new immensity, what a paradise is that to which your stupendous enchantment seems to raise me! where I, wandering in unfamiliar light, forget my earthly condition and everything true. Such, I think, are the dreams of the immortals. . . .")

Not all of the poem reveals the poet in such an attractive Shelleyan light. In the eighth of fourteen stanzas of widely varying length and metrical organization—this is really Leopardi's ode to immortality—he condenses just about everything that later readers have found offensive in his character, the "aristocratic," Catonian features of his "aristocratic humanism."

> *Sempre i codardi, e l'alme*
> *Ingenerose, abbiette*
> *Ebbi in dispregio. Or punge ogni atto indegno*
> *Subito i sensi miei;*
> *Move l'alma ogni esempio*
> *Dell'umana viltà subito a sdegno.*
> *Di questa età superba,*
> *Che di vote speranze si nutrica,*
> *Vaga di ciance, e di virtù nemica;*
> *Stolta, che l'util chiede,*
> *E inutile la vita*
> *Quindi più sempre divenir non vede;*

Maggior mi sento. A scherno
Ho gli umani giudizi; e il vario volgo
A bei pensieri infesto,
E degno tuo disprezzator, calpesto.

("I have always despised cowardly, ungenerous, abject souls. Now every unworthy action stings my senses; every example of human cowardice swiftly moves me to disdain. I consider myself superior to this proud age which feeds on empty hopes, running after chatter, enemy to high quality, silly, which asks for usefulness and fails to see how life becomes thereby more useless. I despise human judgments; and I, a disparager worthy of you, strike down the mindless crowd hostile to high thinking.")

However one may choose to take this stanza, either as only one hypothesis in a body of verse that except for its lyric realizations is all hypothesis; or as a strained attempt to recover pre-Christian *superbia* and *alterigia*; or as the plainest truth of his heart, not unlike the *spagnolisme* cultivated by Stendhal at about the same time, that Mozart magnificently embodied in his "angry arias"—one cannot overlook its force. Perhaps only Blake offers a parallel in English. Nor should any serious student ignore the poem in which it appears, a good reason (alas) for preferring the Flores collection which prints translations with facing text of twenty-five of the forty-one poems in the *Canti,* against only sixteen in the Casale and seventeen in the Heath-Stubbs.

As a boy he had suffered a spell of fervent Catholic piety to satisfy his ultra-devout parents, provincial papal nobility during the post-Napoleonic lapse, in that part of Italy, of nearly every liberal impulse. Late in life his proud and willful but absurdly solicitous, smothering, henpecked father published a widely circulated pamphlet, *Little Dialogues on Current Affairs in the Year 1831,* so reactionary that rather than be confused with its author his son had repudiations printed in well-known journals, and wrote to a cousin: "I really cannot stand it any longer. I will not appear with the stain of having written that infamous, most infamous and wretched book." Shades of the Shelley family in reverse! Yet this was the father who had furnished him with one of the largest, most mixed and seductively accessible private libraries in Italy, buying up every book in the region that went on the market as a result of the disbanding of the monasteries and the prevailing economic misery. In this library, day and night in a thoroughly Coleridgian fashion but with no help from drugs, for at least seven years he "ruined his health," grew hunched over, developed half a dozen vexatious ailments, grew ugly in his own sight if not always in the sight of others. Vital, though generally unexpressed, in his intellectual makeup was an animal faith in the need for good fortune in the composition of *virtù*; good health, good looks, an athlete's body. This was genuinely Aristotelian and perhaps the element that Nietzsche found most congenial. He was a born naturalist who indulged in no self-advertisement as such, whose powers of selection and concentration were extraordinary.

His mother, the former Marchesa Adelaide Antici of the Marches, Professor Di Piero describes as follows:

> Pain, to Leopardi's mother, was a benison, and suffering a passport to salvation. Giacomo was convinced that his mother sincerely envied other mothers whose children died at birth, "for these children, escaping all perils had flown directly to heaven." She thought beauty a great misfortune—the suffering that attends physical deformity was a gift from God. Seeing her children ugly or deformed," wrote her son, the hunchback, "she gave thanks to God."

So much for the atmosphere of that house and town, attractive or tranquil only in inspired imaginative seizures of the poet. Recanati, though situated on a ridge above fertile farming country, was little more than a pitstop on the road to the shrine of Loreto—Napoleon had merely galloped through, offering Count Monaldo no better expression of his wrath than to turn his back in a second-floor study window. Giacomo was eventually to spend months at a time in Rome (disliked), Milan (disliked), Florence (disliked), Bologna and Pisa (liked), and finally Naples (both liked and disliked). His qualities made him a few valuable friends, none of whom could do much to appease his restlessness or his *sacro furore*. One of his first critical acts was to write in 1818 a "Discourse of an Italian about Romantic Poetry." Romanticism had by then acquired its Italian spokesmen, middling men on the whole except for Manzoni's early adherence, in reply to one of whom Leopardi denounced the cult of timely subject matter, novelty for novelty's sake, early Goethean *Sturm und Drang,* the cult of mere *sensibilité.* As a modern critic astutely put it, he was romantic against Empire neo-classicism, but classical against overindulgence in the pathetic. Here at home, where our serious neo-classicism only got underway in the 1920s in the work of Yvor Winters, J. V. Cunningham, and their friends, it is hard to imagine the parity that the two "schools" had reached in Leopardi's Italy, or what complete, healthy, useful confusion he introduced into the discussion.

About Leopardi's justly celebrated gift for reconciling the old and the new, in form, vocabulary, diction, meter, rhythm, and sonic texture, both John Heath-Stubbs and Professor Casale have searching things to say. But both make the Englishing of these qualities sound dangerously easy. Heath-Stubbs, whom Casale professes to admire and whom he clearly, though not slavishly, follows, confesses himself a user of "the middle style, with the language of the English Romantics, especially Wordsworth, in mind." So far so good; most translators keep everything they know in mind, or should. But one scents trouble in the diffidence with which he suggests that Leopardi's two main vehicles—an eleven-syllable blank verse, *endecasillabi sciolti*; and a free-form *canzone libera* consisting of *endecasillabi* alternating freely with seven-syllable lines or *settenari*, plus rhyme ad lib—can be made to seem as normal and inevitable as the experiments of the English Romantics.

This is not the case, for reasons offered above. The *canzone libera*, as Heath-Stubbs suggests, may be "an extension of the classical *canzoni* as developed by the poets of the Middle Ages and the Renaissance" and it may well have been "taken over . . . from the dramatic choruses of Tasso," but after so long a hiatus, not to mention a common ignorance of Tasso's choruses as distinct from the rest of his work, Leopardi's version of it burst on Italy with the freshness and unexpectedness of Whitman's experiments in English. In Leopardi's hand the form was not the exercise in self-conscious restraint that the sonnet became in English, but the subtlest, most elaborate efflorescence of which the era's Italian poetry was capable.

Consider the final lines of *Ultimo canto di Saffo* (Sappho's Last Song), first in the Heath-Stubbs, then the Casale version:

> *E tu cui lungo*
> *Amore indarno, e lunga fede, e vano*
> *D'implacato desio furor mi strinse,*
> *Vivi felice, se felice in terra*
> *Visse nato mortal. Me non asperse*
> *Del soave licor del doglio avaro*
> *Giove, poi che perir gl'inganni e il sogno*

Della mia fanciulezza. Ogni più lieto
Giorno di nostra età prima s'invola.
Sottentra il morbo, e la vecchiezza, e l'ombra
Della gelida morte. Ecco di tante
Sperate palme, e dilettosi errori,
Il Tartaro m'avanza; e il prode ingegno
Han la tenaria Diva,
E l'atra notte, e la silente riva.

And you, for whom vain love and lasting faith
Have held me, and the empty fury of
Unsatisfied desire—live happy, if indeed
Such in this world may be any mortal's lot.
But Jupiter, for me, out of the urn
Whence flows the pleasant wine of happiness,
Dealt with no generous hand, since perished all
The dear illusions and the dreams of youth.
For the most full of joy of all our days
Are first to fly away, and then creep in
Disease, old age, the shade of frigid death.
Behold, for all the palms I might have won,
And sweet deceiving hopes, Tartarus waits;
And the aspiring mind must Proserpine
Possess, forever more,
The sable night, and quiet Stygian shore.

And you for whom I have known useless love,
And kept my trust, and felt the burning bite
Of unfulfilled desire—live, happy love,
If any human be so privileged.
Once my illusions and dear dreams of youth
Had passed the skimping Jove withheld from me
The sweet liquor of joy. The happiest
Of all our days fly by on such swift wings,
And then death insinuates, old age,
And shadows of cold death. Behold. Instead
Of palms I might have won and luring hopes,
Black Tartarus awaits me now. The mind
Which quested for so much goes with the bride
Of Dis who went before,
To the possessing night and silent shore.

Literally more faithful than Casale, Heath-Stubbs is also awfully bland. Leopardi's fourteen-and-a-half lines have become a full sixteen. The Italian has nothing that *sounds* like "the pleasant wine of happiness/ Dealt with no generous hand." The "dear" dreams of youth is an interpellation; "all" our days and "all" the palms are characteristic inflations, not in the interest of precision or eloquence but to keep old Thames smoothly flowing, a stream reflecting more Edwardian sunset hues than the speech of Wordsworth. "Aspiring mind" is feeble for *prode ingegno,* and "sable night, and quiet Stygian shore" takes all the iron out of *l'atra notte, e la silente riva.* (*Atro* is archaic-latinate for black; my modern dictionary doesn't have it but it was a favorite of Leopardi and should be dignified with something stronger in English than "sable.")

Casale has exercised a freer periphrasis with mostly happier results. "Skimping Jove" is fine, more Pope than Wordsworth. The last three lines, freely re-imagined, sound better than in Heath-Stubbs. The Leopardi has no "possessing" night and no going with anyone. But these ironies are implicit. And "silent shore" would seem the inevitable right phrase for *silente riva.*

One must be lenient. In Italian those last three lines have a spine-chilling concentration of sound and association, of gravity and fierceness, that no translator could hope to reproduce. Heath-Stubbs and Casale have obviously proceeded as their age and higher fashions dictated. The first Englishes Leopardi in more ways than one, softens his asperities, reduces his latent drama. In the expected American manner Casale sacrifices any assured familiar idiom, Romantic or otherwise, to the sometimes rewarded hope of being as fierce, imaginative, ironic, or earthy as the original.

Casale's modesty is disarming. His *Reader,* he says, "is directed not at the Italianist but at the general reader of world, comparative, or romantic literature who desires to know Leopardi as more than a name." Within the limits of a 270-page book, that ambition is amply fulfilled. Prose exceeds poetry in bulk. Ten of the *Operette morali* plus several letters, *Zibaldone* and *Pensieri* excerpts are given, the whole carefully annotated and commented upon. Almost exactly the length of the Heath-Stubbs/Iris Origo collection, it is very much worth having.

That non-Italians with a hazy grasp of the language, or none at all, should often have settled for the "little moral dialogues"—like Landor's *Imaginary Conversations* in form but most like *Candide* in spirit—or the

Pensieri, is at least understandable. One of the wealthier publishers should now give us the entire *Zibaldone.* The prose offers few of the insuperable difficulties for translation that protect the poetry from vulgar misappropriation. In his Foreword to the Casale, Glauco Cambon is right to call the *Operette* "saturnine and mercurial." They teeter on the border between hard-nosed eighteenth-century rationalism and romantic fabulation. The spokespersons—Nature, an Icelander, Copernicus, Columbus, Frederick Ruysch and his mummies, a Gnome and a Sylph, Prometheus, and so on —are a random group, not, as it were, taken from repertory, rarely as solidly present as the people in *Candide.* If nothing else, everyone should at least read the splendid "Story of the Human Race."

Nor do the maxims of the *Pensieri* make quite the same points as do his models nor in quite the same way. As Professor Di Piero observes in his admirable Translator's Introduction, the book constitutes "a manual for self-preservation in modern Western society," or as Walter Benjamin tellingly puts it, a "working oracle [that teaches] the art of discretion for rebels." Its author became a rebel only in the service of a single esoteric goal—the writing of lyric and elegiac poetry—so in all its variety and wit it still must be reckoned a diversion. One must agree with Di Piero that "Leopardi's universe is recognizably modern, a blasted place, and nature is *il brutto poter*—brute force, mindless, governed by natural selection empowered by its own necessities, oblivious to man's needs." Still, as Di Piero is also aware, the *Pensieri* are not primarily about the universe but how to survive in a society that such a universe creates. Hence the distinctly old-fashioned Chesterfieldian ring of the advice it gives, advice that Stendhal's Count Mosca or Mozart's Count Almaviva might have given their children *in camera*—the old legitimist hard certitudes stripped of their dynastic animus and pushed as far as logic can take them. Only in the poetry—notably in *La ginestra* (Broom)—does he put this self-protective shrewdness entirely behind him and conjure a world of universal, classless, democratic brotherhood. On the way to that consummation he sang his loves and griefs as very few men have been privileged to do.

A Winter Feast

PAUL SCHMIDT

> And now it's dark. He gets into a sleigh.
> Behind him trails the coachman's cry: "Away!"
> The frost with sparkling silver dusts
> The beaver collar of his winter coat.
> He drives to Talon's restaurant; he is sure
> Kavérin will be waiting for him there.
> He enters, corks go pop, they pour champagne
> (1811, the year the comet came).
> Before them, a roast-beef ensanguine;
> Truffles, that extravagance of youth
> And finest flower of the French cuisine;
> Strasbourg's immortal dish, *foie gras en croûte;*
> Soft, ripening Limburger cheese
> And golden pineapples from overseas.
>
> (*Eugene Onegin,* Chapter One, Canto XVI)

Pushkin's hero Eugene Onegin drives off in a swirl of snow to a dinner that celebrates the birth of the nineteenth century. The celebration is late; 1819 is not the turn of the century; those twenty years would make an adolescent, at least, of anyone. This is a special moment, though, in a special age. The nineteenth century was perhaps the youngest of centuries when it was young; the eighteenth century, for instance, was born old and died older. But the nineteenth century in Europe was born in a thunder-clap; it sprang to life in a fit of revolution, of turmoil, of fire and excite-ment; it was the work of the young. A group of very young people, all of them stimulated to a frenzy by the military exploits, the daring, the very existence of Napoleon. Napoleon, that very young man, whose height kept him a perpetual symbol of adolescence. He was the image that soared over those first decades, as he looms today over Paris on his column in the Place Vendome. He was a supreme symbol of prodigality, an emperor who distributed crowns and kingdoms to his family and friends as if they were Christmas gift baskets. But he was not alone; it was an age of prodigious adolescents: George IV, Pushkin, Shelley, Keats, Byron, Beau Brummel, Chopin, Bellini, Rossini, Mme. de Stael, Mme. Récamier. They strewed their talents lavishly in every direction, all of them spurred on to

From *Parnassus* (vol. 16, no. 1, 1990).

imitate the acts of the emperor himself. They were prodigious eaters and drinkers, prodigious dressers, *bon vivants*—they lived the good life. Dinner for them, like dress, was a symbol of luxury, of triumph; it was a sign that they had conquered. If they could not conquer like the emperor, they could at least eat like him. They assembled feasts that were fantasies: imagined feasts, literary feasts, feasts thought up as much as anything else for the description, simply for the report of the thing. Like the ideal military dispatch, what was important was the image evoked by the words, not the facts of the case.

But the facts of the case were stunning enough. Look at the dinner awaiting Onegin: champagne, roast beef, truffles, a Strasbourg *foie gras,* Limburger cheese, fresh pineapple. None of this is homegrown, especially in a Russian January. Everything is imported, taken by force from the places it comes from. The feast itself was a metaphor of conquest. Cooking and eating came to reflect the incessant heaving to and fro across frontiers and continents that marked the Napoleonic era, and the triumphant movers of that cooking, like the emperor's armies, were French. The mark of France remains upon cooking still; the terminology of the kitchen resists translation. French cooks fed the world, and they fed it in French. Here is Louis-Eustache Udé, a French cook of the period who wrote for an English audience: "Military tactics, fortifications, music, dancing, and millinery, etc., being of foreign extraction . . . it must not be wondered at if in this work I have made use of original, or native expressions."

Food was a metaphor for the age, and the age was a military one. Udé is right: military tactics and food reflected one another. It was all an enormous attempt at the table to live for a while like Napoleon, to conquer as many lands as he had by bringing their produce to the table, to be devoured there like a great living map. We forget, in our simplified age, the visual splendor of those tables. The last vestige of it we see today only in wedding cakes: those white towers are all that a middle-class era preserves—for marriage, that most important of middle-class occasions— of an imaginary architecture. Remember the great dream palaces we see in early nineteenth-century Beaux Arts building projects? None of them were ever built—except by pastry cooks, who covered dinner tables with edible architecture. It was the custom then to lay all the courses on the table at once, so that the table itself looked like a tiny city, an entire state, an empire in miniature, and it was surrounded by the diners the way an attacking army surrounds its target. The table was besieged—the very word means to sit down around something. The more glorious the city, the greater the triumph, and those table-cities were each more glorious than the last. Carême, the greatest cook of the era, has left us a book to describe his obelisks and monuments, his triumphal arches, his hanging gardens, all built of icing and spun sugar. Cakes shaped like castles and obelisks of paté rose over teeming neighborhoods of pastry crusts packed with populations of small birds and lesser beings; platters curved like the shoreline of a port town, the silver scallops and gadroons of their edges winking like the frill of an evening wave, with creamy billows full of fish and crustaceans waiting behind it to tumble in turn upon that silver shore. Long trays lined with glazed domes and molded pinnacles made broad formal avenues that led off to more relaxed suburban sections planted with flower-garden salads; there, cool groves of greenery shaded fountains of champagne. Animals and fruits from all over the world were crammed into this city-table; its treasure was an imperial prize. This was the *ancien régime,* the elegant older civilization, worth the storm of revolution, worth the effort of destruction, worth devouring. And night after night such cities were besieged and sacked by battalions of brilliant, clamoring young men and women. The military dash of such a dinner, the jingling hussars' uniforms, the noise, the flames of a hundred constantly burning candles— it was all a vast piece of poetry, a metaphor. Every banquet a campaign, as every imperial campaign, until the end, had been a banquet.

Our banquets to this day recall those campaigns—some of the great classic dishes of French cooking commemorate Napoleonic victories. Chicken Marengo from the Italian campaign, Chicken Albuféra from the Iberian campaign. Defeats, of course, are not recorded. There is no Cooked Goose Waterloo. There is only that one strange dish where all the main ingredients of Pushkin's menu are combined: Roast beef is covered with *foie gras,* enclosed in a pastry, and served with truffle sauce: Beef Wellington, a case of winner-take-all. (The dish is *not* a French invention.)

Pushkin's dinner, though, is a Russian dinner, and Napoleon never conquered Russia; Moscow burned, true, but the imperial capital St. Petersburg, that distant, frozen city, remained untouched. Untouched? No need of conquest; it had belonged to Europe from the start. The city was the creation of foreigners, of European imaginations. This is a foreign dinner, after all: not only are the ingredients imported, but the restaurant itself is French: Talon's, at no. 15 Nevsky Prospect. Talon, "the well-known restaurant owner," Pushkin calls him; Talon, the Frenchman who had come to Petersburg in the wave of imported artists that swept through the city and created its sensual environment: Didelot the French ballet master, Rastrelli the Italian architect, Cameron the Scottish architect, John Field the Irish pianist, Fabergé the Huguenot jeweller. These were the people who provided the texture of the city, its tastes and styles, the web of sights and sounds and shapes and smells against which Pushkin moved and his verses sounded.

It was a poet, after all, who created this menu, and the menu is perfect Petersburg poetry: As the dishes were imported, so were the words used to describe them. The stanza is full of foreign words as the menu is full of foreign dishes. Roast beef (*rost-bif* in the original: an anglicism), Strasbourg, Limburger, truffles, pineapple (*ananas* in the original: a gallicism)—are these dishes or words? Consider the power of words to make us salivate, to awaken sensation, memory, or even an image of something we've never experienced. This menu is a poem first of all, and so began with words: Pushkin imported it from all over. The English *rost-bif* he found in a French poem by Parny; it replaced a dish he considered for an earlier draft, a *bécasse,* a French woodcock that he'd found in an English poem by Byron. And the *bécasse* was there in the first place not because he liked woodcock but because *bécasse* rhymes with *ananas.* So this stanza is as much an imported delicacy as the menu it describes, for poetry breaks down more frontiers than Napoleon could.

And yet what richness Pushkin offers us, what sensuality, what an imperial meal! Champagne, roast beef, truffles, Strasbourg *foie gras,* Limburger cheese, fresh pineapple. All the senses are put to work in this description: the ear, in the pop and spurt of a newly-opened bottle of iced champagne; the eye, in the crimson of roast beef, the velvet blackness of truffles, the gold of a pineapple; the nose, supremely, in the Limburger, the tactile sense in various textures and temperatures—the icy chill of a glass, the tearing of hot, succulent flesh from a rib bone, the sweet wetness of a piece of pineapple. And the tastebuds, each of them subjected to an elaborate succession of triumphant, conquering experiences. This is poetry not so much about food as about the effects of food on heightened senses, on the finely-tuned palate and the riotous sensual imagination. Words are paramount, but this is a poetry of the flesh—one that borders, perhaps, on pornography. Pushkin knew that. He knew that conquest was not only a military matter, but a sexual one, and that food was ammunition in that crucial war. As his chapter progresses, his hero Onegin becomes gradually disenchanted with the sensual excitements of the life he leads, and Pushkin lumps them all together:

> . . . Was he in vain amid these feasts
> Hale, and hearty, and without a care?
> Yes. His emotions cooled early.
> Society began to weary him.
> Beautiful women were no longer all
> His occupation: betrayals took their toll;
> Friends and friendship got to be a bore.
> Clearly he could not constantly wash down
> Paté and beef with bottles of champagne,
> Nor scatter wit and bright remarks about
> When he was hung over. And even though
> He was a hothead, and a touchy one,
> He grew at last definitively bored
> With duelling pistols, lead, and sword.

The youth of the era was at an end; the disorder of so much violence and richness in the blood was clear. Europe felt bilious and gouty, and turned to plainer local dishes: simple national stews instead of foreign delicacies. The great dinner party was over. It came to an end, like the empire, in a giant crash, as if some firm maternal hand had pulled the tablecloth from the table and everything hit the floor—crystal, dishes, flowers, food, and wine—in a teeth-shattering crash and a clatter of silverware. It all went, all of it, the luxury, the extravagance, the opulence, everything: Sèvres basins broke and dissolved their assemblies of strawberries, bottles of Médoc cracked their necks and rolled into corners, slapping spurts of bloody fluid and drowning the painted flowers of the porcelain plates. The golden candelabra toppled and fell from their sphinx-ridden bases, while the whole debacle was reflected for a moment in the wild eye and wacky grin of an ormolu cupid, astride one sphinx with his arm thrown out, urging the mess on as if he were leading a cavalry charge to the floor. Then he slid face-first into a platter of whipped cream, and over him toppled the spun-sugar temples, the icing Arches of Triumph, the sticky garlands and the carved ice swans, all of it tumbling and smashing, bouncing and skidding across the parquet floor, a torrent of rubbish finally, full of the squish of smeared sauces and congealed grease, a great rolling, rotting mess.

It all vanished. There was nothing left on the polished wooden surface of the table but a plain white Biedemeier coffee pot, two cups of coffee, a plate of bread and butter. And a long domestic silence, broken only by the tick of a clock and a cat's occasional purr.

THE MENU

Foie Gras en Croûte

Truffles

Roast Beef

Limburger

Pineapple

Champagne D'ay, 1811

FOIE GRAS

There is a dark side to food—the inside. Most of what we consider edible is the inside of something, and to get at it we have to open something up: cut it open, crack it open, rip it open, pull it out. The first step in cooking is to get things out in the open.

Of all the inside parts we eat, the richest and rarest is *foie gras,* fat goose liver; the effort and expense of obtaining it are legendary. It is a pleasure we pay dearly for. And yet, a curious thing—once we get the *foie gras,* we almost always serve it covered up again: in a pastry crust as here in Pushkin's menu, in a terrine, or in a block of aspic. Aspic is the most revealing of these coverings, for its transparence emphasizes the innerness of the thing, encased almost in shining crystal. And only by destroying the outside can we get at the inside, ever. To serve the dish we must perform again the act by which we got the liver in the first place—cutting open the goose.

To eat *foie gras en croûte* we must attack it; it is a military operation. It is Brillat-Savarin who says so; he describes a party once where the diners were served "an enormous *foie gras* in pastry from Strasbourg, in the shape of a bastion . . . a real Gibraltar." The image is compelling, and the diners proceeded to conquer the *foie gras* as the British had conquered Gibraltar and taken it from Napoleon not many years before. But in Brillat-Savarin's description that conquest is as much sexual as military. "In effect," he continues, "all conversation ceased as if hearts were too full to go on; all attention was riveted on the skill of the carvers; and when the serving platters had been passed, I saw spread out in succession on every face the fire of desire, the ecstacy of enjoyment, and then the perfect peace of satisfaction."

Perfection, satisfaction—it's true, we strive for satisfaction in love, for perfection in food: That is what every serious dinner for two is all about. But can *foie gras* content us? Can perfection satisfy? That liver, after all, is a triumph of our desire for perfection in food. We do strange and unnatural things to plants and animals in our attempts to perfect them for food. Those geese in Strasbourg, for instance. The facts are known. The geese are kept in stalls, immobilized from goslinghood, and force-fed. They are hourly crammed with corn until their livers, from coping with cholesterol, are swollen many times their normal size. That "fat liver" is a work of art, and its creation begins long before it even reaches the kitchen, long before it even leaves the goose. Delectable monstrosity! Delicious perversion!

We do that to the geese; do we do it to ourselves? We manipulate our bodies this way and that toward perfection, toward fat or thin mostly, back and forth, constantly. Fat yearns toward Thin, Thin strives for Fat; rarely are we content with our casings. The beautiful woman sweating off a last invisible pound in some perfumed retreat, a Greenhouse not for growing but for diminishing, or Arnold Schwarzenegger straining a last metaphysical inch onto a bicep in some clanking gym—what's the difference? Two discontented people, we think, and in a kind of Piranesi prison of their own imaginations: the steel cage and winking windows of the Greenhouse, the steel bars and mirrors of the gym—two views of the same edifice. But suppose we rethink the matter: Is it discontent that moves them to such effort? Or are they rather Platonic philosophers striving toward a perfection of pure form? Both have firmly fixed in mind an image of perfection, and both strive hungrily toward it; that it is a perfection of the flesh doesn't negate the seriousness of their search. The search seems endless, because the flesh is endlessly imperfect, but the very impossibility of the task conveys a certain nobility upon it; we admire that, the way we admire mountain climbers. For these two, though, there is never any fixed summit waiting frozen in the sunshine. The flesh is always unstable; what we see and are pleased with in the evening's mirror we cannot even face in the morning's reflection. But what we see in the morning can give us a goal for the day—at least if we take the matter at all seriously, which Arnold Schwarzenegger and the lady in the Greenhouse do. For both of them the striving and the yearning go on forever, while the image of a beautiful body glows in the air above their heads, always a few inches, just a few inches out of reach.

But who knows what risks they take? Can we manipulate one part and not another? Perhaps Arnold Schwarzenegger himself has a *foie gras,* an enormous glistening liver to accompany the matchless gleaming outside. Perhaps the beautiful lady's insides diminish as she thins her thighs: Perhaps she is left with a skinny, shrivelled heart. There's the real problem, and the real question: Do we prize the inside more than the outside, or the outside more than the inside? Is the beauty of the body somehow within, like a Platonic private part, and are Arnold Schwarzenegger and the beautiful lady both striving to set free something they feel within them, to dig out their *foie gras,* to make an inner perfection visible to the outside world?

Well, we may manipulate inside to make it reflect *out,* or outside to make it reflect *in,* but sooner or later we must come to understand that the one is incomplete without the other: An outside with no inside is empty, and an inside with no outside is helpless. And so we surround *foie gras* with pastry crust, and stuff the goose it came from.

But once surrounded, once inside, the stuff becomes an object of desire. We rush to conquer the bastion, and to conquer we must cut. There's an excitement to the act of opening up—Brillat-Savarin's diners waiting with anticipation the way we all do when something is exposed, the way children wait for a birthday present, or the way we watch a new lover undress for the first time. Conquest, we call it, and the opening can be violent. How often do children rip fiercely at the wrapping, how often do we tear passionately at a new lover's clothes!

Yet that violence bothers me, somehow; I have the feeling it must somehow be paid for, and it may be in a way we little expect. Consider the whole perverse procedure by which we get *foie gras:* Is it really possible to manipulate one part and not affect the whole? If we make the goose livers grow, what about the geese? Mightn't they grow, too? And may there not be, somewhere in the woods back of Strasbourg, great hordes of hulking geese, twelve feet high, honking like fire engines? The goddamn birds by now may even have turned into some sort of strange mutants: Their intelligence may have grown with their livers, as if they had taken a cram course in the awful ways of the world, and they may even now be mobilizing to march upon Paris, out to destroy every three-star restaurant in their path. Revenge! Revenge for perverting Platonic philosophy! Revenge for generations of livers sent to feed the fat-mouthed middle class! There may be hissing firebrands among them, revolutionary geese hoping to bring bourgeois civilization and all its philosophies to its knees. Who knows? We have only the word of a few smiling Alsatian farm ladies that the geese die regularly and gracefully, at normal size.

Perhaps the real expense of *foie gras,* like the price we pay for conquest or for love, is anxiety—the nervous fear of what may be lurking in the dark woods out back. Perfection may be within us, but satisfaction requires something from without, and must somehow be paid.

TRUFFLES

A truffle is a rarity, the way things that require discovery are always rare. It must be discovered quite literally: disclosed, uncovered, dug up. It shares with oysters the quality of being *rock-like:* of lying in silent, undisturbed darkness beneath a surface, and of having to be found out, dragged into the light, like a secret, or like meaning out of a complex event. I think it is this as much as anything that makes truffles attractive to us; anything that must be uncovered—discovered—will yield up more than itself, because we seek in it, as compensation for our search, some meaning beyond the brute fact of its being. So we read a truffle as if it were a text; it means more to us than just another mushroom. It enters our existence more importantly, and lingers longer. Its scarcity, its price, its seldomness, keep it in a metaphoric part of our minds. We say truffle, we write truffle, we imagine truffle, as often as—more often than, perhaps, for most of us—we ever eat truffle. We confront, indeed, in truffle-eating, a dark and hidden behavior. Darkness, after all, is its fundamental quality, its very image, and this may be for us the dark suggestion of an old idea, dragged up from our unconscious as the truffle is dragged up to light. When it is set before us, our imaginations confront a fact: This plaything for grown-ups at their most grown-up may yet bring us in a blink to a buried part of childhood. Are we about to eat *that?* Is a truffle not, perhaps, earth's excrement?

It is certainly something more than itself: The very complication of its provenance assures us of that. A truffle is snuffled out, snorted from the earth, passed from pig to peasant, from village to town, from earth to water; it is washed and polished and cooked and glazed, and sent ceremoniously to a candle-lit table. There it ends its passage from darkness to light, as a great dark eye opens slowly from primordial sleep, and finds reflected in its shiny surface the glance of a lady in satin and diamonds—a glance intended for the gentleman two places down the table from her. And that glance is checked, perhaps, by the sweep of a napkin, and a white wave winks for an instant in the truffle's surface, but as the napkin drops slowly lower and lower, the lady's diamonds are revealed, reflected in the truffle's glaze. Then in both truffle and diamond some kinship is revealed, a cousinage of underground darkness, two lumps of stuff dug out of the earth, brought to light, cleaned and polished and taken finally to the same table, there to reflect each other: perfect darkness and perfect light. In those reflecting surfaces, what secrets may pass! And yet they pass through the diamond, refract, dissolve, and disappear: Diamonds hold nothing. But in the truffle those secrets remain. As darkness embraces all, reveals nothing, so does a truffle. It yields up only an ancient aroma, a black taste, and recalls us to the deepest parts of ourselves. Our latter-day frivolities are judged in that stern earthen eye, the feast darkens, and all the glitter of the diamond is denied. The candles on this table will soon gutter and go out, the truffle tells us, and so will we.

ROAST BEEF

Roast beef is a different phenomenon in different times and in different places, but it is the intractable item in any menu, and the dominant one. All over the world it is called by its English name—it is always roast beef (or roastbeef or rostbif or rosbif or rozbif). Why? Because the English invented it, we say; but the fact is, there was nothing to invent. Roast beef has nothing to do with recipes. It was originally not a matter for the kitchen at all. It is roast meat, grilled meat, a barbecue, something done out-of-doors and done since time immemorial. In a sophisticated age it is the last vestige of our aboriginal past, and to see a slice of roast beef on a Sèvres plate on a candle-lit table is to see an extraordinary combination of things—the gilt and painted flowers of the porcelain glittering in the candle flame, beneath the almost raw hunk of what was once, very obviously, except for its exposure to flame, live meat.

Roast beef is a dish that comes to the table with less human meditation than anything except oysters on the half shell. And except for oysters, which we try to eat live, rare beef is the closest thing to living flesh we eat. We have eaten roast meat in European culture longer than we have eaten anything else. Boiled beef is modern compared to roast beef, and the product of a subtle technology. It takes less art to boil beef than to roast it, but the results are more certain; like most technological innovations, boiled beef is surer than roast beef, but duller. A piece of roast beef is no triumph of the kitchen. It barely belongs in the dining room. It is, rather, the triumph of the principle of conservation, of the idea of habit. Roasting was the first physical meditation of humanity upon the things we eat— again, except for opening oysters. But there it lies, still faintly bleeding, a shocking anachronism. Look closely sometime at a slice of rare roast beef—who brought *that* into the house, we wonder; it shrieks of savagery and the out-of-doors.

The closer the meat seems to the bleeding animal that fell beneath the arrow, the better. Grilled meat is the primal luxury: It means you have been a successful hunter and can afford to offer fresh meat to your friends. And it must be fresh, too; other forms of cookery can disguise tainted meat, but grilling is simple: only flesh and fire. The process is always kept visible, as the fire is always visible, always a focus, always social. All cultures keep grilled meat as a separate item, and most cultures keep some kind of outdoor barbecue for special occasions. A restaurant with a grill almost always displays it. And when we ask the neighbors over, how often is it to the backyard and for grilled meat? An Indian with his slice of bleeding buffalo, an Eskimo with his hunk of bloody seal, a caveman with his messy piece of mammoth, are all cousins to the man in the yard next door with his pile of hamburgers, his grill, and his silly apron. He never went on a hamburger hunt, but that nevertheless is the premise he celebrates.

Outdoor cooking is man's work, too, not woman's. In the primal division of labor, men hunted animals and women gathered plants, and that distinction holds clearly when we think of grilled meat. Not much is ever done to roast beef. It is served without sauces, basted only in its own fat, and its traditional accompaniment is only the complementary food, vegetables. What had been hunted by men is eaten with what had been gathered by women. With the rare, the raw. Salad. Vegetables raw, or only cooked enough, as the meat is ideally, to make them attractive to eat. And as the meat is always basted in its own fat, so a salad is always dressed with vegetable liquids: olive oil and vinegar. There is an immense human satisfaction in this combination of opposites: roast beef and salad, when the masculine activity and the feminine come to rest, side by side, on the same plate. And there we can combine the sexes however we want. As Escoffier notes: ". . . many gourmets like to sop their salad in the meat juice."

LIMBURGER CHEESE

Finding food is an animal problem; preserving it is a human one. To set about preserving food, one must first be aware of time—not merely the fact of it: distinguish day from night, and you can tell time—but rather the effect of time on the world. Time will transform what we eat without touching it; astonishingly, before our very eyes and under our very noses, what used to be food stops being food. At some point it dawned on a caveman, downwind from some stinking mound of mammoth, that the carcass he had been dining off for a week had gone beyond the point of dinner.

But long before that, at some odd, early moment, some thoughtful creature made a curious discovery. She stands—perhaps alone, perhaps with a creature beside her—beneath a tree whose branches are heavy with apples. She eats one. The fruit of the tree tastes "good." But then there is a rustling in the leaves, a cloud for a moment obscures the sun, and the creature near her begins to move away; touched by a certain fear, she starts to follow him—and on an impulse she grabs four or five apples and carries them away with her. Perhaps she offers one of them to the creature near her. Perhaps she eats one of them herself as she goes. Perhaps she decides to keep the others until "later"—and it dawns on her, as she eats another one later, that it tastes "better." Eventually, "much later," she discovers that the last one tastes "bad." Awful, in fact. She has attained a certain knowledge: Things ripen and then they rot, and that is a measure of time.

Ripeness tastes good but rot tastes bad, and the time of the tasting makes all the difference. And from that moment of perception beneath that tree, down an endless chain of grandmothers, comes that knowledge: the idea of preserving food, or trying to make the taste of the apple last forever.

But preserving food is a complex affair: Containers must be invented and proper techniques discovered. Through centuries of trial and error, attempts were made to preserve everything, and apples are an easy matter compared, let's say, to milk. But once we learned to herd cattle and make bowls and baskets, the problem of preserving milk inevitably arose. And so we come to cheese.

To make cheese is to preserve milk. But with cheese the idea of preservation takes a strange turn: The process reverses itself. Time, that we struggle against to preserve food, becomes suddenly beneficial, and the process of ripening is extended to extremes—aging, we call it, and like it. The desirable end of cheese-making is not to preserve youth but to encourage age, not to keep freshness but to lose it, not to safeguard innocence but to ensure an enjoyable corruption. Clearly at some point in the process of corruption, or rot, we draw a line and say: That's it, no further; nobody could eat *that*. But at what point? An attractive gaminess is an acquired taste—acquired with age, at that, and it may simply be that age is drawn to age, decay to decay. What we puke up at six we will gorge on at sixteen; what seems gross at sixteen may be a delicacy at sixty. What sort of progression is this?

The truest understanding of cheese is that it concerns, precisely, milk. Do we ever lose a taste for our first food? The change from mother's milk to other foods is an awful drama of wailing and dribbling and drooling, and it may even be that the messy pain of weaning continues forever. Perhaps it involves more than the lost breast; perhaps it colors the entire world always. Milk sours, as affection sours; do we mark with cheese our disenchantment with the world? Do cheeses provide us with attractive lumps of disappointment?

More than that, I think. Our progress from milk to cheese, and from cheese to stronger cheese, is a change of sexuality. A baby takes only milk, and at some point is noisily and painfully weaned away from the breast; is cheese-eating then a metaphor for the way we relate to our mother's body? Do we attempt to retrieve some other part of what was so forcibly taken from us? As we move from the taste and smell of fresh milk to the taste and smell of aged cheese, do we move from one sexuality to another, from the breast to other parts? The gamey taste and smell of ripened cheese is sexual, and provocative; the smell is maternal still, but now it is the smell of cyclical time. Time is measured constantly and inexorably in the swelling and emptying of maternal organs, and its trace is recalled, surely, in the change of milk to Limburger.

For Limburger is the ultimate palatable state of pure milk. We first drink milk in all innocence; it is the taste of childhood. When we are older and wiser we eat Limburger, and that is the taste of age and decay. One is the odor of life, the other the odor of death, and in the transformation of one to the other, and in the change in our taste for one to the other, we record our body's encounter with time. An interesting encounter, after all. All things are subject to corruption, true; but that's no matter for despair, rather for acceptance, and even for delectation.

Ripeness is indeed all, in cheese as in ourselves, and that's surely the reason we love Limburger.

PINEAPPLES

Pushkin's meal ends with the pineapple, as his poem began with it, for *ananas* was the first rhyme word in Pushkin's stanza. Pineapple poetry? Why not? The pineapple has always been a sign of the high life, of good living, in Russia, all over Europe, and here in America as well: Witness the carved pineapple that crowns eighteenth-century doors, carved mirrors, and furniture.

But it has a deeper meaning, and an older one. When the *ananas* arrived in England, it was called pine-apple because it resembled the pinecone, and the pinecone has an ancient history. The Greeks and Romans associated the pinecone with Bacchus the wine god and the fertility rites of Dionysios, and that association persisted. Beyond luxurious living, the pineapple is a sign of license and sexuality.

Like most tropical fruits, the pineapple provides an astonishing distinction between exterior and interior—the outside never quite prepares us for the inside, which sometimes comes as a shock. That was what fascinated Europe with the tropical fruits brought back from the distant discoveries of the sixteenth, seventeenth, and eighteenth centuries. European fruits were obvious. Cherries and grapes are thin-skinned, or barely skinned at all. Whatever is inside shows through an almost transparent exterior, and colors it. In Europe the only things rough and forbidding-looking but still edible were nuts, but the inside of a nut was also hard, and small. Here suddenly were new fruits, enormous ones; they were scaly, rough, and hurtful on the outside, and yet within they were all softness, paleness, and juice.

Symbol indeed of the deepest hospitality, the pineapple is an androgynous fruit. It does not deny either sex, or equivocate about sexuality, but affords an image of masculinity and femininity totally, one within the other. Think of the whole pineapple: the phallic thrust of the thing displayed erect, as it so often is, over doorways and at the tops of lavish heaps of lesser fruit; and then cut one down the middle: the yonic pattern of the thing, with its pulpy fascicules radiating from a central ovoid cone, and its sticky juice and rich, musty smell. Brought from conquered islands to European tables, and there cut up and eaten, its rough thrust reduced to a yielding wetness, the pineapple is both an image of sexual conquest and as great a military metaphor as any of the columns and arches of Carême's imperial banquets.

But the great masters of the table, if they could, wanted it both ways. Udé's recipe reduces his pineapple to a heap of feminine slices, and then carefully reconstructs it as a phallic pile, in a transparent tower of jelly. And in this form he makes of it, perhaps, the truest phallic symbol of all: That proud, glistening height, as we know all too well, has too often a very shaky foundation. Depending on the temperature of the occasion and the lay of the land, all that shining phallic promise can dissolve, begin to wobble, and at last topple weeping into a puddle.

CHAMPAGNE

They pour champagne? The perfect wine for Russia; only blizzards and snowstorms can ever chill it properly. *1811, the year the comet came?* We need no year to qualify champagne, for every year is comet year: Champagne is just a comet in a bottle. The cork goes pop, it spurts a shower of stars; the foamy moment glitters with wild excitement, the ahs and sighs of satisfaction afterward, always, as it subsides into a bed of bubbles. Bravo! Open a bottle of champagne: The comet always comes.

Headless, With Flares

ROSS FELD

Guillaume Apollinaire. *Calligrammes.* Translated by Anne Hyde Greet.
University of California Press 1980. 513 pp. $19.95.

When Picasso was moved to do an Apollinaire (one good turn deserving
another), what he usually reached for was pen, ink, pencil, sometimes
wash. Acknowledged was that Apollinaire was his own color aplenty. A
friend who was an incomparable genius had only to sketch the shape of
the head (*en forme de poire* like one of Satie's *morceaux,* a pendant drop—
Apollinaire being one of those people to whom was allotted far more
room atop his shoulders than features require; mostly jaw and chin), stick
a little pipe between pursy lips, tug the brows down in an expression of
slight vexation, and top it off with a dozen small unjoined vertical lines
—*voilà,* the banquet years' own cartoon. Surround it with art and watch
it flip into action, becoming adorable and profound and annoying, growing large into the energies of a sentimental heart and a megaphone ego.
His image could have gone up on the street signs of Montmartre. In a
sense it did.

In the 1905 Picasso drawing, it's the top of the head that really matters,
those open lines. In addition to being self-coloring, Apollinaire was also
his own brush: a broad nature which, through steeping, is able to execute
lovely soft twists, get into the smallest corners. Language and culture were
continually beckoning him into the tightest jams: Monte Carlo (where, as
a boy, the Polish-Italian bastard born in Rome learns French—and life-as-
risk?); La Santé prison (six days, accused falsely of complicity in the theft
of the *Mona Lisa*); the war-time trenches of the Champagne. There, when
he was wounded in the head in 1917, shrapnel pierced his helmet; photographed, he looked as dashing thereafter in his pasha-like bandage as he
had years before in his Parisian bowler hat. But the top of the head
. . . You continue to suspect that *he didn't really have one.*

Which would help explain why he was his own solar-heating panel,
sky-comb, one of the last of the great melancholics (Dante, Van Gogh)
utterly available to the sunny or starry heavens. In *"Les Fiançailles,"* in
Alcools, stars are drunk down by the glassful; the moon is cooking like a
fried egg; *L'infiniment petite science/ Que m'imposent mes sens*—the infinitely
teensy skill that my senses force on me—is nonetheless compared to

Review of Guillaume Apollinaire's *Calligrammes* from *Parnassus* (vol. 9, no. 1, 1981).

mountains, cities, the sky, love; and, like the seasons, *Il vit décapité sa tête est le soleil*—it lives headless, its head the sun. Think what brightness must have seemed to Apollinaire to have fallen from the very air directly into his brain-pan. A new language. A clutch of serial, often overlapping mistresses. Friends like Picasso and the Delaunays and Chirico. Fame as aesthetic policy-maker, this after fifteen years of confabulating a personal history without stopping for breath. The shell-bursts of patriotism a war best provides to the previously stateless.

Little surprise, then, that everything boundlessly vertical seemed right to him. Post-Eiffel-Tower Paris asked for a new sort of urban poet, different than say Baudelaire; Apollinaire, in *"Zone,"* takes a street as nothing less than a "fanfare for the sun." Even blasphemous, Apollinaire's tug is a joyful one upward: *ce siècle comme Jésus monte dans l'air*; this century, like Jesus, climbs into the sky—with the religion built around this Flyboy retaining vigor because *Est restée simple comme les hangars de Port-Aviation*; it has kept as simple as the hangars at the airport. The Wrights and Blériot provide what's "modern" about these lines but their soul is as hoary as Icarus.

(Trying to think of a basically Apollinairian work of our much less innocent times—spare yourself from imagining what he might have made of Los Alamos, Eniwetok—I hook very little else besides Fellini's film, *La Dolce Vita,* its opening a nearly direct if coincidental parallel of the first dozen lines and atmosphere of *"Zone."*

But if all Apollinaire was, was simply a swooping sort of Marinetti, bewitched by the thrums of rpms and heavenly altitude, he'd by now be under the same rust that covers the ratchety Italian. Why instead we continue to see fresh skin owes to the fact that in whatever Apollinairian craft, projectile, astral body, or natural prominence that climbs the sky, the passenger (or multiples thereof) is always our Guillaume:

> Au-dessus de Paris un jour
> Combattaient deux grands avions
> L'un était rouge et l'autre noir
> Tandis qu'au zénith flamboyait
> L'éternal avion solaire
>
> L'un était toute ma jeunesse
> Et l'autre c'était l'avenir
> Ils se combattaient avec rage

Ainsi fit contre Lucifer
L'Archange aux ailes radieuses

Ainsi le calcul au problème
Ainsi la nuit contre le jour
Ainsi attaque ce que l'aime
Mon amour ainsi l'ouragan
Déracine l'arbre qui crie

Mais vois quelle douceur partout . . .

("Les Collines")

Anne Hyde Greet's version:

High over Paris one day
Two enormous airplanes fought
One was red and one was black
Meanwhile in the zenith flamed
The eternal solar plane.

One was all my youth
And the other was the future
They raged against each other
So struggled with Lucifer
The radiant-winged Archangel

Thus calculation reckons with the problem
Night strives against day
Thus what I love
My love assails a hurricane
Uproots the shrieking tree

But look what sweetness everywhere . . .

There is, we've come to know, such a thing as the great artist made mostly out of inflatable biography. Little by little a blimp of a self-made life fills, pushes out the creases; it's then grabbed, held to, and risen with. Various gaseous selves march toward us like a kind of Macy's Thanksgiving Day parade: bobbing characteristics of benign generosity, maddening personal and artistic inconsistency, and a strong resistance to being pulled down to one fixed point. Apollinaire was this kind of helium genius (as was, across the channel and contemporary, Ford Madox Ford).

Le tact est relatif mais la vue est oblongue: from "Le Larron" in *Alcools*—and this rounded-off shapeliness is in large part responsible for the classic stature this first volume of Apollinaire's poetry securely achieved. Lushness of music covered Apollinaire while he was getting away, technically, with things a sharper-angled voice and vision (like Max Jacob's) would have been clapped into obscurity for. No punctuation. A gearbox of lubricated pronouns (*Tu n'oses plus regarder tes mains et à tous moments je/ voudrais sangloter;* You don't dare look at your hands anymore, and I am forever/ wanting to cry) that various graduating classes of the New York School of poets continue to have slippery fun with to this day. Alexandrines which weight in the center, promoting a rhythmic rocking that slices any urge to rhetoric neatly in half. He effectively upended masculine and feminine French rhyme, making terminal vowels function as masculine, consonants feminine. And as for the romantic-symbolist tradition: it never recovered from Apollinaire. He had most if not all of its tricks down perfectly. A poem like *"Les Colchiques"* could employ the blunted mood, the spoiling modifier, with which French poetry and painting had been quite merrily objectifying self-pity for fifty years:

> De pré est vénéneux mais joli en automne
> Les vaches y paissant
> Lentement s'empoisonnent
> Le colchique couleur de cerne et de lilas
> Y fleurit tes yeux sont comme cette fleur-là
> Violâtres comme leur cerne et comme cet automne
> Et ma vie pour tes yeux lentement s'empoisonne

William Meredith's translation:

> In fall the fields are poisonous but fair
> Where slowly poisoning the cattle graze.
> The meadow saffron, *colchicum,* thrives there,
> Color of lilacs and the circles under eyes.
> My life pastures so on the autumn hue
> Of your eyes and slowly poisons itself too.

—while the next or previous poem might be *"Le Pont Mirabeau"* or *"Les Sapins"* or *"Automne"* or *"Signe"*: crooned lyrics (Apollinaire insisted he composed much of his work to wandering little melodies of his own creation; friends bore out the assertion, as would anyone with half an ear who reads the French aloud) which hug as close to the conditions of pure affectationless song as any of Villon, Nerval, Verlaine; the uncookedness of some of the feelings expressed startles us to this day. Having donned his climb-every-mountain Promethean costume in *"Le Brasier,"* in order to trumpet above a pot of flames his call for a new vision of miscellania-as-knowledge, Apollinaire can't resist—well towards the climax—dropping in a mischievous, self-mocking, Laforgue-ian aside: *Et le troupeau de sphinx regagne la sphingerie/ A petits pas*; And the flock of sphinxes returns to the sphinxerie/ with little steps. The greatest French poetry always keeps us seriously off-balance; *Alcools* intuitively knew how. What Mallarmé had begun, using the diamantine autonomy of words—abrasion from the surface of French verse of its sheen—Apollinaire finished with an unevenly-textured cloth of conscious *disposition*: whimsy, surprise, enthusiasm, conservatism, sentiment, fluorescent love-sickness, a pornographer's manic feel for pyramiding imagery, a cosmopolitan momma's-boy's sense of optimistic security, and the crowning talent to welcome change, molt, as freedom's grace:

> On sait très bien que l'on se damne
> Mais l'espoir d'aimer en chemin
> Nous fait penser main dans la main
> A ce qu'a prédit la tzigane
>
> ("La Tzigane")

Meredith:

> People who damn themselves are wrong
> To show surprise when they are damned;
> We let Hope lead us hand in hand.
> The gypsy knew it all along.

The art criticism, too, extracts our debt. The skeins of Cubism, pre-war Parisian effervescence, impresario-ship, and Apollinaire's shrewd recognition that France prefers to have at least one art-critic/ poet always on call are by now all tightly of a piece in the weft of retrospect. It's tempting to look back and see one smooth envelope: Apollinaire's foresighted name on it and such blue-chips as Picasso, Braque, Chirico, Matisse, Chagall, Archipenko stuffed chock-a-block inside.

Beautiful myth, of course. The dirty little secret common to art critics (and shared increasingly, awful to say, by art historians) is one compounded of the awareness of art as commodity-capital; of the fact that artists are frequently more attractively convivial than writers; and of a tailor's (let's be honest: a hack's) understanding that you don't need a bolt of cloth to cover an individual pincushion. We have, thanks to scholarship, the notes Apollinaire jotted down into his copy of the catalogue for the Salon des Independants in 1906. On Bonnard: "I have a lithograph signed by him." On Othon Friesz: "His mistress is the sister of Fernande Bellevallée, the mistress of Picasso." On Kees Van Dongen: "I must rent his apartment on Rue Girardon." Because the bulk of Apollinaire's more public writing was for newspapers and journals—*L'Intransigeant, Paris-Journal*—this meant too that the amount of dud pictures and little-fish picture-makers he regularly covered (gently, on the whole) far outweighed those great new jewels he was on to and which now fill our museums. Even on the venerable, already-certified great, Apollinaire was not always that great himself: "But what really shows M. Ingres' affinity with the Greeks and proves that he was their disciple is his ability to discern in each figure the sublime aspect of its particular beauty. And that amounts to nothing more nor less than style."

Yet two years after this felty, dutiful stuff would come *Les Peintres cubistes*—*Méditations esthétiques*—which, along with Vasari's book, and Baudelaire's, stands comfortably as one of the great monuments of art writing in the West. Not that it's flawless: it's the strong reader whose lips will stay level reading Marie Laurencin being described as the Salomé whose art dances between Picasso's cleansing John the Baptist and *le douanier* Rousseau's sentimental Herod. Neither was Apollinaire a major anatomist of criticism. His classifications of "scientific," "physical," "orphic," and "instinctive" Cubisms make for a messy plate, one bleeding into the other until it's better to simply call the whole meal stew. The book's first steps, terse philosophical statements about the plastic unities and the thralldom of nature, simply *wobble* into meaning as if inside brand-new shoes.

Two things stun us, though, as we continue in the book: the almost tale-like use of metaphor and the remarkable moderation, the likes of which the avant-garde manifesto would rarely see again. In Cubism, Apollinaire had staked out a moral moment between the end of the mimetic tradition and the spelunking start of the deep subjective. He saw no call for lugging around "the dead father," nor for nosing down alleys of excessive mystery. What was preferred was something along the lines of mathematics—divorced, elegant, self-proving. Apollinaire calls it "delight"—which, if it sounds vaguely classical, turns out in fact to be so. *We* shall control the universe, not the other way around. The canvas, while eliciting ecstasy, should at the same time defend us from going off "half-cocked. We will not be suddenly turning back. Free spectators, we will not sacrifice our lives to our curiosity. The smugglers of appearances will not be able to get their contraband past the salt statues before our custom houses of reason." In Apollinaire's surprisingly rationalist, even faintly martial hand, the Cubist painting is both pliers and plug.

The channel Apollinaire navigated here (and in his poetry as well) was really a very narrow one. Realism upstream; Freud and the unconscious and surrealism down. Symbolist hermeticism on one bank; the wilder, "half-cocked" raids of modernism on the other. An admirer of the somersaulting *saltimbanques,* he opted instead for change-in-place—and, to his great good fortune, he had found Picasso, that most unique chrysalis, a custodial history of art all by himself. The forty-four paragraphs devoted to Picasso in *Les Peintres cubistes* are perhaps Apollinaire's finest writing, in prose or poetry; certainly they are the most concentrated. Romance, image, and the trembling ground of ceaseless revision are all on view. First Picasso's blue-period and harlequin paintings are fixed with the most touching of clear glues: "This *Malagueño* bruised us like a brief frost. His meditations bared themselves silently." Then, right on his heels, Apollinaire watches Picasso change art forever by making an "inner frame" within a painting by use of either the naked real of collage or the veiled-by-planes nominalism of Cubism. And then this (translated by Lionel Abel):

> There is the poet to whom the muse dictates his chants, there is the artist whose hand is guided by an unknown being using him as an instrument. Such artists never feel fatigue, for they never labor, and produce abundantly day in and day out, no matter what country they are in, no matter what the season: they are not men, but poetic or artistic machines. Their reason cannot impede them, they never struggle, and their works show no signs of strain. They are not divine and can do without their selves. They are like prolongations of nature, and

their works do not pass through the intellect. They can move one without humanizing the harmonies they call forth. On the other hand, there are poets and artists who exert themselves constantly, who turn to nature, but have no direct contact with her; they must draw everything from within themselves, for no demon, no muse inspires them. They live in solitude, and express nothing but what they have babbled and stammered time and again, making effort after effort, attempt after attempt, just to formulate what they wish to express. Men created in the image of God, a time comes when they are able to rest yet admire their work. But what fatigue, imperfections, crudenesses!

Picasso was the first type of artist. Never has there been so fantastic a spectacle as the metamorphosis he underwent in becoming an artist of the second type.

In Picasso, Apollinaire gauged—and was first to be able to precisely describe—new law being irreversibly born. The whole world was going to be changed, made into the short, packed Spaniard's "new representation of it." None of this drama escaped Apollinaire, who immediately, telegraphically, prophetically, adds: "Enormous conflagration."

Finally, there is *Calligrammes,* 1913–1916, the last major corpus of poems. At its overture, less devoted Apollinairians have been known to seize the moment and slip out the side exits. Some of the more committed who stay in their seats wouldn't mind a little editing, and it's the rare faithful who are entirely satisfied with these last works. The honeyed tenor of *Alcools'* love laments is only intermittently on stage; whapping war noises so drown him out that he quickly learns to incorporate them:

Voici de quoi est fait le chant symphonique de l'amour
Il y a le chant de l'amour de jadis
Le bruit des baisers éperdus des amants illustres
Les cris d'amour des mortelles violées par les dieux
Les virilites des heros fabuleux érigées comme des pièces contre avions

("Le Chant d'Amour")

Greet:

This is what love's symphonic hymn is composed of
There's the tune of ancient loves
The sound of mad kisses of famous lovers

> The love cries of mortal women raped by the gods
> The virilities of fabulous heroes erect like guns against planes

Unless one accepts that Apollinaire's First World War was a spectacle of effortfulness rather than a midden of effect, it is hard to make sense of these poems at all. He was more likely to admire the living breathing Senegalese soldier sharing his trench than remark upon the one possibly dead only ten minutes later. The range of his pre-war, mid-war, and post-war labors equably encompassed wasn't-it-wacky enlistment memoirs; painstakingly composed "shaped" poems; simple, often riggish love notes to Madeleine Pagès or to Louise de Coligny-Chatillon; poems that take head-on note of carnage *("Le Palais du Tonnerre," "Merveille de la Guerre")* while refusing to denude it of nobility by calling it waste; and long, touching millenarian odes to the coming age of paradise *("Les Collines," "La Jolie Rousse")* despite a head wound and a lurking death. A far cry from Wilfred Owen, for sure.

Less than a quarter of *Calligrammes* consists of actual "calligrams"—the graphically designed shaped-poems—yet the impression they make is disproportionate. As the book and the war progressed (because, for the most part, Apollinaire wrote and even self-published these poems while actually at the front), there are fewer and fewer. The first major one to appear, *"Lettre-Océan"* (1914), is the richest, most firmly and formally self-assured. Rendered like fat-cracklings out of the occasion of a sea voyage to Mexico made by Apollinaire's brother Albert, the calligram distributes a "simultanist" collage of different typefaces, stamps, place names, slivers of speech and gossip, onomatopoeia, and smutty throwaways into a visual pattern that chiefly apes radio waves and Mayan calendars. Yet despite all the mini-relaxations of its postcard-y parts, the whole displays (as Prof. Greet points out in her notes) a remarkable "sobriety": Da but not yet Dada, a firecracker gone off inside a tightly-lidded box. Apollinaire's inherent orderliness plays some part in this, also the tonguetip-between-teeth sedulousness of labor one can imagine such a poem requiring; as with most conscious experiments in literature, a slight but inescapable just-so fustiness lies over the surface of the composition, defending its newness while also discouraging its re-reading.

With the exception of *"Lettre-Océan"* and a 1915 calligram, *"Aussi Bien que les Cigales,"* whose reiteration of one basic phrase is reminiscent of Gertrude Stein, few of the other calligrams are so theoretically adventurous. Four of the earliest—arrangements of a heart, a crown, and a mirror; a night-train under stars; *"Lettre-Océan"*; a tie and a watch—Apollinaire intended to (but finally didn't) publish under the heading *"Et Moi Aussi Je Suis Peintre"* (See, I'm Also a Painter)—which would seem to tip a rather tame hand. A fountain, in *"La Colombe Poignardée et le Jet d'Eau,"* spouts *ubi-sunt* sighs over friends left back in Paris or, like Apollinaire, sent to battle. Snaky sentences addressed to Lou recommend shared erotic secrets. There are bluntly inked, handwritten nuggets of poster-like phrase. In *"Fumées"* and *"La Mandoline l'OEillet et le Bambou,"* smell is elevated over sight as haven for the sensual appetite during war. Sign-like bombardment impressions, in *"Du Coton dans les Oreilles,"* are collected into a sort of calligram-kiosk. Yet as spikily visual and insistent as they are, all are much simpler in themselves than the effort expended to decipher their pictorial designs. Like jacks in ball-and-jacks, they're perfectly unusable in any context other than their very special own.

Depending, then, on how seriously you take Apollinaire as a poet (and you can love him but still not take him too seriously; for many he's the boy-man, the teddy bear of French literary history); and depending on what you believe his intentions were, you can take these "beautiful writings" as anything from game to poetic breakthrough. As game, a poet's brilliant rebuses sent back to amuse his mistresses, they are very charming. The care that went into them (remembering that Apollinaire is juggling typefaces and paste-ups while resting against a gunnery emplacement) testifies to a faith in invention and sensibility literally unshakable, undislodged by even the worst concussive yap. As documentary souvenirs, mimetically expressing the discontinuities of war, they are at least as effective, coming as they do from behind the lines of Apollinaire's take on life. (In *"SP,"* the tag-like instructions for how to use a primitive gas mask are tweaked: *Les masques seront sim/ plement mouilles des lar/ mes de rire de rire*; The masks will sim/ ply be wet with te/ ars of laughter of laughter.)

And as an arm of the Cubist remaking of reality, speeding up meaning by slowing down recognition, the calligrams surely reach out most hopefully. In *Les Peintres cubistes,* Apollinaire had already described truth as mere communication, "plastic writing" always at the right temperature for perfect elasticity. Yet the calligram, taken down from theory's shelf, is a clunky, näive, nearly pious thing when set next to even the most mediocre Cubist canvas. A dedicated Apollinairian like Prof. Greet will, in her notes, work her scholarly fingers to the bone in order to narrow the gap.

("Graphically, the circular line of the musical instrument echoes the circular movement of thought, while its enclosed shape suggests the self-sufficiency of the aesthetic meditation that it represents. The mandolin contains within itself the violence of war—battles are at the center of its sounding board, and the projecting neck possibly recalls the shape of artillery pieces—but the auditory associations of the instrument transmute the violence into an experience of another order.") But to little avail: exegesis itself is an iron rod thrown into a shaped-poem's combine, bringing it to an immediate halt. It is one of the well-acknowledged foxinesses of language to suggest the purely spatial—only to then presently disappear from and transcend it. One definition of literary style, in fact, could be the speed with which this transcendence is quickened or slowed. If I want to still the choirs of meaning that hover over the plainest sentence or line and thus be able to use it visually, I've got to first make that sentence or line inhospitably numb: shatter or fuse it against its imminent straightening into independent meaning. Contemporary concrete poetry, child of the calligrams, has been illustrating this process of synesthesia-made-anesthesia with some clarity. Hypnosis or else costiveness; the ruined, repeated, or solo-word poem being generally more cozy swaddled in the grey blankets of neurology than sporting the gayer interpretive colors of literary ambiguity, accident, mistake.

It hadn't ever got that far with Apollinaire, however. Big wishes aside, his calligram stayed essentially a primitive pun. And as happens with a pun, it's best left made only once. Though Prof. Greet has set all the calligrams to English—a service of doubtless merit for those who don't read French or can't make out the blurred-by-age photographed originals—the opportunity to reproduce here what she and Apollinaire have wrought is an easy one to pass up. Call me fainthearted. The harder Greet labors to stay unflashily faithful to the shaped French, the worse, I'm afraid, it all ends up. As Apollinaire playfully if a little clumsily rounds a curve with a sprinkle of phonemes, the Greet version obligatorily rounds it too on the facing page—soggying the snap of the original's novelty while at the same time mercilessly exposing its simplemindedness. In English, the calligram comes off as cagier and far more gauche than in French. That wily effects reproduce terribly may be the lesson. That handsome and dangerous-looking translator who accompanied Khrushchev to the United States in the late Fifties: what was he supposed to do, pound his own shoe on the desk also? But in English?

Gesture is always a key to Apollinaire—and since gesture arises from role, the key is at work in the late non-calligram war poems as well. Apollinaire the unhappy lover—the passive *mal-aimé*—is a more comforting figure than Apollinaire the soldier, but the *mal-aimé* had already showed signs of change by 1914. Apollinaire had done some growing-up. *"Le Musicien de Saint-Merry"* (1914) is figured around a Chiricesque mannequin who, with a magic flute, is able to gather in all the women of Paris and lead them into permanent oblivion. Vengeance is mine, saith the Poet—one of the perquisites—but the practical lessons of a strenuous amorous life had finally, too, resulted in a stronger man.

J'ai enfin le droit de saluer des êtres que je ne connais pas
Ils passent devant moi et s'accumulent au loin
Tandis que tout ce que j'en vois m'est inconnu
Et leur espoir n'est pas moins fort que le mien

Je ne chante pas ce monde ni les autres astres
Je chante toutes les possibilités de moi-même hors de ce monde et des astres
Je chante la joie d'errer et le plaisir d'en mourir

Greet:

At last I have the right to hail unknown beings
They pass by me and gather in the distance
While all that I see of them is strange to me
And their hope is no frailer than mine

I sing neither of this world nor of the other stars
I sing of my own possibilities beyond this world and the stars
I sing the joy of wandering and the pleasure of the wanderer's death

Much as we'd like to think otherwise, Apollinaire was not, therefore, lost on the battlefield, wondering helplessly to what bootless pass his life had come that he should suddenly wind up here. What remained in him of the *mal-aimé* could take refuge from rejection in the sole company of other men. The inveterate armchair traveller, forever leaping his poetic imagination over distances to the Rhine, the coast of Texas, Vancouver, the Antilles, Mexico, New York, found the front agreeably foreign: close yet far, like a Kierkegaardian repetition. The sophisticate was treated to fascinating and awesome theater:

Des mitrailleuses d'or coassent les légendes . . .
L'invisible ennemi plaie d'argent au soleil . . .
Le masque bleu comme met Dieu son ciel . . .
Guerre paisable ascèse solitude métaphysique . . .
Enfant aux mains coupées parmi les roses oriflammes

Greet:

Machine guns of gold are croaking legends . . .
The enemy a silver wound in the sunlight . . .
My blue mask as God puts on his sky . . .
War peaceful ascesis metaphysical solitude . . .
Child with severed hands among roses oriflamme

Because many of the earliest war poems are calligrams, like the one above (lines from *"Visée"*), we can for a time excuse them as the stenography of a stunned observer. Uncrabbed, uncrimped, untricky, the non-shaped poems will (our pacifism hopes) be able to ultimately renounce the slaughter. But in a poem like *"La Nuit d'Avril 1915,"* a fire-fight at night: *La fôret merveilleuse où je vis donne un bal/ La mitrailleuse joue un air à triples-croches*; The marvelous forest where I live is giving a ball/ The machine gun plays a tune in three-fourths time. In *"Le Palais du Tonnerre"* (Thunder's Palace), the trenches are described with novelistic scrupulosity (and acceptance). In *"Désir,"* the German lines Apollinaire finds himself firing into blindly evoke a yet more macrocosmic victory:

Je désire
Te serrer dans ma main Main de Massiges
Si décharnée sur la carte

Le boyau Goethe où j'ai tiré
J'ai tiré même sur le boyau Nietzche
Decidément je ne respecte aucune gloire

Greet:

I long
To grasp you in my hand Main de Massiges
So fleshless on the map

> Goethe's trench I have fired at
> I have even fired at the guts of Nietzsche
> Decidedly I respect no glory

in which mix the personae of Genghis Khan, Baedeker, and Don Juan—
a thousand Leporellos around the last in a "Night that is violet and violent
and dark and momentarily full of gold/ Night of men only." In a poem
such as this, or one like *"A l'Italie,"* Apollinaire exhibits no higher ethical
pusillanimity: he wants his army to win, to beat the Boche, to kill them.
When there's horror, it seems to him mostly a product of deceleration.

"Merveille de la Guerre" is perhaps the best summing-up. Flares are
dancing ladies, a daily apotheosis "of all my Berenices whose hair has
turned to/ comets' tails." The light overhead is "as lovely as if life itself
issued from those who are dying." Present at "the feast of this cannibal
Balthazar"

> Qui aurait dit qu'on pût être à ce point anthropophage
> Et qu'il fallût tant de feu pour rôtir le corps humain
> C'est pourquoi l'air a un petit goût empyreumatique qui n'est ma foi pas
>   désagréable
> Mais le festin serait plus beau encore si le ciel y mangeait avec la terre

Greet:

> Who would have said one could be so anthropophagous
> Or that so much fire was needed to roast human flesh
> That's why the air has a slight empyreumatic taste which by God is not
>   unpleasant
> But the feast would be finer still if the sky too dined with the earth

More than anything, it's an astonishment.

> Je lègue à l'avenir l'histoire de Guillaume Apollinaire
> Qui fut à la guerre et sut être partout

Greet:

> I bequeath to the future the story of Guillaume Apollinaire
> Who was in the war and knew how to be everywhere

—in the sweetness, in the death, *Au zénith au nadir aux 4 points cardinaux.*

So it isn't a callous barbarian here. With women, or in exotic places of the imagination, or on the planes of cubism and admixtures of simulta-nism, the many-in-one—riding a parabolic curve—is where to find the true Apollinarian *I.* Roger Shattuck has helpfully isolated it: "He increasingly sought himself *outside* himself. It is as if his *I* were the exterior world from which, once he had radiated himself into it, he could look back wistfully and indulgently upon his old self as a pathetic object." A sleeve turned inside out. And in a recent essay focusing on Dowell, that most eelish narrator of Ford's *The Good Soldier,* Denis Donoghue points out something that applies, I think, as well and snugly to Apollinaire: "The gestures by which he answers contingency make him immune to it. No wonder he survives its attack."

While immunity through gesture could not guarantee Apollinaire safe corporeal passage through war (even his helmet was unable to do that), it did allow the potentials of his art through. And potential—ardor, reach —was for Apollinaire the very crux. (The octopus, three-hearted and ink-throwing, was a favorite autobiographical image; see *"Océan de Terre"* 1915.) It wasn't in Apollinaire's power to too-abruptly categorize war— or anything—as abomination. That would have stunted the image-seeding faculty, would have packed shut the "starry head"—precious rarity in a situation where one was lucky to keep any head at all. If the non-calligram poems of Apollinaire's war never once wholly succeed, at least they still fail from on high. Gliding down off a perch of dogged spiritual innocence that isn't quite—*"Bouche ouverte sur un harmonium/ C'était une voix faite d'yeux"*; Mouth open above a harmonium/ It was a voice composed of eyes *("Souvenirs")*—they are arguably more *possible,* i.e., erotic, than any French poems since those of the troubadors. If Apollinaire could love (and suffer) this, he could love anything.

Atlas of Civilization

Seamus Heaney

At the very end of his life, Socrates' response to his recurring dream, which had instructed him to "practice the art," was to begin to put the fables of Aesop into verse. It was, of course, entirely in character for the philosopher to be attracted to fictions whose *a priori* function was to expose the true shape of things, and it was proper that even this slight brush with the art of poetry should involve an element of didacticism. But imagine what the poems of Socrates would have been like if, instead of doing adaptations, he had composed original work during those hours before he took the poison. It is unlikely that he would have broken up his lines to weep; indeed, it is likely that he would not only have obeyed Yeats's injunction on this score, but that he would have produced an oeuvre sufficient to confound the master's claim that "The intellect of man is forced to choose / Perfection of the life or of the work."

It would be an exaggeration to say that the work of the Polish poet Zbigniew Herbert could pass as a substitute for such an ideal poetry of reality. Yet in the exactions of its logic, the temperance of its tone, and the extremity and equanimity of its recognitions, it does resemble what a twentieth-century poetic version of the examined life might be. Admittedly, in all that follows here, it is an English translation rather than the Polish originals which is being praised or pondered, but what convinces one of the universal resource of Herbert's writing is just this ability which it possesses to lean, without toppling, well beyond the plumb of its native language.

Herbert himself, however, is deeply attracted to that which does not

Review of Zbigniew Herbert's *Barbarian in the Garden, Selected Poems,* and *Report from the Besieged City* from *Parnassus* (vol. 14, no. 1, 1987).

lean but which "trusts geometry, simple numerical rule, the wisdom of the square, balance and weight." He rejoices in the discovery that "Greek architecture originated in the sun" and that "Greek architects knew the art of measuring with shadows. The north-south axis was marked by the shortest shadow cast by the sun's zenith. The problem was to trace the perpendicular, the holy east-west direction." Hence the splendid utility of Pythagoras' theorem, and the justice of Herbert's observation that "the architects of the Doric temples were less concerned with beauty than with the chiselling of the world's order into stone."

These quotations come from the second essay in *Barbarian in the Garden,* a collection of ten meditations on art and history which masquerade as "travel writings" insofar as nine of them are occasioned by visits to specific places, including Lascaux, Sicily, Arles, Orvieto, Siena, Chartres, and the various resting places of the paintings of Piero della Francesca. A tenth one also begins and ends at a single pungent site, the scorched earth of an island in the Seine where on March 18, 1314, Jacques de Molay, Grand Master of the Order of the Templars, burned at the stake along with Geoffroi de Charney and another thirty-six brothers of their order. Yet this section of the book also travels to another domain where Herbert operates with fastidious professional skills: the domain of tyranny, with its police precision, mass arrests, tortures, self-inculpations, purges, and eradications, all those methods which already in the fourteenth century had begun to "enrich the repertoire of power."

Luckily, the poet's capacity for admiration is more than equal to his perception of the atrocious, and *Barbarian in the Garden* is an ironical title. This "barbarian" who makes his pilgrimage to the sacred places is steeped in the culture and history of classical and medieval Europe, and even though there is situated at the center of his consciousness a large burnt-out zone inscribed "what we have learned in modern times and must never forget even though we need hardly dwell upon it," this very consciousness can still muster a sustaining half-trust in man as a civilizer and keeper of civilizations. The book is full of lines which sing out in the highest registers of intellectual rapture. In Paestum, "Greek temples live under the golden sun of geometry." In Orvieto, to enter the cathedral is a surprise, "so much does the façade differ from the interior—as though the gate of life full of birds and colours led into a cold, austere eternity." In the presence of a Piero della Francesca: "He is . . . like a figurative painter who has passed through a cubist phase." In the presence of Piero's *Death of Adam* in Arezzo: "The entire scene appears Hellenic, as though the Old Testament were composed by Aeschylus."

But Herbert never gets too carried away. The ground-hugging sturdiness which he recognizes and cherishes in archaic buildings has its analogue in his own down-to-earthness. His love of "the quiet chanting of the air and the immense planes" does not extend so far as to constitute a betrayal of the human subject, in thrall to gravity and history. His imagination is slightly less skyworthy than that of his great compatriot Czeslaw Milosz, who has nevertheless recognized in the younger poet a kindred spirit and as long ago as 1968 translated, with Peter Dale Scott, the now reissued *Selected Poems*. Deliciously susceptible as he is to the *"lucidus ordo*—an eternal order of light and balance" in the work of Piero, Herbert is still greatly pleasured by the density and miscellany of what he finds in a book by Piero's contemporary, the architect and humanist Leon Battista Alberti:

> Despite its classical structure, technical subjects are mixed with anecdotes and trivia. We may read about foundations, building-sites, bricklaying, doorknobs, wheels, axes, levers, hacks, and how to 'exterminate and destroy snakes, mosquitoes, bed-bugs, fleas, mice, moths and other importunate night creatures.'

Clearly, although he quotes Berenson elsewhere, Herbert would be equally at home with a builder. He is very much the poet of a workers' republic insofar as he possesses a natural affinity with those whose eyes narrow in order to effect an operation or a calculation rather than to study a refinement. Discussing the self-portrait of Luca Signorelli which that painter entered in *The Coming of the Anti-Christ* (in the duomo at Orvieto) alongside a portrait of his master, Fra Angelico, Herbert makes a distinction between the two men. He discerns how Signorelli's eyes "are fixed upon reality . . . Beside him, Fra Angelico dressed in a cassock gazes inwards. Two glances: one visionary, the other observant." It is a distinction which suggests an equivalent division within the poet, deriving from the co-existence within his own deepest self of two conflicting strains. These were identified by A. Alvarez in his introduction to the original 1968 volume as the tender-minded and the tough-minded, and it is some such crossing of a natural readiness to consent upon an instinctive suspicion which constitutes the peculiar fiber of Herbert's mind and art.

There is candor and there is concentration. His vigilance never seems to let up and we feel sure that if he is enjoying himself in print (which is memory), then the original experience was also enjoyed in similar propitious conditions. All through *Barbarian in the Garden,* the tender-minded, desiring side of his nature is limpidly, felicitously engaged. In a church in a Tuscan village where "there is hardly room enough for a coffin," he encounters a Madonna. "She wears a simple, high-waisted dress open from breast to knees. Her left hand rests on a hip, a country bridesmaid's gesture; her right hand touches her belly but without a trace of licentiousness." In a similar fashion, as he reports his ascent of the tower of Senlis Cathedral, the writing unreels like a skein long stored in the cupboard of the senses. "Patches of lichen, grass between the stones, and bright yellow flowers"; then, high up on a gallery, an "especially beautiful Eve. Coarse-grained, big-eyed and plump. A heavy plait of hair falls on her wide, warm back."

Writing of this sort which ensures, in Neruda's words, that "the reality of the world should not be underprized," is valuable in itself, but what reinforces Herbert's contribution and takes it far beyond being just another accomplished print-out of a cultivated man's impressions is his skeptical historical sense of the world's unreliability. He is thus as appreciative of the unfinished part of Siena Cathedral and as unastonished by it as he is entranced by what is exquisitely finished: "The majestic plan remained unfulfilled, interrupted by the Black Death and errors in construction." The elegance of that particular zeugma should not blind us to its outrage; the point is that Herbert is constantly wincing in the jaws of a pincer created by the mutually indifferent intersection of art and suffering. Long habituation to this crux has bred in him a tone which is neither vindictive against art nor occluded to pain. It predisposes him to quote Cicero on the colonies of Sicily as "an ornamental band sown onto the rough cloth of barbarian lands, a golden band that was frequently stained with blood." And it enables him to strike out his own jocund, unnerving sentences, like this one about the Baglioni family of Perugia: "They were vengeful and cruel, though refined enough to slaughter their enemies on beautiful summer evenings."

Once more, this comes from his essay on Piero della Francesca, and it is in writing about this beloved painter that Herbert articulates most clearly the things we would want to say about himself as an artist: "The harmonized background and the principle of tranquillity," "the rule of the demon of perspective," the viewing of the world as "through a pane of ice," an "epic impassiveness," a quality which is "impersonal, supra-individual." All these phrases apply, at one time or another, to Herbert's poetry and adumbrate a little more the shapes of his "tough-mindedness." Yet they should not be taken to suggest any culpable detachment or abstraction. The impassiveness, the perspective, the impersonality, the tranquillity, all derive from his unblindable stare at the facts of pain, the recurrence of injustice and catastrophe; but they derive also from a deep love for the whole Western tradition of religion, literature, and art, which have remained open to him as a spiritual resource, helping him to stand his ground. Herbert is as familiar as any twentieth-century writer with the hollow men and has seen more broken columns with his eyes than most literary people have seen in their imaginations, but this does not end up in a collapse of his trust in the humanist endeavor. On the contrary, it summons back to mind the whole dimensions of that endeavor and enforces it once more upon our awareness for the great boon which it is (not *was*), something we may have thought of as vestigial before we began reading these books but which, by the time we have finished, stands before our understanding once again like "a cathedral in the wilderness."

Barbarian in the Garden was first published in Polish in 1962 and is consequently the work of a much younger man (Herbert was born in 1924) than the one who wrote the poems of *Report from the Besieged City.* But the grave, laconic, instructive prose, translated with such fine regard for cadence and concision by Michael Marsh and Jaroslaw Anders, is recognizably the work of the same writer. It would be wrong to say that in the meantime Herbert has matured, since from the beginning the look he turned upon experience was penetrating, judicial, and absolutely in earnest; but it could be said that he has grown even more secure in his self-possession and now begins to resemble an old judge who has developed the benevolent aspect of a daydreamer while retaining all the readiness and spring of a crouched lion. Where the poems of the reissued *Selected Poems* carry within themselves the battened-down energy and enforced caution of the situation from which they arose in Poland in the 1950s, the poems of the latest volume allow themselves a much greater latitude of voice. They are physically longer, less impacted, more social and genial in tone. They occur within a certain spaciousness, under a vault of winnowed comprehension. One thinks again of the *lucidus ordo,* of that "golden sun of geometry"; yet because of the body heat of the new poetry, its warm breath which keeps stirring the feather of our instinctive nature, one thinks also of Herbert's eloquent valediction to the prehistoric caves of the Dordogne:

> I returned from Lascaux by the same road I arrived. Though I had stared into the 'abyss' of history, I did not emerge from an alien world. Never before had I felt a stronger or more reassuring conviction: I am a citizen of the earth, an inheritor not only of the Greeks and Romans but of almost the whole of infinity. . . .
>
> The road opened to the Greek temples and the Gothic cathedrals. I walked towards them feeling the warm touch of the Lascaux painter on my palm.

It is no wonder, therefore, that Mr. Cogito, the poet's alibi/alias/persona/ventriloquist's doll/permissive correlative, should be so stubbornly attached to the senses of sight and touch. In the second section of "Eschatological Forebodings of Mr. Cogito," after Herbert's several musings about his ultimate fate—"probably he will sweep / the great square of Purgatory"—he imagines him taking courses in the eradication of earthly habits. And yet, in spite of these angelic debriefing sessions, Mr. Cogito

> continues to see
> a pine on a mountain slope
> dawn's seven candlesticks
> a blue-veined stone
>
> he will yield to all tortures
> gentle persuasions
> but to the end he will defend
> the magnificent sensation of pain
>
> and a few weathered images
> on the bottom of the burned-out eye

> 3

> who knows
> perhaps he will manage
> to convince the angels

he is incapable
of heavenly
service

and they will permit him to return
by an overgrown path
at the shore of a white sea
to the cave of the beginning

The poles of the beginning and the end are crossing and at the very
moment when he strains to imagine himself at the shimmering circumference of the imaginable, Mr. Cogito finds himself collapsing back into the
palpable center. Yet all this is lightened of its possible portentousness
because it is happening not to "humanity" or "mankind" but to Mr.
Cogito. Mr. Cogito operates sometimes like a cartoon character, a cosmic
Don Quixote or matchstick Sisyphus; sometimes like a discreet convention
whereby the full frontal of the autobiographical "I" is veiled. It is in this
latter role that he is responsible for one of the book's most unforgettable
poems, "Mr. Cogito—The Return," which, along with "The Abandoned," "Mr. Cogito's Soul," and the title poem, strikes an unusually
intimate and elegiac note.

Mostly, however, Mr. Cogito figures as a stand-in for experimental,
undaunted *Homo sapiens,* or, to be more exact, as a representative of the
most courageous, well-disposed, and unremittingly intelligent members of
the species. The poems where he fulfills this function are no less truly
pitched and sure of their step than the ones I have just mentioned; in fact,
they are more brilliant as intellectual reconnaissance and more deadly as
political resistance; they are on the offensive, and to read them is to put
oneself through the mill of Herbert's own personal selection process, to
be tested for one's comprehension of the necessity of refusal, one's ultimate gumption and awareness. This poetry is far more than "dissident";
it gives no consolation to papmongers or propagandists of whatever stripe.
Its whole intent is to devastate those arrangements which are offered as
truth by power's window dressers everywhere. It can hear the screech of
the fighter bomber behind the righteous huffing of the official spokesman,
yet it is not content with just an exposé or an indictment. Herbert always
wants to probe past official versions of collective experience into the final
ring of the individual's perception and endurance. He does so in order
to discover whether that inner citadel of human being is a selfish bolt hole

or an attentive listening post. To put it another way, he would not be all that interested in discovering the black box after the crash, since he would far prefer to be able to monitor the courage and conscience of each passenger during the minutes before it. Thus, in their introduction, John and Bogdana Carpenter quote him as follows:

> You understand I had words in abundance to express my rebellion and protest. I might have written something of this sort: 'O you cursed, damned people, so and sos, you kill innocent people, wait and a just punishment will fall on you.' I didn't say this because I wanted to bestow a broader dimension on the specific, individual, experienced situation, or rather, to show its deeper, general human perspectives.

This was always his impulse, and it is a pleasure to watch his strategies for showing "deeper, general human perspectives" develop. In the *Selected Poems,* dramatic monologues and adaptations of Greek myth were among his preferred approaches. There can be no more beautiful expression of necessity simultaneously recognized and lamented than the early "Elegy of Fortinbras," just as there can be no poem more aghast at those who have power to hurt and who then do hurt than "Apollo and Marsyas." Both works deserve to be quoted in full, but here is the latter one, in the translation of Czeslaw Milosz:

> The real duel of Apollo
> with Marsyas
> (absolute ear
> versus immense range)
> takes place in the evening
> when as we already know
> the judges
> have awarded victory to the god
>
> bound tight to a tree
> meticulously stripped of his skin
> Marsyas
> howls
> before the howl reaches his tall ears
> he reposes in the shadow of that howl

shaken by a shudder of disgust
Apollo is cleaning his instrument

only seemingly
is the voice of Marsyas
monotonous
and composed of a single vowel
Aaa

in reality
Marsyas relates
the inexhaustible wealth
of his body

bald mountains of liver
white ravines of aliment
rustling forests of lung
sweet hillocks of muscle
joints bile blood and shudders
the wintry wind of bone
over the salt of memory
shaken by a shudder of disgust
Apollo is cleaning his instrument

now to the chorus
is joined the backbone of Marsyas
in principle the same A
only deeper with the addition of rust

this is already beyond the endurance
of the god with nerves of artificial fibre

along a gravel path
hedged with box
the victor departs
wondering
whether out of Marsyas' howling
there will not some day arise
a new kind
of art—let us say—concrete

suddenly
at his feet
falls a petrified nightingale

> he looks back
> and sees
> that the hair of the tree to which Marsyas was fastened
> is white
> completely

About suffering, he was never wrong, this young master. The Polish experience of cruelty lies behind the poem, and when it first appeared it would have had the extra jangle of anti-poetry about it. There is the affront of the subject matter, the flirtation with horror-movie violence, and the conscious avoidance of anything "tender-minded." Yet the triumph of the thing is that while it remains set upon an emotional collision course, it still manages to keep faith with "whatever shares / The eternal reciprocity of tears." Indeed, this is just the poetry which Yeats would have needed to convince him of the complacency of his objection to Wilfred Owen's work (passive suffering is not a subject for poetry), although, in fact, it is probably only Wilfred Owen (tender-minded) and Yeats (tough-minded) who brought into poetry in English a "vision of reality" as adequate to our times as this one.

"Apollo and Marsyas" is a poem, not a diagram. By now, the anti-poetry element has evaporated or been inhaled so that in spite of that devastating A note, the poem's overall music dwells in the sorrowing registers of cello or pibroch. The petrified nightingale, the tree with white hair, the monotonous Aaa of the new art, each of these inventions is as terrible as it is artful, each is uttered from the dry well of an objective voice. The demon of perspective rules while the supra-individual principle reads history through a pane of Francescan ice, tranquilly, impassively, as if the story were chiseled into stone.

The most celebrated instance of Herbert's capacity to outface what the stone ordains occurs in his poem "Pebble." Once again, this is an *ars poetica,* but the world implied by the poem would exclude any discourse that was so fancied-up as to admit a term like *ars poetica* in the first place. Yet "Pebble" is several steps ahead of satire and even one or two steps beyond the tragic gesture. It is written by a poet who grew up, as it were, under the white-haired tree but who possessed no sense either of the oddity or the election of his birthright. Insofar as it accepts the universe with a sort of disappointed relief—as though at the last minute faith were to renege on its boast that it could move mountains and settle back into stoicism—it demonstrates the truth of Patrick Kavanagh's contention that tragedy is half-born comedy. The poem's force certainly resides in its impersonality, yet its tone is almost ready to play itself on through into the altogether more lenient weather of personality itself.

> The pebble
> is a perfect creature
>
> equal to itself
> mindful of its limits
>
> filled exactly
> with pebbly meaning
>
> with a scent which does not remind one of anything
> does not frighten anything away does not arouse desire
>
> its ardour and coldness
> are just and full of dignity
>
> I feel a heavy remorse
> when I hold it in my hand
> and its noble body
> is permeated by false warmth
>
>   —Pebbles cannot be tamed
>   to the end they will look at us
>   with a calm and very clear eye

This has about it all the triumph and completion of the "finished man among his enemies." You wonder where else an art that is so contained and self-verifying can possibly go—until you open *Report from the Besieged City.* There you discover that the perfect moral health of the earlier poetry was like the hard pure green of the ripening apple: now the core of the thing is less packed with tartness and the whole oeuvre seems to mellow and sway on the bough of some tree of unforbidden knowledge.

There remain, however, traces of the acerbic observer; this, for example, in the poem where Damastes (also known as Procrustes) speaks:

> I invented a bed with the measurements of a perfect man
> I compared the travelers I caught with this bed
> it was hard to avoid—I admit—stretching limbs cutting legs

the patients died but the more there were who perished
the more I was certain my research was right
the goal was noble progress demands victims

This voice is stereophonic in that we are listening to it through two speakers, one from the setup Damastes, the other from the privileged poet, and we always know whose side we are on. We are meant to read the thing exactly as it is laid out for us. We stand with Signorelli at the side of the picture, observantly. We are still, in other words, in the late spring of impersonality. But when we come to the poem on the Emperor Claudius, we are in the summer of fullest personality. It is not that Herbert has grown lax or that any phony tolerance—understanding all and therefore forgiving all—has infected his attitude. It is more that he has eased up on his own grimness, as if realizing that the stern brows he turns upon the world merely contribute to the weight of the world's anxiety instead of lightening it; therefore, he can afford to become more genial personally without becoming one whit less impersonal in his judgments and perceptions. So, in his treatment of "The Divine Claudius," the blood and the executions and the infernal whimsicality are not passed over, yet Herbert ends up speaking for his villain with a less than usually forked tongue:

I expanded the frontiers of the empire
by Brittany Mauretania
and if I recall correctly Thrace

my death was caused by my wife Agrippina
and an uncontrollable passion for boletus
mushrooms—the essence of the forest—became the essence of death

descendants—remember with proper respect and honor
at least one merit of the divine Claudius
I added new signs and sounds to our alphabet
expanded the limits of speech that is the limits of freedom

the letters I discovered—beloved daughters—Digamma and Antisigma
led my shadow
as I pursued the path with tottering steps to the dark land of Orkus

There is more of the inward gaze of Fra Angelico here, and indeed, all through the new book, Herbert's mind is fixed constantly on last things.

Classical and Christian visions of the afterlife are drawn upon time and again, and in "Mr. Cogito—Notes from the House of the Dead," we have an opportunity of hearing how the terrible cry of Marsyas sounds in the new acoustic of the later work. Mr. Cogito, who lies with his fellows "in the depths of the temple of the absurd," hears there, at ten o'clock in the evening, "a voice // masculine / slow / commanding / the rising / of the dead." The second section of the poem proceeds:

> we called him Adam
> meaning taken from the earth
>
> at ten in the evening
> when the lights were switched off
> Adam would begin his concert
>
> to the ears of the profane
> it sounded
> like the howl of a person in fetters
>
> for us
> an epiphany
>
> he was
> anointed
> the sacrificial animal
> author of psalms
>
> he sang
> the inconceivable desert
> the call of the abyss
> the noose on the heights
>
> Adam's cry
> was made
> of two or three vowels
> stretched out like ribs on the horizon

This new Adam has brought us as far as the old Marsyas took us, but now the older Herbert takes up the burden and, in a third section, brings the poem further still:

after a few concerts
he fell silent

the illumination of his voice
lasted a brief time

he didn't redeem
his followers

they took Adam away
or he retreated
into eternity

the source
of the rebellion
was extinguished

and perhaps
only I
still hear
the echo
of his voice

more and more slender
quieter
further and further away

like music of the spheres
the harmony of the universe

so perfect
it is inaudible.

Mr. Cogito's being depends upon such cogitations (one remembers his defense of "the magnificent sensation of pain"), though unlike Hamlet, in Fortinbras's elegy, who "crunched the air only to vomit," Mr. Cogito's digestion of the empty spaces is curiously salutary. Reading these poems is a beneficent experience: they amplify immensely Thomas Hardy's assertion that "if a way to the Better there be, it exacts a full look at the Worst." By the end of the book, after such undaunted poems as "The Power of Taste"—"Yes taste / in which there are fibers of soul the cartilage of conscience"—and such tender ones as "Lament," to the memory of his mother—"she sails on the bottom of a boat through foamy nebulas,"— after these and the other poems I have mentioned, and many more which

I have not, the reader feels the kind of gratitude the gods of Troy must have felt when they saw Aeneas creep from the lurid fires, bearing ancestry on his shoulders and the sacred objects in his hands.

The book's true subject is survival of the valid self, of the city, of the good and the beautiful; or rather, the subject is the responsibility of each person to ensure that survival. So it is possible in the end to think that a poet who writes so ethically about the *res publica* might even be admitted by Plato as first laureate of the ideal republic; though it is also necessary to think that through to the point where this particular poet would be sure to decline the office as a dangerous compromise:

> now as I write these words the advocates of conciliation
> have won the upper hand over the party of inflexibles
> a normal hesitation of moods fate still hangs in the balance
>
> cemeteries grow larger the number of the defenders is smaller
> yet the defense continues it will continue to the end
> and if the City falls but a single man escapes
> he will carry the City within himself on the roads of exile
> he will be the City
>
> we look in the face of hunger the face of fire face of death
> worst of all—the face of betrayal
>
> and only our dreams have not been humiliated

(1982)

The title poem, to which these lines form the conclusion, is pivoted at the moment of martial law and will always belong in the annals of patriotic Polish verse. It witnesses new developments and makes old connections within the native story and is only one of several poems throughout the volume which sweeps the string of Polish national memory. If I have been less attentive to this indigenous witnessing function of the book than I might have been, it is not because I undervalue that function of Herbert's poetry. On the contrary, it is precisely because I am convinced of its obdurate worth on the home front that I feel free to elaborate in the luxurious margin. Anyhow, John and Bogdana Carpenter have annotated the relevant dates and names so that the reader is kept alert to the allusions and connections which provide the book's oblique discharge of political energy. As well as providing this editorial service, they seem to have managed the task of translating well; I had no sense of their coming between me and the poem's first life, no sense of their having interfered.

Zbigniew Herbert is a poet with all the strengths of an Antaeus, yet he finally emerges more like the figure of an Atlas. Refreshed time and again by being thrown back upon his native earth, standing his ground determinedly in the local plight, he nevertheless shoulders the whole sky and scope of human dignity and responsibility. These various translations provide a clear view of the power and beauty of the profile which he has established, and leave no doubt about the essential function which his work performs, that of keeping a trustworthy poetic canopy, if not a perfect heaven, above our vulnerable heads.